Interpersonal Sexuality

David F. Shope

Continuing Education
Pennsylvania State University

W. B. SAUNDERS COMPANY

PHILADELPHIA • LONDON • TORONTO

W. B. Saunders Company: West Washington Square
Philadelphia, Pa. 19105

12 Dyott Street
London, WC1A 1DB

833 Oxford Street
Toronto, Ontario M8Z 5T9, Canada

Library of Congress Cataloging in Publication Data
Shope, David F
Interpersonal sexuality.
Includes bibliographical references and indexes.
1. Sex.   I. Title.
HQ21.S482   155.3   74–6692
ISBN 0–7216–8253–7

Front cover photograph, title page photograph and all chapter opening photographs courtesy of H. Armstrong Roberts Company.

Interpersonal Sexuality   ISBN 0-7216-8253-7

Last digit is the print number: 9   8   7   6   5   4   3   2

To Mary

—for the hours of toil, patience, arguing, correcting, and the myriad other things a friend and partner becomes involved in when a spouse decides to write a book.

ABOUT THIS TEXT

The general purpose of this book is to discuss human sexuality from a psychosocial perspective. The term "sexual behavior" is used throughout with the understanding that it includes the thoughts, feelings, motivations, interactions, and subtleties associated with it. Sex is analyzed part of the time as though it could stand alone from the rest of humanness, but this is simply a device to make discussion easier. Whatever else can be said of sex, it does not operate as an isolated phenomenon.

Man's sexual adjustment is an achievement dependent upon the ability to integrate one's sexual and nonsexual lives into a unitary whole. Fragmentation of human life into isolated categories is suitable only for the purpose of studying man as a living organism. The process of living, as opposed to studying life, requires consolidation. Living humans are whole beings, and it is unlikely that any one facet of life is entirely free from all the other influences that go to make up the world of the living. Our religious-philosophical valuing system inspires everything we do. Biophysical functions affect every part of our lives, and psychosocial processes interact with the rest of our being. Yet there is more to it than that, because each of these systems not only interacts but when isolated presents at least a partial lie, since the human being is a functional whole. The methods of science have a tendency to find truth in isolated fragments, but in the interactive processes of the total human being are found the greatest truths. This gestalt view—the figure-background unity—will be noted frequently throughout the text. What is true of the rest of man is also true of his sexual behavior. Sex is found to some degree in everything man does and is.

Interpersonal Sexuality endeavors to present human sexuality in a simplified and brief form. Sometimes it adheres closely to empirical evidence, and sometimes it does not. I have tried to make clear the distinction between those generalities about which there is some consensus of research opinion and those based on personal impressions, whether they be my own or another's. At times the book, which deals with a not overly well-studied area of human life, may not do justice to those men who have contributed to our sexual knowledge, but the student who is interested in more depth than it provides is encouraged to seek further understanding by consulting the original sources of information upon which it is based.

The major emphasis of the book is on relationships. The text is organized according to a developmental sequence: beginning with theories of sexuality and role-taking, progressing through relationships in general and through marriage, with its accompanying role adjustments, continuing as though children had been added to the marriage, and concluding with a discussion of sexual morality and atypical sexual behavior. It is recognized that a good deal of nonmarital sexual interaction takes place both before and after marriage, and these important aspects of interpersonal behavior have not been neglected.

Yet like the separation of sexuality from other facets of human life for purposes of discussion, any chapter-by-chapter assignment of aspects of sexual behavior is clearly arbitrary. It is evident that the psychology of interpersonal dynamics finds certain of its roots in the individual's personality makeup, and each affects the other continually. Much of our thinking concerning love and sexual interaction — two of our most precious commodities — is muddled because we have feared to face ourselves as loving, emotional, passionate sexual beings. This fear is reflected in our steady refusal to expose our intimate nature to objective study. Furthermore, although in assigning certain personality functions to one sex or the other I have followed the accepted analyses of male and female sexuality, the reader should bear in mind that such characteristics can and do transcend sexual barriers. Aggression is not an exclusive prerogative of men, and masochism is today more a stereotype belonging to the past than a universal characteristic of modern women.

Finally, despite the developmental sequencing of the chapters, each may also, to a degree, stand alone. It is not absolutely essential that the chapters be read in order, or even that all be read. Individual needs and programs may dictate that they be studied in an order other than the one presented here. The attention of both instructors and students, however, is drawn to the appendices, which summarize the major anatomical features of the sexual and reproductive organs, review contraception, and discuss venereal diseases. A glossary of terms basic to the study of human sexuality has also been provided.

ACKNOWLEDGMENTS

The existence of this book owes much to a large number of people and the long, tiring hours that they worked in helping me to achieve some perspective on and integration of the volumes of material on human sexuality. Dr. Clifford Adams, my first mentor and personal friend, read the entire manuscript critically and made many valuable suggestions. Paul Weikert also studied the manuscript in an earlier draft and gave me many useful ideas. Special thanks are due to Carlfred Broderick, who reviewed the chapter on children; to Ira Reiss, who provided insights into the chapter on nonmarital sexual relationships; and to Harold Christensen, who studied the chapter on sexual morality. Each of these men made important contributions not only to the book itself but also to my understanding of human sexuality as a whole.

Two prepublication reviewers were especially helpful with their evaluations and suggestions. These were Professors Donn Byrne, Purdue University, and James Geer, State University of New York, Stony Brook.

Baxter Venable, Psychology Editor of the W. B. Saunders Company, guided me with special skill and expertise through the final draft and kept me pointed in the right direction when I had a tendency to stray. His patience with me through this, my first book, was monumental. Marie Low, who edited the manuscript at Saunders, not only helped me in many technical ways but also assisted me greatly by contributing a woman's point of view.

Sandy Evans, who typed each draft and never seemed to tire of correcting my mistakes, deserves my special gratitude.

Finally, to the many other students, friends, and coworkers who helped to make this text a living reality, my thanks.

Under no circumstances are any errors in this book attributable to anyone but the author.

DAVID F. SHOPE

CONTENTS

Chapter 15

Appendix A

Appendix B

Appendix C

CHAPTER 1

INTRODUCTION TO THE STUDY OF SEXUALITY

SEX RESEARCH

The word *science* has many meanings, but as it is used in this book it refers to a method of study. The scientific method consists of making observations, collecting and evaluating data, forming hypotheses based on these observations, and eventually combining the hypotheses into an interrelated series known as a theory.

The scientific study of human sexual behavior has not found its own identity as a separate discipline. Human sexuality has been the object of research by biologists, sociologists, theologians, psychologists, anthropologists, and members of sundry other disciplines. This multi disciplinary approach has both advantages and drawbacks. Among the advantages are the variety of ideas that have been advanced, the avoidance of lopsided views based on a single discipline, and a continuing freshness of approach. The major disadvantage seems to lie in the lack of integration between the competing viewpoints that have produced valid cross-disciplinary findings.

Our current knowledge of sexual behavior comprises many hypothetical constructs based on learning theory, symbolic interaction theory, humanism, and various sociological viewpoints. Psychoanalysis presents the most complete theory at this time, but what is needed is a well-developed social-psychological theory based on testable propositions. Nevertheless, scientific methods deserve our further attention.

LIMITATIONS

Generalizations deriving from scientific studies of human sexuality are limited by several important factors. The foremost of these is the nature of the subjects under study. The most reliable and valid information would come from a random sample of subjects, but such samples are rarely possible with humans. This lack of randomness means we cannot always be certain which of the many possible intervening variables is affecting our results, nor can we always know the direction of these effects. A good deal of sexual research uses college students as subjects, but we

1

cannot be certain that statistics obtained from college populations apply to noncollege groups as well. Fortunately, with an increase in the percentage and variety of persons attending college, research using students may become more generally applicable. At any rate, the reader of sexual reports ought to know the nature of the subjects on which such reports are based.

Another factor which must be considered when reading sex research is that experimental work, such as that of Masters and Johnson (1966), in which subjects are observed in controlled situations is rare. Moral issues limit the procedures any researcher may conduct with his subjects. Thus far, society has not given adequate sanction to experimental studies of human sexuality, even with volunteer subjects. This limits our knowledge of cause and effect and circumscribes our capacity to develop new approaches.

Furthermore, since observations must be made by someone and research results must be interpreted, the personal bias of the investigator may, intentionally or unintentionally, influence the outcome of a study. This can be an acute problem in any human research, but it is especially crucial in research on sex. The scientist, when he fits the pure role, is nonjudgmental in terms of allowing his personal biases to influence his decisions. However, it is likely that few generalizations about human sexuality are free from the personal biases of the investigator. His moral values and theoretical leanings are very apt to affect his evaluation of sexual data. Thus the most valid way to read sexual literature is probably to delve into a variety of offerings. In this way one can make comparisons and arrive at one's own conclusions.

Of course, value-free thinking may not necessarily be the best, because values are themselves part and parcel of every interaction. The quality of sexuality is highly dependent upon the values of the participants. This means that the researcher needs some appreciation of his subjects' values regarding both science and sexuality. In some cases the investigator might do well to act in the role of participant-observer, considering the results of his data in terms of both objective science and his own personal feelings. Presumably, the combination will give him more insight and "feel" for the nature of the problem he is studying. It would be more honest and more precise if the reporter of sexual research spelled out the values that guide him in his work.

TYPES OF RESEARCH

The study of a single individual has been called the *idiographic* approach and is usually characterized by a richness and depth not often found in the study of groups. The group approach has been labeled the *nomethetic* approach (Allport, 1940). The case study helps us to see in action many of the generalizations that stem from research with groups.

Sexuality can also be studied by following the changes of a single individual or group through a definite period of time. This is the *longitudinal* study. *Cross-sectional* research uses data gathered from a sample of individuals at one time. This is the most widely used method of collecting information, since the subjects need not be followed for long periods of time and it is thus usually possible to deal with greater numbers of persons. Very often cross-sectional research will be in the form of surveys of various types.

The most accurate way of establishing cause and effect is through the experimental method, which permits all factors to be controlled. By holding all but one variable constant, it is possible to manipulate that one (the *independent variable*) and to study the consequences of that manipulation. These consequences are the *dependent variables*. Ideally, there would be only one dependent variable and it would follow the controlled application of the independent variable. If this were the case, there would be strong evidence that the independent *caused* the dependent variable to occur. However, this situation is rare in human research, and we must be content with less specific information about cause and effect.

Predictions based on human research findings are very tenuous and fallible. For example, in 1938 Lewis Terman, the noted research psychologist, predicted that virginity at marriage would practically disappear within three or four decades, but virginity has not and does not seem destined to become a social relic. Part of this lack of predictability stems from the fact that most human behavior is affected by many factors, and it is not clear which will have the most influence on the final behavioral act.

THE SEX RESEARCHERS

A number of landmark research studies of human sexual behavior have been conducted, primarily through the use of the interview and questionnaire methods, content analysis, and scaling techniques dependent upon quantitative data. Sex research has also been done on animals. In these major reports, each scientist has been aware of the limitations of his method of study. For instance, it is unclear to just what degree animal research is applicable to human behavior. With the interview and questionnaire methods, the need to give socially approved answers, failure of memory, the influence of subconscious defenses, and the different types of questions that various investigators ask all reduce the comparability among studies. As one example, the Kinsey studies (1948, 1953) have been criticized because they used orgasm as a criterion of sexual responsiveness and emphasized the biological foundations of sexuality more than some sexologists would have liked.

An important distinction which sex researchers have made is that of sexual attitudes versus sexual behavior. The counting of reported behavioral acts permits a more quantitative control of generalizations but fails to get at the important, personally determined internal mediators of that behavior. Reported attitudes can, of course, be quantified and correlated with actual behavior. Newer statistical tools have permitted recent research to be more sophisticated. Nevertheless, as Clayton (1972) has pointed out, the relationship between reported attitudes and actual behavior is often weak, and controversy over the effect of attitudes on behavior and of behavior on attitudes continues.

Edward M. Brecher (1969) has highlighted some of the history of early and modern sex research. He cites the pioneer work of Havelock Ellis as an anticipation of later findings. The early appearance of sexual behavior in both boys and girls, the fact that females develop sexual behavior at a later date than males, the fact that masturbation is a common phenomenon at all ages, the notion that homosexuality and heterosexuality are both present to varying degrees in each individual, the importance of psychological factors in impotence and frigidity, and the similarity of orgasm in men and women all were described by Ellis long before modern researchers analyzed them in greater detail.

Another early sex writer was Richard von Krafft-Ebing, whose famous book, *Psychopathia Sexualis* (first published in 1886), focused on sexual practices deemed by him to be deviant. As Brecher notes, the general tone of Krafft-Ebing's book is antisexual (pp. 50–60).

From these two opposites, Ellis and Krafft-Ebing, Brecher goes on to describe the contributions of other giants of sex research, including Freud, Hendrik van de Velde, John Money, Kinsey and his associates, Masters and Johnson, and others. Brecher does not forget the contributions of women researchers, such as Katharine B. Davis, Karen Horney, Margaret Mead, and Mary Jane Sherfey.

Along with Brecher's book, students interested in further studying the processes of sex research might wish to read Grummon and Barclay: *Sexuality: A Search for Perspective* (1971), Beigel: *Advances in Sex Research* (1963), or Money: *Sex Research: New Developments* (1965). It should be remembered, however, that although human sexual behavior has long been the object of scientific study, the science of sexuality does not and cannot have all the answers for which society or the individual might wish. There is room for subjective experience and for fitting the available facts into the context of personal encounters.

SOME NATIONAL STATISTICS

The majority of the studies reported in this book are based on various population samples that are more or less representative. They are basically correlational studies, with a very few based on the laboratory-experimental method. Few sex research studies match the probability sampling of the United States Bureau of Census, with its representations of large sections of the American public.

Since this text is devoted primarily to sexuality in the United States, a brief review of national statistics will give us a picture of the population as a whole and provide a background for our continued study. The characteristics described are the outcome of the application of the scientific method to the collection of sociological data. The material is based on *USA Statistics in Brief 1973* and *Statistical Abstract of the United States 1973*.

THE POPULATION

In 1970 the estimated population of the United States was 204.9 million persons, and this had grown to 208.8 million by 1972. The median age of this population in 1972 was 28.1 years, with about half the population being between the ages of 15 and 54, the most active sexual years.

In 1960 there were 88.6 million males, a figure which increased to 101.5 million by 1972. The 91.3 million females in 1960 had increased to 106.8 million by 1972. Today there are 5.3 million more women than men in the United States. Just 12 years ago the excess of women amounted to only 2.7 million. The consequences of an increasing ratio of females to males are difficult to predict, but the effects are apt to be felt mostly by older women. Until about age 24 there are slightly more males than females, and between the ages of 25 and 44 the excess of females to males is about three-fourths of a million. Beginning at age 45, for every 10-year age bracket there are about 1 to 2 million more women than men, with the gap widening as age goes up. Thus at the very time that love, comfort, and support are most needed, there are fewer males. Greater acceptance of polygamous marriage models, comarital relationships, homosexuality, or other forms of person to person interaction may be more functional with advancing age than earlier in life.

The ratio of blacks to whites has remained about 11 per cent. Other nonwhites amount to about 2 ½ per cent of the population.

In 1970 there were 18.2 live births per 1000 population, but this figure had dropped to 15.6 live births per 1000 population by 1972. Out of every 1000 live births, 16.8 white infants and 30.2 black or other minority infants died. The detrimental effects of poor living conditions upon low-income blacks are quite clear, despite the fact that middle-income blacks are about as well off as middle-class whites.

SOME FAMILY STATISTICS

More people than ever are marrying. In 1960 there were 8.5 marriages per 1000 population, but this figure had risen to 10.9 per 1000 by

1972. There were an estimated 2,269,000 marriages in 1972, reflecting a continuing increase each year since 1960, when 1,523,000 marriages took place. In 1971, among the population born between 1900 and 1954, 23.2 per cent of men were single, 66.5 per cent had been married only once, and 10.3 per cent had been married twice or more. Seventeen and one-half per cent of American women born between 1900 and 1954 were single. Among the married women, 85.5 per cent had been married only once, and 14.5 per cent had been married twice or more. Twelve per cent of the ever-married women were widowed, and 15 per cent were divorced according to the 1971 figures, the latest available at this writing.

Divorce, like marriage, is increasing. The median duration of marriage before divorce is 7 years. In 1960 there were 2.2 divorces per 1000 population, but by 1972 this rate had increased to 4.0 divorces per 1000 population. A total of 839,000 divorces were reported in 1972. Marriage and divorce will be discussed again in a later chapter, but this running account of national statistics reminds us that while marriage is more popular than ever as a life style, divorce is an increasingly acceptable solution to the difficulties inherent in that life style.

BEYOND OBJECTIVITY

Up to this point, we have emphasized objectively derived data derived from rationalistic and consensually validated approaches to the study of sexuality—the scientific method. Yet while the scientific view of mankind provides us with one focus for the study of human life, there are other vantage points that permit insights not currently available to behavioral observation. Individual experiences, as perceived and understood by the experiencing person, are a valuable source of knowledge. Humanistic orientations, existentialism, and innumerable but personally felt religious or philosophical frameworks assist man in understanding himself.

This direct focus on the experiencing individual can and often does have its own methods of validating interpretations of life, including feelings, beliefs, attitudes, thought processes, and behavior. Thus the quantification of behavior may be supplemented by qualitative (personal) experiences. It is difficult to communicate quality with the precision characteristic of valid statistical statements, but few of us subject all the ramifications of our personal lives to scientific scrutiny. For the individual experiencing love, the categorizing of love into various dimensions may have little relevance. Some men and women have a spiritual life. The inability of mankind to quantify this spiritual life, at least with precision, may leave the incessant objectivist with a sense that the unmeasurable may not even exist, but it also leaves the spiritual person with a sense of mystery.

SPECULATION

In general, this text is based on the scientific study of human sexuality, but many shades and hues of the human sexual experience have not been studied. These unresearched areas often lead to speculation about mankind. We speculate about humans on the basis of our personal experience when scientific data are not available or are not taken into account. But even when science has provided material concerning human sexuality, we still apply this scientific knowledge in terms of our conditioned perceptions. In a sense most sexual research is speculative to a degree, since each reader will interpret the data according to his or her understanding and will apply most statements to the extent that they seem relevant to and congruent with his or her individual experience. All texts thus mix conjecture with fact to one degree or another, and this one is no exception. If the reader interprets the statements made in terms of his or her personal experience, acceptance or rejection of the material presented will perhaps be most personally meaningful.

Throughout the remainder of this text, we will examine some of the problems and answer some of the questions concerning human sexuality. By mapping out the pitfalls of others, we may more easily avoid these pitfalls ourselves. In seeking to know the joys of sexuality, it is well to know the paths to joy that others have found.

CHAPTER 2

THEORIES OF SEXUALITY

ABOUT THEORY

This brief look at sexual theory is intended to provide a broad view of current explanations of human sexual behavior. Actually, except for Freud's work, there are no comprehensive theories of human sexuality; consequently, most explanations of sexuality are found within general personality and sociological constructs. The majority of these ideas are in the form of individual hypotheses that have not been fitted together to form adequate theory. Such hypothetical guidelines are, nevertheless, essential to the full development of a theory. They might be considered "little or immature theories" awaiting further development. What then is the role of theory?

A theory is an integrated set of hypotheses bound together by logical explanations and interconnections which is intended to explain data, relate facts, assist in focusing on a problem, or open new avenues of thought. Because of its functions, a theory is neither good nor bad but rather useful or useless. If the theory fulfills the demands made upon it without seriously interfering with new learning, it is useful. Unfortunately, many times the theory blinds its adherents to other equally logical explanations; when this occurs, the theory loses some of its usefulness. One result of a theory opening up new avenues of investigation is the necessity of continually modifying it in the light of new evidence. This process of refinement is never-ending. Nonetheless, such organized speculation is necessary if learning and understanding are to take place, and this is as true for human sexual behavior as for any other endeavor. What is known today may be considered misinformation tomorrow.

The translation of sexual data into hypotheses suffers the same fate as all classification attempts; that is, the purity of interpretation is reduced because of overlap among classes. Whenever data are forced into a mold, they are subject to the assumptions of the one who designed the mold and thus take on certain biases inherent in the mold design.

Much overlap is found among sexual theories, and one finds within most of them elements of the biological, learning, developmental, and social factors. Consequently, for our purposes sexual theories have been divided, on a purely arbitrary basis, into three major types based on whether their major emphasis is the biological, social, or learning approach.

BIOLOGICAL THEORY

Attempts have been made to explain human sexuality in terms of biology or instinct. That is, humans have a basic biological drive to be sexual, although learning may define the types of sexual acts one will permit oneself. Learning may also enhance or retard the direct expression of the basic biological drive. Genetics, hormones, physiology, and physical structure have been used as explanatory models.

GENETICS

Genetic theorists postulate that man has inherited his basic sex drive from his ancestors, and since the need to reproduce is instinctual, it is virtually impossible to inhibit it completely. Within the human, the seed of sexual awareness is already implanted at birth, and only time is needed for this seed to come to fruit. If left unhampered, even infants show signs of sexual behavior. The chief aim of the sex drive is to reproduce in the service of the species. In this sense, the biological theory continues, the sex drive is approximately like the needs for air, food, and thirst quenchers, although it is not nearly as far up the biological survival hierarchy. This is because the sex drive is aimed at the species as a whole, while the other three drives are part of individual survival. Sexual behavior for the individual can be highly inhibited, but this is not true for the species.

FREUD'S THEORY

In its original form, Freudianism is steeped with the flavor of the biogenetic theories. Thus although concern with learning (especially social learning) is important to Freudians, the fundamental component of Freud's work is instinct—the "push toward sexual behavior."

Freud termed the energy of sex the *libido* and believed that it is this energy which sparks many of man's endeavors. The libido is a form of energy that is set apart from other kinds of psychic energy by virtue of its focus on sex (Freud, 1962, p. 75). This sexual energy, along with hostility and aggressiveness, accounts for most of the motivation behind human behavior.

Freud's division of man's psyche into id, ego, and superego is well known. The *id* comprises those baser instincts of man which seek fulfillment at any cost; the *superego*, in contrast, is composed of those absolute morals (learned primarily from one's parents) which allow almost no behavior at all, sexual or otherwise. Neither the id nor the superego is aware of outer reality and each seeks to impose its demands upon the other, so that a struggle is constantly going on between the two. The id operates only to seek pleasure for the organism; the frustration of this *pleasure principle* is the goal of the superego. The *ego* is the aspect of man's psyche that is in touch with external reality. Its task is to mediate the battle between the id and superego by bringing the forces of environmental reality into the picture. In this way the ego censors the id. The ego operates on the *reality principle*.

According to Freud, the libido may be entirely masculine in nature (1962, p. 77). In a sense androgen, the male sex hormone, is somewhat analogous to libido, since there is evidence that administration of androgen in proper amounts to females can sometimes increase their sexual desires (Kupperman, 1961, p. 497). Freud, however, seemed to prefer instincts to hormones for his explanation of human sexual behavior.

More than anyone else up to his time, Freud recognized the sexual responses that prevail in infants and young children. He divided the development of the individual into several life stages, based primarily on presumed connections between physiological events and psychological factors. These stages of development are nothing more than convenient devices for bringing order to a large number of observations. The first stage, the *oral* stage, extends from birth (or before) to about 18 months and is that period when the infant is concerned primarily with searching the world through his or her mouth. The ending of this stage is purely arbitrary, for it may extend with some individuals into adulthood, while others may regress to it under stress. The *anal* stage, the second of Freud's pregenital stages, is that period in which the child's concern with defecation and his own anus is paramount. Like all the Freudian stages, the anal period has no really discrete end, and its consequences may persist into adulthood. Adult stinginess and miserliness are often considered outcomes of a failure to move beyond the anal stage.

The next period in early childhood is that in which the youngster becomes keenly aware of his genital organs. Roughly, this *phallic* stage extends from the age of three to that of five or six. The child moves from anal preoccupations into an awareness that he has a genital area which is pleasurable to touch (Freud, 1962, p. 57). This, Freudians feel, is a period of major importance in human life, for during this time little boys learn not to compete with their fathers for their mothers' sexual favors. The desire of sons to consume completely the sexual favors of their mothers is the well-known *Oedipus complex,** and the fear of reprisal from the larger, stronger father is *castration anxiety.* Little girls who see a man's penis realize that they do not have such an organ and the advantages that go with it, and this is *penis envy.* According to traditional Freudian psychoanalytic theory, penis envy, castration anxiety, and the

---

*Following Freud's original writings, some authors still label the companion desire of daughters to engage in sexual activity with their fathers the *Electra complex,* but the term "Oedipus complex" is now generally used to refer to both sexes.

Oedipus complex can all be roots of adult neuroses if not satisfactorily resolved.

The so-called *latent* period extends from the time when the Oedipus complex is worked through, chiefly by identification with the father, until puberty. During this period the child is comparatively quiescent as far as sex interest is concerned.

Puberty begins a second period of sexual interest, the *genital* stage, characterized by a reawakening of sexual impulses. This revived interest is continuous with adult sexual needs and normally is not lost until very late in life. Usually, the child goes through a period during which interest in members of his own sex is high, and it is this period that Freud likened to homosexuality. Freud believed that if the male goes through this period successfully, he becomes mature and heterosexually oriented. If the woman matures successfully, she passes through a period of recognizing that her clitoris is somewhat like a little penis, but escapes this form of "male sexuality" in adulthood (Freud, 1962, p. 32). Puberty, then, is the time when the general sexual excitability of the body becomes concentrated in the genitals. For the man this represents nothing more than the developmental sequence by which general infant sexual excitability matures into adult sexuality, but for the woman it means outgrowing her bisexuality by repressing the male (clitoral) aspect of her sexual nature (Freud, 1962, pp. 76–79). Women develop a vaginal orgasm upon completing the Freudian developmental sequences.

Some Criticisms of Freud.   The Freudian constructions have been criticized on several grounds. Because most of the developmental changes take place at unconscious levels, they are difficult to verify empirically. Generalizations from traditional Freudianism have been applied too broadly and indiscriminately. Furthermore, clitoral orgasm has been demonstrated to be highly satisfactory and for many women more pleasurable than coitally induced orgasm. The absence of touch cells in the vagina casts doubt on any physiological vaginal orgasm and suggests that the stronger feelings supposedly associated with coital activity are psychologically based. Freud's belief that the latent period is characterized by a temporary suspension of sexual interest has not been verified, and just recently (1973) the American Psychiatric Association has removed homosexuality from its list of psychiatric disabilities.

For a more detailed view and criticism of psychoanalysis, the reader is referred to books such as Jastrow: *Freud: His Dream and Sex Theories* (1960).

MODIFICATIONS OF FREUDIAN THEORY

Freudian theory has been highly modified by many of those who follow Freud's thinking. Both Karen Horney and Harry S. Sullivan through his interpersonal theory have emphasized social learning rather than sex as the chief source of personality development. Horney was able to classify individuals according to their inclinations to interact with others. She used three major classifications: moving against people, moving away from people, and moving toward people. The aggressive, competitive individual who is somewhat indifferent is apt to move against others in many of his relationships. The moving away person tends to isolate himself from others or to deny his need to interact with them, while those who move toward others tend to nurture interpersonal relationships.

Sullivan's formulations emphasize the importance of relating to others, especially those with whom one first interacts. Thus the *mothering one*, to use Sullivan's term for the individual most responsible for the infant, exerts a primary and lasting influence. Those aspects of a relationship that satisfy the individual, such as being fed when hungry, tend to be selected out for attention, while those that lack satisfying consequences tend to be ignored. Thus the individual learns to *selectively inattend* to designated aspects of his or her interpersonal relationships by becoming unaware of those that are unsatisfying or pose a threat to the self concept. Selective inattention is more than ignoring; it is unawareness that the distasteful stimuli exist.

Sandor Ferenczi, a pupil of Freud, proposed in a 1938 edition of the *Psychoanalytic Quarterly* that each organ of the body is originally imbued with its own source of libidinal energy. This energy becomes repressed and is finally concentrated in a "special pleasure reservoir," the genitals, from which it is periodically discharged. The entire coital sequence is symbolic of man's earlier existence as a carefree sea creature and of the struggles associated with man's becoming a land creature. Ferenczi likens coitus to sleep, which he regards as a regressive state. According to Ferenczi, "the principal difference between sleep and coitus may, however, consist in this, that in sleep only the happy existence within the womb is represented, but in coitus [are also represented] the struggles. . . which the 'expulsion from the Garden of Eden' brought in its train (cosmic catastrophes, birth, weaning, efforts at adjustment)" (1968, p. 80).

Mankind's existence in the womb, then, is a recapitulation of his earlier existence in the sea, and it is to this comparatively comfortable situation that he seeks to return. The womb environment is physically and psychologically pleasurable, and man's attempt to return to it means that he has a biological drive for pleasure much the same as his biological need to reproduce. Coital behavior satisfies this individual drive for pleasure because all the comforts of man's existence before coming from the sea, repeated in utero, are again reproduced symbolically during coitus, the final outcome of which is equated with sleep.

There are other offshoots of Freudian theory, many of which emphasize biological propensities and the conflicting requirements of various cultures.

FORD AND BEACH

The monumental study (1951) in which Clellan S. Ford and Frank A. Beach related and integrated biological and social data should not be forgotten. Ford and Beach studied sexual behavior across cultures and within infrahuman species in an attempt to discover differences and commonalities. They assumed (1) that sexual behavior common to man and animals was probably evidence of a common genetic inheritance, (2) that one could not understand one's own sexuality by introspection alone, and (3) that the only valid way to separate the learned aspects of sexuality from the instinctual was by cross-cultural and cross-species comparisons.

After reviewing the evidence of a large number of investigators, Ford and Beach concluded that all primates masturbate, engage in homosexual activities with large numbers of individuals, not just a few deviates, engage in coitus, and have methods of attracting a sexual partner. Variations between animal and human sexual behavior involve primarily methods of attracting a sexual partner, duration and type of precoital play, preference for coital positions, and aggressiveness associated with sexual arousal. Humans permit mild pain-producing techniques by both men and women, but lower animals generally limit this type of activity to males. Some societies permit bestiality but most do not. Preferred coital positions vary widely among human cultures, and only humans seem to practice kissing and breast-fondling to any extent.

The general thesis of Ford and Beach is that a fundamental biological propensity to act sexually exists, but this propensity can be modified by learning. Cultural conditioning accounts for the extent and type of sexual expression humans will allow themselves. The sexual behavior of humans falls far short of their biological potential.

The conclusions of Ford and Beach are representative of those theorists espousing a predominantly biological orientation. Instincts may well have their most profound influence on hormonal physiology, however, and along with nutrition and genetics may account for individual and gender differences in hormone production. It is to this important aspect of human sexuality that we now turn.

HORMONAL INFLUENCES

The effect of hormones on behavior is just beginning to be understood. June Reinisch (1974) surveyed the literature with regard to the effects of hormones on sexually dimorphic (differentiated) behavior. The general hypothesis of this survey and investigation was that during the critical fetal period of central nervous system development, hormones have a "fundamental influence on the organization and differentiation of neural tissues (substratum) destined to mediate, at least partially, dimorphic behavior in human males and females" (p. 52). Further, the organizing effect of androgens is best understood as setting a response bias in the system, so that differential sensitivity and responsiveness are built into the organism. The tendency to be differentially responsive to various types of stimuli affecting the maleness or femaleness of the individual is thus built into the nervous system before birth. Learning may overcome some of these built-in tendencies, but in the absence of specific environmental influences, the individual is apt to select, automatically, stimuli compatible with his or her nervous system. Androgen, the male sex hormone, appears to be the significant factor in fetal differentiation of the central nervous system substratum.

Neumann and Steinbeck (1972) reached conclusions similar to those of Reinisch. Males develop only if the embryonic testis releases its hormonal messenger; that is, from the same homologous embryonic structure, male gonads develop if androgens are released at the critical time. If no male hormones are released, female gonadic structures develop, and these latter grow without needing estrogen to stimulate them. In other words, in the absence of androgens, embryonic sexual organs automatically develop as female.

Money and Ehrhardt (1971) found the brain to be bipotential as to maleness or femaleness unless the androgens are introduced during the critical period of fetal development—a period not yet specified. Bipotentiality appears to persist if the individual is hormonally feminine.

If androgen is present during the critical period, which occurs sometime before birth, the individual will tend to be more aggressive, less sensitive to skin exposure as a neonate, less influenced by female hormones, and more receptive to a variety of stimuli considered masculine in our culture. All of these variations in receptivity will occur regardless of the gender of the individual, for it is the central nervous system that is affected, not gonadal structures.

Although some of these sex differences persist throughout life, the processes of social conditioning and learning reduce many of them in later childhood and adulthood. It is important to note that except for ejaculation there is no sex-related behavior that is exclusive to one gender or the other.

Luttge (1971) concluded that gonadal hormones apparently aid in the induction, maintenance, and control of sexual behavior in both rhesus monkeys and humans, but that they are not absolutely essential for its display in all individuals.

The use of testosterone, the hormone responsible for male secondary sexual characteristics, has led to definite increases in sexual appetite for some women (Kupperman, 1963; Salmon, 1941). However, hormones have been less successful in increasing the male's sexual potency. Males who have their testicles removed after reaching maturity are often capable of continued sexual interest and activity, especially if they are regularly administered hormone therapy. On the other hand, males castrated before puberty are not likely to be sexually active, although they may indicate an interest in erotica simply because to do so is socially desirable (Potts, 1969; Molitar, 1970).

It is the male sex hormone that in both genders has the greatest effect on increasing libido. Indeed, estrogen, a female hormone, often has a suppressing effect on sexual potency and occasionally has been used by physicians in an attempt to control excessive sexual urges in men and women. There are, however, so many factors other than hormones influencing sexual urges that the long-term effectiveness of both estrogen and androgen on normally healthy people remains uncertain.

Nevertheless, there is one time when estrogen therapy may be especially helpful in re-establishing female sexual interests, and this is following long periods during which natural estrogen production has been quite low, for instance, following menopause. Additional estrogen at these times helps keep the vaginal mucosa from deteriorating and thus may reduce painful coitus for the postmenopausal woman. But even estrogen treatment as a routine procedure following menopause is disputed as recommended medical therapy (Pinker and Roberts, 1967, pp. 32–34). That hormones contribute to human welfare and thus to sexuality cannot be disputed. Less clear is the direct effect of androgen and estrogen on human libido.

Raboch and Starka (1973) found that the level of circulating testosterone was not significantly related to the reported coital activity of the male subjects they studied. These researchers found that under favorable social conditions, males with circulating levels of testosterone previously considered "eunuchoid" were able to engage in normal coital activity.

In brief, assessing the effect of hormones on human sexual behavior and attitudes is particularly difficult, since a multiplicity of intervening factors influence the sex lives of men and women. The data do suggest the hypothesis that androgen-mediated central nervous system variations account for initial and early responses, but that continuous reinforcement or nonreinforcement accounts for behavioral maintenance or disappearance.

SOME CONCLUSIONS

Biological theories of sexuality account for man's generalized propensity to respond to sexual stimuli, give us one focus for considering individual differences in receptivity to stimuli, and indicate possible methods of intrapersonal transmissions of sexual stimuli. Taken as a whole, the biological theories seem to imply a generalized emotional tendency to respond, but give us little information about the processes whereby one selects the types of responses to be made.

There is some suggestion that biological potential, to a limited degree, can be enhanced or retarded by the social environment and learning conditions under which the individual is reared. Only masturbation, coitus, and homosexuality appear to be practiced by all species and all cultures, but coitus is the most widely used sexual practice in the animal world, man included. Biological theory could be interpreted as suggesting that all other sexual activity, perhaps masturbation excepted, is aimed at the final act of coition.

Biology has not accounted for variations within the individual from time to time, the development of values and beliefs surrounding mankind's sexuality, or the varying sexual practices that appear in different cultures. While much more biosexual research is needed, it is safe to state at this time that nearly all of the human's sexual activities can be at least partially accounted for by learning.

SOCIAL-PSYCHOLOGICAL THEORIES

Social-psychological formulations of mankind's behavior recognize biological considerations but concentrate primarily on the dynamics of interpersonal relationships. The power of social conditioning to shape the manner in which humans relate to one another is considered an essential aspect of human behavior, while the unique psychological perceptions of the individual are accepted by many as the consequence of physical status, past learning, and current environmental pressures — especially those of an interpersonal nature. Several important social-psychological theories are presently recognized.

SYMBOLIC INTERACTION THEORY

From the outset it should be realized that among the social-psychological theorists there is no central figure of Freud's stature. Consequently, from the mainstream of social-psychological theory arise many divergent viewpoints. In this book only the broadest and most general outlines can be discussed. That there are many exceptions to, disagreements about, and modifications of the views presented here is self-evident.

A leader in the social-psychological field has been George H. Mead. As summarized by Meltzer (1967, pp. 5–24), Mead's theory states principally that humans do not respond directly to the activities of others but rather to their intentions; that is, they respond to the future intended behavior of others and not merely to their present actions. This is a distinctly human characteristic which depends upon man's ability to use abstract symbols. Gestures by animals (snarling dogs, for example) elicit predetermined responses, but gestures by humans are responded to on the basis of their meaning or intent, as when one shakes his fist at another. Gestures are symbolic representations of an act. People's responses to the communications of others are governed by the meanings they attach to these communications. In order to engage in cooperative interaction, those who are themselves interacting must similarly interpret their communications and fill in the imaginative gaps left by others. This imaginative completion of the meaning of the other person's act requires the taking of the other person's role through mental activity and the responding to one's own communication through symbolic completion of the meaning of that communication. The ability to respond to oneself precedes the capacity to respond to others. It is the acquired ability to respond to shared symbols that makes human cooperative relationships possible.

By the term *self* Mead meant the ability of the individual to respond to himself or herself socially. That is, the individual may praise, blame, or encourage himself or herself; or he or she may seek punishment, become disgusted, and develop a variety of other attitudes toward the self, just as one develops a variety of attitudes toward others. The self initially develops through imitation of the roles of others. Imitation is followed by actually playing the roles—for example, those of wife, mother, or husband. The third stage finds the child assuming a number of roles simultaneously in response to a variety of persons. In time the individual tends to generalize certain aspects of his or her self, and these generalizations are manifest in a wide variety of situations. The individual has learned to define himself or herself in a rather consistent manner. Thus it is possible to say "This is like me," or "This is so unlike me."

According to Mead's formulation, the structure of the self is made up of two major components, the *I* and the *Me*. The I aspect initiates all acts performed by the individual and represents the more or less impulsive, spontaneous, and unorganized aspect of human experience. The Me component is the standardized set of meanings concerning values, beliefs, attitudes, and behavior common to the significant reference group with which the individual identifies. The I aspect of an individual's self initiates any action, while the Me carries the act to completion. Thus the I and the Me components of the self work cooperatively to further the person's functionality. This cooperativeness between the I and Me differs from the antagonism between man's impulsive nature and his moralistic learning represented by the psychoanalytic concepts of id and superego. When environmental conditions permit, the I and the Me work together in harmony to help the individual create a positive self.

The possession of a self resembling a miniature democracy makes it possible to have imaginative inner experiences that need not reach overt expression. Through the interpretation of covert or overt stimuli via inner imaginative processes, the individual is able to direct, check, and organize his or her behavior. He or she acts upon the environment instead of being merely a passive respondent to stimuli.

All behavior involves the selection of stimuli which will be responded to according to their relevance. Individuals select certain stimuli and perceive these stimuli in accordance with their self concepts. This *selective attention* is related to Sullivan's concept of *selective inattention,* but it is also essentially different, for it is an *active* process in which stimuli are judged as to their relative importance, while selective inattention is the *avoidance* or *denial* of stimuli perceived as threatening.

Apart from reflexes and habits, human behavior is built up as it goes along; that is, people act, not simply react. The act is the total process of initiating, constructing, organizing, and completing behavior. Acts may be short or they may encompass large portions of an individual's life. Courtship may be an act, and so may sexual intercourse within that courtship. Thus acts may build one upon another, implying that much behavior is interrelated and not merely discrete and separate responses to a stimulus or a set of stimuli.

To summarize, symbolic interaction begins with the imaginative completion of one's own and others' communication through mutually understood symbolizations. Eventually, through various role-taking stages, the individual builds a self that strongly reflects the teachings and experiences of significant others. The individual then receives stimuli from others, interprets them through his or her idiosyncratic perceptual processes, and responds accordingly.

THE PHENOMENOLOGICAL, EXISTENTIAL, SELF THEORY STREAM

In addition to Mead and other symbolic interaction theorists, there are others who view the individual's psychology as stemming from his or her perceptions of environment, especially perceptions of interpersonal relationships. It is the individual's interpretation, which in turn is shaped largely by past interpretations of experience, that accounts for individual personality development.

Kinch (1967) sees the individual's self conceptions as arising from social interaction and as directing the behavior of the person. In turn, this personal behavior causes others to react in terms of their personal interpretations of it. This latter interpretation is, of course, highly influenced by the second person's self concepts. In this manner each individual influences others, and the result is the modification of everyone's self concepts. These self concept modifications may be so slight that they are unnoticeable, or they may be drastic changes.

Rogers (1964) discusses three ways of knowing. The first of these is *subjective* knowing. Subjective knowing is awareness from an internal frame of reference. This subjectiveness impels one to say "I know I love her," or "I wonder how I do feel about that." Since all knowing is ultimately a matter of hypothesis-making, subjective knowing, like all knowing, requires that subjectively generated hypotheses be tested for validity. One important way of validating subjective knowing is by checking the inner flow of personal experience for congruency with what one subjectively knows. Thus if one says subjectively of another "I know he hates me," the experiences that come from one's interpersonal relationships with this other person provide a basis for validating the hypothesis.

Objective knowing, Rogers continues, is the knowing that comes about through validation of knowledge by sources outside the individual, primarily by reference groups. Thus, if there is a high level of agreement that such and such is true within the reference group, the individual hypothesis is regarded as valid. It is true because those with whom the hypothesis is checked agree that it is true. Harry S. Sullivan called this kind of group agreement *consensual validation.* Whereas subjective knowing directs empathy inward, objective knowing is based on the flow of empathy outward toward the reference group as a whole. Of course, one can select reference group members who agree with one's hypotheses about life and "stack the deck," so to speak. A good deal of scientific effort is based on objective knowing.

The third type of knowing Rogers names *interpersonal* knowing or *phenomenological knowledge.* In interpersonal knowing empathy is directed toward another individual. The individual hypothesizes that he or she knows something about another. "I know how you feel." "I understand you." "I know how deep your convictions are." These are all examples of knowing interpersonally. Like all hypotheses, these knowings need to be validated by simply asking the other person about his true thoughts, or better still, by providing the kind of environment in which the other can feel free to reveal inner feelings, thoughts, and beliefs spontaneously. Interpersonal knowing is a way of getting at the other's phenomenological field, of getting inside his private world of meanings to check the accuracy of one's own understanding.

The healthy person, Rogers says, will use all three methods of knowing, generating within himself or herself the subjective feelings, beliefs, and thoughts that give individuality its richest meaning. At other times or in conjunction with subjective knowledge, the individual will acquire objective pieces of knowledge, and these, along with considerable interpersonal knowledge, assist in developing the fullest relationships with others.

The subjective experiences of the individual have both temporal and spatial dimensions (Ford and Urban, 1963). Time may be personal, as when a given period seems shorter or longer than the period of time that actually elapsed. Activities that are pleasurable or require concentration may make time seem short, while boring or enforced periods of attention may seem longer than they actually are. The estimate of space that occurs in subjective awareness can, like the estimate of time, be shorter, longer, wider, or narrower than actual space. *Oriented* space is experienced as having a vertical and horizontal axis. This gives the individual some sense of his position in relation to his physical surroundings. *Attuned* space is experienced when one interprets one's spatial positions according to one's affective state at the time. Attributes of attuned space include feelings of constriction, fullness, emptiness, clearness, darkness, and so forth. Ford and Urban have mentioned two other attributes of subjective experience: *causality,* experienced as chance, intentionality, or determinism, and *materiality,* which they describe as the experience of the physical qualities of the world.

The theories just discussed all emphasize subjective experience as reality to the individual — a reality into which no one else can fully enter and which leaves the individual in a state of *existential loneliness.* The self is born from interaction with others and the more or less gradual internalizing of the norms, symbols, and meanings of significant others. A most important aspect of these theories is their emphasis on the possibility of the individual actively controlling himself or herself, rather than being a passive pawn of the environment.

Other social theories emphasize the gain or loss aspects of interpersonal bargaining (exchange theory), role performance, game theory, or general systems theory. None of these theoretical formulations have been developed adequately in their application to family or sexual behavior (Broderick, 1971). Thus attempts to apply them to sexuality seem premature at this time, except in the case of special and specific aspects. One could, for instance, conceive of sexual relationships in terms of an exchange in which the actors reciprocate sexually according to symbolic interpretations of costs, rewards, and profits. However, although power wielding within dyadic groups has been studied, the results have not clearly supported an exchange theory.

All theories have their limitations. For example, if we conclude that significant others influence our self concepts, sexual behavior, and so forth, we might ask as Rosenberg (1973) did, "Which significant others?" Rosenberg found that we err to some extent in taking the role of another and differentiate levels of significance attributed to others on the basis of our trust in them. The consistency of our feedback from others affects our images of ourselves. Also, abstractions that infer internal processes are difficult to verify. Many of the conceptualizations of social psychological theories lack refinement.

For these and other reasons, many researchers prefer behavioral theory with its more observable conditions. Increasingly complex levels of abstraction and reduction, many behaviorists feel, only add confusion to our understanding of ourselves. Accessible facts lend themselves to verification, while unavailable data (including many hypotheses from nonbehavioral theory) are useless. For the true behaviorist, speculation about internal processes is most unscientific. Opponents of behaviorism point out that much of humanity and humanism is lost to study by those who persist in regarding objectivity as superior to subjective methods. Most likely, to the extent that it is possible, the behavioral verification of humanistic psychology through the process of consensual validation (shared observations) would add considerably to our knowledge of the sexual behavior of men and women. For this reason, as much as any, both sexes should participate in the investigation of human sexuality.

LEARNING THEORY

INTRODUCTION

There is little doubt that most human sexual behavior is learned, and that this learning affects not only genitally oriented sexual expression but also the more generalized function we have labeled sexuality. It is this author's opinion that no matter what other theory one espouses, the fundamentals of learning theory will apply.

There are several ways individuals learn, including trial and error, association, specific tutoring, and conditioning. Certain conditions seem to facilitate conscious learning, such as a desire to learn, the psychological capacity to drop older, undesirable habits, and the availability of adequate neurological apparatus. Without some degree of motivation to find new methods of behaving sexually, sexual learning will be inhibited. If one is fearful of giving up behavior, opinions, or values which interfere with adaptation, the old habits will remain and new learning will not take place. If the nervous system of the organism cannot accommodate a new behavior, that behavior is impossible. Consequently, sexual behavior which is impossible to perform physically, a disinterest in sex, or a fear of the consequences of sexuality all reduce the potential for learning new sexual responses.

A considerable amount of human behavior is learned by trial and error; that is, the individual tries out a response, and if it is successful and rewarding, he is likely to continue it. If the response does not satisfy the original need, it will not be repeated: an error has been made, and a new and different response must be tried. For example, the girl who accidentally discovers the pleasant feeling that comes from touching her clitoris is apt to repeat the touching unless the idea that she has touched herself is so negative that she is overwhelmed with guilt or shame. At this point it should be noted that women are more likely than men to discover self-stimulation accidentally and through trial and error can find the ways that sexually excite them most. When guilt is a factor, the individual often must seek alternative responses by means of trial and error.

One learns much behavior, sexual or otherwise, through association with others. Originally, this association will be with the parents or parent substitutes, and the individual will imitate much of the behavior he sees, eventually introjecting the values of those significant to him until at last he achieves a high degree of identification with them.

Teaching sexual behavior by direct tutoring is not very acceptable in our society, yet there is little or nothing about sexual expression which should be known instinctively. Even animals learn much of their behavior rather than depend only upon instinct. Anthropologists tell us that in some cultures sexual behavior is learned by having the older men teach the younger girls, while older women teach the young men. In our own culture, counselors often teach their clients sexual behavior within limited degrees, but some have also combined direct sexual instruction with analysis (McCartney, 1966, pp. 227–237). Whether more direct methods of teaching sexual interaction would serve society better is a matter of speculation. Yet acceptable or not, there is much informal sexual "tutoring," such as might take place in a wife-exchanging club or "behind the barn," and it is not likely to lessen in the future. The quality of some of this "education" might, however, be in doubt.

CONDITIONING

Basic to much learning is the conditioning paradigm. In its simplest form, conditioning occurs when a response is made in the presence of anything that will cause it to be repeated. When the response is repeated it is said to have been *reinforced*, and that which brought about the repetition is called the *reinforcer* or reward. Time is an important element in this type of learning. If the reinforcement comes either too early or too late, a response other than the one intended will be learned. Time is less critical with humans than with animals, but much learned human sexual behavior can nevertheless be explained by differences in the time of reinforcement. For example, the coed who engages in premarital coitus satisfactorily will have immediate reinforcement from her sexual behavior. Any guilt that occurs later, unless it is very strong, may be too far away in time to negatively reinforce (punish) her sexual behavior. The later guilt is more apt to reinforce the concept of herself as a "bad" person. Thus, she continues coitus even though her concept of herself plunges increasingly lower. However, if she is negatively reinforced while engaging in the coital act (perhaps by being caught by her parents), she may temporarily discontinue her behavior. At some time later, unless the negative conditioning is continued, she may resume coitus.

The strength of any reward for the individual is related to the extent to which he values it and is another important factor in determining whether or not learning will take place. The more the individual desires the reward, the greater is the likelihood that he will respond in a manner to get it.

According to Dollard and Miller, a stimulus, cue, response, and reinforcement are part of most learning situations (1950). A *drive* may be innate or learned and has been defined by Dollard and Miller as "that which impels to action." In other words, the sex drive is the combination of forces, biological and learned, which pressures the individual toward action specifically defined by him as sexual. A *cue* is that aspect of the learning situation which defines more specifically the manner in which the drive will be relieved. A man entering a room sees several women and becomes sexually excited by seeing all of them. Among them is his wife, and it is with her that he relieves his sexual desires. The women in the room are the direct stimuli which "cause" a desire for sex; his wife is the cue telling him the one with whom he will fulfill this desire. Other conditions may provide further clues as to the way she will relieve him—through coitus, fellatio, masturbation, or some other method. His response is his total reaction to the situation and could be further divided into his internal responses and his overt or external responses. The latter constitute his directly observable behavior, and the former are inferred from his behavior as seen by others. Reinforcement occurs when the drive which originally propelled the behavior is reduced or controlled.

Dollard and Miller also describe two very important kinds of responses that man can make. These are speech and fear, and both are of critical importance in human sexuality.

FEAR

Fear is both a stimulus and a response; that is, it stimulates a person to action or freezes him in inaction. As a stimulus fear can be useful in motivating a person to constructive or remedial action. As a response fear is a warning that the organism is approaching a dangerous situation. Fear can become a learned response to sexual stimuli which may be useful, for example, in protecting oneself from strangers. Unfortunately, however, fear of sexual stimuli can be generalized to people and situations other than those that would be dangerous. This fear generalization is learned but no less irrational when it hampers constructive relationships. Fright, phobias, and anxiety are usually made of the same stuff; they all stem from fear of the consequences of dealing with others.

Since fear is for the most part a conditioned response, it can be unlearned. If the conditioning has been long and intensive or otherwise quite dramatic, the help of a trained therapist may be necessary to get rid of it. However, most sexual fears are eliminated by virtue of the fact that sex is pleasurable: the presence of a positive reinforcement (pleasure from sex) simply extinguishes the fear response. Thus, everyday sexual behavior does most to decondition sex fear. If fear or disgust (a form of fear) with sex is overly strong, however, no pleasure will result from sexual responses and no positive reinforcement will occur. As a consequence the fear remains and sexual acts become negative reinforcement (punishment). When sex becomes its own punishment, the end result will surely be dissatisfaction, more and more disgust, shame, and guilt, and less and less desire to engage in sexual behavior.

The wife who is forced to enter a sexual relationship with her husband and has deep-seated negative feelings about sex is apt to become conditioned to dislike him. Fortunately, the majority of Americans are not intensely taught that sexuality is negative. On the other hand, they are also not taught the positiveness of sex, and most sexual dissatisfaction comes about through this lack of positive reinforcement.

INTERNAL MEDIATORS

The conditioning of humans is not as straightforward as that of animals because humans think and speak—responses which in and of themselves can be reinforcing. Consequently, most of man's responses are filtered through *internal mediators*, the most important of which are cognitive processes. Words both signify and attach values to behavior, with the result that it is sometimes difficult to be sure what is and is not rewarding. The manipulation of words and thoughts can change the entire meaning of a sexual relationship, and when sexual partners derive different meanings from the same word, trouble can result. To be fallated is the same, behaviorally speaking, as to have love made to you, but the words carry quite different meanings to particular individuals. Both are symbols, as is sexual behavior itself, but the phrase "to have love made to you" avoids direct mention of out-and-out sexual intercourse and thus helps avoid some of the stigma attached to sexual behavior by impuning to it a "proper motive." Fallate, which means to perform the act of sexual intercourse, is a verb; it denotes action.

The majority of sexologists consider learning the fundamental key to human sexuality. So do antisexual moralists. Two opposite influences exert strain upon the individual who is involved in making choices about his sexual behavior. Often there is no possible choice he can make without some feeling of bewilderment as to which is right. This conflict situation is termed an *approach-avoidance* conflict by psychologists and constitutes what Dollard and Miller have described as a *learning dilemma*; that is, a drive or need exists for which there is no possible answer. Any choice the individual makes is apt to be both rewarding and damning at the same time. A major task for many Americans is the developmental one of "coming to terms with one's own conscience." Since each side (actually there are many more than two) can be both rewarding and punishing, in the final analysis it is the amount and intensity of exposure to the pros and cons, along with one's own internal mediating forces, that help the individual decide which items from each side will be rewarding and which will not. He can simply ignore the opinions, ideas, and values that are inimical to his goals; that is, he often uses the defense mechanisms of denial and repression when sexual conflict exists.

THE HALO EFFECT

Everyone knows that a financially secure couple have a better chance of making a satisfactory adjustment if other things are equal. Financial security affects all aspects of marriage, and this notion that one part of marriage will affect the other parts is akin to the psychological mechanism called the "halo effect."

Halo occurs when judgment is affected by factors which logically should not affect it; for instance, the good athlete may find himself getting better grades than his academic work warrants. He receives the better grades because of his athletic ability, but the instructor who gives them does so without conscious awareness. Negative attitudes toward sex can and do adversely affect the marriage of those so conditioned. Consequently, much earlier conditioning must be unlearned after marriage, but this is possible only if the couple are willing and patient enough to wait for new conditioning to take effect. Sometimes this process is rather fast, but for other couples it can be painfully slow. The important idea is that at least some negative earlier learning can be overcome, especially if a specific effort is made to overcome it. Sexuality, like other aspects of personality, is not so fixed during childhood that it cannot be modified, although the longer one lives with undesired sexual traits the more difficult it will be to eliminate them.

MODELING BEHAVIOR

Imitation of others begins at a behavioral level and may extend not only to concrete actions but also to abstract values and beliefs. The child learns the role of male or female by observing the behavior of others, especially those upon whom he or she depends, and models himself after it.

Identification, the process of assimilating roles, is a major part of the modeling process. The psychoanalytic view is that the little boy identifies with his father as a defense against the latter's superior strength, which would be used against the child if the Oedipus complex were actually carried out. Tharp (1963), however, has summarized evidence indicating that boys apparently achieve identification with their fathers through affectionate bonds, not fear of castration as the psychoanalysts would have us believe.

Essentially, modeling behavior is a means of acquiring new behavioral patterns through the observation of behavior and its consequences. Bandura (1969, pp. 118-126) cited extensive research data indicating that both behavioral and affective responses can be gained through observing and imitating the behavior of others. Imitation, when practiced extensively, may take on the qualities of a habitual response and thus may become an actual part of the individual's makeup.

Rose (1973, pp. 107–109) has given us some prerequisites for effective modeling: (1) the observer must give attention to the model's behavior; (2) it may be necessary to point out to the child the behaviors most useful to him; (3) the modeling person should be held in positive regard by the observer; and (4) the observer should be able to give feedback to the model concerning his (the observer's) perception of the behavior modeled. Modeling is most effective when it is combined with reinforcement procedures, especially when the model is reinforced in the presence of the observer.

When Johnny, age four, sees his father tenderly relating to his mother, and when he sees father rewarded with a kiss from mother, Johnny has observed a model in the marital pair and may be led to imitate their behavior. If Johnny sees enough of this mother-father interaction, he is more likely to accept warmth and responsiveness as part of his own makeup. However, if Johnny is told that mother and father love each other but never sees the consequences of this love in behavior that he can understand, he is apt to be mystified about love and to accept his peers' definition of love's meaning, or he may think that love is whatever his parents have shown him it is. Even indifference might be learned as part of love.

Calonico and Thomas (1973) have delineated some factors in modeling processes using role theory as their basis of explanation. They believe that the "accuracy of role taking is a function of the level of affect in interpersonal relationships together with the degree of similarity of value systems." Persons holding similar value systems will advocate similar responses in behavioral situations. Calonico and Thomas then present evidence that for parents accuracy of role-taking is related only to similarity of value systems, while for children it is related to both high levels of affect and perceived similarity of values.

Calonico and Thomas state: "For parents, as the similarity between the value systems of parents and children increases so does the parents' accuracy in taking the roles of their children. The level of affect between parents and children does not seem to play an important part in parental role taking ability" (p. 663). On the other hand, high affect together with similarity of values assists the child in taking on the parents' roles, while high affect associated with dissimilarity of values results in inaccurate parental role interpretations by the children. In low affect homes in which value similarity is high, there is an increase in the accuracy of the child's perception of parental roles. Thus congruence of values between parent and child seems related most to accurate role-taking on the child's part, and thus to effective modeling.

According to Brim (1968), there are two ways in which the actor imitates the roles of the model. In the first of these, the role of the model is taken directly and adapted to a parallel status of one's own, as when an older son performs the role of father to younger siblings. The second form of model imitation is more covert: the roles of admired others (or of those in a position of power) are assimilated, and incorporation of certain elements of the roles takes place. This may come about because the imitator notes that the model is successful in particular role behavior. Or it may take place because for the imitator one set of roles has already failed, and rather than try new and untested responses, he is more apt to rely on role behavior proved successful in other cases. A third reason modeling behavior may be copied is that the individual, especially the young child, may have difficulty distinguishing between reality and fantasy in role-taking because the roles are performed in interaction with others, making it difficult to ascertain whose roles are being performed, the model's or one's own.

It thus becomes clear that as the child grows, he or she performs various roles based on the models with whom he or she interacts. Such roles may be copied directly but are more likely to be learned implicitly. The modeling individual who is demanding, indifferent to others, and aggressive in a hostile sense can expect those who imitate him or her to be of the same temperament. Siblings, peers, and others will, of course, modify what is learned from parents.

SUBSTANTIVE THEORY DEVELOPMENTS

Theoretical propositions aimed at specific aspects of human sexuality — substantive theories — are more useful, it seems to this author, than general theories applied to human sexuality. This is because our current polymorphous knowledge of sexually oriented behavior, beliefs, values, and feelings has yet to lend itself to an integrated view. Three well-known paradigms of human sexual behavior will be presented here, but it should be noted that several others exist. Some of these will be discussed in later chapters. For the present, it is sufficient to use these three as illustrations of the manner in which theory is built.

REISS' THEORY

Ira Reiss (1967) has presented a theory of premarital sexual permissiveness based on seven propositions that he developed from his investigations in this area. He emphasizes family and courtship institutions as key determinants of the norms governing premarital sexual behavior. Reiss believes that the courtship system of a society reflects basic family values, but that the greater the independence of the courtship system from family influence, the more likely it is that biological sex drives will exact pressure for greater permissiveness. In America, courtship roles are more permissive and less demanding than family roles; consequently, those more closely tied to the family tend to be less sexually permissive. Females, being traditionally more family-centered, could be expected to be less permissive than males and to direct their permissiveness toward the possibility of a stable relationship, such as marriage or living together with one person.

Other social institutions and groups with differing norms tend to discourage independent thought and permissiveness among young individuals. Therefore, even in participant-run courtship systems, individuals will express varying degrees of permissiveness in response to these outside social pressures.

Reiss believes that the potential permissiveness deriving from parental values is a key determinant of the number, rate, and direction of changes in one's premarital sexual standards. Children with highly permissive parents are apt to be high in permissiveness themselves. Parental values limit the extent of permissive "push" that social forces can alter.

According to Reiss, parents, older siblings, those with increased family responsibilities, and those with a large number of children tend to be less sexually permissive.

Reiss summarizes his theory as follows: "The degree of acceptable premarital sexual permissiveness in a courtship group varies directly with the degree of autonomy of the courtship group and with the degree of acceptable premarital sexual permissiveness in the social and cultural setting outside the group" (1967, p. 167).

Any given individual, according to Reiss' theory, could be expected to conform to the norms of his peer group while a member of that group, but after marriage would likely return to the more conservative family norms, since culturally defined family norms would then be the point of reference.

Premarital sexual permissiveness is greatest within a culture that is generally liberal in sexual attitudes and within courtship groups relatively free to set their own norms. Equality between the sexes is also greatest in sexually liberated groups, a point made by Harold Christensen (Christensen and Gregg, 1970) as well as by Reiss.

Another force that might be expected to alter the individual expression of premarital sex is religion, which according to Reiss should have its greatest influence upon individuals belonging to courtship groups upholding the tradition of premarital abstinence. Within such conservative, low permissive groups, Reiss believes, religious standards are assumedly reinforced by other social forces, such as family attitudes. The effect of religion on more permissive groups should be less. According to Reiss' Proposition One: "The lower the traditional level of sexual permissiveness in a group, the greater the likelihood that social forces [such as religion and the family] will alter individual levels of sexual permissiveness" (1967, p. 51).

Reiss (1967) interprets this proposition to mean that the traditionally high permissive subculture has greater power and independence than the traditionally low permissive subculture, and that social forces thus have less power to affect the level of sexual permissiveness of individuals in the high permissive groups than they have to influence individual permissiveness in the low permissive groups. The individual in low permissive groups is more responsive to demands for social conformity.

Heltsley and Broderick (1969) tested Reiss' Proposition One by using religion as a social influence. They found that religion was less effective in controlling blacks than in controlling whites, but no support for Proposition One was found when other groups, such as males and females, were compared. According to Heltsley and Broderick, all that is needed to explain the racial discrepancy is the different degree to which black and white churches stress premarital restraint. Thus, these researchers claim, Reiss' more elaborate explanation is not needed.

Reiss himself (1969) argues that Heltsley and Broderick have misinterpreted the essential idea presented in his Proposition One. Furthermore, the sample Heltsley and Broderick used was composed "largely of single, female, white, Protestant, middle-class southerners" (Heltsley and Broderick, 1969, p. 442). Bardis' religion scale was used to test the degree of religiosity. It is apparent that the use of only one social force, the nature of the sample, and the use of an ideological scale as a measure of religiosity limit the general applications of this research. By indicating some need for further elaboration of Proposition One, however, the study does show the process whereby hypotheses gradually become modified.

Ruppel (1970), in a later study, tended to support the Heltsley-Broderick findings. However, he pointed out that measuring religiosity by church attendance (as Reiss did) is qualitatively different from measuring it by inventories (such as Heltsley and Broderick and he himself used), because inventories get at ideological dimensions.

In another study, Middendorp, Brinkman, and Koomen (1970) analyzed their data and concluded that the major determinants of premarital sexual permissiveness are religion and age, with place of residence showing a positive but weaker influence. These researchers used a sample from the Netherlands consisting of 1704 individuals and a scale of premarital permissiveness that they themselves devised. The Middendorp group does not feel that its data support Reiss' Proposition One, but as Reiss himself (1970) points out, the group's methodology is not comparable to his own and thus little deduction concerning the Reiss theory can be made from its data. The subjective measurement of premarital permissiveness, the inadequate conceptualization of Reiss' propositions, and the tendency of the Middendorp article to wander away from the major hypothesis that it sought to test, namely, that an empirical relationship exists between social class and premarital permissiveness, all lessen the study's usefulness.

In general, the propositions from which Reiss formulated his theory are founded on hard data collected before the theory-building attempt, and as a result are empirically based. What is needed at this point is research based on Reiss' methods but carried out with different populations. The Reiss data are older now and perhaps less relevant than formerly. Nevertheless, Reiss' propositions should be refined, not abandoned.

CHRISTENSEN'S THEORY OF RELATIVE CONSEQUENCES

Another contribution to sexual theory has been made by Harold Christensen (1966, 1967, 1969a, 1970), who has made cross-cultural comparisons of attitudes toward premarital sexual relations. Christensen compared a permissive, a moderate, and a restrictive culture and also studied the effects of premarital pregnancy on marriage. From his studies he postulated several effects of a discrepancy between values and behavior. He concluded that when differences between what a culture permits and the actual behavior of its inhabitants are small, there is less guilt following premarital coitus. In other words, the general strength of cultural attitudes concerning premarital sexual behavior has a direct effect on the amount of guilt felt by those members who violate cultural norms. Those with the strictest standards had the highest proportion of individuals who violated them. Christensen also found that forced weddings due to premarital pregnancy are less likely in permissive cultures, and that these same cultures produce fewer drastic effects on the individual who becomes premaritally pregnant.

Although these are comparisons of cross-cultural norms, Christensen believes that "personal norms are the individual counterparts of cultural norms, and we can assume the value variation among individuals within a society will show the same relationship to behavior and behavior-consequences as does norm variation across cultures" (1969a, p. 20). In a sense, then, Christensen casts sociological findings in psychological language. One's value system is derived partly from the sociocultural milieu in which one lives, and the seriousness of the effect of violating one's personal moral code is a function of the strength of that code. The individual is less likely to violate the values he or she holds most highly when these values are congruent with those of the larger society, but when values held in high esteem are violated, the psychological consequences to the individual are greater than when less meaningful values are violated.

AN EXTRAMARITAL INVOLVEMENT THEORY

Edwards (1973) has described the beginnings of a theory of what he terms extramarital involvement, although evidently the theory could also apply to comarital relationships. Extramarital involvement implies a continuum, ranging from flirtation through various phases of noncoital sex to actual sexual intercourse. Edwards has formulated seven empirically derived statements from which he generates three formal theoretical propositions. The empirical statements, which depend heavily upon data published during the 1950's and 1960's, are as follows:

1. The lower the socioeconomic status, the more likely is extramarital involvement.
2. The lower the person's intensity of religious devoutness, the more likely is extramarital involvement.
3. The more urban the person's background, the more likely is extramarital involvement.
4. The more extensive the individual's premarital experience, the more likely is extramarital involvement.
5. The longer the duration of the marriage, the more likely is extramarital involvement.
6. The lower the person's satisfaction with the marital relationship, the more likely is extramarital involvement.
7. The greater the individual's sense of alienation, the more likely is extramarital involvement.

These empirical statements will need revision as we gain new insights and produce newer data. For example, for women extramarital involvement is not as related to marital dissatisfaction as it is for men. Comarital relationships (if Edwards meant to include these) are often the consequence of high levels of marital satisfaction and agreement. Social class differences in sexual attitudes and behavior may be disappearing as increased integration takes place. Nevertheless, Edwards' propositions at least recognize the need for theory pertaining especially to extramarital sexual behavior and attitudes.

The three theoretical hypotheses that Edwards derived from his seven empirical statements are:

1. The higher the normative level of sexual permissiveness prevailing in a group or collectivity, the more likely is extramarital involvement.
2. The greater the person's heterosexual involvement, the more likely is extramarital involvement.
3. The greater the positive discrepancy between personal and relational satisfaction a person desires and receives from marriage, the more likely is extramarital involvement.

The data which tend to support Edwards' theoretical formulations include the facts that those involved in higher degrees of heterosexuality (dating, etc.) become involved in sexual activity more quickly, that the religiously inactive are the most sexually active, and that the level of sexual permissiveness within a society is associated with greater willingness to act out sexual desires. Furthermore, as commitment increases for most individuals, especially women, so does willingness to become sexually involved. Disenchantment with marriage, coming earlier for men than for women (Pineo, 1961), has as one of its effects extramarital involvement. Not yet studied fully nor admitted by many is the fact that the same marital partner may over a period of time simply become boring or uninteresting, regardless of the techniques used to keep interest from waning. This must be an important reason for much nonmarital sexual behavior among the married.

SUMMARY

Although it is clearly evident that no acceptable, comprehensive theory of human sexuality exists at this time, some hypothetical derivatives based on the material in this chapter are possible. It must be kept in mind that these are *possible* explanations for the sexual data currently available and that other hypotheses may be equally plausible.

1. The manner in which sex drives are expressed is learned primarily through psychosocial conditioning.
2. Psychosocial factors can, to some unknown degree, override biological inheritance. Consequently, low sex drive people can learn to develop stronger drives, while high drive individuals can be taught to reduce the strength of their drives. In other words, individual sex drives are a mixture of biological and learning conditions. Learning either enhances or retards the individual's biological potential.
3. The strength of a sex drive will vary from time to time because of the interactional effects of biological and learning factors. This variation may be manifested over the designated developmental periods or even from day to day. The sex drive of an individual is *not* a constant.
4. Those individuals with high sex drives will have the most difficulty conforming to inhibitory regulations, while those with low sex drives will experience frustrations when trying to keep pace with expectations of high sexual expression.
5. A permissive culture is apt to produce more sexual behavior, with fewer disastrous consequences to its inhabitants than would be imposed by a nonpermissive culture. Fewer sexually frustrated people should be found in a permissive culture.
6. Sexual adjustment affects and is affected by one's self concepts. Consequently, the individual who has the best sexual adjustment is also most satisfied with his or her personal moral code of conduct and is least confused about his or her gender identity.

CHAPTER 3

LOVE AND SEXUALITY

THE LOVE-SEX RELATIONSHIP

Love and sex are related in many ways, and most students have expressed a strong interest in such love-sex connections. It might be well to begin our study of these relationships by pointing out some fundamental ideas concerning love and sex. Some individuals consider every physical act of an intimate nature between adults to be erotically tinged; others consider the same act to be affectional. Obviously, many types of behavior are neither clearly sexual nor merely affectionate but will be interpreted according to the needs and past experiences of the individuals involved. Another factor is the general nature of love and sex. Love is sharing and giving, while sex, separated from affectionate feelings, often is utterly selfish, seeks its own relief, and is unconcerned about others.

Freud thought of love as aim-inhibited sex; that is, the original biological urge for being with others was sexual desire. Love is simply a way to divert the basic biological urge toward more socially acceptable motivations. It sublimates socially forbidden sexual desires, such as those for close relatives or casual friends. To Freud, then, love was the psychological outcome of the cultural thwarting of a biological intention.

What Freud has given us is a biological basis whose assumed aim is reproduction of the species. Today some psychologists are continuing this Freudian tradition, but others have rejected it. Ira Reiss (1960), for instance, has postulated a sociological theory of love. According to his formulation, the first element in falling in love is a feeling of relaxation and openness that makes possible self-revelation and a willingness to learn about the other person. This openness to mutually revealing exchanges leads to mutual dependency, which in turn leads to personality need fulfillment as the couple make their needs and wishes known to each other. In brief, the process is one of rapport, self-revelation, and mutual dependency, followed by personality need fulfillment. Reiss likens this sequence to a wheel: the wheel can turn in a positive direction to enhance love, or reverse itself and destroy love. Failure to fill the loved one's needs would be the likely first step in the dissolution of love.

Another theory of love is that of Robert Winch (1963), who has proposed that individuals with complementary needs are more likely to be attracted to each other. Those with opposite needs or with differing degrees of the same need should be able to find the greatest fulfillment with each other. Although this theory is intriguing, it needs further development and has not yet been adequately supported. It makes sense that an individual who has a need to dominate would find more fulfillment of that need with an individual who needs to be submissive. The difficulty is that needs keep changing from time to time and that a dynamic equilibrium exists among them.

William Goode (1959) notes that love must be channeled by the larger society because of its potentially disruptive aspects. Love could lead to unions that might weaken social stratification or lineage patterns. In America, love is channeled through such social devices as parental control of the young person's associates, peer group pressures, specific definition of eligible spouses, and other socialization processes.

In my own thinking, love stems from the sensuous need to be near others, to be touched and to experience this touch as psychologically satisfying. Love grows out of a biological need, sensuousness, and is differentiated in awareness from sexuality because of social conditioning.

SEXUALITY DEFINED

Sexuality refers to the total characteristics of an individual—social, personality, and emotional—that are manifest in his or her relationships with others and that reflect his or her gender-genital orientation. By this definition it is meant that human sexuality is more than sexual behavior, feelings, attitudes, and beliefs. Sexuality encompasses the whole person, including his or her personality, general emotional tone, intellect, physical makeup, and spiritual functioning. The individual expresses his or her attributes in relation to a set of socialized expectations that are gender-oriented on a broad, general level. Usually, but not always, these culturally defined methods of gender expression are associated with the physical genitals of the individual. In other words, those with male sexual organs have much of their personal expressiveness directed by societal norms for men, while those with female genitals are directed, in their self-expression, by societal norms for women. There is, of course, a large middle ground and much overlap in the expression of sexuality, but within the context of interpersonal relationships, the sexuality of the individual usually expresses and identifies his or her genital structure.

POSITIVE SEXUAL ADJUSTMENT

Positive sexual adjustment, as we shall see later, contributes to personal happiness, and this is reason enough for studying sex. Happiness and positive sexual attitudes are related, and to some extent each depends upon the other: if irrational fears of the erotic exist, happiness, once the immediate pleasure of sexual interaction is over, may give way to despondency. The joy of relating physically is lost to many because of their fear or disgust of eroticism. Some are unaware that many so-called "nonsexual" feelings have an element of the sensuous associated with them. Thus they may be frightened by their emotions upon experiences such as touching a stranger's face, because they do not realize that non-sexual physical contacts can result in feelings similar to genital responses. This combination of innocence and fear does as much as anything to discourage all sorts of human relationships. The result is an intensification of alienation and loneliness among those fearful of their own sexuality. The study of sensuality and sexuality can help to alleviate these fears by focusing on their roots.

THE INTERACTIONAL EFFECTS OF SEXUALITY

The simple fact that sex exists can be quite disturbing to some when they view it in isolation. Yet sexuality is part of the interaction of human relationships, and while it can be studied in isolation to define its borders more clearly, it is, like all functions, an interrelated part of the whole. Set apart from the rest of living, sexual relationships often lose their essence, but when woven into the fabric of life, they help to slow down the process of depersonalization — the process whereby one feels less and less like a person and more and more like an object. However, if sexuality is to help one attain individuality — the subjective awareness that one is truly a person — it must be viewed as wholesome. "Dirty sex," primarily a product of the culture, kills self-worth. This unifying effect of personally acceptable sexuality is reason for searching out one's individual responses to eroticism.

PERSONAL VALUES

In the United States, the current trend in sexual training is to recognize sexuality as part of the whole person and to put it into context with the rest of personality. In itself sex education yields few, if any, answers in terms of abstract values, but it can provide a realistic basis for the evaluation of one's standards when the developmental aspects of morality are understood (Maddock, 1972). These personal values are a major integrating force if they fuse realistically with one's needs, but they are quite the opposite otherwise. Unrealistic beliefs based more on myth than on fact may be antithetical to one's biological inheritance and incapable of uniting life into a functional unit. At any rate, impulsive acts without consideration of their personal consequences can have negative outcomes for the individual.

LEARNING

The bulk of human behavior is learned; indeed, even one's biological potential is enhanced or decreased through the learning process. Learning, not biology or physiology, is the keystone. Attitudes, conditioned either intentionally or through modeling from the individual's environment, are the important determinants of human sexual behavior.

MOTIVATION

Love and sexual feelings are major motives for many kinds of interpersonal relationships. The degree, type, and direction of this motivation are not constants. This fact is well understood in regard to sex, but many will not accept the notion that love also varies, sometimes substantially, in degree, type, and direction. Furthermore, individuals themselves vary considerably in the manner in which they translate the feelings of either love or sex into overt acts. The translation is intimately bound up in the perceptual processes of each person. Past learning, along with the expectation of certain outcomes, results in feelings being acted upon in specific ways peculiar to the demands made by the situation, the partner, and the self.

The existence of love or sexual feeling in another is inferred from his behavioral acts, including his verbalizations. Incorrect judgments may thus arise from faulty perception. Perceptual processes are idiosyncratic and are affected by past learning, current needs, and the individual's self concepts. Consequently, some perceive love in another when in fact it does not exist, perhaps because they have strong but unfulfilled needs for affection or perhaps because they have not coped successfully with the narcissistic yearning for an ever-present, all-consuming love (Boyd, 1968).

Love and sexual behavior may be expressed according to standardized, social stereotypes or may take a more individualized and adventuresome route. When the critical motive for establishing or continuing a relationship is one of predictable comfort and security, the first approach, with its low-key passions, may be most suitable. Those who seek a dynamic, intensely passionate relationship are more apt to follow the adventuresome course, even though it is less predictable. To some extent the choice will depend upon the individual's inclination to enjoy the experience of the unknown in human relationships.

RELATIONSHIPS

The relationship aspect is the outstanding function by which the goodness or usefulness of love or sexuality is usually judged. If the outcome of engaging in intimacy is positive for those involved, intimacy is apt to be evaluated as good and worthwhile, but if negative results occur either to the rest of the relationship or to the individual's self image, intimacy may be devalued. For some, love and sexuality are so intertwined with the rest of their relationship that anything affecting one part may modify the total relationship. Others may have a generally poor relationship but enjoy unlimited sexual encounters with their mates. Actually, most will judge the functionality of each intimate session on the basis of many personally relevant variables, and this, in turn, has the effect of producing the lack of constancy mentioned earlier.

As relationships, both love and sex can stand alone, become paired, or be integrated with other aspects of the interpersonal transaction. They may be permanent or temporary. More often than not, the inability to form satisfactory relationships is of greater significance than sexual inadequacy. Relationship inadequacy accounts for more failures among lovers and sexual partners than any other single factor.

SYMBOLIC FUNCTION

As important as any aspect is the symbolic function of either love or sexuality. Love and sexuality are usually overt portrayals of the individual's inner psychodynamics. The manner in which intimate actions are carried out may be a representation of the individual's self image or of his idealized self. Some types of intimacy may be performed as rebellion to undesired but persistent conditioning. The symbolic function of loving or sexual relationships may also be evident in the choice of partners. Almost everyone has certain criteria for choosing a long-term mate or even a short-term sexual partner. Few can enjoy sexual relations with just anyone who is willing. These learned value systems apparently include a desire for complementary need fulfillment, which will permit symbolization through sexual interaction. Karen is a case in point:

> I never got along well with my father, but I don't hate men because of it. I do like to tease them and to lead them on, and I have been to bed with quite a few, so I'm not just a torment to them. One thing, though, every step along the way I keep the upper hand and allow them only as much progress as I choose. One wrong remark, and I'll shut them off so quick they won't know what happened.

It is not too difficult to glean from the above conversation that Karen uses sex to obtain a high degree of control over her sexual partners, something she was unable to do with her punitive father. Most of her partners do not return after one or two times, and those with whom she has had the longest relationships are males with strongly submissive needs.

Up to this point I have stated that love and sex are primarily learned behaviors, that it is through behavioral acts that we infer the existence of either, that both are motives for many types of interpersonal relationships, and that as motives they are individually determined by idiosyncratic perceptual processes. A major point has been the role of love and sex as developers of interpersonal relationships.

LOVE, SENSUOUSNESS, AND SEXUALITY

Shortly I will discuss love, sensuousness, and sexuality separately, but it is their wholeness and unity that I wish to stress at this time. In my thinking love and sex can never be fully separated, because they arise from similar biosocial needs. One or the other may be quite faint and not consciously experienced, but some positive attraction must be present in every sexual situation. I do not mean that love is necessary to develop an intense sexual relationship nor that erotic awareness is necessarily a part of every form of love, but I am inclined to believe that the two stem from similar biological roots. Love is not sex and sex is not love. My point is simply that a part of the source of each is to be found in man's biological makeup, and that when human love-sex feelings are reduced to this biological level, they are undifferentiated. Social conditioning is the vital factor in determining if either or both will come to the individual's conscious awareness.

The taproot of love and sexuality is sensuousness. I have chosen this term to symbolize the biologically based need for tactile stimulation. Sensuousness is the need to be held, fondled, caressed, and touched. Later we will discuss sensuousness more fully, but for now it is enough to state that the three – love, sensuousness, and sexuality – are interconnected and functioning aspects of human intimacy. Together they *are* intimacy. Love is a necessary condition for true intimacy; so is sexuality. Neither is itself a sufficient condition to produce human intimacy. As we shall see later, true intimacy really begins with self-knowledge, that is, intimacy with oneself.

LOVING RELATIONSHIPS

There is a vast literature on the subject of love, most of it folklore or literary creation. Robert Hazo (1967) has systematically analyzed the ideas of love that he found advanced in this literature. He discovered that most authors agree that love is a tendency to action, a desire to be with the beloved in a union of wholeness, and complete communication—a wish to give more to the beloved than to others. Some writers have emphasized the *judgmental* aspects of love, in which the worth of the beloved is valued as good. Others have emphasized love's *interactional* facets, pressing either for the notion that love is unselfish or for the belief that no love can really exist in which the giver does not also have a self-centered interest in receiving.

Certain authors have sought to classify love into types, insisting that infatuation, romantic love, and conjugal love can be clearly differentiated. Very often, however, their categories overlap because their criteria for classification are unclear. For example, infatuation is supposed to be superficial and a romance that has ended is often classified as such, but during the time that the couple were functioning together smoothly, no one could have convinced them that theirs was not "true" love. Romantic love is supposed to be more inclusive of the total personality than infatuation, but the partner may be overidealized and reality factors underemphasized. Conjugal love—love supposed to typify the marital relationship—is often considered a companionship type of love. In conjugal love more realism is expected; the partners are available to each other at all levels, and mutuality of desires is of paramount importance. This is considered by many to be the most mature form of love.

Some authors emphasize the giving function of love. Rollo May (1969, p. 103) suggests that "[t]he capacity for surrender, for giving one's self up, must exist in love. . . ." Those who love must have the ability to give and to receive; otherwise, those who give but cannot accept the return of love may dominate and control their partners through their giving. Such relationships are more power struggles than love affairs. Giving, an active function of love, is the capacity to contribute some of one's personality, time, efforts, and feelings to another. Lovers can both love and be loved—freely, naturally, and without inhibition. The giving and receiving is mutual sharing in a comfortable atmosphere.

In general, it is the *feelings* of love that have been emphasized by many authors, along with certain culturally defined notions. Among these love myths are the beliefs that lovers will somehow know when they "truly find the right person," that genuine love is necessarily eternal, and that love is somehow qualitatively different from other types of friendship. One trouble with these ideas is that they are ambiguous, and this lack of clarity often leads to confusion and distortion. Love, whatever it is, seems to be personally and privately defined by each individual as he or she experiences it.

Important as they may be, my concern is not with the feelings of love but with the behavioral interaction which should result from a sense of love for others. It is the overt behavior of love that makes it important to most of us. Rather than describe *love,* I prefer to discuss the *loving relationship,* that is, the active consequences of a sense of love for others. The loving relationship is based on mutually given and received acts of an affectionate nature and can be described on the basis of these acts. Elements of the loving relationship can be found in all human contacts of a positive nature: in friendship, companionship, chums, buddies, or other positively construed interpersonal relationships. Each of these is a form of love.

Not every act within a loving relationship must be of a positive nature, but enough rewarding interaction must occur for the participants to evaluate the overall relationship as positive. Mutually favorable outcomes or tolerance for those that are less than desirable is a general expectation of loving relationships.

The continued existence of love for others depends upon interaction with them directly, imaginatively, or more often both. Once certain acts have come to denote love to us and we have participated in them, our affectional emotions become reinforced. In other words, love to the individual is exactly what he has learned it should be, in both feeling and behavioral terms. The interaction between behavior and feelings has led me to define love as follows:

> Love is that relationship in which two or more individuals interact in a mutually perceived positive manner and in which each is free to develop his or her full potential with the unrestricted help of the other(s). Choices for personal growth are always made so that no significant lessening of the cohesion between the beloved is intended and are based on mutual understanding and respect.

This definition emphasizes the points that love may exist for more than one person at the same time, that personal growth is enhanced within the loving relationship, and that freedom of choice and mutuality are inherent aspects of love. Freedom may be given up, but this is an act of free will. The definition also points out that love is the intentional and purposeful impulse to act in behalf of others. All within the loving relationship receive some benefit from the growth and enhancement of the others; consequently, love is not truly sacrificial.

A loving relationship begins within the individual, since both giving and receiving are explicit outcomes. A capacity to put one's trust in others and to have faith in oneself is essential to this give and take. This capacity for faith is *basic trust.* Without basic trust it is difficult to engage in cooperative, caring, sharing, and life-giving human adventures.

The exchange of deepest emotions through the development of *emotional interdependence* is one of the most exciting and demanding functions of the loving relationship. Such interdependence recognizes the necessity of giving up some independence, but at the same time it emphasizes the cooperative nature of emotional exchanges. Each partner is both source of arousal and satisfier of needs. The essence of love is shared feelings that are given and received graciously. This comes about through attachment, mutual support, interpersonal empathy, and awareness of changing needs. One important aspect of emotional interdependence is the capacity and willingness to permit one's partner to regress psychologically from time to time. Love demands the occasional acceptance of more primitive responses if passion and intimacy are to grow.

The loving relationship is a singular communication system in which honesty and expressiveness combine to form an experience that is greater than mere words. Interactional communication is sensitivity to the needs of self and others. It is freedom from fear and jealousy and results in open discussion when this is deemed advisable. Fear, jealousy, and possessiveness are not elements of love and drastically interfere with the genuine communication of feelings. Communication, both verbal and nonverbal, is the life blood of the loving relationship.

Other elements of the loving relationship include such personality traits as agreeableness, tolerance, and patience. Kindness, itself a form of warm, personal concern, is fundamental to the continuance of love. So are forgiveness and forgetting.

A sometimes forgotten function of viable relationships is that of service to the beloved. The service of love is distinguished by its volunteer nature and lack of expectation of specific rewards. The willingness to do things, to help, to lend assistance, to set aside personal desires, to be generally useful is important to those in love.

The loving relationship is the one human-to-human situation in which the opportunity to test one's free will should be most evident. Making interpersonal choices, willingly submitting to another, trying out various approaches, and experimenting with openness and honesty should be possible within the loving relationship. Indeed, the position of lover is the major status-role position in which a sense of self may be gained and affirmed. Restrictions forced upon those within the loving relationship by either society or self serve primarily to isolate and negate personal identity. It is through the relationship of love that one can transcend the everyday, the mundane, and the restrictions of the physical. It is within an affectional context that a new self can be created or an old one modified. Love, then, is important, because it allows the inner core of personal existence to be examined, acted upon, and recast in light of ever-changing needs. When the road to inner awareness is blocked permanently, a loving relationship does not exist.

To sum up, the loving relationship is one in which the individual is awe-struck with the qualities of the beloved, acquires the other's needs as his or her own, has high feelings of generosity toward the beloved, drops distance-maintaining psychological defenses, disregards the faults and shortcomings of the beloved by ignoring or accepting them, and looks upon love as an end in itself. Those who love do so by choice, because love is the behavioral consequence of inner feelings of affection.

Among those who love there is a great desire for physical and psychological intimacy. This wish for physical closeness is one of the first and most important bases for loving relationships, and it is to this need for tactile experience that we now turn.

SENSUOUSNESS

Primarily, love comprises socially defined characteristics that are identifiable through behavioral outcomes, but there is a definite physical basis upon which love rests. This is the need for tactile stimulation and close, personal contact in which warmth, gentleness, softness, and caring affirmation are critical. The place of this intimate contact in primate development has been demonstrated by Harlow and his associates (Harlow, 1958, pp. 673–685; Harlow and Zimmerman, 1959, pp. 421–432; Harlow and Suomi, 1970, pp. 161–168). These researchers have discovered that a strong need for all types of affirmative tactile stimulation exists from earliest life and is probably inborn through a long evolutionary process. At any rate, those primates denied close, affectional warmth are retarded in their capacity to respond to others in a normal manner. Many psychologists studying human development feel the satisfaction of this need for affection is equally important to the full psychological growth and development of man. Those deprived of physical closeness in their first years have greater difficulty accepting adult love in later life. Maslow (1969, pp. 35–36) asserts this when he discusses the biological rooting of values held to be important to life. According to Maslow, those who have had their basic needs gratified can then be motivated to seek higher life goals. They are not anxiety-ridden, rootless, isolated, nor suffering from other crippling feelings such as inferiority—at least not for any length of time.

I have chosen the term *sensuousness* to designate this biologically based need for physical closeness. As I use the word, sensuousness refers to heightened sensations of warmth, security, and psychological satisfaction growing out of physical contact of an affectional nature. Sensuousness is a generalized feeling throughout the body, under the influence of which physical sensations are experienced as psychologically pleasing. This intertwining of physiology and psychology produces emotional security and is a fundamental source of basic trust. Sensual feelings are among the most intense of emotional experiences. There are many examples, including the wonder of a child who has just discovered some new plant or bug, the exquisite existence of young lovers who have recovered themselves after a quarrel, or the meditations of a religious man who has just found God within himself. One of the most profound instances of sensual reality is the mother who has just given birth to a child and suddenly grasps the momentously personal importance of the unity between the physical, emotional, and spiritual.

Despite its biological basis, sensuousness can be enhanced or retarded through learning. If sensual needs are satisfied, they tend to be reinforced and to continue, but if they are not they will appear in disguised and distorted form, since it is impossible for them to go unacted upon. Aggression, hostility, and withdrawal are the chief means by which sensual expression comes to the surface masked. As a human need, sensuousness will be met at any cost, and this is perhaps one of its most outstanding characteristics. Although sensuousness is primarily biological in nature, sensual expression is clearly psychophysical.

There can be two possible outcomes of unmasked sensual expression. One of these is the generalized feeling in awareness that is considered to be and is perceived as love. Sensuousness can also be experienced as sexual feeling, in which case sex-organ awareness has become the focal point of concern. Sensual feelings precede love, sex, or the combination of the two. They are part of the roots of both love and sex, and this rooting source may make it impossible ever clearly to distinguish one from the other except by arbitrary definition. Sensuousness is the connecting link between man's biological nature and his interpersonal experiences. When sensuality is minimized, both love and sex become more mechanical, because acknowledgment of the need for sensual contact is an important source of passion.

Rollo May (1969), in his book *Love and Will,* makes the point that some of our most intense responses toward those we love occur when we are in danger of losing them. Anyone who has watched a loved one depart knows something of these feelings. The young bride walking up the aisle also knows these feelings well, although in a more positive sense. Later as she waits for her husband on her wedding night, she undergoes greater anticipation because of her feelings at the marriage ceremony. These conditions intensify sensual longings.

Sensuousness, to conclude, may be enhanced or retarded through learning. It must find expression, either through positive reality experiences or through distorted means. In interpersonal relationships, sensuousness may be experienced as love or sex or both. Love and sexuality are connected through sensuousness and exist in awareness simultaneously, alternately, or not at all. Most importantly, purposeful and conscious goals, aimed at sensual need fulfillment, are essential throughout the life span.

SEXUALITY

The need for sexual experience is biologically rooted, primarily through the drive for sensual fulfillment. Sexuality is the wholeness of interaction in which genital sensations occur, sex preferences are established, and erotic awareness is in ascendency. Yet unlike the biological drives for air, food, and water, sexual relief is not necessary to the life of the individual. The so-called sexual instincts exist only in conjunction with sensuousness or such socially learned needs as reproduction or pleasure. Both the need for sexual interaction and the methods of expressing this need are culturally conditioned and can be repressed in favor of nonerotic forms of sensuousness.

There are wide individual differences in human sexual potential. If sensuousness could be measured apart from the effects of learning, I suspect that something approximating the normal curve would result. Following this theoretical curve of biological sensual potential, we would find that some individuals have little need to express themselves sexually while others are driven almost continuously by sexual urges. It is also important to recognize that individual differences within the sexes are greater than any that may exist between them. There is little reason to believe that the male's biological needs are greater than those of the female. Cultural standards of permissiveness seem to better account for any observed differences in sexual expression, and it is becoming increasingly clear that women may actually have a greater sexual potential than men.

The effects of learning may be seen in some of the differences between the sexes in sensual expression. Women generally prefer affectionate expression of their sensual needs before they acquire a desire for sexual involvement. With men it may be just the opposite, for often their initial attraction to a woman is physical. It is worth noting that affectionate types of expression may come to include a desire for sexual interchange, while conversely, initial sexual urges may later lead to a desire for affectionate interaction.

Frank Shuttleworth (1959), noting the traditional differences between women and men (women are physically weaker, possess equipment to carry out specifically the full reproductive process, have no external organ such as a penis, and do not build up seminal fluid), has postulated that these differences account for the variation between the sexes in responses to sexual stimuli. It is known, however, that in permissive cultures women do respond to sexual stimuli more than in restrictive ones. Greater freedom to develop an awareness of their sexuality might be helpful in gaining a new responsiveness for women. Pressure on the surface of the vulva, perhaps not as evident as that on the penis, may result in high levels of sexual excitement. A moist vagina can be a powerful reminder of erotic potential, and breasts can be used for purposes other than nursing babies.

The notion that sexual needs are based on a biological drive to reproduce is also tenuous. Judging by our lack of concern over the environment, our propensity to find excuses for war, and our failure to provide proper nutrition for vast numbers of people, we seem to possess little innate interest in the species as a whole. Furthermore, there is theoretical justification for the belief that any innate sexual drive is fed by a pleasure principle. Ferenczi (1968), as noted in Chapter 2, has hypothesized that psychic security through the reduction of psychological tension is an important unconscious aim of coital encounters. This tension reduction is pleasurable because of the psychic relief it brings. In my own thinking the pleasure comes about more from reduction of pressures for sensual contact than through symbolic psychic relief. Nevertheless, the need for psychosexual pleasure seems to have a biological basis which is much more important than any need to reproduce.

Sexual fulfillment is a major source of sensual gratification. From birth until the time that it is modified through learning, genital manipulation is a prime sensory activity through which relief is possible. Even though learning may distort, disguise, or cause denial or introversion of the need for genital routes to sensual comfort, a program for reassertion of genital interests is continually in effect.* Social learning may temporarily force this awakening into other molds, such as achievement, status-seeking, or even love, but once on their own, most individuals seek some sort of sexual interaction. Sexuality, like love, is a natural extension of sensual needs.

The discouragement of sexuality may, to some extent, hinder the development of love by inhibiting direct sensual expression, but by the same reasoning an overly emphatic or too rapid approach to sexuality may also inhibit love. In the first instance high levels of sex regulation by society or parents produce inhibition, while in the second the couple themselves become involved with sex too exclusively and overlook any feeling of affection that may have developed.

In brief, sexuality is the individual's total biosocial and personality makeup as manifested in genitally focused behavior. It is a major outcome of sensual needs, is primarily learned, and is present in both men and women in approximately equal strength. It is an important source of sensual relief and when inhibited may result in denial or distortion of desire. Physical sexual interaction can be enjoyed without the intimacy created by the love-sex union. Whereas love is essentially altruistic, sex without love is primarily narcissistic and seeks its own relief without regard for the partner.

DEVELOPMENTAL STANDARDS OF SEXUALITY

Human sexual development proceeds along certain recognizable lines. Brown and Lynn (1966) have outlined some of these components

---

*See the discussion of preadolescent sexual development in Chapter 9.

for us. They believe that the psychosexual status of the individual is un-differentiated at birth but develops from three major variables: the biological-constitutional component, sex-role preference as defined by society, and genital-sex object preference.

Heredity, along with congenital and maturational factors, makes up the constitutional component. Brown and Lynn use the terms maleness and femaleness to distinguish between physical characteristics and those of a psychosocial nature, for which they use the terms masculinity and femininity. The degree of one's maleness or femaleness is defined by the chromosomes (XX or XY), the presence of ovarian or testicular tis-sue, and the hormone balance, especially between androgen and es-trogen. The internal and external sex organs are the structures of the biological-constitutional component.

Brown and Lynn discuss a standard expected outcome for each com-ponent, based on sociocultural expectations. The expected outcome of the biological-constitutional component is an individual with a prepon-derance of anatomical structures and a physiology typical of one sex or the other. Hermaphrodites are examples of a nonstandard outcome.

The sex-role component is learned as a result of social conditioning and is expected to be related to the primary sexual organs. Normally, one's sex roles fit one's maleness or femaleness and are typical of those expected by the culture. Sex-role preference is the desire to adopt a par-ticular role, while sex-role adoption is the actual assumption of behavior characteristics of one sex or the other.

The standard expected outcome of sex-role development is the adoption of roles related to the individual's makeup. Males accept soci-ety's definition of masculinity and adopt it as their own, while females adopt the societal concept of femininity. Brown and Lynn suggest that transvestism is a nonstandard outcome of the sex-role component.

According to Brown and Lynn, "Genital-sex object preference is defined as the source of genital sex arousal, the aim and direction of the genital sex drive, and the nature of the object and situation with which genital satisfaction or orgasm occur" (p. 161). This component deals with genital arousal, behavior, and satisfaction. Genital excitement and grati-fication may be observable, or they may be present only through dreams or imagination.

In our society, the expected outcome of this component is what Brown and Lynn term "monogamous heterosexuality" (p. 161). Nonstan-dard outcomes might be exclusive or predominant masturbation or homosexuality.

SUMMARY

The capacities for love, sensual expression, and sexuality are developmental aspects of living. Genetic inheritance and individual learning are their guiding forces. The openness, honesty, and wholeness with which the three are communicated to others is a major aspect of personality and interpersonal competence. The denial of any one of the three crucial components of intimacy can be expected to have an effect on the others.

Below are some of the major propositions set forth in this chapter:

1. The capacity to love or to engage in sexual interaction is learned primarily through social conditioning and interpersonal experience.
2. For most individuals, both love and sexual responses have strong symbolic functions and may be behavioral representations of the individual's inner dynamics.
3. Love is best defined by its behavioral acts and their feeling consequences.
4. Sensuousness—the biologically based need for close, personal, tactile contact of an affectionate nature—may give rise to feelings of love or to erotic sensations.
5. There is greater variation among individuals within each sex than there is between the sexes, both in sexual potential and in the need to express that potential.
6. Sexual arousal and relief are important sources of sensual satisfaction, but eroticism is not absolutely essential to sensuous expression.
7. Human sexual development follows a fairly standard sequence and is thus quite predictable, although less so in its psychosocial aspects than in its anatomical and physiological aspects.

CHAPTER 4

GENERAL SEXUALITY

The very fact that the bulk of human sexuality is learned does much to differentiate human from animal sexualness. The mechanical quality of animal sexual relationships has little in common with human eroticism. In man, both biological makeup and cultural expectations are aspects of sexuality, and it is this biocultural premise that humans will be sexual that produces the many shades and hues of erotic interaction. The great variety of types and intensities of sexual interaction among humans is itself a noteworthy phenomenon. Despite this variety, however, there are certain generalities that seem to apply across the human species, and it is to these basics that we now direct our attention.

BIOLOGY AND SEXUALITY

THEORETICAL VARIATION

First, let us turn to some theoretical and applied biological bases of human sexual responding. In theory, the biological potential for human sexuality should follow an approximately normal curve pattern, as most biological phenomena seem to do. Thus one individual's biological sexual potential might be quite low, while another individual's sexual urge might have an extremely strong biological push. Most persons would lie near the hypothetical average of sexuality, while a smaller number (roughly 5 per cent) would have much more or much less "sex drive." About one person out of each 100 would be extremely high or low in biological sexual potential. This curve might parallel the curve for intelligence. Figure 4–1 demonstrates a perfectly normal distribution of human sexual potential.

Because of the moderating effects of learning, it is doubtful that the validity of this hypothetical curve of human biological sexual potential can ever be established; nevertheless, a good many aspects of human sexuality as currently measured seem roughly to fit a normal curve pattern. It is important to remember, however, that many researchers use the normal curve as their statistical basis without really establishing whether or not their findings are normally distributed. Such findings may thus give us erroneous ideas about the nature of human sexuality. If our biological potential does vary to some degree from individual to in-

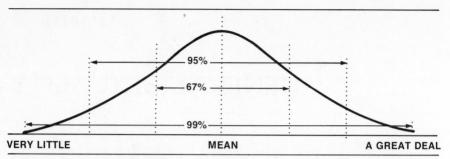

Figure 4–1. A hypothetical normal probability curve of human biological sexual potential. Two out of three persons would have a biological sex drive plus or minus one unit* from the average, 95 per cent of the people would be within two units of the mean, and almost all (99 per cent) of the people would be within three units above or below the mean.

*Technically, these units are known as *standard deviations.*

dividual, and within the same individual from time to time, this fact has considerable implication for both the individual and society. How can one moral code justly apply to a variety of biological sexual intensities? How can satisfactory sexual adjustment take place between two persons whose sexual urges are very unequal? How can one build self-esteem if his or her biological potential is vastly different from permitted or required social expectations?

Thus a genetic (instinctual) basis for human sexuality may be postulated, but the fundamentals of any genetic influence are extremely unclear at this time. One possibility, mentioned in Chapter 2, is that one's inherited gene pool contributes to the production of various sex hormones, and it is through these hormones that biological sexual urges are mediated.

SIMILAR PHYSIOLOGY

The basic physiological processes of sexual responding are not vastly different in men and women. Masters and Johnson (1966) have established the fact that women respond to effective stimulation about as quickly as men. Blood engorgement, general myotonic responses, and the sex flush are part of sexual responsiveness regardless of gender. One can use the four phases of sexual arousal and release — from excitement through the plateau period to orgasm and finally resolution — to describe either gender's progress through the sexual encounter. These four phases are not discrete, as Masters and Johnson note, but are convenient points on a continuum of responsiveness used to describe an individual's state of arousal.

Both men and women tend to pull their legs together in a squeezing action as they near orgasm. In both sexes blood pressure rises, breathing becomes faster, and heart rate increases as sexual tension mounts. The rectal sphincter may contract involuntarily as orgasm approaches.

Although neurological data are less clearly understood than other physiological aspects of sexual responding, there is little reason to believe that the sexes function very differently. The role of the cerebral cortex in inhibiting or otherwise modifying erotic responses is well known. What has not been fully determined is the extent to which specific brain areas control sexual desire. Nevertheless, Heath (1972) presents evidence that high levels of activity, as measured by electroencephalograms, occur in the septal region of the brain during sexual arousal and orgasm. Heath's data substantiate other research indicating that septal region activity is related to subjectively felt pleasurable responses in man.

Many theorists feel that the central nervous system functions as a unit and that no one part of the brain has exclusive or dominant control over man's sexual sensations. The cerebral cortex, with its emphasis on cognitive-intellectual functioning, modifies erotic responding in many individuals. Regarding brain functions, Frank (1968) writes:

> Unlike most reactions sexual desire does not originate in one brain center. It is triggered by an intricate network of many specialized areas that coordinate the impulses through the spinal cord to a group of nerve cells called the erection center in both men and women (p. 68).

The erection center is located in the lower back in the lumbosacral area of the spine, the area through which genital and pelvic impulses are transmitted to and from the brain. The continuity of lumbar area nerve connections with both peripheral nerves and the brain is believed necessary for such sexual functions as erection to occur. In man then, as Kinsey and his associates (1953, p. 693) have pointed out, the *coordination* of sexual impulses is probably a major function of the nervous system as far as erotic responding is concerned. It is this coordinating function that permits the person to respond sexually with his or her entire body. Malfunctioning nervous systems, whether due to faulty learning, inadequate physiology, or incomplete physical structure, interfere with the sexual responding of the whole person.

From the physiological standpoint, it appears to make little difference whether a sexual stimulus is supplied by oneself or by a person of the same or opposite sex. Erotic stimulation through self means, mechanical devices, coitus, or fantasy seems to affect only the speed of responding, not the basic physiological processes.

PSYCHOSOMATIC NATURE OF SEXUALITY

PSYCHOSOMATIC UNITY

Probably no other human activity is more dependent upon concordant functioning between the body and cognitive processes than sexuality. A refusal to admit sexuality into awareness can cause the actual disappearance and disintegration of one's sexual potential. Unlike other physical needs, sexual expression is not necessary to the individual's life. Respiration, elimination, thirst, and hunger must be carried out or relieved if the individual is to survive. Sexual desires need not even be admitted, let alone acted upon, and not a few individuals go through life purposely smothering any sexual feelings that they could have experienced. Yet while sexual awareness may be relegated to the unconscious, sensuousness, as I stated earlier, must find expression in some form. At any rate, a disparity between thought processes and body functions can engender many illnesses, and when one considers the essential psychosomatic nature of sexual arousal and responsiveness, it is easy to understand that failure to integrate these systems can lead to a variety of sexual disasters.

RELATIONSHIP OF SEXUALITY TO OTHER EMOTIONS

It has been claimed (Kinsey et al., 1953, pp. 703–705) that certain other emotions mediated through the autonomic nervous system (and less dependent upon the "higher" and mediating brain functions) have many aspects similar to the sexual response. Anger has most in common with sexual responsiveness. All the physiological responses that occur during sexual arousal — except genital secretions, facial and skin flushing of a ruddy color (angry people sometimes turn white), tumescence, pelvic thrusting, and orgasm — are also found in anger. Indeed, it is not unusual for angry feelings to result in sexual arousal, although some wives are surprised when immediately after a fight their husbands ask for coitus. Other emotions having many of the physiological concomitants of sexual responsiveness according to Kinsey are fear and pain. Sexually dissatisfied mates often relieve their tensions through hostility toward others or withdraw in painful frustration.*

It appears that the autonomic nervous system functions in a relatively stable manner throughout the life span of the individual, and that a very narrow range of autonomic patterns gives rise to a wide variety of emotions, from anger to sexual arousal. The cluster of physiological responses associated with sexual output has been termed by Kinsey (1953, p. 703) "the sexual syndrome."

---

*It should be noted that sexual arousal is capable of inhibiting anxiety and that this method of suppressing anxiety can sometimes be a useful adjunct to some forms of therapy (Brown, 1973).

CAPACITY, DRIVE, AND PERFORMANCE

Lester Kirkendall (1961b, pp. 939–947) has proposed the division of "sex drive" into three major areas: capacity, drive, and performance. Capacity is one's physical ability to respond to the point of orgasm and to recuperate to the point at which orgasm is again possible. Performance is what one actually does, while drive is the desire or motivation to perform sexually.

At the present time, it does not seem possible to measure Kirkendall's three factors in a meaningful manner. In the first place, capacity, in a physical sense, tends to vary with such conditions as fatigue, need for nourishment, and muscular strength. Again, it is difficult to ascertain whether capacity or motivation is most affected by the manipulation of sexual stimuli — for instance, by the introduction of a new partner. Both capacity and motivation must be inferred largely from performance, but for the most part sexual performance must be measured by the subjective reports of respondents, and these are subject to a variety of influences, including the tendency of individuals to answer in a socially desirable manner. Thus the literature continues to use the terms drive, capacity, and performance interchangeably, and while this ambiguity has not helped, it does not seem that Kirkendall's scheme vastly improves the situation.

Kirkendall correctly points out that performance is not necessarily a valid measure of capacity, and this fact might be useful in practical, everyday sexual activity. The couple who feel that their sexual life is growing stale might remember that many new ideas can be introduced that would increase motivation and thus performance. Also, many reduce their performance as they grow older, but to infer that their capacity has been reduced accordingly may result in a vicious cycle in which further reductions in performance are seen as the inevitable consequence of ever-decreasing vitality. By the introduction of new sources of erotic stimulation, the cycle can be reversed, since increased performance may foster the idea that one's capacity is not as low as one might have thought. Certainly, being aware of capacity as a physical function reminds us that many variations in people's sexual needs occur in conjunction with their physical health.

In this text I am using the term drive in its behavioral sense; that is, a drive is that which impels an organism to action, whether the source be physical, psychological, or both. By capacity I mean the theoretical maximum potential of an individual or group. Performance will mean what an individual or group actually does. With these definitions in mind, it is clear that the culture promotes a greater sex drive in men and that men as a group do perform more sexual acts than women. On the other hand, some theorists, basing their judgments on the demonstrated capacity of a few women, have questioned male sexual superiority and have concluded that the performance of women is inhibited largely by a male-dominated culture. Under proper cultural conditions, women's sexual drive and performance should theoretically exceed men's if indeed their sexual capacity is greater. The question that remains to be answered is whether the capacity shown by females who have been released of their inhibitions applies to women generally.

SENSUOUS NEEDS AND SEXUALITY

The need for sensual experience as a basis for human sexuality has been discussed in Chapter 3. Sensuousness, it will be recalled, is the general psychophysical drive toward close, personal, tactile contact with others. Sensuousness is expanded through association with external events having a sense of mystery about them. In this way, anticipation, primarily through fantasied expectations, acquires a sensual element without the necessity in every instance of actual physical contact. This mystery, the unknown of the human condition, adds passion to the whole process of sexual fulfillment. Sensuousness contributes more directly to sexuality because it means in practice the ability to sense, to become aware of others' needs and inner responses, and to admit into consciousness one's inner self and hidden or latent potentials. As it increases in genital focus, sensuousness brings us into a sense of awareness of that conglomerate of wholeness by which inner feelings of sexual desire are felt, communicated, and appreciated.

Lack of sensual fulfillment can be found in many marriages, as when a woman complains that her husband never holds her close without quickly beginning breast or genital fondling. She wants her husband to appreciate her entire body but feels that he is interested in her only as a sexual partner:

> Reubin's wife, Jean, complained that after six months of marriage he seldom approached her physically unless he expected the outcome to be coitus and that rather quickly. Jean explained to her husband that she wanted to be appreciated for herself and could respond best to his touch if occasionally he would caress her romantically. Once Reubin felt that he could meet Jean's request without feeling unmanly, their total relationship and sexual adjustment improved dramatically.

SIMILARITIES IN PSYCHOSEXUAL MAKEUP

I shall use the term psychosexual makeup to refer to those factors that affect the individual's ability to respond through genital arousal to his or her need for sensual gratification—that is, those factors that are associated with the person's ability to respond sexually. Sexual responsiveness is the conscious awareness of generally recognizable erotic feelings in relation to external or internal stimuli. This awareness may come about through physical, social, or psychological stimulation and ranges from the first consciousness of erotic feelings to their final relief. Sometimes holding hands will give rise to sexual awareness; at other times elaborate forms of stimulation clearly intended to be sexually arousing will be necessary. But regardless of the source or degree, the individual must be aware of an erotic element in his or her response before it can be clearly established as sexual.

SEXUAL INDIVIDUALITY

The capacity to turn inner feelings of sensuousness into personally satisfying sexual responsiveness is without doubt a learned art. Because it is learned it is subject to the usual laws of learning, but as an art it is highly personalized. Inability to recognize the laws of learning common to all relationships interferes with the acquisition of new knowledge and makes growth-promoting practices unnecessarily difficult. On the other hand, failure to recognize the uniqueness of each relationship may result in depersonalization, dissatisfaction, and stunted personal growth.

At some ambiguous point, various forms of sensuousness may become sexuality. This point may shift from time to time within the individual and may vary from person to person, because the critical issue in differentiating sensual from sexual responses is the individual's awareness of a shift from generalized feelings and responses to a specifically genital focus. This differential shift from sensuousness to sexuality is one contribution to each individual's uniqueness. As J. Dudley Chapman (1967) has stated, the varying sexual responses both within the individual and between couples and groups of individuals may be as different as fingerprints. Important aspects of one's sensitivity to one's mate are the recognition of the uniqueness of each sexual encounter and the awareness of the degree to which sensual feelings have become specifically sexual. Empathic feelings are also enhanced by a realization of the many sexual functions that the genders share. Increasing one's awareness of the similarities and differences between oneself and one's mate is one of the continuing developmental tasks of married life.

UNITY OF AROUSAL-RELIEF IN SEXUAL RESPONSES

Technically, sexual arousal comprises those psychophysiological processes by which erotic tensions are increased, while sexual relief consists of those processes by which tension is released. Both the arousal and relief processes, however, include physiological and behavioral responses. Since both sexual tension and relief are normally perceived as satisfying, it is often convenient to consider the two processes as a unity. Sexual responding, much like fear, is a complex phenomenon in that it can be both stimulus and response. Just as fear in an individual may produce greater fear, so sexual tension may produce even more intense erotic feelings. Very often frightened individuals will react in ways that tend to increase their fear. Similarly, sexually aroused persons may act by focusing on stimuli that increase their erotic tensions. Others, viewing the arousal-release behavior of the sexually responding individual, may through imaginative, positive empathy become aroused themselves. The thought of the explosive release of orgasm can actually build up sexual tension both in the responding individual and in any onlookers. Producers of pornography know this fact well.

PLEASURE OF AROUSAL-RELIEF

Because sexual tension is usually sought for the intense pleasure derived from its release, I have stated that sex can be (perhaps should be) very self-centered; that is, the need to build tension to a high degree demands, from the point of view of sexuality, that the individual concentrate on his or her self. Helping one's partner to increase his or her erotic tensions is part of love, although the very act of stimulating another also gives rise to sexual feelings in the stimulator. In this respect it must be recognized that any given stimulator may not consider his or her act love but simply ego-building for self. In addition, others may willingly stimulate a partner because of some anticipated gain. Calling the act of willingly stimulating a partner love, however, is consistent with my thesis that any behavior of a positive nature be termed an act of love.

The idea that pleasurable behavior is not in itself good and must be accompanied by additional values is, I believe, one of the major inhibitors of sexual satisfaction for many persons. Thus, some will not consider masturbation because its only meaning for them is pleasure. A particularly difficult pattern to deal with is what I call the *No Response Pattern*. The No Response Pattern follows this order:

1. I *should* not respond.
2. I *will* not respond.
3. I *cannot* respond.

A value not to respond is followed by a willful attitude to avoid responding, which finally becomes conditioned as an inability to respond. Such a pattern can be expected to interfere with all learning.

In the case of human sexuality, the person who believes that responding to sexual stimuli is undesirable either avoids erotic stimulation or interprets such stimuli negatively. Sooner or later many of these same individuals wish to respond sexually but find it impossible. As long as they continue to avoid sexual stimuli, they are likely to have reduced responsiveness. However, many virgins, once married, focus on sexuality and soon catch up to those with previous sexual experience (Popenoe, 1961). When they were avoiding sex they appeared to be unresponsive, but after accepting it as right and proper they quickly overcome any deficits. At this time it is impossible to know validly whether or not there is a *critical period* for the learning of sexual pleasure, the critical period being that period beyond which new learning is difficult or impossible.

THE PASSION-INTIMACY PATTERN

Passion (the intensity of responsiveness and the extent of one's experience of that responsiveness) and intimacy (the level of interaction with another or with others) are part of the unity of sexual arousal-release. The dimensions of passion as I understand them are sensuousness, sexuality, and transcendence. Sensuousness and sexuality have already been defined. By transcendence I mean the phenomenological experiencing of one's own emotions as well as those of one's partner. The transcendental aspects of one's relationships are those functions that cannot be accurately described but are subjectively felt. Often the transcendental processes are not recognized during any particular phase of the relationship and thus are viewed as consequences. Shortly, we will look at transcendental experiences again, but for now, as we explore the role of transcendence in sexual interaction, we should be aware that passion and intimacy are part of many types of relationships.

The three major dimensions of human passion and their subparts are set forth in Table 4-1. These dimensions are seen from three perspectives, all relating to the manner in which an individual can experience his or her relationships and personal attributes.

According to this formulation, one would need to develop considerable sensitivity to one's own sensual, sexual, and transcendental qualities in order to become a fully functioning person. One would need to be sensitive to one's partner's bodily and psychological responses and to develop a high degree of appreciation for those responses. Personality, gender roles, and interpersonal relationships should be emphasized, so that one may be both aware of the processes taking place and appreciative of those processes from a humanistic viewpoint. If one is involved in a personal relationship, especially a relationship of love, one needs to be aware of the awe-inspiring aspects of that relationship. One should also be alert to the feeling that the relationship transcends the ordinary and is unique. Furthermore, the limitations on the relationship and the degree

TABLE 4-1. PERSPECTIVES AND DIMENSIONS OF HUMAN PASSION

Personal Perspective	Three Major Dimensions and Their Subparts		
	Sensuousness	Sexuality	Transcendence
One's sensitivity to	Body awareness Self awareness Other awareness	Personality Gender roles Interpersonal exchanges	Awe Uniqueness Limitlessness The unearned
One's type of responsiveness	Global physical Existential and behavioral	Gender-related Genitally focused	Inspirational Personified Inclusive
Focus of one's appreciation on	Physical world Relationship of self to nature	Interpersonal processes and outcomes	The unexplainable aspects of life The general beauty of life and its relation to human intimacy

to which it must be psychologically earned will determine its outcome. Certainly a very satisfying relationship cannot be fully explained and thus leads to increasing appreciation of the inexplicable aspects of life. Obviously, then, sensuousness, sexuality, and transcendence are functions of life that are never complete but always in the process of becoming. Many erotic relationships die of boredom simply because the individuals involved have failed to grow in awareness, responsiveness, and appreciation of their own sensuousness, sexuality, and ability to transcend the commonplace. Two cases will illustrate.

> Betty and Bob have been married 4 years and are the parents of two children. Betty does not work outside their home by her own choice, and the couple consider themselves moderately happy. Both, however, are dissatisfied with the quality of their intimate life and are less interested in sex than they used to be. Bob tends to intellectualize much of their relationship, controls the everyday functioning of the family without real involvement in family problems, and keeps busy in an apparent effort to avoid communicating his feelings to Betty. Both feel that each must meet a number of standards (earned) if their marriage is to continue. Each feels that exclusiveness of behavior is more important than the unique manner in which they should relate to each other, and both feel that their relationship has not helped them transcend the ordinary humdrum of everyday living. Thus more and more they have controlled each other through excessive demands, ignored each other's needs, and depended upon the capacity to explain rationally everything in life as well as in their relationship. Betty and Bob have had little concern for their subjective experience, and this has drastically reduced the pleasurable dynamics of their life together. For them even sex has become boring.

> Evelyn and Gilbert have been married 10 years and also have two children. Like Betty, Evelyn has preferred being a housewife, even though she was employed outside the home for a short period. In contrast to Betty and Bob, however, Evelyn and Gilbert have very few rules governing their personal relationship, are openly emotional, and ac-

cept each other quite completely. Gilbert has no wish to control Evelyn's life or her feelings and encourages her to have a wide variety of friends of both sexes. Evelyn and Gilbert are quite intimate with two or three other couples, often spend an evening with them exploring personal relationships, and live in both a rational and feeling world. Both have spent considerable time investigating their bodily and psychological responses, experiment with new ways of relating interpersonally, and are often an inspiration to others who come to know them. Evelyn and Gilbert are awe-struck with each other's qualities, prefer the uniqueness of their personalized style of responding to demanding exclusiveness of behavior, feel there are no limits to the possibilities of their relationship, and generally find a good deal of satisfaction in the beauty of life and in helping their children to grow into loving human beings. For Evelyn and Gilbert the sensual life even embodies religion, and both regard their personal relationship as one method of worshipping God.

THE SIGNIFICANCE OF TRANSCENDENTAL EXPERIENCE

As the experience of Evelyn and Gilbert testifies, the attempt to respond sensitively to the transcendental aspects of one's interpersonal relationships is but one aspect of modern man's purposeful search for new and unique life experiences. Our need to experience both our inner and outer world in ways beyond those imposed by social and physical limitations is evident everywhere. Increased interest in astrology, spiritualism, and the Eastern occult religions is evidence. So are the new Christian communes and what Billy Graham calls the reawakening to Christ as a personal experience rather than a religious ritual. Man, the sexual creature, is also man the worshipping creature, and these two, sexuality and transcendence, have much in common and are capable of contributing to each other. Peak experiences, to use Abraham Maslow's term, are often sought through sexual encounters, and some segments of society teach their young that sexual intercourse with love is the most intense human experience possible.

One author (Rockberger, 1969) has written about the search for what he calls the *orgiastic experience*. The term orgiastic, he reminds us, does not refer to sexual orgasm but to group phenomena characterized by an atmosphere of abandon, trance, religious rite, symbolic movement, and the like. Some use drugs in their attempts to find the orgiastic experience, although drugs and alcohol are more frequently used in nonorgiastic subcultures.

Rockberger believes that the search for orgiastic experience may be motivated either by a need for tension relief or by a desire for growth-promoting activity. The orgiastic phenomenon in the sexual realm may be thought of as the experience of letting go without the usual feeling of threat associated with complete emotional release. Both real and imaginary threats are negated during orgiastic freedom. A desirable outcome of the orgiastic experience is a recognition of the unity among bodily functioning, emotional awareness, and increased sensitivity to spiritual possibilities.

Rockberger feels that we cannot expect sexual encounters alone to bring on the feeling stage of the orgiastic. Janeway (1971) agrees when she states: "An unforeseen danger in the situation is that sex, in gathering such significance to itself, may become too important, overwhelming, frightening" (p. 268). Janeway is referring to the current status of sex as the one body sensation that can still be enjoyed as it was in the distant past. Other bodily skills needed to master life-threatening situations are minimal, nonexistent, or artificially created. Many dangerous situations of the past encouraged bonding between men and women and carried, within the situation, the ability to bring the individual into contact with his or her wholeness of self—physical, psychological, and spiritual. Janeway tells us that to overinvest in sex as an emotional relief is to ask more than is possible in the general course of events (p. 271).

Many other authors also remind us that the search for personal identity, unity, and completeness cannot be found through any one medium. Using sexual relationships as the exclusive path to finding oneself produces a schism in personality functioning. Indeed, the very emphasis on achieving high levels of sexual responsiveness may be one of the most important factors inhibiting satisfactory relationships. Pleasure in our society carries with it guilt by association for many, perhaps most, individuals. Failure may also have a guilt component attached to it. Sexual failure—that is, the failure to reach some specific standard of erotic responsiveness—is thus a double failure. In order for sexual encounters to be fully enjoyable, an atmosphere free from compulsion and guilt must exist. Freedom from set standards of responsiveness which must be lived up to in each and every sexual encounter is more helpful to interpersonal satisfaction than attempts to meet absolute and ideal criteria.

The orgiastic experience—with its emphasis on a variety of approaches, naturalness, and freedom from anxiety—seems to have considerable potential for enhancing sexual responsiveness.

Fullness of sexual satisfaction then, according to the passion-intimacy formulation, very much depends upon the ability to fuse sensual, sexual, and transcendental functions into a unity. This fusion may arise in a long-term loving relationship, provided both individuals have grown toward it, for if only one has grown a whole-couple relationship is not possible. A long-term relationship is not necessary, however, for unity among the sensual, sexual, and transcendental to occur, because some individuals have been reared in families emphasizing whole person development or have made efforts toward personal growth on their own. But no matter how the unity arises, sensuousness, sexuality, and transcendence are not accidents of nature. They are learned as part of the art of human living and loving.

SIMILARITIES IN ATTITUDE

For some time, the attitudes of the sexes have apparently been converging. It will be pointed out in Chapter 5 that many members of both sexes expect the modern woman to be as sexually proficient as her mate. Studies by Rainwater (1964), Reiss (1967), and Christensen (1971) make it clear that, although there are educational, ethnic and social class differences in sexual behavior and attitudes, within each of these categories there is much homogeneity. Furthermore, social class differences in sexuality appear to be lessening. Rainwater, Reiss, and Christensen conclude that sexual attitudes are becoming more liberal and that women's attitudes are changing faster than men's, but that generally women remain more conservative than men.

On the other hand, Robinson, King, and Balswick (1972), studying behavior and attitudes toward premarital sexual relations, found that the men in their southern college-level subject population were slightly more conservative than those in an earlier but similar study done in 1965. The women in their study were more liberal than those in the earlier group, but Robinson, King, and Balswick believe that the finding of more conservative males might indicate the beginning of a masculine backlash against female sexual liberation.

Since in almost every study males have been found to be more interested in sex than females, and since that interest is usually so positive, men's attitudes would not be expected to increase in liberality as rapidly as women's.

One very important concept that has developed is the idea that one's private sexual behavior is his or her own business. Especially among college students, a live-and-let-live attitude to sexuality has come into prominence. Many individuals who will not engage in a particular type of behavior nevertheless see no reason to interfere with other people's activities. The author asked college students who were part of a larger study whether they considered legal control over premarital, extramarital, and homosexual behavior desirable. Each subject was also asked about his or her attitudes to sexual experimentation of the Masters and Johnson type, and about the desirability of teaching young people age 17 or over specific sexual techniques when they requested such training. The subjects were then compared on the basis of whether or not they reported having engaged in coitus. No subject had ever been married, and all were between the ages of 18 and 23. All were attending colleges in Pennsylvania at the time, although many had attended colleges in other states or were permanent residents of other Eastern seaboard states. Significantly, nearly twice as many women as men participated in the study (170 females versus 90 males); thus the importance of the group percentages (Column 4) in Table 4-2, which summarizes the subjects' attitudes.

One would expect—and finds—high levels of permissiveness among

TABLE 4–2. CERTAIN ATTITUDES OF VIRGIN AND NONVIRGIN COLLEGE STUDENTS

Question Asked	Group	Number of Yes Answers	Per Cent of Group Answering Yes
Should premarital coitus be illegal?	MV*	2	5†
	FV	4	5
	MNV	0	0
	FNV	1	1
	Total	7	3
Should extramarital coitus be illegal?	MV	8	20
	FV	13	16
	MNV	9	18
	FNV	6	7
	Total	36	14
Should homosexual relationships be illegal?	MV	8	20
	FV	11	14
	MNV	6	12
	FNV	2	2
	Total	27	10
Should scientific sexual experiments be permitted using volunteer subjects?	MV	32	80
	FV	73	91
	MNV	47	94
	FNV	86	95
	Total	248	92
Should individuals age 17 or above be taught specific sexual techniques if they request such training?	MV	36	90
	FV	69	86
	MNV	47	94
	FNV	85	94
	Total	239	92

*MV = male virgins; FV = female virgins; MNV = males with coital experience; FNV = females with coital experience.

†Approximate percentages.

Ns (number of subjects in each group) were as follows: MV = 40; FV = 80; MNV = 50; FNV = 90.

these students. Although males, both coitally experienced and coitally inexperienced, were more restrictive than females about extramarital intercourse, and although male virgins (coitally inexperienced) were more restrictive about permitting the legalization of homosexuality — findings that might corroborate the conclusions of Robinson, King, and Balswick concerning the possible increase in conservatism among college males — few members of either sex demonstrated conservative attitudes. This broad homogeneity of attitudes between the sexes seems to disprove the expectation that one would find greater homogeneity within other classifications (such as religious affiliation, educational level, or virgin-nonvirgin) than between the sexes in general. The reported attitudes of the men and women in this study were on the whole quite similar, with some tendency toward agreement among virgins and nonvirgins of either sex.

Extroverts could be expected to engage more extensively in sexual behavior and to have more liberal attitudes if social outgoingness is positively correlated with above-average liberality. H. J. Eysenck (1972) presents evidence that the attitudes of unmarried students can be classified by their degree of extroversion or introversion as measured by a scale he devised. He postulates that extroverts undertake intercourse earlier and more frequently than introverts, that they engage in coitus with more persons per unit of time, and that they engage in more noncoital sexual activities, such as oral-genital relations. Eysenck's hypotheses are corroborated not only by his own evidence but also by that of many other authorities whom he cites in support of his views. Regardless of gender, the Eysenck findings hold.

ATTITUDES AND BEHAVIOR OF BLACKS

Staples (1972, 1973) has compared the sexual behavior and attitudes of blacks and whites and reminds us that judging black sexuality by white standards of permissiveness is invalid because blacks, especially those in lower socioeconomic classes, view sexual relationships as natural. Whites are more prone to tie sexuality to socially approved unions. Middle-class blacks are more sexually free than middle-class whites but not as uninhibited as lower-class blacks.

Another attitudinal difference between blacks and whites is the greater tendency of white people to use a variety of noncoital techniques. Petting, as a substitute for coitus, masturbation, and oral-genital relations, occurs more frequently among whites, according to unpublished Kinsey data cited by Staples. Consequently, the so-called greater sexual restraint of whites may be a labeling artifact. Whites are not sexually inhibited; they simply employ more noncoital techniques and rely less on intercourse for sexual fulfillment (Rainwater, 1966).

Yet despite the fact that whites may be less inhibited sexually than is often thought, black sexual behavior, at least in the lower classes, is more extensive than that of whites. Although Staples reports only a 1 per cent variation in black and white male premarital sexual activity—99 per cent of his black subjects and 98 per cent of his white subjects engaged in premarital sexual relations—his figure for whites is significantly higher than that found in most studies. He reports that by age 19 over half of unmarried black females had engaged in coitus and did so with a larger number of partners than did white women. After age 20, black women engage in premarital coitus at about the same rate as white women. The attitudes of black college-educated women are closer to those of white college-educated women than are those of non-college-educated whites to those of their college-educated white sisters. Apparently, college education irons out many social-class differences and results in greater attitudinal variations among those with and without college education than exist between the races in general.

Black sexuality, then, is affected not only by racial background but also by social class, educational level, and economic opportunity. Although social-class differences are less pronounced than formerly, there is still a long way to go before real equality is achieved. As blacks rise in educational and financial achievement, they tend to become more like whites in their attitudes toward sexuality. Furthermore, as communication and understanding increase among various educational and social levels, the movement of all groups toward homogeneous standards can be expected. We might then find other factors, such as degree of religious devoutness, stability of interpersonal relationships, and a willingness to forsake sexual norms taught in childhood, to be important determinants of sexual participation.

SOCIAL CLASS

In this section we shall further explore the effects of low socioeconomic status on sexuality. Rainwater (1964, 1966), analyzing lower-class sexuality among both blacks and whites, found the central sexual norm among the poor in four cultures (Mexico, Puerto Rico, England, and the United States) to be: "Sex is a man's pleasure and woman's duty" (1964, p. 457). The idea that the male is by "nature" more sexually inclined than the female is likely to lead the woman to suppress erotic emotions of a positive nature, to bring greater acceptance of male extramarital sexual activities by both sexes, and to lessen acceptance of female sexuality by both women and men. Of the middle-class American women subjects studied by Rainwater, 50 per cent were "highly accepting of sexual relations." While 53 per cent of the upper-lower class were in this category, only 20 per cent of the lower-lower class were highly accepting of their marital sexual activities: 54 per cent expressed avoidance or rejecting attitudes toward sexual relations. Only 14 per cent of middle-class women were not accepting of their marital relationships.

Rainwater also found that marital sexual relations provide the major source of sexual outlet for most men and women during their sexual life. As one moves from higher to lower social status, both men and women report less enjoyment of sexual relations. (Men may engage in coitus more frequently, but coitus seems much more an ego trip among lower-class males.) Foreplay techniques, especially oral-genital relations, are less important among lower-class couples. As is true in all social classes, the longer a lower-class man is married, the less likely he is to report enjoyment of sexual relations with his wife and the lower will be the frequency of reported coitus.

A major variable related to lower-class sexuality is the quality of the conjugal relationship. Sharply defined sex roles (which tend to segregate the couple, hinder communication, depress empathy, and interfere with nonerotic intimacy) are found more often among the lower socioeconomic classes and among the less educated. Women in these role-defined couplings find it especially difficult to appreciate sexuality. Although their wives' sexual gratification is more dependent upon the general quality of their interpersonal relationships, males of lower social status either appear insufficiently interested in this overall quality or are simply unaware of ways to improve their interaction with their partners. Indeed, whatever the couple's social status, role-segregated relationships may produce less interest in mutually satisfying sexual behavior.

In general, then, the lower classes in the four cultures studied by Rainwater contain fewer persons who think of sexual intimacy as truly social and interpersonal in nature. Unmarried males brag of their "conquests," yet they label a girl who permits premarital coitus negatively and seek as married partners those with limited or no experience. Much of this assumed male superiority in sexual interests and abilities carries over to marriage.

One would expect this pattern to change as more of the poor and less educated rise in social status, since changes of social class are usually accompanied by greater interaction with others. Both Rainwater (1966) and Komarovsky (1964) discuss this possibility. They predict that the traditional style just discussed will be replaced by a "working-class style" in which role segregation gives way to cooperative sharing in family roles, greater interest in mutual gratification, and increased self-expression. Those who do not share in the country's prosperity can be expected to be even more exploitative and competitive in their sexual relationships.

Data available at this time verify that such changes are already taking place. After studying working-class West Germans, Sigusch and Schmidt (1971) concluded that their subjects were nearly the same in sexual outlook and behavior as the West German middle class. Love and affection within a stable and mutually satisfying relationship provided the basis for much sexual interaction among these respondents. Most of the German men and women intended to marry and rear families, accepted their partners' previous sexual relationships yet would not accept infidelity on the part of a mate, and expected women to be sexually responsive. One interesting finding was that 7 per cent of the women and 5 per cent of the men thought women should be free to masturbate more often than men.

Although expectations of postmarital roles were somewhat stereotyped for these unmarried Germans, mutual friendship and companionship was more highly desired by both sexes than any form of sexual encounter. Since they valued sharing and supportive actions in all realms of their relationships, communication on sexual and emotional matters was high.

Sigusch and Schmidt concluded that the attitudes of their lower-class subjects were almost identical to those others have found in lower-class Scandinavians and were practically indistinguishable from those of the middle class. They do not think that the sexuality of the individuals they studied is much like that of the American lower socioeconomic classes. However, it should be pointed out that they compared their own findings with American studies done in the 1960's. Perhaps newer studies would show more uniformity among American social and educational classes.

Summary. The variables that contribute to social stratification seem to have more effect on the lower socioeconomic class view of sexual participation. Regardless of their race, members of the lower classes demonstrate sexual exploitation and competitiveness and less erotic enjoyment.

RESPONSES TO EROTICA

Human attitudes toward sexual feelings and behavior are intricately entwined with the general social atmosphere. In America and western Europe there has been an increasing tendency toward sexual permissiveness. Until a 1973 ruling of the United States Supreme Court left the definition of pornography to local authorities, erotic material was widely distributed and easily available to most adults. Whether this decision will redirect social attitudes toward conservatism cannot be ascertained at this time. This section deals with the personal and interpersonal effects of sexually stimulating material, but the studies on which it is based were done prior to the Supreme Court decision.

Recent evidence (Commission on Obscenity and Pornography, 1970; Berger, Simon, and Gagnon, 1973; Gaughan and Gaynor, 1973; Schmidt, Sigusch, and Schafer, 1973) indicates that women and men are about equally responsive to erotic materials. Men still respond with more overt interest and take the lead in procuring sexually stimulating material, but more and more women are enjoying the pleasures than the joint viewing of erotica can bring. Sexually stimulating material—pictorial, written, spoken, fantasy, or live action—has become highly acceptable to many Americans. According to the Commission on Obscenity and Pornography (hereafter called the Commission), 85 per cent of adult men and 70 per cent of adult women in the United States have at some time or another seen sexually explicit material (p. 19). Some of the effects of viewing pornography will be discussed in the chapters on male sexuality and female sexuality. In this section we will examine some generalities about pornographic material.

After reviewing a large number of studies, the Commission concluded that there are no long-term effects from viewing pornography, that most persons see erotic productions before age 21, that those who are tolerant and liberal in their general sexual attitudes are most likely to have seen erotica, and that there is no consensus among Americans about the effects of reading or viewing sexually stimulating material. Research cited by the Commission indicates that arousal from the use of erotica is more likely among the young, religiously inactive, college educated, and sexually experienced.

Generally, the Commission found, conventional sexual acts are regarded as more arousing than unconventional acts. Petting and coitus are more arousing than oral themes, which in turn are more arousing than sadomasochistic actions. There are wide individual differences in pornographic preferences, however.

Some individuals increase their sexual activity and a few decrease it following exposure to sexually stimulating material, but the great majority report no change in their behavior. Any changes that do occur are apt to be transitory and disappear within 48 hours. Thus pornography seems no different than other forms of noncontinued sexual stimulation. It stimulates sexual patterns that have already been established but does not initiate new patterns. Masturbation increases when a partner is not available, but coitus increases if a mate is available. The individual who has never masturbated is unlikely to do so merely because he sees an X-rated movie. An increase in dreams of an erotic nature, in conversation about sexuality, and in levels of sexual fantasy may occur following exposure to pornographic art.

Individuals who have never been exposed to pornography are most likely to condemn it or to have ambivalent emotional responses to it. For this reason it is best to introduce pornography to a lover gradually and with some caution. What is objectionable may derive both from the stimulus itself and from the personality of the person doing the perceiving. Like beauty, much of what is pornographic is in the eye of the beholder. Nevertheless, the joint viewing of pornography can do much to assist a waning marriage or love relationship to recover needed communication, increased empathy, and the excitement of experimental interpersonal approaches.

Parents may ask about the effects of pornography on their children. The Commission, in a majority statement, had this to say:

> In sum, empirical research designed to clarify the question has found no evidence to date that exposure to explicit sexual materials plays a significant role in the causation of delinquent or criminal behavior among youth or adults. The Commission cannot conclude that exposure to erotic materials is a factor in the causation of sex crime or sex delinquency (p. 27).

In fact, the available evidence indicates that sex offenders have had less experience with erotica than other adults. When one considers the large numbers of Americans who have seen sexually explicit material, it is self-evident that the simple fact of having been entertained by such material is not enough to make one a sexual psychopath or rapist.

The viewing of pornography is usually a social activity. According to the Commission report (p. 123), most individuals attend X-rated movies with others. Men are likely to be accompanied by another man or group, while women generally attend with a man or mixed group. Only about 14 per cent of men usually attend alone. A small number of people appear to buy pornography and then share it with friends or spouse.

Pornography, then, is an aspect of Americana and has useful psychosocial functions, such as enhancing communication, increasing knowledge about sexual activity, providing relaxed entertainment, producing greater capacity for accurate empathy, and acting as a nucleus for the developmental socialization of the adolescent and adult.

Since the dissolution of the Commission, a number of studies have supported the majority position that all legislation prohibiting consenting adults from procuring pornography be abandoned.

Reed and Reed (1972) found that frequent church attenders, blue-collar workers, children of farmers and ministers, females, and those without sexual experience are most apt to rate material as pornographic on the basis of its content or presumed effects. Those who consider stimuli pornographic only in relation to the context in which it is viewed are more likely to be urban, the sons and daughters of managers or professionals, more mobile, and sexually experienced. Reed and Reed conclude that the definition of what is or is not pornographic is a product of socialization.

Gaughan and Gaynor (1973) found general support for the Commission's findings, especially that pornography is not an efficient arouser of long-lasting sexual feelings for normal subjects.

Berger, Simon, and Gagnon (1973) questioned urban, working-class adolescents mostly between the ages of 13 and 18 and also a group of college-level subjects. They found that males were more likely to have been exposed to sexually explicit material than females. Pictorial representations, textual material, and movies of coitus were the most frequently viewed objects, in that order. They found that the larger the number of friends (especially for males) and the greater the frequency of dating (especially for females), the more likely it was that the individual would have seen sexually explicit material. Those who had seen the most erotic material also reported the highest rates of masturbation and coital activity. The more sexually active college students were also the most likely to have seen pornography and to have been sexually active while in high school.

Berger, Simon, and Gagnon feel that viewing pornography is, for most young people, an aspect of psychosocialization and can be an important source of sexual information, filling in the blanks left by inadequate adult-sponsored sex education. Thus if sexually explicit material depicts through word and picture the love-sex combination that most adult Americans perceive as morally correct, it can act as an important adjunct to adult-taught sex and as an important modifier of peer-taught sex. In this manner acceptable pornography adds significant dimension to the sociosexual developmental tasks of both adults and adolescents.

Schmidt, Sigusch, and Schafer (1973) studied the responses of German men and women to reading erotic material. They found that their subjects rated the stories used as stimuli only moderately arousing. During the study and the 24 hours following, the general level of emotional activation rose, there was a slight to moderate rise in sexual behavior and fantasy, and only slight gender differences were demonstrated in all measured responses. Women displayed less emotional activation and greater emotional instability than men during the 24-hour period following the experiment but were more coitally active than the men.

Although men and women seem increasingly similar and often quite compatible in their responses to erotica, there remain some important differences. These differences will be discussed in Chapters 10 and 11. Suffice it here to state that the many similarities in physiological response to erotica leave little doubt that the differences in psychological and behavioral responses are culturally conditioned. As in other aspects of human erotic life, liberalism reduces differences between the sexes while conservatism leads to greater emphasis on dissimilarities.

The convergence of behavior is less striking than the growth of attitudinal similarities between the sexes. Nevertheless, there are some signs that the sexes have been behaving more alike in recent years. We shall examine this proposition next.

CONVERGING SEXUAL BEHAVIOR

TRANSLATION OF ATTITUDES TO BEHAVIOR

Hunt, reporting in the December 1973 issue of *Playboy*, reveals that marital coitus has increased in frequency for all age groups. The duration of coitus has also increased from an estimated 2 minutes (based on Kinsey data) to a median of 10 minutes. Foreplay is longer within marriage; coital positions are more varied, and the percentage of wives reaching orgasm has grown. Especially among the younger marrieds, fellatio and cunnilingus have increased so that 90 per cent of those under 25 years of age report at least occasionally engaging in oral-genital stimulation, and this has occurred regardless of educational level. Women, it appears, have become more sexually oriented, while men have permitted themselves to become generally more sensuous and willing to see their mates as whole persons as well as sexual partners. This greater sexual satisfaction, in the presence of other marital rewards, should intensify the depth of many of today's marriages.

Although studies dealing with apparent contemporary increases in sexual activity are few and recent, speculation about the possible increase did begin before the publication of Hunt's *Playboy* article. This author, along with others (Bell and Chaskes, 1970; Christensen and Gregg, 1970; Schmidt and Sigusch, 1972), believes that sexual behavior has been rising in both incidence and variety. While men have not altered their sexual behavior drastically over the last 20 years (Packard,

TABLE 4–3. APPROXIMATE FREQUENCY OF COITAL ACTIVITY
REPORTED BY VARIOUS RESEARCHERS

Source	Sample	Age	Activity	Rate
Kinsey et al. (1948, 1953)	Married couples	35 or less	Marital coitus	Median 2.0 times weekly
Nedoma and Sipova (1970)	Czechoslovakian married couples	30 or less	Marital coitus	48% reported 3.5 times weekly 33% reported 2.0 times weekly 10% reported 1.0 time weekly
Hunt (Dec., 1973)	Urban married couples	34 or less	Marital coitus	Median 2.5 times weekly
Kinsey et al. (1948, 1953)	Unmarried males Unmarried females	25 or less	Premarital coitus	68% had engaged 35% had engaged
Bell and Chaskes (1970)	Unmarried college coeds	25 or less	Premarital coitus	Percent engaging in by dating status: 1958 1968 Dating 10 23 Steady 15 28 Engaged 31 39
Christensen and Gregg (1970)	American unmarried males American unmarried females Danish unmarried males Danish unmarried females	25 or less	Premarital coitus	Average percent engaging in: 1958 1968 45 44 16 33 64 95 60 97
Hunt (1973)	Unmarried males Unmarried females	25 or less	Premarital coitus	About same as Kinsey 70% had engaged
Arnold (1972)	Inner-city adolescents	Median 18.2	Premarital coitus	Median 2.1 times per week Median age coitus began: 14.3

1968, p. 186), women have significantly enhanced their sexual activity, translating the attitude of sexual equality into action. One must be cautious, however, about interpreting studies of a normative type, because they may be affected by sampling differences, variations in population backgrounds, bias and judgment errors of the researchers, and other statistical considerations. There may be only an upsurge of erotic behavior rather than a long-term increase. A reasonable hypothesis is that sexual behavior in the United States has increased slightly for men and significantly for women, beginning in the latter part of the 1960's. This general hypothesis needs, no doubt, several subsections; for example, I would suggest that males have been more accepting of general sensuousness during the last 5 years than they were previously. If this is true, we have a valid convergence of psychosexual behavior, rather than a simple instance of women increasing their sexual activities in accordance with men's standards. Both these hypotheses require greater investigation.

The convergence of attitudes and behavior, especially for women, is demonstrated in a lessening need for commitment before acceptance of coitus and in broader participation in oral-genital, anal, and other non-vaginal forms of sexual interaction. Table 4–3, summarizing selected results of some studies, hypothesizes an increase in coital activity since the latter part of the 1960's.

MASTURBATION

Hunt (Oct., 1973) and Schmidt and Sigusch (1972) give us evidence that both American and German girls have increased their masturbation activities. Hunt found that about 70 per cent of his single American women between the ages of 25 and 34 reported masturbating to orgasm within the past year. Approximately one out of three single American women aged 18 to 24 also indicated to Hunt that they had masturbated to orgasm within the past year. Schmidt and Sigusch found that only among their more educated women was there a significant change in the cumulative incidence of masturbation. Masturbation among Schmidt and Sigusch's University-level German females doubled during the 1960's. Fifty-eight of 108 female subjects in their 1970 study had masturbated by age 16 (these were girls born in 1953 and 1954). In an earlier study, only 30 out of 212 girls born in 1945 or 1946 reported masturbating. Schmidt and Sigusch remind us, however, that although the cumulative incidence of masturbation rose, the active rate of masturbation did not. More girls were trying masturbation, but on a sporadic, irregular basis—a finding similar to Kinsey's.

Weikert (1970), in opting for formal education in regard to self-stimulation, has prepared a summary of surveys on masturbation. He concluded that the more recent surveys show both greater incidence of masturbation and the beginning of masturbation at an earlier age. Weikert surveyed studies from 1897 to 1968. The wide range of reported incidences of self-stimulation that he found in these various studies prompts one to be most careful about interpreting investigations of masturbation. Undoubtedly, conditions such as personal and cultural values, the availability of a partner, and so forth affect whether or not one will masturbate. It does appear that self-stimulation has been practiced by many more men than women, but women, especially more highly educated ones, are finding this activity increasingly acceptable.

SUMMARY

Clearly, symbolic costs and gains to the actors in an interpersonal sexual situation are made up of many things. Against the biological inheritance of the individual, learning through a variety of mediums conditions the person to interpret through perceptual processes the meaning of each interaction, as well as the relationship as a whole. Continued participation, level of enjoyment, effect on self concepts, and willingness to accept the mutuality of sexual decisions all become conditioned through experience. This experience is itself shaped by a variety of social factors and processes, such as social class, educational level, degree of mobility, and vocational opportunity. Those denied the benefits of society are more apt to symbolize sexuality as one method of compensating, and this compensation can be as competitive and exploitative as any within the industrial sphere. Those who have more can afford to explore relationships and can symbolize sexual interaction as love, personalized freedom, or the many other values found within the middle class.

Many more studies are needed to reduce the amount of speculation about human sexuality, and concepts such as transcendence, passion, and cost and gain exchange should be made more operational. Refinement of concepts is always the goal of future research. In the meantime, the similar conclusions reached in several studies suggest some hypothetical statements, but the reader is cautioned that these are not established facts.

1. In theory, the biological impetus of human sexual urges should be distributed along the dimensions of the normal probability curve.
2. Although any postulated genetic function in human sexual behavior is currently quite unrefined, there is little doubt that some inheritable factors do exist. These genetic functions may be mediated through hormonal influences.
3. Mental process about sexuality are correlated with physiological

responses, and the greater the congruence between sexual mentality and physiology, the more likely the individual will accept his or her level of responsiveness, other things being equal. This is the psychosomatic nature of human sexuality.

4. Many other emotions, such as anger and fear, produce most of the physiological responses in sexual arousal, and it is possible to reduce anxiety in some individuals by sexually arousing them.

5. One can condition oneself not to respond through a mental sequence that sees sexual responding as undesirable: practicing mental thoughts that view sexuality as negative and finally arriving at the point at which responding does not occur (or at least awareness of any marked degree of responsiveness is lost).

6. Sexual relationships, at least among the middle and upper classes, may have as at least one symbolic function the triumph over ordinary and explainable; for example, sexual interaction may be a concrete way of showing feelings of love that are fully explainable neither by the individual nor by others. This dimension of humanness I have labeled transcendence.

7. Men and women are becoming more alike in their attitudes toward sexual behavior, and this melting of attitudes operates in both directions. Men are increasing their emotional responsiveness to sex, and women are increasingly accepting themselves as sexual beings and acting on that new self concept.

8. Current evidence suggests that a wider variety of sexual behaviors are occurring and at greater frequencies than 15 or 20 years ago. These increases in sexual behavior are occurring premaritally, within marriage, and extramaritally or comaritally.

9. By far the greatest increase in sexual behavior has been among women, with men remaining about the same or increasing slightly.

10. The poor and those with lower educational attainment may be more exploitative and competitive in their sexual activity. The relationship aspects of sexuality seem to be less functional among individuals within the lower social strata.

11. In this writer's opinion, the bargaining aspects of human sexual interaction are more clearly defined in the lower classes but exist in varying degrees within many (perhaps most) human relationships.

12. There is some belief that a convergence of sexual attitudes across social classes is occurring, but there is no real evidence to support this belief.

The generalities concerning male sexuality in Chapter 10 and those concerning female sexuality in Chapter 11 provide us with some insights into stereotypes of the sexes and individualized functioning as differentiated from those stereotypes. This chapter has emphasized the fact that the genders are very much alike in many ways and are becoming more alike as time goes by, especially among the young.

CHAPTER 5

MASCULINE AND FEMININE

Although, as we have seen, the differences between masculinity and femininity are not as great as they once were, there remains an essential core of attributes by which each sex is described. Masculinity has traditionally been defined as more object-centered, task-oriented, and active—that is, more instrumental—than femininity. Femininity has traditionally referred to those traits that are person-centered, interpersonally oriented, and affectionate. Such traits are said to be expressive. Each individual possesses not merely masculine or merely feminine characteristics but rather a mixture of both. It is clear that masculinity-femininity ranges over a broad continuum, varies widely from individual to individual, and from time to time within the same individual. However, it is important to observe the general nature of the masculinity-femininity concept.

THE CONCEPT

MEASUREMENT

Terman and Miles' (1936) work set the pattern followed by most researchers who have sought to measure masculine and feminine traits. Terman and Miles gave a large number of test items to men and women of varied ages and occupational backgrounds. They then proceeded to construct a masculinity-femininity scale based on those answers that were given predominantly by one sex or the other. Answers that were given mainly by males and by only a few females were considered indicative of masculine attitudes and interests, while those answers largely or almost exclusively given by females were classified as feminine.

It is clear that the measurement of masculinity and femininity is highly dependent upon the culture in which one is reared and varies from generation to generation in a fast-changing society such as ours. The relativity of the masculinity-femininity concept means that its measurement is less reliable, and consequently research results have not always been clear-cut. Thus the concept is less valid than many other psychosocial ideas. Nevertheless, the characteristics associated with masculinity and femininity play an important part both in individual lives and in the social structure.

IMPORTANCE

It is partly through the process of socially correct sex-role integration that the individual achieves a sense of identity. We will assume that gender-role assignments are learned psychosocial characteristics and that few of them are irreversibly innate. Many scholars think the pressure to find satisfactory sexual identification is greatest during adolescence, and certainly the longer such identification is delayed, the more difficult it is to achieve. Glandular development and body build become associated with certain activities, and social recognition is accorded in relation to particular stereotypes. Vocational aspirations vie with sexuality for the male's chief attention, while girls must reconcile the sometimes conflicting claims of marriage, motherhood, and vocation.

Recognition that many traits may belong to either sex, adoption of roles traditionally assigned to the opposite sex, and attempts to integrate equalitarian attitudes into the dynamics of everyday living have blurred the usefulness of sex roles as a source of identification. No longer are differences between the sexes epitomized in the image of harsh, brutish, larger, stronger male pitted against the often weaker but more cunning female.* Nevertheless, many vestiges of these extremes still exist, and some individuals, fighting for identity, act in accordance with them.

The masculine-feminine concept has a second important function in addition to its association with self-identity: it provides us with highly useful norms to guide our social and personal conduct. In some heterosexual relationships, gender roles may become personalized in response to *intra*personal and *inter*personal expectations. As long as role switching, disguised role expression, or other modifications are understood and agreed upon, no difficulty need be experienced. Partners lacking long experience with each other, however, are apt to find socially prescribed manners of interacting their surest guides.

The concepts of masculinity and femininity have a third important function. A good deal of the sexual behavior that occurs between a couple, within a group, or individually is drastically affected by "nonsexual" dynamics. In the intimate relationship the symbolic importance of such sex-role symbols as power, independence, daring, submission,

---

*Our concern will be with the generalities of American sex-role learning. Other cultures may present modifications or even reversals of American stereotypes. For some cross-cultural comparisons, see Ruth Benedict's *Patterns of Culture*, Margaret Mead's *Sex and Temperament in Three Primitive Societies*, or a wide variety of other anthropological studies.

attractiveness, and others is enhanced or reduced by children, financial matters, daily living routines, vocational considerations, and health. Thus an understanding of masculinity-femininity as it is affected by socially prescribed functions should help us to understand the importance of sound overall adjustment to more positive sexual adjustment.

LIMITATIONS

The description of masculinity and femininity that follows applies chiefly, but not exclusively, to the broad middle class. There are differences in the manner in which various subcultures and social classes expect men and women to express their needs, but these are primarily a matter of intensity rather than of kind. Although various factors influencing particular class categories may alter traditional role expectations, they do not change the broad social definitions of masculinity and femininity. Religion, race, formal education, and family expectations are among the variables affecting sex-role expression. Since this book is limited to a discussion of human sexuality, it is impossible to explore all the subcultural modifications that might affect the individual. Regardless of other considerations, those who have not achieved sufficient sex-role identification can be expected to act erratically when compared with a standardized group.

SOME LEARNING FACTORS

The situations in which sex-role training occurs can have important consequences. David Lynn (1966) has given us a number of hypotheses based on his own work and a summary of other studies. He postulates that (1) males tend to identify with a culturally defined masculinity concept, whereas females tend to identify with their own mothers; (2) both males and females identify more closely with mother than with father; and (3) the closer identification of males with their mothers than with their fathers is revealed most frequently in personality characteristics not clearly sex-typed, and therefore males have more difficulty achieving same-sex identification than females do. Lynn also suggests that males are more anxious about sex-role identification, since they are taught chiefly by mothers and female teachers and have less opportunity than girls have for direct observation of a sex-role model. Females are apt to react strongly to enforce masculinity in their male charges and may do so with negative sanctions, such as reminding a boy he is a sissy or teasing him about acting like a girl. In the absence of clear understanding, such sanctions may become sources of anxiety, and this anxiety may reappear in later relationships.

Lynn believes that this female-generated anxiety may be partially responsible for the hostility that some men feel toward women. But he also theorizes that because of the extensive social reinforcement of masculine concepts, males become more firmly identified with masculine roles as they grow older. The social rewards of masculinity may cause some females to *prefer* certain male roles, although they do not necessarily identify with them.

GENDER DIFFERENCES IN LEARNING SEX ROLES

The process of sex-role learning is believed to be different in some aspects for males than for females. One difference is the fact that males usually first identify with their mothers in expressive roles but later identify with the more abstract social idea of masculinity (Lynn, 1966; M. M. Johnson, 1963; Ward, 1973). The social model of masculinity is probably more universal within the American population than the ideas concerning role-appropriate behavior for girls. The less universal model of role-appropriate behavior, along with the presence of a specific learning model—mother—means that females probably show greater variability in their sex-role behaviors and preferences (Lynn, 1962). It is the continuity of interacting expressively with the mother while tending to maintain affectionate relationships with the father that reinforces femininity in girls (Johnson, 1963).

Since neither parent is imitated consistently, both instrumental and expressive traits are found in both sexes, but the introjection of masculinity in the male is apt to be highly expected by both parents (Ward, 1973). This greater parental stress on masculinity than on femininity is another important difference between the genders in the learning of correct sex roles. As boys grow older, they are increasingly discouraged from engaging in sex-specific feminine behavior. Cooking, sewing, and playing with dolls, all activities that set the tone for later interest in family life, become more and more inappropriate for boys. There is usually less pressure on girls to stop certain "masculine-oriented activities," such as interest in science, mathematics, or sports, since these may later lead to career possibilities. Ideally, the middle-class girl may have her choice of being a wife and mother, a career girl, or even both, but her male counterpart must be appropriately educated, seek the best employment, find a suitable wife, and see that his family gets settled as an integral part of the community. Most evidence strongly suggests that lower socioeconomic classes also aspire to this ideal model, although they may differ in their definitions of the standards they regard as ideal and in their methods of achieving those standards. All this can be exasperating for the male who is forced into this mold against his wishes. On the other hand, the choices available to the female may produce marked anxiety and dissatisfaction. Unless there is a willing male she may not have the opportunity for marriage or motherhood, and despite the advances in this area in recent years, her career possibilities remain culturally limited.

THE MODEL

An important learning factor is the model, and during the most crucial stages this is the parents or parent substitutes. Although fathers may be less important than mothers as major identification models, they have a definite place in teaching their sons and daughters. As a father becomes more involved in caring for his children and helping them to make decisions, his role as a model for interaction with them is enhanced. The extent of a father's influence appears related to the amount of interaction he has with his children, and to the warmth and affection he extends to them.

According to the findings of Barclay and Cusumano (1967), males reared in father-absent homes are less aggressive, more dependent, show greater field dependency (dependency upon the environment for cues), and when in competition with boys from father-present homes, tend to employ feminine tactics. To cover up their sex-role confusion, father-absent boys may also act in a compulsive and exaggerated manner in their denial of anything feminine. These findings are in general agreement with most other research on the effects of father-absence on boys. Bernard (1966) cites Pettigrew's similar findings in Negro males reared in fatherless homes, and she suggests that "lack of marital aptitude" is one of the most relevant results of father-absence on later family life. Highly nurturing fathers who are also quite masculine tend to have sons similar to themselves. In general, research indicates a greater degree of masculinity for boys reared in father-present homes.

Fathers are also important to girls, because it is with their fathers that daughters first learn to interact and express their femininity in an appropriate manner. It is from the interaction with her father that a female usually learns to evaluate males. If a girl has learned to accept her father both in his functions and as a person, and if she has in return been sufficiently rewarded for this acceptance, she is more likely positively to evaluate men in general. If her father has failed to recognize her needs or has belittled her, a girl may learn to be suspicious and distrustful of all men.

Thomes (1968) found few differences between those of her 9- to 11-year-old subjects who were reared with and those who were reared without the presence of fathers. She found both sexes were affected by the absence of a father in the home, but primarily in the area of interpersonal relations. Her female subjects who were reared in father-present homes tended to evaluate "most fathers" more favorably than those reared in father-absent homes. She also found that girls reared in father-present homes had a greater degree of affectionate feeling for and of attitudinal involvement with their fathers.

Mothers provide the earliest and most influential role models for their young. Consequently, mothers are expected to have considerable interest in their children. In the absence of the natural mother, a mother surrogate may take over her functions. These surrogates may be professional baby sitters, friends, neighbors, or extended kin if they live nearby. Sometimes an older brother or sister fills in for the natural mother. Occasionally grandparents exert considerable influence upon their growing grandchildren. A mother's absence can be expected to have varying influences upon masculine or feminine development. However, since there are very few homes in which a mother or mother substitute is not present, more concern is shown with regard to homes in which the mother is absent only part of the day, such as those in which she works or is involved in community activities on a regular basis. Because women are generally more affectionate and expressive than men, the period when they are home is likely to be one of greater parent-child involvement. Still, a mother's part-time absence, especially as her children age beyond the preschool years, does not seem to have as many important negative consequences as was once suspected.

In summary, research suggests that homes in which both parents are not only present but functionally and affectionately involved with their children are more apt to produce offspring who meet the social expectations of masculinity and femininity. Such homes are the initial training grounds for testing sex-role expression.

OTHER INFLUENCES ON SEX-ROLE LEARNING

Additional influences, such as mass media, peer groups, religious training, and formal education, alter home training but usually do little more than add variety to the expression of masculinity-femininity. The *Playboy* philosophy, for instance, reinforces the notion of male aggressiveness and competitiveness and at the same time seems to suggest that "manly virtues" include no real depth of involvement. Peers have a tremendous influence, but as the nature of the peer group changes so does the type of norms it will support. The Judeo-Christian religions support and are the source of many traditional sex-role concepts.

Although divergent subcultures, such as the hippie subgroups, often alter sex roles, they seldom do more than this. Those within these subcultures tend to ignore role-taking on a specifically gender basis. Nevertheless, those subcultures that have remained intact have had to set up rules governing the division of labor, delegation of responsibility, and expectations of conformity (Kanter, 1970, 1972). These subcultures seem to allow more freedom of individual choice in regard to role expression. For example, there is more instrumental response on the part of females and greater freedom of emotional expression among males. As a subculture becomes more specialized, greater delegation of specific tasks becomes necessary, but the assignment of specialized tasks may be on a basis other than sex. To some extent, as we shall see shortly, general social demands concerning sex roles are becoming more relaxed. Consequently, in the area of sex-role expectations, the hippie subcultures and the general society are becoming a little more alike.

SEX-ROLE COMPONENTS

TRADITIONAL ATTRIBUTES

The attributes of masculinity and femininity are meant to complement each other. An examination of Table 5–1 reveals that in our culture the decision-making attributes of humanness have been traditionally assigned to the male. It is he who is most daring, self-reliant, and controlling, while his female partner has traditionally been regarded as passively dependent, unrealistic, and highly introverted. The male, to a greater extent than the female, is in control of his own behavior. Many of the rules surrounding sexual behavior are more concerned with reduc-

TABLE 5–1. TRADITIONAL MASCULINE-FEMININE ATTRIBUTES

Masculinity	Femininity	Both Sexes
Aggressive	Passive	Flexible
Competitive	Cooperative	Self-controlled
Voyeuristic	Physically attractive	Reliable
Dominant	Submissive	Honest
Adventuresome	Inhibited	
Independent	Dependent	
Realistic	Idealistic	
Sexually oriented	Love-oriented	
Fearless	Fearful	
Mechanically minded	Artistic	
Job-centered	Family-centered	

This table was derived from a wide variety of sources dating from the early 1900 era until 1960.

ing the threat to one male by another than with the rights of females. Further examination of Table 5–1 indicates that the locus of control for females has been in the male, either directly as in some ancient and primitive cultures, or through a variety of social sanctions, as in our present-day society. The female exerts control through her appeal as a cooperative person, through her overt acknowledgment of dependency and the effect of this acknowledgment on the male's sympathy, or through her sexuality.

TODAY'S CONCEPTS

Evidently, many of the traditional concepts of masculinity and femininity are still desirable in the opinion of both sexes. Table 5–2 summarizes the abilities and attributes considered by young men and women to be desirable in both sexes but of more desirability in one sex than the other. The study was conducted to provide insight into which human

TABLE 5–2. COLLEGE STUDENTS' CURRENT RATINGS OF DESIRABLE MALE AND FEMALE CHARACTERISTICS

Abilities and Aptitudes Considered by Majorities of Both Sexes to Be More Desirable for Males	Abilities and Aptitudes Considered by Majorities of Both Sexes to Be More Desirable for Females
Athletic ability	Social ability
Mechanical ability*	Interpersonal understanding
Leadership	Art appreciation
Economic ability	Art-creative ability
Entertaining ability	Moral-spiritual understanding
Erotic ability†	Domestic ability
Observational ability	Affectional ability
Intellectual ability	Sartorial ability
Scientific understanding	Physical attractiveness
Theoretical ability	
Common sense	
Achievement and mastery	
Occupational ability	

Adapted from Centers, R. Evaluating the loved one. *J. Pers.* 39 (June, 1971), p. 311. Copyright 1971 by Duke University Press. Reprinted by permission.

*Mechanical ability was considered by both sexes to be below average in desirability as a female trait.

†This item was a practical tie. Only a small fraction of a rating point determined its being placed in the male category.

characteristics should be assigned to each gender and surveyed the average thinking of 296 undergraduates at a large Western university.

The results presented in Table 5–2 are paralleled by the findings of other researchers. Broverman (1972) found masculine traits to be more highly valued than feminine traits as these latter are defined by culture. Physical prowess, abstract reasoning powers, a keen sense of observation, and mastery of most of one's undertakings are more expected of the male. While males hopefully also develop some of the traits assigned to females, it is clear that noninterpersonal, intellectualized, and achievement-oriented behavior is highly associated with maleness. In the Centers study, mechanical aptitude in particular was associated with men by both sexes. The abilities assigned to males reveal the power and control orientation most individuals of both sexes expect of men.

The aptitudes associated with women by both sexes in the Centers study reflect only moderate modification of the traditional female roles. Interest in understanding others rather than in controlling them remained a major aspect of femininity. Traits that contribute to homemaking and child-rearing were considered significantly more important for women than for men. Two attributes of women, physical attractiveness and erotic ability, underscore their capacity to interact with men on a purely sexual level. The notion that females should have as much erotic ability as men perhaps indicates a modernization of the thoughts of men and women on feminine sexuality, but this finding may not hold across noncollege populations.

In a study of 23-year-olds in Hamburg, Germany, Pfeil (1968) found this same mixture of traditional and modern expectations concerning masculine and feminine roles. Sixty per cent of her male respondents expected certain personality traits in their spouses or future spouses. Among these were open-mindedness, reliability, warmth, understanding, and the ability to enter into the interests of the respective mate. Fifty-five per cent of the German men rated domestic qualities and motherliness as important characteristics of their mates, and 44 per cent mentioned certain external criteria, such as (1) the husband should be three to five years older than the wife; (2) girls should be married no later than 25; (3) the best age for a man to marry is between 25 and 28; and (4) the more educated the man the longer he may delay marriage. Not one German male listed professional competence as a desirable trait for his spouse.

Seventy-two per cent of Pfeil's female subjects felt that their mates should possess the same personality traits that the males desired in them; 38 per cent wanted a satisfactory level of work efficiency (professional competence) in their men; but not one German woman listed domestic qualities as desirable in her mate, despite the fact that many of these same women's husbands were helping them with the rearing of children. One might conclude that although men are expected to assist with domestic duties, they are not expected to be highly efficient at or very interested in the job. Adult males who must stay home and do household chores while their wives work (perhaps because the husbands lack employment opportunities) are apt to react with intense and exaggerated behavior designed to bolster their sagging masculine self-images.

OCCUPATIONAL SUCCESS

There is little reason to doubt that most Americans attach great importance to occupational success for the male. As Brenton (1966) points out, vocational success is valued more highly today than during the Great Depression, when men were expected to be out of work. Brenton believes that the shift to a consumer economy has made level of income a more important criterion of job success than personal satisfaction. This consumer orientation has also meant that a man's wife and children may, because of their increased need to buy, place greater stress upon his monetary success in the vocational world. Or this stress may be self-imposed with the husband-father feeling guilty because he does not provide for his family as well as he wishes. Thus in the area in which he is most vulnerable — occupational achievement — the criteria of success seem not to have lessened and may actually be more demanding than is often realized.

Employment as a status variable is highly significant to most males' sense of self-worth. The male is very ego-involved in his occupation and heavily relies on it as a source of identification. Even though he may work at jobs that are considered boring, the average male finds some source of satisfaction in the mere fact that he is working. While a female may choose to work out of boredom, out of a need for self-fulfillment, or because of an intense interest in a particular vocation, a male is apt to find that his occupation is a major aspect of his life style. Unemployed males are often considered a little less than fully masculine, even in their own eyes. Most men create all sorts of activity for themselves, since being very active at least looks productive.

There is little doubt that the two critical elements of the adult male's gender identity are occupational and sexual success. Factors such as time of life, background training, interpersonal competence, and success in one of the two critical elements seem to vary the relative importance of these factors. A male who feels he is achieving satisfactorily in the sexual area may increase his attention to vocational success, or if vocational success seems assured he may show greater interest in sex. The occupationally unsuccessful male may turn to promiscuity as compensation. The ideal, of course, is the occupationally competent, sexually sophisticated male depicted in *Playboy* magazine. But like all idealistic standards, this one is seldom reached.

The high-status-conferring properties of vocational success are frequently denied women. A female who has achieved well in the work world is not accorded the wholeness of status that a male may achieve. Women, even top-notch professionals, are more fully accepted as whole persons if they have also been successful with marriage and a family. Thus females achieve little identity through occupational acumen. But although they are freed from the anxiety of demands for success, they may develop another type of crisis. Homemaking, wifehood, and child-rearing receive less recognition in the status hierarchy because they are consumer- rather than producer-oriented. Wise and careful spending by a housewife may add significantly to the real income of the family but will not receive the public recognition that a high salary does, no matter how frivolously that salary is spent. Consequently, a wife's contribution through wise spending habits earns her little recognition outside her immediate family. The greater social importance of being a high producer than of being a wise consumer has left women with no sex-role status comparable to vocational success for the male. If women turn to the occupational world, the general society still recognizes this as an attempt to imitate men. Thus many women have been unable to invent a social phenomenon equal to the status of employed male, for the majority social attitude does not consider failure on the job a real threat to their femininity.

CONSEQUENCES

Training for masculinity and femininity has produced mixed blessings. On the positive side, it is easier to perform well-spelled-out role expectations; behavior is more predictable; less personal disorientation occurs when role expectations are agreed upon; and cultural notions of masculinity and femininity provide secure identification models when adequately introjected. On the negative side, relationships are apt to be more role-centered than person-centered, resulting in feelings of depersonalization; self-expression is apt to be stymied; personal growth may be retarded; and individual needs may go unmet or unrecognized.

ROLE EXPRESSION

That lasting relationships must be built around some social roles is generally accepted. However, these are times of rapid change and new expectations about gender roles have not yet been refined to the point at which clearly understood models can be presented. One result of rapid change has been the ambiguity surrounding the *manner* in which various roles should be expressed. It seems clear that most couples expect the male to be the nominal head of the house and to take a leadership role in heterosexual relationships. But just how much dominance, aggression, and competitiveness goes into this leadership role is uncertain.

As the barriers to role-sharing are reduced, men are faced with the important learning task of assimilating affective-expressive roles. This they must do without attendant guilt feelings and without losing their sense of masculinity. Since masculine activities are more highly valued by society, it is probably easier for women to accept and adopt elements of masculine behavior than for men to acknowledge femininity in themselves. The failure of men to accept themselves as emotional beings with fears and dependency strivings reduces their capacity to become intimately involved with others, including their wives and children. When emotional expression is limited, sensual development is retarded. Decreased sensitivity to his own needs limits the individual's capacity to be sensitive to the needs of others.

As men become more affectionate, they more nearly meet the needs of women. It has long been noted that men in love are less sexually demanding before marriage than women, who tend to be more sexually permissive with the man they love. Thus the acceptance of femininity in the male by both sexes can have definite positive consequences. Bruce (1967) suggests that masculinity be redefined around new constructs, such as gentleness, tenderness, openness, and the capacity to engage in affective relationships. An important point concerning male emotional expression is that women must be willing to accept it and must be ready to assist whenever their mates have difficulty in this area.

IDENTITY CONCERNS

Although most changes in masculinity-femininity concepts have been favorable to women, as women have gained in personal freedom their psychosexual identity has become a problem. This fear of losing identity is, I believe, an important reason why many women prefer traditional roles and expect to marry and bear children. It is also one reason why some women block any feminine expression in their mates or male children.

For the most part, a woman's identity is closely linked with her husband's occupational success and his standing in the community. This phenomenon may itself produce some splitting of a couple. Since love is partly dependent upon respect and since the sexual attractiveness of a woman's mate is dependent (to some degree) on the amount of affection she feels toward him, failure of the male to achieve occupationally according to his own or his wife's expectations can result in loss of her respect. On the other hand, the demands of work can be so great that the man is unable to function sexually at an optimum level. Either way sexuality and personal intimacy seem to lose out.

To the male who is highly dependent upon his occupation as a source of identity, technological advances and change may bring about a feeling of rootlessness if he fails to keep pace. In addition, technological requirements have meant an increased emphasis on intellectual and cognitive processes, further reducing the exercising of affective responses in both sexes. Much of our modern system of education underscores rational processes while excluding education for feelings or increased interpersonal competence. Emotions can be intelligently evaluated, but intelligence can never fulfill the functions of emotions.

Certain changes in female functioning may also increase a man's awareness of his partial femininity and at the same time highlight the limitations of masculinity, especially as practiced in urban and suburban America. For example, the entry of women into occupations previously reserved for men tends to feminize one of the few remaining strongholds by which males could secure a definite masculine identity. Even though the office worker only vicariously identifies with the lumberjacks he sees on television, a picture of lady lumberjacks can dilute this image seriously. Working women may be viewed as competitors, but this competition may lose some of its harshness and aggressiveness when compared with male-to-male competition. One of the supposed reasons for the popularity of professional football and hockey is that men can identify with the roughness and power displayed in the game and thus gain some measure of masculine identity. Preoccupation with sports has kept many a man from his wife's bed. In short, the current tendency is toward reducing the male's image of himself as powerful, emotionally strong, and dependable. To offset this tendency he must find other routes to masculinity.

POWER SHIFTS

One of the most important changes that has occurred is in the power position of males over females. Husbands remain the nominal "heads of the house," but their position is one of arbitrator, analyst, and advisor in a joint decision-making process. Leadership is expected of men, and if a final decision must be made by one person, many women believe that the husband should make it. Pfeil, cited earlier, found that exactly half of her German women felt that the man should make the decision on important matters that cannot be agreed upon, and she cites evidence of a similar situation in America. In today's heterosexual pairings, nevertheless, male dominance seems to be shifting from command to intelligent leadership.

In times past, and in some marriages today, men enforced their superiority by withholding information concerning family income or finances, threatening to leave their wives or behave in other socially embarrassing manners, by using their children as co-conspirators in undermining the wife's authority, and by insisting on the double standard for sexual behavior. Joint bank accounts, working wives, greater respectability for divorced individuals, increased concern for children's psychological development, and more personal awareness of women's needs have all reduced the male's traditional methods of maintaining his position of power. A man may still have considerable power over his wife, but he often possesses this power because she chooses to give it to him. In democratically run homes, the power of any family member is more likely to be a function of his ability to *influence* (rather than autocratically control) the decisions of others within the family circle.

Actually, women have always had considerable influence on decision-making, regardless of generalizations about the past. In the first place, many women held power through the fact that their husbands loved them and thus wished well for them. Love has been and will continue to be the great leveler of power in primary relationships. Secondly, the patriarch who uses his wife as a sounding board for his opinions becomes vulnerable to her, for she can give negative connotations to his ideas anytime she chooses. The more a woman becomes a mirror of her mate's image, the greater is the power she has over him.

WOMEN'S LIBERATION

The women's liberation movement is one result of society's emphasis on sex roles and the superior position of males. Betty Friedan (1963) has set much of the tone for modern women's liberationists. She developed the thesis that society has played up the "mysterious" aspects of femininity by continuously throughout history detouring women back to housewifery and child-bearing. This, she says, has been done through a variety of brainwashing techniques calculated to convince women that home is the only place where they can really be comfortable and find their "true" feminine identity. She states:

> Toying with the question, how can one hour of housework expand to fill six hours (same house, same work, same wife), I came back again to the basic paradox of the feminine mystique: that it emerged to glorify woman's role as housewife at the very moment when the barriers to her full participation in society were lowered, at the very moment when science and education and her own ingenuity made it possible for a woman to be both wife and mother and to take an active part in the world outside the home (p. 238).

Women, Friedan feels, have either been placed upon a pedestal or condemned to housework, both of which are contemptuous denials of their real ability to contribute to society. She notes that new gadgets should have helped free the housewife of hours of drudgery, but instead harried wives have actually spent more time keeping house. Friedan interprets this as evidence that most of these women are made to feel that they have no other useful function in society. This the overworked housewife, surrounded by her labor-saving devices, can understand. Newer and more radical forms of women's liberation have sprung up.

The aims of the different women's liberation organizations vary from basic demands for social, political, and occupational equality to pronouncements that freedom from motherhood, housework, and subservience to men includes the need to be free of men themselves. Sexual liberation means not only the freedom to enjoy eroticism but also freedom to seek an identity other than as a sexual object. Kate Millett (1970) has described the use of the arts and literature to subjugate women sexually and has been attacked by Norman Mailer (1971), whose thesis seems to be that feminists (at least Millett) do not interpret literary sexualism correctly. While Millett sees Henry Miller as denigrating women, her perception of Miller's intentions is not necessarily correct, Mailer believes. Identity of their own is the goal of many feminists, but they do not want this identity to be an exclusively sexual one. Lucy Komisar (1971) writes:

> Feminists are concerned that the new sexual freedom should not become a means of exploitation of women — that women should not be forced into sex merely because it is the thing to do and that they should not be treated as sexual objects in the same way that prostitutes have been treated as sexual objects throughout history. It will be no great victory to extend that exploitation to the population at large. Feminists do not want the return of the time when women did not have the right to say "yes," but they insist that the mores of society give women the right to say "no" (pp. 162–163).

Many feminist groups seek more child-care facilities provided at government expense, abortions on demand, freer access to contraceptive devices, and the freedom to *enjoy* sexual relationships without *demands* that they do so. Some groups seek sexual freedom in regard to the choice of a partner, whether that partner be of the same or of the opposite sex.

Much of what the feminists hope to accomplish would also be beneficial to males, who are as "stuck" with masculine stereotypes as females are with femininity. However, even among women themselves there exist grave scientific doubts as to the validity of the extreme feminists' views. Florence Ruderman (1971, pp. 48–54) makes a case for bona fide biological differences between the sexes, including not only differences in reproductive functions but also the extension of biologically based differences between the sexes to "personality and mental organizations" (p. 50). Furthermore, the existence of a biologically based male "bonding" has been postulated. Tiger (1969) presents evidence which he interprets as indicating that males have biologically based bonds which may partly account for their banding together to wage war, hunt, carry on political activity, or simply be together. Sometimes these male bonds are stronger than heterosexual attraction, and the woman who insists on being a "good companion" when her husband prefers being alone with the "boys" is apt to be resented.

FEMALE FREEDOM

As women are liberated from societal restrictions, they gain more freedom to be themselves erotically. Both men and women need to understand this growing female freedom and its impact on both sexes. The double standard tends to be eliminated among the more liberated, and women are more apt to initiate sexual encounters and introduce new ideas to their sexual partners. Sexual companionship replaces competitiveness when those involved feel free to express themselves, and this companionship outlook on eroticism can be functional for women in increasing their sexual responsiveness. Cooperativeness, the byword of companionship, is likely to be greater among those who feel they are equals. High levels of continuous agreement, necessary to the maintenance of long-term intimacy, are more likely when equality is genuinely practiced.

However, there are also negative consequences of women's liberation, sexual or otherwise. Men, despite their claim to enjoy high levels of eroticism in their mates, are likely to respond to women's freedom negatively when that freedom is perceived as a threat to their masculinity. On the other hand, some women may overreact to the liberated feeling by deliberately provoking men through a variety of strategies. Overreaction on the part of either men or women hinders sexual companionship. Aggressiveness by women is not socially encouraged as feminine, yet many husbands complain because their wives do not initiate sexual play often enough. Since most, if not all, sexual codes in the Western world have been set up by men, a cooperative effort to lessen the sexual restrictions on women is sorely needed.

Although sex-role differentiation may be less important than formerly, ambiguity and confusion still exist, since many individuals have internalized traditional role expectations side by side with more modern codes. This is especially true in relation to female sexuality. A fuller understanding of feminine sexual and emotional needs should provide greater appreciation of women as erotic beings.

In brief, women's liberation is adding new dimensions not only for females but for men and children as well. The movement appears to represent a series of loosely knit organizations and efforts aimed at bringing about more personal freedom and individual identity for women. To the extent that individual freedom is an important issue for all Americans, all should benefit, at least from the less radical efforts of women's organizations. To some extent, then, the liberation of women should enhance the genuineness of their sexuality.

SOME SOLUTIONS TO SEX-ROLE CONFLICT

The idea that females suffer from severe role conflict may be overdone. Actually, the great majority of women seem to find solutions that they can live with, and while these solutions are not always ideal, they are at least practical, given today's social milieu. One solution to role conflict is to redefine the roles to fit more appropriately one's needs and situations. Research evidence and the experiences of women themselves verify that this is a workable answer. Rand (1968) compared career-oriented with homemaking-oriented college freshman girls and found that the career-oriented girls were able to redefine their roles to include many "masculine" traits while retaining several traits usually considered feminine. She found that her home-oriented girls remained closer to traditional concepts of femininity and had higher feminine personality and social characteristics. Sanford (1966, p. 201), reviewing an earlier study of Vassar girls, noted that they tended to score higher on masculinity scales as they progressed through college. He feels these girls were not really becoming less feminine but rather were acquiring the ability to see themselves in a greater variety of roles. The expansion into more and varied roles does not necessarily mean the loss of one's basic femininity or masculinity.

The male has long compartmentalized his roles, being the active, competitive, and aggressive man in his occupation but playing a more moderate role when with his family. There is no reason why women should not also follow this pattern, and many do. Some wives have compartmentalized their day into periods of employment, time for the children, and time set aside for the husband. As long as this compartmentalization is attuned to the needs of those one loves, little harm will be done, and guilt because of neglect need not arise.

Perhaps the most satisfactory way of managing differences in masculine-feminine expectations is consciously to modify or obliterate the whole concept of masculinity and femininity. Rather than demanding of oneself or one's mate that socially stereotyped roles be performed in a culturally determined manner, any person in a group of two or more individuals living in an intimate and long-lasting relationship can perform many of the roles needed to remain functional. Fathers cannot nurse babies, but they can change diapers and bathe their offspring. Women can learn the elementary mechanics needed to paint, fix furniture, or repair a broken latch. The concept becomes one of role-sharing, with both housewives and househusbands cooperating. According to this view, the traditional assignment of certain roles to one sex or another is, to a large extent, nothing more than cultural lag.

The cost of this cultural lag to full development of a viable, intensely passionate relationship can be high. In fact throughout this text we will see examples of failures at every stage of intimacy because of expectations that sex roles must be fulfilled. Louise and Bing are one such example:

> Louise and Bing had been married about three years when Louise began to rebel at her husband's rather dictatorial attitudes. Bing never refused to permit her to see her friends, but the fact that he expected her to ask his permission every time and his constant belittling of her for not being "satisfied to stay at home like a good wife should" irritated her. Although her friends were mostly female and of long acquaintance, Bing felt that they interfered with their marriage, since in his words "They are always trying to get her to take shortcuts in her housework. Sometimes they even think she should go out and leave me to do the dishes." Although he had bought his wife many appliances to reduce the drudgery of her work, Bing clung to the idea that a woman's place is in the home. About the only change Bing permitted from traditional sex-role expectations was during sexual interplay. There he encouraged and demanded that Louise be active and often take on the aggressor role.
>
> Louise retaliated by demeaning Bing's occupational accomplishments (which were many). She constantly reminded him that he was a poor father and not very good at making repairs around the house. She enjoyed the aggressor role in sex but complained that the whole sex act was too mechanical.
>
> The entire relationship was based on keeping records of who had done what to whom and who had not fulfilled his "proper" (traditional) sex-role expectations. Bing was never able to give up his patriarchal notions of marriage, and no real sensuousness ever developed between him and his wife. This made no difference to Bing, who felt that anything emotional beyond sexual fulfillment was foolishness. Louise remained disappointed for years but finally found herself a lover with whom she was more satisfied. A year later, in spite of her strong religious upbringing, Louise divorced Bing.

The demands of modern mechanized society, coupled with traditional sex-role expectations, stultify the development of spontaneous, highly intense sensual responses, for sensuousness cannot be mechanized or planned. Many couples, nevertheless, find the solution to their intimacy problem by denouncing the sex-role concept of division of labor and in the husband's acceptance of affectional-expressive roles as a part of modern manhood.

SUMMARY

The following generalizations may be derived from our study of masculinity and femininity:

1. Masculine and feminine roles can assist the individual to establish his or her identification as a functioning person.
2. The socially prescribed roles associated with one's gender are learned early in life, and the predominant masculine or feminine orientation is normally established before adolescence.
3. Males tend to be more anxious about their traditional sex roles, have fewer role options than females, find much of their identity in either occupational or sexual roles, and are expected to have greater command of their situations than females and to exert leadership in their roles as husbands and fathers. In addition, men are expected to have greater physical prowess, higher abstract reasoning powers, and a keener sense of observation than is generally accorded to women.
4. Large numbers of women consider men to be generally superior to them, and it is thus women as much as men who support the traditional models of masculinity and femininity.
5. An expansion of the roles available to both sexes need not reduce individual feelings of femininity or masculinity.
6. Sex-role divisions have emphasized the differences between men and women and have been the cause of much distress between the sexes, especially when these divisions have been used to bolster sagging self concepts.
7. Some modern couples interpret role fulfillment in terms of the needs and dynamics of their relationship rather than on a gender basis.
8. New concepts of masculinity that include gentleness and similar ideas are needed to cope with today's changing world and the demands it makes on interpersonal relationships.

CHAPTER 6

PSYCHOSEXUAL PARTNERS

COMING TOGETHER

The isolated individual satisfying himself through masturbation interacts symbolically with a partner who will respond exactly as he wishes, but when two or more persons come together to form a union, fantasies must give way to reality. Each brings to the situation highly individualized expectations out of which he or she hopes to build a relationship. Often these idiosyncratic expectancies exist on a romanticized plane, the individual imagining his partner and himself blending with minimal effort. Even important anticipated differences may be glossed over. However, the reality is that neither individual is apt to have all his wishes fulfilled. Many factors interfere with the ongoing process of relating, including the inability or refusal to drop inappropriate responses, inefficient communication, unrealistic expectations, misunderstood personal needs, and inadequate sexual information.

NEW LEARNING

The process of sexual interaction follows the general laws of learning and includes considerable trial and error behavior, especially in the beginning phases. New responses must be tried, and if they are found to be undesirable, they must be either modified or discarded altogether. Conditions must be favorable to new learning. An atmosphere of openness, trust, and acceptance must be established. Satisfaction, the necessary reward of any continuing relationship, must be felt and communicated if deepening intimacy is to take place.

When unsatisfactory but habitual responses exist, their replacement is subject to three important considerations. First, the individual must prize the relationship enough to want to make it work. The general direction of his motivation toward the relationship must be positive, consciously acknowledged, and relatively free from unconscious interferences. Second, the individual must possess the necessary neurological apparatus needed to learn new and varied responses. Pressures to learn or develop insights beyond one's capacity can undermine any relationship, whether these pressures are internally or externally produced. Third, the individual must have the psychological capacity to give up the old, inappropriate responses in favor of new ones. Broadly, this implies that the more the individual's sexual habits are under his conscious control and not part of his defense armor, the easier it will be to bring about desired changes. When deeply entrenched sexual habits help defend the individual against overwhelming anxiety, new interpersonal learning is impossible. When one or both partners sense a long-term dissatisfaction but neither is able to change, it is time to call on professional help. These three factors—level of motivation, adequacy of neurological apparatus, and psychological adaptiveness—are recognized as basic elements necessary to most learning. They are especially important in the sexual relationship because it is usually an intense affair full of symbolic meanings for the participants. Failure to consider what is possible as opposed to what is expected or hoped for can lead to the destruction of an otherwise sound relationship. Susan and Jim were one such couple:

> Both Susan and Jim claimed to have a high degree of interest in each other and in maintaining their relationship of four months. Other factors, such as similarity of education, social class, and religion, appeared to be satisfactory. However Jim, an engineering student, insisted that Susan comprehend what he considered to be elementary engineering principles. This she had been unable to do in spite of her best efforts, but he would not give up, pressuring her to meet his demands. Susan's response to this pressure was to cry and cling to Jim while promising to try harder. This usually tended to make Jim angry, and he would walk out. Following each of these episodes, things would go well again for several days and then the pattern would repeat itself. Susan had not yet experienced coitus but had offered to try it with Jim on several occasions when he had pressured her to learn engineering, but each time he had refused, explaining that he had too much respect for her.

Susan and Jim responded to each other with the same old habits that had worked well for them in other relationships. In spite of the fact that their relationship was dying, neither seemed to understand the cause nor have any idea how to handle the situation. The overt demands had, of course, changed from those of previous relationships, but the underlying dynamics had not.

Consideration of a few facts might have helped this couple. Each had developed certain responses as a defense against anxiety related to the masculine-feminine dimension. Susan's dependency needs are readily recognized in her crying and clinging and in her offer of coitus. Jim's doubts about his masculinity underlie his demands on Susan. His insistence upon judging her by her ability to meet his own criterion (learning engineering principles) protects him from any direct assault on his masculine pride and at the same time places her in a dilemma by exposing her "weakness." Jim's dependency needs are neatly hidden beneath his charade, and one cannot ignore the fact that he makes preposterous demands on Susan on the one hand while claiming a high degree of respect for her on the other. There may be other underlying dynamics of even deeper significance than these, but consideration of those defenses I have mentioned may be all that is necessary to bring about changes.

SEXUAL COMMUNICATION

As soon as two individuals initiate a relationship, communication becomes a vital issue. Communication is the ability to send and receive messages accurately. Messages may be classified into two major levels. There may be messages of intent, fact, or expectation, or messages may be sent and received at the emotional-feeling level. The first are expositions of the way conditions are perceived, while the second level is the individual's personal evaluation of the facts. Often both types of messages are embodied within the same communication. Feeling level messages are frequently involved in the maintenance of loyalty, morale, or control over the other.

Communication takes place both verbally and nonverbally through shared symbols, but when symbolic meanings are not understood and agreed upon, trouble can be expected. Sexual behavior ordinarily is an overt representation of internally and socially mediated needs, and communications involving erotic material often have highly intense personal meaning to both the sender and the receiver. Consequently, much of the sexual interchange between a couple has possible connotations for the self-image of each participant and is easily misinterpreted, thus limiting the possibility of personal enhancement through sexuality. Clearly, the words and other symbols of sex must be understood and their meanings agreed upon in the context of the couple's relationship. The special intentions of the partners take precedence over social definitions. Not only is it important to share one's sexual feelings, ideas, values, and beliefs through the token of sexual interaction; if deeper relations are sought, appreciation of the internalized meanings of these symbols ought to occur. Howard and Georgia are a case in point:

> Howard and Georgia had been married only a few weeks when one night while engaging in coitus Howard, in a high state of passion, expressed his appreciation for her in this manner: "I love the way you screw; you sure make a wonderful piece." Georgia was shocked and dismayed, but waited until the next day to approach Howard with her feelings. He carefully explained that he meant only that she was something very special to him and an excellent sexual partner who could really let herself go. Georgia considered the fact that he never used these words in his everyday language, nor did he use them often even when highly aroused. Consequently, she decided he genuinely did mean to communicate extraordinary feelings for her. Now that she has become more used to this and other so-called unacceptable verbalizations, they tend to increase her own passions.

Undoubtedly, some might be tempted to extract more from this intimate interchange and to analyze it at "deeper" levels, but the fact is that this couple has found a special way of exchanging their feelings that works well for them. Further interpretation would only serve to reduce the passion between them and perhaps destroy the relationship, and would seem to be based more on sociomoral considerations than on their own needs. This point is made to emphasize that dwelling on the negative can be harmful, regardless of whether the couple themselves, well-meaning friends, or counselors do so.

Messages are sent and received idiosyncratically. Past experiences, current psychological sets, personal needs, and individual value systems guide the internal processes that modify messages from the form in which they originally fall on our senses. Individual perceptions can distort both the messages we send and those we receive.

In his tape recording, "Married Couple Group Therapy," Blinder has given us some important insights into the problem of perceptual distortion, and the following discussion is adapted from his work.* Faulty perception occurs when the partner is seen only according to the expectations of the perceiver, when unconscious attitudes are projected, or when ambivalent attitudes toward the partner or to sex exist. Furthermore, if the adaptive defenses of either partner are seriously challenged, or if it is feared that the kind of response desired will not be forthcoming, sexual communication will be inhibited.

Everyone develops psychological response sets—expectations of obtaining similar responses from standard situations. These sets may cause us to misinterpret or to fail to understand the full meaning of a communication. Very often certain aspects of sexual communications will be misinterpreted while the remaining aspects are understood. The consequence of this may be that ambiguity, mistrust, and hurt feelings exist side by side with love and sexual attraction.

The ability to listen is a major component of effective interpersonal communication. We tend to decode messages in the light of our past experiences. Threatening, boring, or irrelevant material may be heard, but no meaning will be absorbed from it. We simply "turn off" those persons who are not meeting our needs of the moment. Often as not the transmission of irrelevant material or the failure to abstract what is important is a subconscious defense against involvement. At other times, of course, it is deliberately done. One major reason for the failure of communications is the inability of senders to perceive their own messages. Communicators often concentrate so much on what they are going to say next that they

---

*The sound tape recording "Married Couple Group Therapy" is tape 75508 in the McGraw-Hill Sound Seminar Series and may be purchased from: College Division, McGraw-Hill Book Company, P.O. Box 402, Hightstown, N.J., 08520.

miss the implications of their present transmissions, and when they do hear and decode them, they discover that their intentions were not correctly conveyed. Those who can hear themselves as their partners do have the best chance of projecting the sexual image they intend.

Until partners become so involved with their passion that they lose contact with the external world, nonverbal signs may be the chief means of communicating during sexual interaction. Body movement, muscle tone, and facial expressions may transmit as much or more to the partner as verbalizations. As long as verbal and nonverbal communication are consistent, they add assurance that the interplay is acceptable. But when spoken material does not harmonize with the nonverbal signs, confusion may occur, resulting in loss of zest. Physical signs of sexual arousal can be simulated, especially by the good actor or actress, and this may generate the feeling that a good deal of involvement exists when in fact it does not. More often (and perhaps more serious because of the consequences), absence of the motor signs of sexual arousal may lead to the conclusion that the partner is not very passionate. Acutally, the vagaries of sex are such that some very passionate individuals exhibit only a few motor signs during arousal while others less passionate may respond with many. The individual himself also varies from time to time in the number and intensity of overt signs, even though subjectively felt passion is high.

In the final analysis, the best communicators are those who have gained an adequate measure of self-knowledge, are relatively free from gross personality disturbance, have purposely practiced the art of telling and listening, and consciously wish open, honest interchange.

Everything need not be communicated. Part of the continuing allure of any sexual partner is the mystery surrounding those aspects of the inner self that have not yet been revealed. A mild degree of unpredictability adds excitement and passion to any sexual relationship. Furthermore, everyone needs a private sector of his life that is not subject to the scrutiny and judgment of others. Attempts to absorb each other fully while allowing few if any private thoughts, feelings, or behaviors end up as futile gestures which more often destroy than enhance love, for to rob the ego of its essential function of maintaining a sense of autonomy is certain to bring about neurotic psychological defense mechanisms. Attempts should not be made to reveal all or to extract from a partner details of his or her past sexual life. If confessions must be made, society has provided priests, ministers, rabbis, psychiatrists, and counselors of all sorts. Experienced and wise sexual partners realize the critical place of personal autonomy and privacy in sexual interaction.

In summary, good sexual communication is the ability to experience the other person at all levels while allowing oneself enough openness for the other to reciprocate. At the same time, each partner should respect the other's right to privacy in certain areas and at particular times.

THE COUPLE PATTERN

If they interact over a long enough period of time, each and every couple will develop a pattern of responsiveness idiosyncratic to their needs and situation. Patterns of sexual interaction that were successful with others will, to some extent, need to be modified to fit the specific needs of a new partner. If they are attuned to the finer aspects of their relationship, a couple will realize that theirs is a unique alliance, different from any other they may have experienced. Comparisons with former relationships should not be made.

Sexual adequacy inheres primarily in the individual. The person who is sexually capable can relate to a number of partners and is not dependent upon others to compensate for his defects. The sexually self-assured may or may not choose to have relations with more than one person, for he is compelled neither to prove himself nor to refrain because of fears. Considerations other than sex enter into his decisions. The adequate person may find a particular individual with whom he can enjoy sexual relations to a greater extent than with others, but this is because he recognizes that his partner's personality traits complement his own. A couple pattern based on the fact that one partner is compensating for the other's deficiencies is not likely to be enduring. The fearful, reluctant, indifferent, or unskillful partner must overcome these barriers if he desires a self-enhancing sexual relationship.

CHANGING NEEDS

Some individuals have fairly constant day-to-day psychosexual needs; others vary considerably in their daily demands. In either case many couples reach a high degree of stability in the pattern of their relationship, and for some this general pattern of need-responsiveness lasts for a lifetime of satisfaction. Many persons, however, find that their sociopsychological or sexual needs change as a result of certain variables. Although the personal pressures on the individual may be gradually shifting in response to vocational, family, social, or personal demands, they sometimes appear in the conscious relationship of a couple to produce a sudden disequilibrium. This apparent suddenness occurs because the participants in the relationship were not attentive enough, or lived the fantasy that no changes were taking place, or, believing that the necessary changes would somehow come about, expected them to shift in accordance with certain social stereotypes. One such social stereotype is the expectation that a couple should "settle down" after marriage. Another is the belief that sexual interests will wane drastically as the individual becomes older. There are many such stereotypes, some of which may become self-fulfilling prophecies.

The failure to notice or cope with changing needs, whether these changes are gradual or sudden, is a psychological defense mechanism against the overwhelming anxiety that can result from equilibrium shifts. Changes may occur in many areas, but some of the more usual shifts involve dependency needs, patterns of dominance-submission, social or personal prejudices, altering of social patterns, acquisition of new values and rejection of old ones, reduction or elevation of sexual desire, increases or decreases in tolerance, and switches in the type of sexual activity sought. This is but a small list of the many "gut-level" changes that can take place within the personal-interpersonal structure of the couple's relationship. The list makes clear the necessity of continuously active communication if a viable, aware, and fully functioning relationship is to be achieved.

DEPERSONALIZATION

Under certain conditions, the sexual relationship can become devastatingly impersonal. The process of depersonalization begins when one partner (or both) is persistently critical of the other, or tends to remember the worst times, or attempts to extract confessions from the other — when spontaneous behavior in the intimate situation is discouraged, when honest differences cannot be tolerated, when love is either lacking or unexpressed, or when either partner implies that the other is a bad or immoral person. The case of Jack and Jenny illustrates the process of depersonalization that both results from a deteriorating relationship and adds to that deterioration:

> Shortly after their marriage, Jack, who had been widely known on campus for his high degree of erotic activity, began losing interest in Jenny. He claimed that beginning a new career along with the heavy work load of graduate study was draining most of his energy. If Jenny indicated a desire for sexual relations, he would answer in a manner implying that he was indifferent, that she was not an important part of his life, and that she was oversexed. His response to her most provocative gestures went something like this: "Well, if you need it get your clothes off, and I'll put it in. I realize you get like a hot bitch once a month, but remember I haven't all night to fool around. Jenny never has anything on her mind but her ass. She just can't seem to settle down — can you?"

No wonder that after three months of marriage Jenny decided to leave her husband; in this short time he had successfully reduced her self-image to a shambles. Although Jack was cruder than most, several common elements of depersonalization are evident in his conversation. The change from the use of her first name to the pronouns is one example. His last sentences are confusing and sound as though he is talking to a third person instead of to his wife. The degrading reference to Jenny as a bitch and his impersonal "command" that she remove her clothes are elements that can be found in many faltering relationships.

All of Jack's language suggests that Jenny is personally repugnant to him. The sooner patterns of sexual interaction which are dehumanizing and alienating are discovered the better, for the effects of one such relationship can be carried for a lifetime.

FACTORS LIMITING CHANGE

The sexual aspect of a relationship may or may not influence or be influenced by the other parts. Some couples continue to have a satisfactory sex life despite the fact that other phases of their partnership are unfulfilling, but for most, disruption of the nonsexual functions reduces sexual gratification as well. In most cases, the nonerotic dynamics of a relationship do more to reduce sexual satisfaction than poor sexual functioning itself.

Certain personal deficiencies limit the possibility of adjustment to change. Some individuals have anti-interpersonal attitudes, beliefs, or values. Simply put, they believe that a deep, personal attachment is dangerous or wrong. Other factors limiting the possibility of change include a tendency to become highly involved in outside activities, pressure from bad experiences of the past or from repressed material, a tendency to ignore subtle changes in one's mate, or the fear that one is inadequate to deal with changing needs.

Changing needs must be coped with in some manner. For some couples, sensitivity to each other, open communication, a deep interest in maintaining the relationship, and large amounts of day-to-day interaction mean that changing needs will be met. For others, however, need changes produce fears, which result in overt defensive and deploying reactions. The most widely used methods of expressing sexually related fears, inadequacies, or indifferences include the outright refusal to engage in sexual relations, noncooperation during precoital activities, denial of sexual desire, claims that the partner is no longer exciting, protestations of fatigue or illness, and claims of disgust with the partner's requests. Each of these, of course, may have some basis in fact, but it is clear from clinical observation that all may be used as avoidance devices.

Limiting factors help avoid the immediate anxiety often attached to changes in interpersonal equilibrium, but in the long run become increasingly disruptive as the need for change increases.

ILLNESS OR OTHER CONTINGENCY

Some couples find that their pattern of sexual interaction is seriously interrupted by illness, surgery, or pregnancy. Nevertheless, several recent studies suggest that sexual interest following illness or surgery can be quite complete and is frequently dependent upon psychological attitudes (Twombly, 1968).

Several factors must be considered when predicting a change in sexual desire due to surgery or disease processes. The first of these is the premorbid state of the individual. A low sexual drive may be accented by the illness, while those with greater interest may be less affected or affected for a shorter period of time. Some surgery, such as a hysterectomy, may actually increase sexual desire.

A second important factor involves the effects of the disease process itself, such as pain, fatigue, or fever. Illness, according to Dengrove (1968), produces a constriction of the ego, a tendency toward depression, and a need to cope with a sense of helplessness. These in turn produce anxiety and further depression, which result in a loss of sexual interest.

Thirdly, the psychological state of the individual must be considered. Those for whom particular organs symbolize sexual potency or who believe, consciously or subconsciously, that their misery is punishment for sexual activity may lose interest if that organ is removed or if a morbid condition develops.

Fourthly, the effects of treatment vary. Surgery or irradiation may reduce sexual desire, but different drugs produce different effects. Drugs that reduce anxiety may increase libido, as does testosterone when administered to women. In contrast, estrogen, when given to men, may reduce their sex drives.

A fifth factor in post-surgery sexual response is the attitude of the partner. If the mate shows a loss of interest, the patient may fail to maintain or recover previous interests. In general, research indicates that coitus does not excessively drain energy, that no physical reasons usually exist for avoiding coitus during menstruation, that some form of sexual activity can take place during most illnesses, that sexual interests are not lost following brain damage or among paraplegics, and that sexual activity, including coitus, is no harder on the heart than many everyday activities, such as employment or anger (Zehv, 1970b).

To sum up, satisfactory patterns of sexual adjustment may be spoiled by failing to cope with basic personality, social, vocational, or other changes in individual needs, by attitudes which are or which become anti-interpersonal, by depersonalizing the relationship, by using defensive measures during particular contingencies such as illness or surgery, and by expectations that the sexual aspect of a relationship will compensate for nonerotic, negative conditions. Inadequate communication and conditions that inhibit change add to the likelihood of sexual maladjustment.

ENHANCING SEXUAL ADJUSTMENT

AGREEMENT

Certain factors have been found by researchers positively to enhance sexual adjustment. One is the amount of agreement concerning the types of sexual acts in which the couple will engage. Usually, the longer a pair interact sexually, the more likely they are to engage in variety. In addition, each partner may feel more free to make requests for specific acts that were once thought forbidden. Some individuals participate in particular kinds of sexual behavior just to please a partner. If the couple are compatible in other areas, this may be no problem, for part of sexual satisfaction is pleasing each other. When frustration must be kept hidden because of violent opposition, continual engaging in unwanted sexual acts may bring mounting guilt feelings with eventual projection of those feelings onto the partner. Such projected defenses are apt to appear consciously as anger, disgust, hatred, or withdrawal.

There is evidence that those partners who believe that their sex drives are about equally strong have a better chance of achieving adjustment both sexually and nonsexually. Thus couples who perceive the wife's sexual drive as greater than the husband's are apt to experience extra difficulty in their adjustment (Wallin and Clark, 1958). The cultivation of shared sexual interests can be helpful in equalizing erotic needs. The introjection of romance into the relationship can also be helpful, since it tends to erase differences that may be due to the male's greater interest in direct sexual expression. One of the major factors in bringing about an equality between sexual partners is the establishment of common values for both sexual and nonsexual behavior. The axiom in this regard is that the more agreement there is on major issues, the easier it will be to achieve adjustment generally. Close agreement in psychosocial and spiritual areas will be of assistance in establishing a feeling of equality in the sexual relationship. Equality of sex drive, then, is not limited to a belief that physiological desires are about the same, but includes agreement on the amount and kind of sexual interaction that is to take place, on satisfactory levels of romance, and on mutually arrived at couple values.

THE COUPLE PHILOSOPHY

Needs must be fused with values in a complementary manner if a sound sexual partnership is to be built. Satisfaction is difficult to maintain if the needs of any individual within the relationship are antagonistic to his own or to the other's value system. Every couple who plan on spending any considerable part of their lives together ought to develop a "couple philosophy" of life. The couple philosophy is based on the personal needs and values of each partner, molded so that these needs and values become the essential outlook of the relationship. The couple philosophy is essentially the broad, philosophical guide that will steer the couple in their relationship with each other. If more than two persons are involved in a sexual association, the couple philosophy simply becomes a group philosophy.

By working out a broad, general outline for functioning, beliefs, and values, the partners acquire a means of predicting each other's behavior and responses. Such generalized foreseeing helps minimize personal distress and aids in planning for more positive relational enhancement. Included in the couple philosophy might be agreement on moral values, the general importance of sex, love, and passion to the relationship, the extent and limits of personal involvement with others, rights of privacy, the place of certain status positions such as marriage, lover-mistress, or fiancé, general views of life, and other matters of importance to the couple.

A couple philosophy provides a broad base for settling disputes and for seeking new horizons. It is a dynamic concept calling for periodic revision as conditions change. For some couples the philosophy underlying their relationship will not be spelled out, but I believe that those who can most clearly specify their joint views of life have the best chance of succeeding.

RELATING NEEDS

Many psychosexual needs are the same for both sexes, although the intensity of such needs will be individually determined and will vary from time to time. Men can and do develop strong needs for sentimental, emotional, and affectional relationships, and women generally do develop a greater need for direct physical expression of sex as they grow older and gain experience.

Men, of course, have been conditioned to be aggressive and to inhibit any impulse to show profound emotional feelings, but this does not mean that those feelings do not exist. Since sex is an active form of expression (as is aggression), it is easy and natural for men to make a psychological connection and to use sex as a form of affectional expression. For many men sex is an active means of showing their affectional desires toward women. I do not mean that the desire to show affection is the chief or only motive for engaging in sexual relations, but I believe that both sexes need to be more fully aware that sex is an active, instrumental way of expressing love and affection well suited to the cultural conditioning of the male.

As females gain freedom, both socially and personally, they too may tend to accept direct sexual participation as a form of affectional expression. Since they are often trained to be less active and more sentimental in their general demeanor, they associate tenderness, softness, and psychophysical warmth with their physical feelings to a greater degree than men. For almost 100 per cent of women, affectional expression from a sexual partner (temporary or not) adds a dimension of unity or wholeness to erotic acts.

UNACCEPTABLE NEEDS

Each sex has learned not only the roles of his own gender but also the socially acceptable roles of the other. Within the individual's personal experience, social stereotypes of the various statuses have developed: husband, boy-friend, lover, or casual date; wife, girl-friend, mistress, or pickup. In the group situation, group partner may be an assigned status. It takes some time to be fully assured which type of sexual behavior is and is not acceptable, since each individual has had private experiences that do not exactly match those of any other person. Consequently, because they fear loss of respect, personal guilt, or other negative reactions, many individuals hold in check those aspects of their sexual desires that they assume their partners will find unacceptable. In other cases, intimate wishes are kept secret because the individual himself cannot accept his desires. Often another partner will be sought on a temporary basis and the "unacceptable" acts will be carried out with that person. In this way the more meaningful relationship with a permanent partner is believed to be less threatened.

Very often "secret" longings are not strictly in the sexual realm and include the desires for greater affection, for increased masculinity, for improvements in the general relationship, and for greater experimentation both sexually and nonsexually. There is a real danger in exposing one's wish for forbidden relationships or acts, since the partner may devalue not only the acts themselves but also those persons who desire or engage in them. One cannot ask a mate to go beyond his or her conscience. Some couples solve this dilemma by stifling unacceptable desires, while others agree to some modification. Still others permit extrasexual relationships, hoping that need satisfaction will be gained in the erotic area while leaving the rest of the partnership intact. As in all good communication, the only way to check out the assumption that certain desires or acts are unacceptable is to make them known.

Certain hidden feelings tend to spoil sex (Adams, 1968). A desire to examine each other's genitals closely and minutely often must be kept secret because of embarrassment or shame. Other attitudes that are often suppressed include a wish on the part of the male that his partner be more aggressive, impatience with prolonged foreplay and a desire to get on with coitus, a feeling of being cheated because of missed orgasm, disgust with one's mate for ignoring one following coitus, and the belief that one is being used in a sexually exploitative manner.

Beigel (1969) delineates other attitudes and feelings that tend to interfere with sexual adjustment. As he points out, "acts, attire, words, smells and sights which are enormously stimulating during sex play may have a disenchanting effect in a sexually neutral situation." Power politics within the couple relationship, overly critical attitudes during the day, quarrels not resolved (at least partially), and a desire to force pregnancy upon a partner against her will all reduce cooperativeness. Fear, clumsiness, or some other inadequacy lies at the bottom of many unsatisfactory relationships. Hidden feelings may be present regardless of the degree of sexual liberation of the individual or the depth of involvement.

GOOD SEX MANNERS

Nothing is more apt to interfere with the progress of successful sexual adjustment than bad manners. An individual whose general life style is tactless and discourteous will, of course, find friendship only with others of his kind, but even those with acceptable general manners may react differently in the bedroom. Sexual manners become a matter of indifference for some who are no longer committed to a partnership, and indeed may even represent overt rejection of the partner. But perhaps more often unmannerliness is a by-product of thoughtlessness, not really intentional but growing out of a lack of appreciation for the importance of sexual courtesy. Sometimes poor sexual etiquette occurs because those involved do not have sufficient knowledge of sexual amenities.

Dengrove (1969) has given us some rules for acceptable bedroom manners based on his wide experience as a psychiatrist dealing with marital problems.

First, take your time with each other. Regardless of other considerations, moments spent in sexual interaction with a caring partner can be some of the most precious in life. Sexual excitement may come easily, but interpersonal passion of a more inclusive nature takes time. Hurrying through precoital play or speeding up intercourse for the sake of getting it done not only reflect poor taste, interpersonal incompetency, or a low opinion of sex but also are often a sign of disdain for the partner. Speeding through sexual intimacies is one of the quickest and surest ways of turning your partner off both sexually and lovingly.

Secondly, do not be afraid or ashamed to look or be seen. Although a woman may not be as easily stimulated by the sight of her mate's nude body as he is of hers, it is not correct to assume that she has no interest in seeing him. A hairy chest, erected penis, or muscular build may be as interesting to some women as the mons pubis, pointed nipples, and curvaceous buttocks of a woman are to most men. It pays to know your partner's tastes in this matter. Some men like a good deal of continuous nudity or near-nudity when alone with their mates; others prefer periods in which the partner is fully clothed. The more sophisticated a couple become through experience of openness and togetherness, the more likely they are to understand and appreciate subtle, temporary changes in each other's voyeuristic preferences.

Thirdly, be sure your partner is not offended by your method of stimulation. Men are often overly brusque and rough early in the sexual session, and this tends to spoil responsiveness for their mates. Most women can stand a good deal of roughness after they have become very sexually aroused, provided the action is not brutal in its intensity. The matter of using sexual words that are unacceptable in nonsexual situations has already been discussed, but the reader should be reminded to check his mate's feelings about the use of four-letter words. Offensive words having highly personal meanings symbolically attached to the mate's self concept are not likely to increase sexual desires. Some men are offended if their women sexual partners use obscene language, while others find such language exciting. Both men and women enjoy sexual stimulation, but many have strong preferences both for and against specific types of precoital and coital activity.

Fourthly, although most women and a good many men enjoy physical and psychological closeness following sexual relations, this is often neglected, especially after a couple have "gotten used to each other." Of course, most individuals are aware of the importance of not abruptly ending an intimate relationship and of the need to enjoy a postcoital romantic interlude with the partner, but knowledge of this fact without carrying it out will not help. Sometimes romance is not desired by either partner following coitus, or the lateness of the hour precludes the possibility of long-continuing loveplay. In all cases after-love should occur because it is a natural desire. If one partner habitually shows no interest in romance after sex while the other does, special effort must be made to bring the relationship into better equilibrium, since this difference in desire is a major component in sexual incompatibility.

Fifthly, make as clear as possible your answer to the other's approach. Do not let internal feelings pile up or become involved in uncommunicated resentments. In today's sexual pairings, real feelings on the part of both sexes can and should be made known. Appreciation and understanding of these feelings are important, but absolute agreement on them is not always essential. Clarity of response must of necessity include elucidation of feelings, similarity of desire or counter-desire, understanding of meanings, and other factors, such as those discussed earlier in this chapter under Communication. At any rate it is more than dysfunctional not to communicate; it is downright impolite. Sexual compatibility grows when responses to sexual questions, requests, facts, and implications are unambiguous.

If certain types of sexual interaction are esthetically unpleasant from the point of view of one partner or the other, this should be a subject for open discussion. There are no reasons beyond esthetic ones for not engaging in most forms of sexual interaction during the woman's menstrual periods. Many couples, however, avoid coitus during this time. Likewise, pregnancy ordinarily does not interfere with the capacity to engage in all forms of sexual interaction, but some view intercourse during the latter months of pregnancy as repugnant. Others consider oral-genital relations "dirty." Certain people do not like the "mess" made by genital lubricants or ejaculate and they seem almost anxious that coitus end so that they can make their way to the bathroom to clean up. The person who is very upset by all such matters may need to work through his disgust with professional help unless he has a partner of like mind. At any rate, failure to consider the partner's sexual tastes is poor sexual etiquette.

All the preceding conditions are of importance for at least two reasons. They are a matter of kindness and considerateness toward one's partner and as such apply as much to casual sexual couples as to more permanent ones. In addition, they are factors upon which agreement is generally needed if sexual compatibility is to be satisfactory.

HELPING EACH OTHER

In general, most individuals are anxious to please their partners, and some achieve as much or more satisfaction from this as from their own sexual release. Broadly speaking, an attitude that each sexual encounter is a kind of new adventure in which the outcome is dependent upon cooperation, willingness to try new methods, and freedom from inhibitions can be considered the "experimental attitude." Gaining full joy from the sexual relationship is more nearly assured when both members of the team relate without fixed ideas as to how the erotic interaction should proceed and end. My own research with both men and women has indicated that those who are highly enthusiastic about experimenting with new ideas and approaches are likely to report the highest degree of sexual satisfaction and adjustment. This does not mean that one must begin a frantic search for something new because the old is unsatisfactory; it simply represents an attitude of willingness to try new methods.

THINGS SHE MAY ENJOY

Cooperativeness with the feminine partner includes an awareness of some of the sexual approaches she likes best. She may or may not enjoy a variety of approaches, methods, and outcomes. While I cannot detail the idiosyncratic desires of each woman, I can suggest several things that seem to apply to females generally, Before doing this, however, I wish to emphasize my belief that the feminine personality functions differently in the erotic encounter than in nonintimate situations, and that these changes are in a direction supporting a woman's self picture as a feminine person. In the intimate heterosexual situation, most females want to fulfill the culturally prescribed roles assigned to them. (This point will be discussed further in Chapter 11).

A woman obtains much pleasure from those things that assist her in feeling womanly. Many men are not as aggressive or as insistent as their partners think they should be. A woman may sometimes purposely resist, refuse, or try to detour her partner, hoping or expecting that he will assert what she herself considers his sexual rights or opportunities. When he gives up too easily, she may be disappointed, confused, or disgusted, but the modern male, having learned that he should be most considerate of his female, is often simply following social dictates. Assuming that the couple have already established a good erotic relationship, there is no reason not to be assertive with her once in awhile, for the sexual encounter is one place where social taboos can often be minimized and forgotten.

Although some girls may be "shocked" at their lover's suggestions, the majority prefer that he lead the relationship by opening up new ideas. Most modern women are willing to bring some of their own notions of sexual interaction to the relationship but do not want to be the ones who carry the encounter throughout. As long as he is considerate of her, where he leads she will usually follow. His leadership and considerateness assure both of their roles while providing automatic mutuality of desire. She does not want to feel coerced into the sexual act but will gladly be led into it by the right man. Most women welcome frank discussions about sex in general and about their particular relationship of the moment. She will simply appreciate the fact that he can verbalize any just complaints as well as compliments, for as long as he is not constantly nagging about her sexual ability, she can interpret occasional murmurs as signs that he is willing to take risks with the relationship.

She will often respect him more deeply if he does not force certain objectives upon her. These include insistence that she always reach orgasm, demands that she achieve the same degree of arousal as he (no less and no more), and pressure to form sexual attitudes exactly like his own.

Sometimes she will look upon his willingness to abstain totally from all sex for a period as quite positive. Some couples purposely go without sexual encounters for a period of time and find increased enjoyment and passion in the reunion which follows. Other factors that she will appreciate are generally well known; gentleness, kindness, appreciativeness, and loyalty are the outstanding examples.

THINGS HE MAY ENJOY

Many of the things a woman enjoys bring pleasure to the man who can do them for her. Some women are reluctant or shy about certain kinds of sexual participation or are unaware of the types of interaction that men enjoy. Almost every male appreciates it when his partner occasionally initiates the sexual relationship. Men admire seductive dress and movements as well as the sight of a partner's nude body. Men usually enjoy sex for the sake of sex alone, and most hope that their partners will feel likewise. A man simply enjoys watching or knowing that his partner is becoming highly aroused and that he is the cause of this arousal. Pornographers well know the importance of feminine facial expressions in their portrayal of female eroticism, and research indicates that pornographic pictures without faces are apt to be viewed with more disdain than pleasure by most adult males.

Many men prefer sexual relations in a well-lighted room because the sight of their partners in the ecstasy of sexual arousal is a fetish for them. The majority of men also enjoy a variety of coital positions and techniques.

Perhaps as important as any other single factor is the fact that most men have periods during which they are either indifferent to or wish to avoid sexual relations. At these times they are apt to resent subtle female pressures, such as seductiveness, erotic movements, or other forms of suggestiveness.

ADVANCING THE RELATIONSHIP

Many writers seem to feel that comparative freedom from sexual inhibitions adds a positive dimension to a relationship. However, I believe that it is more important and more realistic that the couple have similar inhibitions. As long as both members of a pair agree on the prohibitions they will follow and have inhibitions of about the same kind, there is little reason to believe that the relationship will not be satisfying. When one or the other has sexual inhibitions that interfere with the goals of the relationship, these, of course, must be reduced or eliminated.

Garai (1969) has listed five ways in which a sexual relationship may be improved. He suggests that sexual relations should not be enforced in the face of the partner's refusal, that sex should not be used to prove one's virility and potency, that the use of sex as a bargaining tool or for blackmail of the partner should be avoided, that sexual practices which one's partner finds distasteful should not be insisted upon, and finally that the idea that sex must be carried out in a perfectionist manner should be relinquished. Garai tells us that tender loving concern, gentleness of approach, avoidance of mechanistic attitudes, and frank discussion of likes and dislikes all contribute toward sexual agreement and reduce inhibitions. Seduction through loving interaction rather than force is most apt to bring the results wanted.

The variety of erotica that may be enjoyed is wide; as Frank Caprio (1969), the noted psychiatrist, reminds us, "anything goes in lovemaking." Assuming that those involved do not consider any sexual behavior a perversion, mouth-genital contacts or other extracoital activities, group sex, exotic methods of stimulation, and playacting can all add to sexual pleasure. Probably as exciting as anything is the sheer *willingness* of both partners to search for new methods of approaching each other sexually while concentrating on the passions involved rather than on the mechanics.

The sexual relationship may be furthered by special concern and patience with any problems that may develop. Among males there will be times when an erection cannot be obtained or when it is achieved only at great expense. Men are always very sensitive to female negativism about their sexual capabilities, but during temporary periods of impotency, any ridiculing of a man's prowess or any pressure upon him to perform sexually is likely to lead to further sexual disaster and alienation. Subconsciously, he may carry feelings of resentment toward females for the rest of his life. It is equally unwise to make seemingly "innocent" remarks during the highly sensitive period of impotency; verbalized sympathy is often more harmful than silence. This is the time when concern for his welfare in the nonerotic areas of the relationship can be shown most profoundly. Following his lead both in open discussion of his impotency and in suggestive sexual overtures is best. If the problem persists longer than either can tolerate, professional help should be sought.

Premature ejaculation requires some of the same considerations, but if he is actively interested in helping his mate secure sexual satisfaction, the male may be helped by some of her activities. It may be necessary to help him reach a first climax as quickly as possible; if this is followed by a period of rest, he may be able to delay further ejaculation until his mate has gained satisfaction. Some suggest that the woman masturbate her mate almost to the point of climax, allow a period of rest for his sexual excitement to die down, and then again masturbate him almost to ejaculation. Repetition of this process will condition him to more self-control.

The same tolerance and patience that can be so helpful to a man also apply to the woman who is experiencing sexual problems. If a woman tends to be indifferent or withdrawn, she should be permitted open expression of any hostile feelings. It is usually wise to encourage full unfolding of her sexual impulses. Ridicule of these impulses should be avoided, and if her interests are greater than her male partner's the couple should attempt to develop a couple philosophy that will permit her as much expression as possible without becoming intolerably threatening to him. If professional help is needed to develop this agreement, it should be sought.

Nonresponsiveness either to the male's sexual advances or in reaching a desirable degree of excitement occurs in most women at some time. If, however, unresponsiveness continues or becomes a threat to the relationship, active cooperation may be necessary to relieve the situation. Very often temporary lack of responsiveness is due to situational conditions and will clear up when these conditions are changed. At other times, however, even temporary nonresponsiveness is highly associated with attitudes toward the partner. He may, for example, make requests for or engage in behavior against which she has strong feelings. At first she may focus on the behavior, but later she will project her dislike of it onto him as a person, and when this point is reached, she may become either temporarily or permanently unresponsive to him.

At other times, unresponsiveness is toward men in general and may be due to competitive attitudes, dominance feelings, or inward projections of guilt onto the partner. He causes her to act or feel guilty, and she, usually quite subconsciously, reacts as she would to any negative stimulus — by not responding or by limiting her responsiveness. A general attitude that sex is dirty or sinful may be projected onto the partner, since he, by his very presence, is a reminder of her erotic potential. Nonresponsiveness by refusing or failing to achieve the level of sexual excitement he has hoped for can sublimate any unwanted feelings of subjugation she may possess. If these attitudes are not too deeply ingrained, an understanding male who takes the time, patience, and persistence necessary to change them may be all that is needed. In other cases professional help will be required, but given the absence of a congenial partner, such help will be of no use in cementing the relationship. If the mate is unwilling, all that can be done is to seek a new partner.

HOMOSEXUALITY

AN OVERVIEW

The same criteria that apply to atypical heterosexual behavior may also be applied to homosexuality; that is, the qualities of a successful relationship are nearly the same, regardless of the gender of one's partner. As double standards fall in other areas of interpersonal relationships, it becomes increasingly illogical, insensitive, and irresponsible to judge gay people on the basis that the worthiness of one's relationship is dependent upon the object of one's attention.

In the past (and in many areas of the United States presently), homosexual behavior was looked upon as sinful, sick, and illegal. Shortly we will take a brief look at these three labels. They do little to help us understand homosexuals. But what do we mean by "homosexual"? The ambiguity of the word has been discussed by Fisher (1972). The lack of precision in describing homosexuals generally and the failure of most "scientific" studies to define the phenomenon operationally become clear as one reads Fisher's book. Individuals are stereotyped as homosexual for a variety of reasons, but Fisher reminds us that homosexuality is not a word that can define a human being. Where do homosexual feelings and inclinations begin and end? Is the individual who has only one or very few homosexual contacts a homosexual? Some persons go through temporary periods during which they are predominantly or exclusively homosexual. Others have excursions into same-sex sexuality throughout their lives. Still others have a strong preference for homosexual interaction but are willing on occasion to have heterosexual relationships. Not a few have one or more homosexual experiences while under the influence of drugs or alcohol.

All this makes it difficult to decide whether one is truly homosexual or even to define exactly what is meant by the term. Homosexuality appears to be on a continuum from little interest to the almost exclusive focus which some show. Consequently, vast numbers of individuals engage in homosexual acts but do not consider themselves homosexual.

Many of the more exclusively homosexual persons seem to believe that those who claim to be bisexual are simply using their bisexuality as a rationalization because they cannot bear to think of themselves as homosexual. The term *ambisexual* is preferred in some quarters, since it implies the capacity and willingness to be turned on by a wide variety of sexual stimuli. Martin and Lyon (1972) discuss the matter of bisexuals and note that even among homosexuals there is apt to be some aping of the heterosexual life style. A homosexual can be psychologically heterosexual and thus unattracted to persons of like homosexual orientation. For example, one "butch" (lesbian who fulfills the male role) would not likely be attracted to another. A butch would more likely be attracted to a "femme" (lesbian filling the feminine role).

The lack of clarity in terms referring to homosexuality is not helped by the concept of *latent versus overt homosexuality*. Freud, by popularizing the assumption of a psychic unconscious, elaborated the notion that homosexual desires might be out of the realm of awareness. Thus the latent homosexual is not always conscious of his or her desire for same-sex erotic relationships. In fact, the latent homosexual probably exhibits many defenses against the anxiety which such feelings arouse. For instance, the antihomosexual crusader might actually be a latent homosexual whose overt behavior is a reaction-formation against hated and dreaded homosexual desires. Overt homosexual behavior might imply that one is aware of at least temporary homosexual desires, but we have already seen that this is not consistently true, as in the case of the drunk who cannot remember his actions the day after a homosexual relationship has occurred.

Hooker (1969), summarizing the *Final Report of the Task Force on Homosexuality*, reminds us that homosexuals are a heterogeneous group and that homosexuality cannot be understood as a single phenomenon. Not only do the three to four million adults who are predominantly homosexual come from all walks of life; so also do the millions of others who participate sporadically in homosexual behavior.* Like their heterosexual counterparts, homosexually inclined persons vary extensively in their social and emotional adjustment. Undoubtedly, some psychologically distressed persons do turn to homosexuality for relief of their erotic tensions, but others exhibit a compulsively heterosexual sex drive.

That there is wide variation within the category "homosexual" seems well established. Our discussion will focus primarily on persons who are predominantly homosexual within environmental circumstances affording an opportunity to choose the object of one's sexual attentions. Circumstantial homosexuality, in which the individual chooses homosexual interaction because of the unavailability of opposite sex partners (as, for example, in a prison), will enter only tangentially into our treatment of the subject.

HOMOSEXUALITY AS SINFUL

The earliest instances of condemnation of homosexuals are found in the Christian concept of sin as interpreted by various religious organizations. Both the homosexual act and the impulse or desire to engage in homosexual behavior have been condemned as sinful. Traditional interpretations of Biblical passages alluding to homosexuality—such as Genesis 19:3–5, Leviticus 18:22, Judges 1:22–30, Romans 1:27, and I Corinthians 6:9—have emphasized divine condemnation of homosexual behavior. For example, the King James version of Romans 1:27 states: "And likewise also the men, leaving the natural use of the woman, burned in their lust one toward another; men with men working that which is unseemly, and receiving in themselves that recompense of their error which was meet." Romans 1:26 similarly condemns female homosexuality, according to the usual interpretation of these verses. Genesis tells of two angels visiting Lot in the city of Sodom. Within a few sentences of the opening of the story, these angels are described as men. All the men in Sodom sought to "know" the strangers and threatened Lot if he would not turn them over to them. In their place Lot of-

---

*Hooker states that these are tentative figures, since it would be difficult to establish actual incidences of homosexual behavior in our society.

fered his virgin daughters, but the men of Sodom refused, preferring to know the male strangers who were Lot's guests. Traditionalists have interpreted the word "know" to mean that the men of Sodom desired sexual relations with the strangers and have pointed out that in the context of Lot's offer of his daughters, the sexual thesis acquires added validity.

However, certain questions concerning the sexual interpretation of these verses have not been satisfactorily answered. One wonders how many men could be entertained sexually by just two other persons, especially by two other males. Pragmatically, there may have been very few men in Sodom, a situation unlikely to promote extensive homosexuality. Or, once the men of Sodom had wrested the strangers from Lot, they may have had a small war among themselves to determine who would engage in sex with them. One underlying assumption of traditional interpretations is that angels always appeared in male form when physically visible, and much of the interpretation of the Genesis verses depends upon the validity of this assumption. Again, it is not always possible to obtain a literal rendering of Greek and Hebrew into modern English. Although today we usually equate the word "lust" with strong sexual striving, the more general Greek words for lust imply not sexuality but an insatiable, greedy desire. The object of that desire can be anything including (but not restricted to) sex. Thus a nonsexual basis can be argued for many Biblical verses interpreted as sexual by traditionalists. Whatever one chooses to believe about this subject, the fact remains that much of our revulsion at homosexuality stems from the Christian concept that recreational sexual relations are sinful.

Practicing homosexuals must come to terms with their childhood training, which has very rarely been prohomosexual. One aspect of the negative training that homosexuals must confront is the value that homosexual acts and thoughts are sinful. Speaking of lesbians, Martin and Lyon (1972) state: ". . . because [a lesbian's] sexual expression is not procreative, she is 'unnatural' and therefore 'sinful'—a religiously inspired attitude which permeates our culture" (p. 35). These authors then discuss some of the difficulties in accepting themselves that some lesbians have had because of their early religious training. Accepting one's dominant interest in same-sex sexual partners seems to be a developmental task for practicing homosexuals, and the psychological and spiritual reworking of one's childhood introjects—a task of all maturing persons—seems doubly difficult for them.

Although the mainstream of American religion continues to condemn homosexuality regardless of the gay person's needs, some religions have accepted homosexuals. A United Church of Christ candidate for the ministry who openly declared his homosexual preferences was ordained in 1972, after this church organization began accepting the possibility that homosexuality, in and of itself, was not necessarily sin. Some major religious groups have formed committees to study the need for further elaboration of Biblical interpretations of homosexuality, and a few have concluded that they should support the repeal of laws which make private sexual behavior between two consenting adults illegal. The need for religious acceptance has also resulted in the development of homosexual churches. The Metropolitan Community Church, founded in Los Angeles, is fully open to homosexuals, although heterosexuals are also welcome.

Some writers, such as Jones (1966) and Oberholtzer (1971), have added to the acceptance of homosexuals by both society and the Christian religion. The Christian community has been slow to acknowledge homosexuality, however, and the concept that it is categorically sinful regardless of personal and interpersonal needs remains. One might expect that acceptance of situational ethics would provide considerably more tolerance for homosexuals, and it is among those who espouse this form of ethics that the greatest acceptance does occur. Yet although most people today are not as concerned with sin as formerly, this has not relieved the onus on active homosexuals. Instead of sinfulness, the psychiatric idea of "sickness" frequently plagues them.

THE "SICKNESS" DEBATE

A number of books written by practicing homosexuals and some articles by professional psychologists have attacked the notion that homosexual preferences or inclinations are necessarily pathological (Fisher, 1972; Martin and Lyon, 1972; Siegelman, 1972; Szasz, 1972). These authors point out that although there may be homosexuals who are psychologically malfunctional and in need of psychiatric care, this does not make homosexuality a sickness any more than malfunctioning heterosexuals make heterosexuality an illness. Fisher, Martin and Lyon, and Szasz argue that the psychiatric concept of homosexuality as a form of mental illness is based on dubious theories not well supported by research. They further point out that many of those who have researched homosexual behavior have begun their work with the psychological set that homosexuality is an illness and have simply generated data to support their thesis. Szasz, a respected gadfly to organized psychiatry, has this to say concerning the movement of antihomosexuality from religion to psychiatry: "In one of those ironic reversals of roles which occur every so often in human history, the homosexual is now persecuted by physicians, and defended by clergymen" (p. 115).

A number of students of sexual behavior have debated the "sickness" question, but these are mostly persons with a psychoanalytical orientation. Irving Bieber and his associates (1962) have advanced the hypothesis that homosexuals are individuals who have developed an ordinate fear of the opposite sex and severe anxiety about heterosexual relationships. These anxieties arise especially from overdependence upon a sexually provocative mother and in the absence of warmth, closeness, and interest on the part of the father. The parents of homosexual sons are described as having an unsatisfactory marital relationship, with the homosexual son becoming the butt of marital frustrations. Thus, according to this view, mothers of homosexuals are too romantically attached to their sons, partly because they are seeking a substitute for the fulfillment they fail to receive from their husbands. This absence of strong parental figures—the combination of indifferent father and seductive mother—has also been described by other clinical workers. Bieber, however, informs us that the biological norm is heterosexuality and suggests that through therapy homosexuals may set the goal of change to this norm. Apparently he believes that this untested assumption is fact.

Loney (1973) studied a "relatively well-functioning group of lesbians" to gather information about their upbringing. He found significant differences between his lesbian subjects and a matched group of heterosexual women on the number of adverse factors attributed to child-rearing. The lesbian group reported more negative attitudes toward both parents. They described being rejected as children and acquiring the belief that their families were inferior and that they must escape and assert their independence. Fathers were frequently neglecting and churlish and mothers were martyred and preoccupied. Studies such as Loney's lend support to the thesis that malfunctioning family relationships may be one component in an individual's need to feel that he or she is predominantly homosexual. But since many heterosexuals have also been reared in homes where family relationships were inadequate, this fact alone cannot fully explain a homosexual orientation.

Other theories advanced to account for the supposed "sickness" of homosexuality include the notion that homosexuality is a defense against schizophrenia; that is, if one has homosexual inclinations and attempts to suppress them, one will become schizophrenic. Bieber (1962), however, suggests that homosexuality and schizophrenia are two distinct types of personality development that may or may not coexist. Another line of thought focuses on the idea that homosexuality represents arrested development: the homosexual is an individual who for one reason or another is fixated at an earlier developmental stage. Still others have argued that homosexuals are individuals who reject their masculinity or femininity.

Siegelman (1972) found that male homosexuals who scored similarly to heterosexual males on measures of masculinity were very much like the heterosexuals in their general adjustment, and he notes that his findings concur with those of other researchers studying nonclinical samples. Siegelman's more effeminate homosexuals scored less well on his measures of adjustment than either the masculine homosexuals or the heterosexuals. He explains that the effeminate male always has greater difficulty adjusting to social demands, and the homosexual effeminate male has a double problem in this area. It is not merely homosexual activity that is unacceptable to the general society but also the refusal or inability of some persons to embrace cultural definitions of masculine or feminine behavior and attitudes. Possibly many negative beliefs about homosexuality stem from the stereotyped equation of male homosexuality with femininity. In this regard it is noteworthy that lesbianism is often more socially acceptable than male homosexuality.

Persons who are insecure, some think, may become homosexual for many reasons. Among the more important of these are fear of pregnancy or fear of one's inability to function satisfactorily in a heterosexual relationship. Others include seduction by a same-sex person in adolescence, disappointment with a heterosexual love affair, renunciation of authority, rebellion against puritanical attitudes, concentration on athletics, and defensiveness against male authority. Some suggest that mixed or reversed gender roles account for homosexual predispositions, but most homosexuals are not given to transvestism.

Behavioral scientists have not established the validity of these "causes" of homosexuality. Seduction of adolescents has not been a major factor in promoting homosexual behavior, and when older individuals and adolescents have had homosexual relations, most of the time it is the adolescent who has sought out the relationship (Hoffman, 1972). Conversely, assertions that homosexuality is "natural" also cannot be validated. Bieber (1962) notes that although animals do make many homosexual contacts, they quickly return to heterosexual behavior. Thus exclusive homosexuality cannot be validly compared with the oral contacts in which animals engage.

Recently (1973), the American Psychiatric Association has stricken homosexuality from its manual of pathological behaviors. Nevertheless, the subject of the pathology of homosexual attitudes and behavior continues to be hotly debated by professionals and laymen alike.

LEGALITY

Whatever the truth about homosexuality in relation to causes and sickness, the law has taken a fundamentally pragmatic view. In most states the old ambiguous sodomy laws remain, and to date the United States Supreme Court has not seen fit to examine them. According to

Fisher (1972, pp. 142–143), the Supreme Court has failed to act on numerous appeals on the ground that the cases involved were not sufficiently serious. One decision favorable to the homosexual world might invalidate all state sodomy laws. But state laws are changing, although quite often those acts most likely to be performed by homosexuals, oral-genital relations and anal intercourse, are expressly forbidden except between married adults. Thus the law continues to reinforce both the sin and sickness concepts of homosexuality, despite the supposed separation of church and government in the United States. The law is pragmatic because it is concerned with acts, not attitudes. It is the *behavior* of homosexuality that is illegal. A single act of anal intercourse, oral-genital contact, or other forms of "lewdness" as defined by law is all that is needed to make one a criminal.

Although there has been a growing recognition among law enforcement agents well trained in humanistic psychology that no minority members, including homosexuals, should be unfairly treated, many police (perhaps the majority) continue to deal with homosexual behavior just as they would with open, public heterosexual acts. The homosexual who practices in private is not very likely to be molested, but harassment of male gays and the use of public nuisance and solicitation laws to embarrass and control homosexuals are still common police practices in some areas. Fisher (1972, p. 144) states that the homosexual is still a second-class citizen, despite the constitutional guarantees granted to all Americans.

Certain law reform groups are currently seeking to abolish all laws prohibiting private, mutually agreed upon sexual behavior between adults, and some states, notably Illinois, Connecticut, Colorado, Idaho, and Oregon (Fisher, 1972, p. 129), have repealed their laws against consensual sodomy. In other states, Pennsylvania for example, oral and anal intercourse between consenting but unmarried adults are illegal, even when these acts are carried out in private. The assumption that private, unforced sexual behavior should be controlled because that behavior might be socially dysfunctional needs to be re-examined continually. It made more sense to inhibit homosexual behavior in an underpopulated world, but in today's world homosexuality could be an effective form of contraception for some. The onus should be on the state to prove that private, mutually agreed upon sexual behavior is socially disruptive.

•

HOMOSEXUAL INTERACTION

One of the major myths concerning homosexuals is that their lives are almost completely saturated with sex and sexual interests. The facts about homosexuals — and their own testimony — fail to bear out this myth. Homosexuals come from almost all occupational fields and are interested in political and social reform and in religious affiliation. Some enjoy a variety of social relationships, such as dances or parties, while others prefer camping, boating, or other sports. Homosexuals participate in all the activities that can be found in the heterosexual world, including, on some occasions, heterosexual erotic liaisons. Martin and Lyon (1972) report that three-fourths of the lesbians that they knew had experienced heterosexual intercourse at least once. Hedblom (1972) found that 37 of his 65 female homosexuals had engaged in sexual relationships with a man. Furthermore, half of those lesbians who had engaged in heterosexual relationships had reached orgasm with their male partners. At least for some homosexual women, dissatisfaction with heterosexual levels of responsiveness is not the sole reason for their choice of homosexuality.

What do homosexuals do in bed? The three major ways that male homosexuals relate sexually are mutual masturbation, oral-genital contacts, and anal intercourse. Depending upon the circumstances, erotic petting and foreplay similar to heterosexual interaction may occur, especially if the actors have formed a long-term relationship and are in a private place. A male who cruises homosexual bars and other places where pickups may be found, for example, a public toilet, is less apt to engage in preliminary play. Male homosexuals in general appear to be more promiscuous than lesbians, and like men in general, are less apt to be socialized.

The more effeminate homosexual may dress and act as though a transvestite, but the true transvestite is not necessarily homosexual. Both homosexual genders may also engage in sadomasochism, analingus, group sex, bondage and discipline, and other extragenital forms of sexual behavior. In the homosexual world, males probably engage in these forms of activity to a greater extent than females.

Martin and Lyon (1972) discuss the various ways in which lesbians relate sexually and state that they are very similar to some of the sexual interchanges between a man and a woman. Sexual gratification may occur through mutual masturbation, cunnilingus, and tribadism. Martin and Lyon describe tribadism as the position in which one woman lies on the other and makes a series of rhythmic movements that stimulate the vulva. Some compare this act to heterosexual coitus without penetration. Other forms of lesbian lovemaking are analingus and various types of foreplay, such as mouth-kissing, breast-fondling and sucking, nibbling the ear, and touching or stroking various erogenous zones. Dildos are also used, but less commonly than more personal approaches, according to Martin and Lyon. A lesbian relationship is one of sexual-emotional responses of a gestalt-like quality. Martin and Lyon decry the notion of vaginal orgasm and state: "The quality of the orgasm differs — not within the body, but within the head" (p. 84). A penis or penis substitute is not necessary to a woman's sexual gratification.

SUMMARY OF HOMOSEXUALITY

Homosexually and heterosexually inclined individuals are more alike than different. Homosexuality has been labeled sinful and psychologically sick, but only homosexual *acts* are illegal in most sections of the United States. Although the general adjustment of homosexuals has been described as pathological by many psychoanalysts, other researchers (Manosevitz, 1970; Thompson, McCandless, and Strickland, 1971; Evans, 1970) have failed to find support for such clinical impressions. Object choice rather than confused thinking seems to be the critical issue in homosexuality. To the extent that this is possible, homosexuals behave erotically much as heterosexuals do. The homosexual is apt to think of sexual interaction as especially important in his or her life and to have initiated sexual behavior at an earlier age (Fisher, 1972; Hedblom, 1973). However, the lives of homosexuals are not saturated with sexual interests as many heterosexuals think. Perhaps most importantly, the wide variety of individuals who engage in homosexual acts makes any stereotyping of homosexuality inaccurate and adds to the difficulty of defining it.

SUMMARY

A satisfactory psychosexual relationship is one in which both partners are willing to give and take in a mutually satisfying manner. Much of the relationship depends upon the intactness of individual personalities, since those who must act defensively as psychological protection have greater difficulty achieving openness of communication, freedom of expression, and willingness to tolerate periods of sexual abstinence. The development of a productive attitude in which sex is an integrating aspect of the total relationship includes a general agreement on the manner in which the relationship should function. This agreement I have called the "couple philosophy." Other interpersonal factors that contribute to the betterment of the relationship include using good sex manners, giving special attention to changes in personal needs, developing as fully as possible similar needs, and working toward continually greater involvement at all levels.

The suggestions and considerations in this chapter apply to all human sexual liaisons, whether they be casual, temporary, or permanent. They apply as much to the lover-mistress relationship as to marital partners and are as pertinent to homosexual relationships as to heterosexual ones.

MARRIAGE AND SEXUALITY

A great American dream has been the attainment of a lifelong, sexually exclusive relationship with a person of the opposite sex, with whom a thoroughly wholesome (and sometimes idealistically envisioned) adjustment can be made. That this stereotype of marital bliss often fails is evident to anyone studying American marriages. Despite the high rate of marital failure, however, more Americans than ever are marrying in the hope of finding love and security (see the statistics on pp. 5–6).

The best marital prediction tests, parental advice, guidance from experts, or premarital experience will not accurately predict the outcome of any given marriage. We must be content with generalities, and generalities are easily rationalized away by couples in love who wish to marry. It is only later, when reality does not consistently support their early ideals, that some of those who were once in love become disillusioned.

MARITAL ADVICE

Much advice about the sexual side of their relationship has been given to married couples, and for the most part the material communicated to them has reflected the social ethos of the time. Early books stressed the importance of the male as head of the family, the necessity of bearing children, the wife's place as a homemaker, and other morally oriented goals. Correct role fit was emphasized above family dynamics.

Brisset and Lewis (1970) studied 15 popular marital sex manuals and found that practically all portrayed the role of the male as more complex and significant than that of his partner; the man receives either most or all the attention of the authors of these manuals and is expected not only to give his wife pleasure but also to lead her step by step through the sexual interaction process. A major task given to males by the manuals is the thwarting of personal pleasure in the service of their mates. Furthermore, the man is usually expected to "keep the upper hand" in his sexual relations, initiating his wife gently but firmly into erotic ecstasy. In brief, the male that Brisset and Lewis found in the manuals "is saddled with the actual fashioning of the form and content of sexual relations. His responsibilities range from educating his partner to the proper use of special equipment. He is the person who establishes and maintains the direction and intensity of sexual conduct" (p. 44).

The woman of most sex manuals, on the other hand, has the responsibility to assure her husband's success and serve his needs. She passively submits to his wishes and willingly accepts sexual intercourse whenever he desires it. Much of the satisfaction that a woman receives from erotic interaction, according to these manuals, is knowing that she has pleased and sexually satisfied her husband. In general, then, these widely read manuals regard clear-cut role divisions as an integral part of sexual partnerships, and proceed to advise and to advocate role reciprocity. The man is assumed most fit for the active, instrumental, and initiating role, while the woman is pictured as fitting the passive, expressive, and recipient role.

Recently there has been more willingness on the part of some writers to advocate roles other than those that are socially determined. Drury (1968), drawing on her experiences as a mistress, offers this advice: "Society has a set of rigid rules as to what constitutes a good wife, but a mistress is one lone man's business. An affair is free to make its own rules." Later she adds: ". . . a mistress is not constrained to catechize herself as 'good,' for it is evident from the beginning that there is no such thing. She is herself and that suffices or it does not." Drury believes that "marriage radically needs more of this public be damned attitude. Unpremeditated joy, a disregard for consequences is one of the special ingredients of a love affair" (pp. 113–114). Recent existential and humanistic writing also opts for a more dynamic, self-fulfilling concept of marriage.

CONTRIBUTIONS OF SEX TO MARRIAGE

The importance of sex to any given marriage varies with the length of the marriage, the effect of the children, the philosophy of the couple, the degree to which the couple have achieved an adjustment through earlier phases, and other sociocultural background factors, such as type of upbringing and intensity of religious affiliation. Correlational studies have demonstrated a degree of relationship among marital happiness, sexual adjustment, and sexual responsiveness, and it is upon these studies that we will chiefly rely.

THE HONEYMOON PERIOD

The honeymoon is the major transitional period between individual identity and the social adjustment necessitated not only by the process of sexual interaction but also by day-to-day living with another person. As such, the honeymoon performs a number of important functions. Rapoport and Rapoport (1964) see the honeymoon as a period of "critical role transition" and as a subphase of "getting married." The change in roles brings about a state of disequilibrium from established premarital patterns, and to the extent that later adjustment is dependent upon successful honeymoon adjustment, the period is a crucial one.

Rapoport and Rapoport identify four tasks that are specifically related to the honeymoon period. Although some of these tasks may be accomplished through premarital sex or unmarried cohabitation, they acquire added significance when they must be confronted in the context of the formal commitment of marriage. Two tasks are *intra*personal: development of personal competence to participate in an appropriate sexual relationship and development of the capacity to live in close association with a marital partner. The honeymoon is, for many persons, the first time of living in an intimate relationship with a person of the opposite sex, and one consequence of this may be the reawakening of old anxieties about intimacy and identity. A test of the capacity to give and take in the marital situation may take place at this time. Major issues with which the individual must cope are dependence, autonomy, and interdependence, as the case of Beth and Jim testifies:

> Soon after their marriage, Beth and Jim began to quarrel and complain almost daily. She accused him of indifference, while he blamed her for "constantly nagging." Both felt guilty afterward and each was aware that the other was attempting to project his or her individual guilt on to the other. After examining their behavior, they realized that their quarrels seemed to follow attempts at nonerotic intimacy. Sexually, they worked together without difficulty, but neither seemed able to tolerate exclusively sentimental moments. A review of their past history indicated that neither had come from a home where the parents were openly warm and affectionate. Furthermore, Beth's mother had been the dominant person in her home, and Beth had made up her mind that she would not let this happen to her. She had learned (quite subtly) to regard male sentimentality as a sign of weakness, and when she was approached by Jim, the old disgust she had felt toward her father because of his submission to her mother arose within her. In order to preserve her image of herself as feminine and submissive, she filled with anger and hostility and projected these feelings to her husband. Thus desirable intimacy never came about.

The second pair of tasks is *inter*personal in nature: developing a foundation for a mutually satisfactory sexual relationship and gaining mutually satisfactory experiences as a basis for agreeable husband-wife roles. The Rapoports feel that some basic sexual relationship must be attained by the end of the honeymoon, since this is the one time the couple will have an opportunity to relate sexually without the interference of everyday responsibilities. The honeymoon should not only provide the couple with the *experience* of cooperation; it should also help them *estimate* their ability to be cooperative as a marital pair. Concerning the basis for later development of husband-wife roles, the Rapoports state:

> What appears to be focal is the crystallization of some kind of positive emotional toning in relation to whatever pattern the relationship has taken by the end of the honeymoon. This emotional tone (e.g., of interpersonal trust, relaxation, security, admiration, or more negative counterparts) may form the basis for a set of stereotypes developing within the interpersonal relationship. The way one perceives one's spouse on one's honeymoon and the concomitant set of experiences seem to set up images and expectations between the couple that are later difficult to alter (p. 255).

The functional aspects of the honeymoon are accomplished by reducing the strain of everyday living, by separating the couple from relatives or others who might interfere, and through the transitional device of a wedding trip. The honeymoon trip is more apt to be taken by those who have abstained from premarital intercourse (Kanin and Howard, 1958). In America, considerable effort has gone into the commercialization of the honeymoon. Gersuny (1970) believes that the essence of this effort is the stressing of romantic idealism: evocation of exotic places, sensuous imagery, and extolling the virtues of the beds and baths available at honeymoon resorts. The rhetoric of the entrepreneurs of the honeymoon industry, he reminds us, is designed to attract customers, thus the saturation with romanticism. However, this very antirealistic emphasis may, to some extent, detract from the functional usefulness of the honeymoon as a preparation for cooperative living.

SEXUAL ADJUSTMENT

Sexual adjustment in marriage is a lifelong process affected by many variables, some of which are nonsexual in nature. The idea of adjustment implies an ability to express desires and to meet each other's needs, a capacity to deal with new and changing desires, and a willingness to function in a pliable manner. Sound adjustment means a workable program of give and take, based on everyday dynamics and recognition of the fact that disequilibrium is an inherent part of couple interaction.

Sexual adjustment is a part of every individual's life process, beginning at the time he was born if not before, but it is usually at adolescence that one's interest in matters specifically sexual deepens. Continued involvement in the courtship process is a constant reminder of one's sexual potential. As marriage nears, sex looms as increasingly important, and attention is concentrated more and more on the wedding night, especially if the couple are still virgins.

Obviously, then, sexual adjustment does not begin only with the first coitus, although the "deflowering" ritual receives widespread attention in many cultures, including our own. For centuries, art and literature have represented the losing of virginity as one of the rites of passage to adulthood, and in some sections of our country considerable importance continues to be attached to it, both by the community in general and by individuals in particular. The losing of one's virginity is taken as a sign of maturity, an indication that one has definitely crossed from the state of "innocence" to that of "experience."

Some of those who are still virgins at marriage prefer to delay coitus a day or two beyond the wedding night, on the assumption that it is best not to begin such an important experience under the harried conditions that often accompany the wedding ceremony and attendant social activities. However, if the courtship process has been successful, many rewarding premarital erotic experiences should have reduced fears of coital contact.

An important myth concerning a woman's first coital experience is that she will necessarily suffer pain as her hymen is torn and stretched. But pain is not always a part of first coitus, since many modern girls stretch or lose the hymen through vigorous physical activity. At any rate, a thorough premarital examination by a qualified physician can do much to relieve anxiety if it exists. Terman (1938, p. 344) reported that those women who had had very painful or distressing first coitus were more apt to experience subsequent marital difficulty. However, these same women may have been more poorly adjusted initially. It cannot be assumed that painful first intercourse was the *cause* of their later problems.

In general, nonetheless, first coitus is important to later adjustment to the extent that it sets the tone for that which is to follow.

MARITAL HAPPINESS AND SEXUAL ADJUSTMENT

Marital happiness, sexual adjustment, and sexual responsiveness are correlated, although sexual responsiveness seems less important to marital happiness than is often assumed. In general, the factors that affect a sense of sexual well-being are less directly related to physical eroticism for a woman than they are for her husband.

All studies have made it plain that affection, tenderness, and considerateness are of utmost importance to a wife's sexual adjustment. No amount of prowess on the part of a man can make up for his failure to treat his wife with loving concern. In other words, tender loving care is as important to good sexual adjustment as it is to child development. Along with this tenderness, many women also desire their mates to be decisive, to exert leadership in the sexual situation, and to work toward the achievement of democratic principles within the family.

Considerable emphasis has been placed on the wife's attainment of sexual equilibrium, on the assumption that she is apt to have greater difficulty achieving responsiveness and the enjoyment of sexual activity. In their classic study, Burgess and Wallin (1953) reported that the enjoyment of sexual intercourse can vary over a wide range. This can be as true for men as for women, however, and it is unrealistic to expect that the male will invariably enjoy sexual activity to the maximum. A part of sexual adjustment is coping with variation in desire: from time to time the degrees of desire felt by each partner will fail to coincide.

A major factor causing sexual disappointment is the disparity between what was expected and what one receives. Very often this disappointment is manifest following first coitus or after the conclusion of the honeymoon period. If the desired level of response either from one's mate or from oneself has not been reached, a tendency may develop to blame one or the other. But blaming is not a positive adjustment process, and if allowed to continue it can easily invade other aspects of the marriage. We have sufficient evidence that for both sexes reaching a satisfactory level of sexual adjustment takes time and that it is a continuing and fluctuating process throughout marriage.

For some, an initial failure to achieve satisfaction may stem from poor self attitudes, while for others such failure is the beginning of self-degradation. Sex can be especially disappointing if either consciously or unconsciously it is expected to make up for a lack in other areas. Again, part of the problem is setting up unrealistic standards. But time, in terms of an expectation of immediate results, is not the only aspect that can be disappointing. All too often a maximum level of adjustment is anticipated, with a high level of optimum interaction throughout the marriage. While many men and women acknowledge that they cannot reach such a level, they continue, because of subconscious needs, to seek it desperately. Failure to find the idealized level may engender a variety of psychological defense mechanisms that only defeat the marriage further.

Adams (1953) has given us statistical correlations for the relationship between the marital happiness of college wives and three variables: sexual adjustment, sexual responsiveness, and aging. (Responsiveness and aging will be discussed later.) He found that sexual adjustment correlated .51 with marital happiness. In other words, about one-fourth of the marital happiness of the wives in his study could be accounted for by their sexual adjustment. Factors that positively contributed to a wife's sexual adjustment included a mutual desire for intercourse, an equal strength of sexual desire, high sexual attractiveness of her husband, awareness that he did extra things to make sex more enjoyable for her, and her willingness to do things to make sex more enjoyable for him. Conditions adversely affecting the sexual adjustment of these wives were, however, frequently nonerotic: military service or other enforced separation, disagreement over the economic aspect of marriage, an unsettled philosophy of life, and differences of opinion about child-rearing.

In short, Adams found that nonerotic variables frequently had a more profound effect on the sexual adjustment of his college wives than did actual sexual technique. Subsequently, he conducted similar studies on men, asking them the same questions that he had used to measure and define the wives' sexual adjustment. He discovered that certain functions correlated positively with marital happiness and sexual adjustment for both sexes. As a result, he formulated the *Adams Marital Happiness Prediction Inventory,* a series of 12 criteria that he believed could be used to anticipate the likely degree of sexual adjustment for individual men and women. His theories have been confirmed by other major studies of marital adjustment. P. Rossi (1955), factor analyzing the Marital Happiness Prediction Inventory, discovered that Adams' 12 personality and background conditions* could be grouped into a smaller number of factors. Sexual responsiveness, compliance, patience, and cultural integration were the labels he attached to the factors he found important in a woman's sexual adjustment. These factors comprised such personality traits as sociability, agreeableness, seriousness, tolerance, and equanimity. The factors he found to be most significant for males he labeled considerateness and ethical values. The latter factor reflects a generally conservative attitude on the part of the men in the study.

From these factors it may be assumed that the woman who is most apt to achieve satisfactory sexual adjustment is sexually responsive to her husband, tends readily to accept socially defined feminine roles, and has developed such personality traits as patience and tolerance. Collaterally, males who tend to be conservative in their general outlook, who look upon women positively, and who are sensitive and considerate of their partners' needs have the best chance of adjusting.

Obviously, when both husband and wife possess the qualities most conducive to sexual adjustment, their chances for a satisfying sexual relationship are increased. Underlying the entire structure of adjustment is the simple yet critical element of agreement. Those most in agreement are most likely to achieve the goal of sexual compatibility.

FAMILY AND BACKGROUND FACTORS

Both marital happiness and sexual adjustment are profoundly affected by the type of learning that takes place during childhood within the family of orientation. Although peers may greatly influence later interpersonal learning (once a couple marries they tend to direct their per-

---

*Enumerated on p. 227.

sonal norms toward those generally acceptable to the married community), many of the earlier methods of coping with others remain. Unless a
special effort is made to overcome any negative habits learned early in
life, such habits are apt, intentionally or unintentionally, to be continued
with one's mate and children. Since it is primarily nonerotic functions
that affect sexual adjustment, family and orientation influences are often
indirect and subtle.

One of the most important influences on marital happiness and sexual adjustment is the type of parental relationship that the individual has
experienced. The manner in which one's parents' marriage is viewed is
highly predictive of the outcome of one's own marriage. Those who perceive their parents as happily married are apt to achieve marital happiness themselves. Little conflict with parents, a good deal of attachment
to them, firm but not harsh discipline, a memory of a happy childhood—all increase the potential for a happy and well-adjusted married
life.

Terman (1938) found that frank and encouraging answers to sex
questions asked of parents and an attitude of interest and pleasant anticipation contribute to marital happiness and sexual adjustment. He also
discovered that an eager and passionate longing for sex is associated
with maladjustment and a lower degree of happiness. Other premarital
factors indicative of more satisfactory adjustment include learning about
sex from parents or teachers, a belief that the sex instruction received
was entirely or reasonably adequate, and freedom from shocking or
disgusting sexual encounters before age 16.

MARITAL FAILURE

A recent study comparing intact and divorced couples confirms
many findings of older studies such as Terman's. Coombs and Zumeta
(1970) discovered that marital failure, as exemplified in divorced couples, is more likely when the couple are of low socioeconomic status,
when they marry before age 20, when the wife is pregnant at marriage,
and when the husband has less than a high school education and thus
low upward mobility. They also found that their divorced couples were
less in agreement on the number of children they desired and that the
birth intervals between children were shorter than had been anticipated.
Coombs and Zumeta conclude that in dissolved marriages wives expect
to perform their roles less traditionally but actually perform them in the
most traditional manner. For example, in their study the husbands made
all the major decisions, did the heavy work around the house, and
handled the money. One of the most important factors in stable marriages, according to Coombs and Zumeta, is the belief and intention of
the couple that their marriage should be lasting. The expectation that
marriage will fail is often a self-fulfilling prophecy.

EMOTIONAL MATURITY AND MARRIAGE

Much investigative thought has gone into the idea that emotional maturity is necessary to productive and satisfying marital relationships. The emotionally mature person is evaluated as capable of meeting everyday stresses without undue tension, as able to handle anger and frustration in a useful and socially acceptable manner, as integrating his philosophy of life into the process of living, and as usually exercising sound judgment and adequate self-control. Such a person has positive attitudes toward responsibility, can communicate effectively, feels emotionally secure most of the time, and tends to refrain from excessive ego-centered activity.

Dean (1966) used the *Nye Marital Adjustment Scale* and a scale designed to measure the attributes of the emotionally mature person just described to gather information on the relationship between marital adjustment and emotional maturity. Husbands and wives from an Ohio city of 6000 and primarily of middle class rated themselves and their mates on the two scales. The correlation between the marital adjustment ratings of the wives and husbands was .59, a figure which indicates one fact about adjustment: husbands and wives usually do not fully agree on the extent of their adjustment when making ratings on which they cannot collaborate. In general, Dean found that in this sample emotional maturity and marital adjustment were related. Significant correlations ranged from .28 for the husband's self-rated emotional maturity to .55 for the husband's emotional maturity as rated by his wife. He points out, however, that while this evidence indicates that emotional maturity is related to marital happiness, we have no way of knowing how much emotional maturity is prerequisite to successful marriage. Conversely, it is also not possible to ascertain from a study such as Dean's the extent to which marital happiness has contributed to emotional maturity. The two are related, but it is impossible to know which is cause and which is effect.

Boxer (1970) studied the relationship between personality congruency and serious emotional disorder in a group of couples in which one of the partners had been hospitalized for psychiatric disability. She found that the higher the degree of personality incongruency, the more likely one was to find a hospitalization for psychiatric disability. A highly dependent husband unable to accept his dependency needs and married to a dominating but conflict-ridden female was especially likely to have psychiatric problems. Boxer sums up her study this way:

> What can be tentatively inferred from these findings is that marriage is certainly not a panacea for the emotional equilibrium of all individuals; and that for certain individuals, previously existing emotional difficulties may be intensified and aggravated by an unfortunate selection of an incompatible mate. This study tentatively suggests that the highly dependent male, who cannot accept his dependency needs, experiences extreme and dire conflict if he marries a woman with strong needs for domination and emasculation (pp. 177–178).

Some couples hope that through a high-quality sexual adjustment they will be able to overcome or mask unacceptable personality patterns. When it is used to circumvent confrontation with the real issues in a relationship, however, sex becomes a defense mechanism — a form of denial that is a primitive and infantile means of coping with adjustment. While the masking effect may be initially helpful, the evidence indicates that sex used as a defense mechanism is not apt to work for long nor to be fully adequate.

SUMMING UP THUS FAR

Marital and sexual adjustment are interdependent entities. The probability of achieving a satisfactory adjustment is enhanced if earlier learning, especially in the home, has produced a positive psychological set toward marriage and the family. Many factors are believed important to successful sexual adjustment, regardless of how adjustment is defined. The person who is adequately socialized, well integrated into the mainstream of the culture, concerned about others, tolerant and patient, and who has achieved a satisfactory level of self-esteem is most apt to attain a healthy sexual adjustment. Partners whose personality patterns are congruent have a better chance of marital happiness than those whose personalities are different. Although the evidence concerning complimentary and homogeneous needs is conflicting and final judgment must thus be suspended at this time, it is certainly true that those who are from similar sociocultural backgrounds have more probability of marital success than those whose backgrounds have led them to develop different marital expectations and values. It is not clear how much emotional stability is needed to help marriage succeed, but at least a nominal amount seems necessary. The single most important variable in marital and sexual adjustment may well be the difference between expectations and outcomes.

SEXUAL RESPONSIVENESS IN WIVES

The relationship between sexual responsiveness and sexual adjustment is somewhat dependent upon the manner in which responsiveness is defined. If sexual responsiveness is the ability to respond positively in a warm, accepting fashion to a total sexual situation, including the sheer pleasure of helping one's mate to a satisfactory conclusion, it is evident that responsiveness is closely tied to adjustment. If, on the other hand, sexual responsiveness is defined as the ability to achieve an orgasm from coitus, most studies show little relationship between responsiveness and adjustment.

As measured by Adams (1953), a wife's sexual responsiveness was based on her answers to 51 separate questions designed to probe her feelings and responses during foreplay, intercourse, and climax, and after intercourse had concluded. Adams found that general sexual responsiveness and marital happiness correlated only .13 for his college wives. However, he also found that sexual responsiveness correlated .46 with sexual adjustment. He concluded that sexual responsiveness affects sexual adjustment, which in turn affects marital happiness. (As we have seen, sexual adjustment correlated .51 with marital happiness in the Adams study.) Sexual responsiveness, then, is an indirect and partial determinant of marital happiness, brought into play primarily through the medium of the husband. The husband enjoys the things that a responsive wife does, and in turn reacts to her in a manner that he understands will increase her happiness. A wife's marital happiness is very dependent not only upon her husband's erotic reactions but also on his willingness to participate with her in activities characterized by affectionate companionship. The husband who offers this companionship will interpret his wife's ensuing sexual responses as signs of warmth and love toward him, and in this way each contributes to the happiness of the other. Since the wife may be investing a larger part of her life in the marriage than the husband, she is more apt to be dependent upon him for her total happiness.

Terman (1938) found that marital happiness was correlated with sexual responsiveness .26 — a figure not statistically significant — for the wives in his sample. He also found that the wife's attainment of orgasm was not significantly related to her husband's happiness. However, in the author's own ongoing study, 80 per cent of the male subjects of college age and background have expressed the belief that their happiness would suffer seriously if their future wives did not achieve orgasm. This is a possible indication that modern men do expect considerable sexual responsiveness from their wives. In another study of marital orgasm, Gebhard (1966, pp. 88–95) found that orgasm was related only to those wives who reported their marriages as "very happy." Sixty per cent of the "very happy" wives reached orgasm from 90 to 100 per cent of the time. There was no relationship between lower reported degrees of happiness and the attainment of orgasm.

SOME SPECIAL ASPECTS OF ADJUSTMENT

CHILDREN

As with so many other aspects of marriage, the arrival of children is often idealized, and expectations far exceed likely results. Some major roles change with the coming of children, but most importantly the new role of parent is introduced and begins to compete with the roles of husband and wife. If the relationship was sagging anyway, new role strains are not apt to bolster it. With the availability of modern contraceptive methods, today's couples of child-bearing age would do well to be sure that children are wanted by both marital partners and that these children will be brought into an intact, on-going relationship. Several studies have been made of the effects of children upon marriage, and we will consider a few of these here.

Alice Rossi (1968) discusses the transition to parenthood from several standpoints. The assumption of the parent role is an especially important transition point for women. Early in marriage and before pregnancy, the wife may have worked and supplemented her husband's income. This gave her considerable opportunity to press for an egalitarian relationship, but with the advent of a child her contributions often cease. The equality may continue, however, resulting in the building of a barrier between parents and children that may eventuate in a coalition of mother and children versus husband and father. Rossi, in her analysis, points out that the birth of a child produces an irrevocable situation: one cannot give up the biological fact of parenthood, and for intact families this means permanent parenthood in all its implications throughout the life span.

Rossi demonstrates that for some women parenthood means not the reaching of a higher level of maturity but rather depression and a sense of lowered self-worth. This feeling may be due to several factors, including social conditioning favoring the male, lack of sound preparation for parenthood, absence of real training during pregnancy, the abruptness of the transition from partner to parent, and our current inability to define guidelines for successful parenthood.

Christensen (1968) has studied the relationship between marital success and the number and spacing of children. He cites evidence that the presence or absence of children is not associated with marital success. When the couple have the desired number of children, satisfactorily spaced and in the phase of marriage that they choose, their behavior is in line with their values. When value-behavior discrepancies occur in this area, marital adjustment may be negatively affected.

McCandless (1969) reminds us that child-rearing in our mobile society must take into account certain factors, such as teaching the child to live with change, dealing with power structure within the family, and setting goals such as impulse control, acceptance of others of a different race or socioeconomic class, and openness to new experiences. Obviously, parents who are experiencing severe differences in their own values will have some difficulty implementing some of these goals, particularly those involving sexual behavior. Does openness to new experiences include erotic ones? Should our daughter marry someone of another race? Should she engage in premarital sexual relations? Questions such as these can and do occur between parents and sometimes result in lowered sexual interest. The student might try to imagine himself in the role of a parent who must answer these questions, or better still, one might try them out with a favorite girl- or boy-friend, pretending he or she is the other parent.

In the final analysis, it appears that accidental parenthood is less conducive to marital adjustment than parenthood chosen on the basis of mutual desire. Parental adjustment, not yet widely studied, is conceivably a factor in sexual adjustment. Here, as elsewhere in the marital situation both agreement and action to fulfill that agreement are necessary to insure success. Unfortunately, our knowledge of the effects of children on sexual adjustment and responsiveness is currently almost nonexistent.*

AGING

The effects of aging and length of marriage are difficult to separate. Most evidence indicates that as marriage continues, satisfaction goes down. Pineo (1969) found an increasing tendency for couples to diverge in both behavior and attitudes — a process which he conceptualizes as one of disenchantment and loss of adjustment. Among his subjects, incidentally, women made no greater adjustment than men. He also found that those least satisfied made the most extensive changes in their behavior and attitudes — a fact that would be expected in light of other evidence suggesting that continued marital happiness is most likely for those who have been happy during the first years.

Adams (1953) found little relationship between age and the marital happiness of his college wives. He felt that the wife's sexual adjustment was more influential than her sexual responsiveness in offsetting the negative effects of aging. He also thought that sexual responsiveness which has grown stronger with age moderates the loss of happiness.

Kinsey and his fellow workers have provided us with evidence that females increase in sexual responsiveness to a pinnacle at the late 20's or early 30's, remaining on a plateau for much of their lives. Men, on the other hand, reach their peak earlier and gradually decline. The activity of older men and women will be discussed in Chapters 10 and 11. An important point, however, is that the sheer belief that one will not — or should not — be interested in sex during later life is very often the reason why sexual desires are lost during this period.

---

*For a review of several studies and the methodology of studying the transition to parenthood, see Jacoby, A. P.: Transition to parenthood: A reassessment. *Marriage and the Family*, 31 (Nov., 1969), pp. 720–727.

Peterson (1968, pp. 81–101) has elucidated the sexual problems of those at midlife. He thinks martial relationships ought to be communicating love and devotion, an important reason for not denying sexual interaction during the middle and later years. It is during middle age that the undeniable discrepancy between achievement and idealistic expectations becomes most apparent. It is also during middle age, especially after the children have left home, that the wife's need for affectional expression from her husband increases. Peterson remarks: "It is understandable that many middle-aged persons who have allowed their total marriage to become passive would likewise find their sexual mate uninspired" (p. 95). Peterson describes apathy, overly used habits, failure to experiment and create from the beginning of marriage, and boredom with the same old sexual stimuli as problems of the middle and upper aged.

Throughout marriage, most authors agree, it is necessary to maintain an interest if things erotic are not to diminish in significance. It is easier to maintain a healthy sexual life than to try to restore a lost one. Again, communication of one's desires and expectations should be as clear as possible. In her discussion of reconciliation, Mueller (1970) points out that although most wives have a need for greater affectional response, they mean something quite different than their husbands think. Her perceptive finding emphasizes the need for clarity in communication. By affection a wife means a diffuse and varied attitude, including such things as talking for sociability, being told she is a good wife and mother, and having support for her decisions about such family matters as child-rearing and finances. A man specifically includes under wifely affection an interest in greater sexual responsiveness and more willingness on her part to initiate sex play. Apparently, both mates often use the same word but attach different meanings to it. When the physical drive for sex is lower, the need for affection to enhance sexual interaction increases.

Aging does not necessarily mean the loss of sexual prowess or interest. Men may become more mellow and women more aggressive, so that the partners converge in their sexual needs. If marriage and sexual relations are to succeed as the couple grow older, it is usually essential that they be successful at earlier stages. Aging, then, may bring on a new awareness of the importance of nonerotic factors to marital and sexual adjustment (Stinnett, Collins, and Montgomery, 1970).

SPACE

Perhaps as important as anything is the need to establish or maintain a personal identity after marriage. Two can become one only when both exist as cooperative but individualized entities. Fast (1970), in his text on body language, discusses the manner in which space is used to both transmit messages and maintain personal identity.

According to Fast, there is personal, social, and public space, and some rather well-defined norms exist as to who may or may not invade these spaces. He describes Edwin Hall's work, in which "zones of territory" are used to define various distances between people that are acceptable to them. These zones are based on culturally recognized degrees of intimacy. As the distance between persons narrows, there is an increasing awareness of each other's personal aspects. At the close, intimate distance (the distance at which physical contact is easily achieved), partners become "overwhelmingly aware of each other," as Fast puts it. At a few feet away, personal conversation without touch is possible. Social distance emphasizes the social status characteristics of the situation and of the persons involved. It too has a close phase, as when a housewife talks to the repairman, and a far phase, as when one is in the presence of one's boss. The public zone of distance also has its close and far phases: the teacher in a classroom versus a politician giving a speech to a large crowd. The intimacy of the interaction determines public space.

The assumption that marriage is a contract in which social and public space between partners is obliterated is absurd. Intrusion—being where you are not wanted—is highly distasteful and inconsiderate. Fast speaks of acting toward the invaded person as though he or she is a nonperson, an object. Some intimate personal space is so private that to intrude upon it is a major violation and a threat to love.

It is critically important to be able to touch and be touched, but it is equally important to know when not to touch. Sometimes a mate is intent upon not being touched, and forced attention at this time is apt to be either repulsed or permitted with resentment. Folded arms, shrugged shoulders, a bent-over torso, and other bodily signs shouting "leave me alone" need to be recognized and respected.

Many individuals establish some part of their dwelling as off limits to others in the household. Parents of teenagers understand this well. A marital partner may also need the privacy of certain household space that is more or less understood as his or her own. Some individuals resent the excursions of others into the bathroom when they are using it; invasions of this nature to them are unwelcome signs of ego intrusion. Although sex may be becoming less private and personal, core ego activities are not, and efforts to make them so may be interpreted as attempts to be all-consuming of the partner. As I have said before, such overconsumption of the mate can be detrimental or even fatal to love.

NEW MARRIAGE FORMS

Exposure of the major failings of monogamous marriage has led some individuals to propose new marriage forms. Attempts have been made to assist the young in setting more realistic marital standards and to prepare them for the rigors of marriage. That this effort has not fully succeeded is evident; as Sporakowski (1968) discovered, those who are approaching marriage feel more sure of their readiness for it than those already married. Thus some among the young are experimenting with the newer forms of marriage.

Group marriage, marriage in two steps, an "intimate network of families," and other alternate models to monogamy have been proposed. The two-step scheme suggested by Margaret Mead (1970, pp. 75–84) would allow a trial period of marriage which, if successful, could be followed by a permanent marriage license. Mead's first step—individual marriage—would be childless by decree, while the second would be established with the possibility of creating a family.

Group marriage is now being tried by a few people within our own as well as other societies. In such a marriage, a small group of individuals usually consider themselves spiritually married to one another, with each having equal conjugal rights over the others. Those within this arrangement expect that the responsibilities of marriage will be shared by all and that the woes of monogamy, such as loneliness during crisis periods and absolute separation after death, will be minimized. Companionship can be a shared and mutually enjoyable activity, increased by the availability of partners. Monogamy, many of the adherents of group marriage assert, tends to increase possessiveness and jealousy by exaggerating threats of loss.

Frederick Stoller (1970a, pp. 145–159) has described the "intimate network of families" as a new structure on the marital scene. This network of families would have many of the attributes of the extended family, but it would not be confined to relatives. Nuclear families, whatever their origin, would meet regularly and frequently, share intimacies, influence one another's values, and engage in other activities typical of the clan. Services would be exchanged, and in general each nuclear family would seek to promote the welfare of the others. Stoller offers this model because he believes that there is little propensity in America to do away with monogamy or the nuclear family, yet society is so highly mobile that the extended kin network is not functional for many.

Improvement of the dynamics of the nuclear family is the aim of many advocates of new marriage forms. Otto (1970, pp. 111–118) has described some ideal dynamics of the new family. There should be clear acknowledgment by both partners that even the healthy individual functions at only a fraction of his potential. Love and understanding are the dynamic elements, enabling the family members to enhance their potential for deeper interpersonal understanding, and the knowledge that each marital partner is devoted to turning the other on helps to build a mutually satisfying family relationship. Partners (and children are also essential partners) are interested in growth groups and other means of achieving personal development through relationships with people. The members of the marital team recognize the important influence of the physical environment upon their family. The new marriage will be more here-and-now-oriented. Both partners will conceive of marriage as an evolving, flexible union. The family will have an interest in discovering the spiritual dimensions of their togetherness. The couple will also explore, Otto continues, the spiritual dimensions of their sexual relationship as they seek to deepen their understanding of God. The family members will plan action and commit themselves to the achievement of ever deeper fulfillment of their individual and collective potential. A high degree of respect for one another and for the individual rights of each will be implicitly felt within the new family.

The new family as Otto has conceived it is an ideal and a goal to be sought by many couples. The worthy assumption of the new family concept is its effort to bring to marriage and family life a creative endeavor aimed at helping all members actualize their latent potentials to the fullest. The openness in the "open marriage" described by George and Nena O'Neill in their book (1972) means simultaneous honesty between marital partners and the reduction of some of the negative aspects of the monogamous marriage model idealized by American society. In an open marriage, both personal and couple growth are sought while constant revision of the couple's expectations in light of changing needs is stressed (O'Neill and O'Neill, 1973). A function of many new marriage forms is the inclusion of others on a personal and emotional level as potentially intimate friends and sources of psychological, emotional, spiritual, and sexual support. Open marriage does not necessarily mean sexual liaisons with others, nor does it preclude this possibility. It is simply more honest about nonmarital relationships than most traditional monogamous marriages.

Our primary concern in this chapter is with legally or socially sanctioned marriage forms, but group marriage is here mentioned briefly because it is considered by its adherents as a form of marital union.

Although the legally sanctioned forms of monogamous marriage have not always worked well for a number of reasons, including most prominently the emphasis on exclusiveness of sexual-emotional relationships, unions of three or more persons have not worked well for many either. Probably the social conditioning for ideological monogamous forms has hindered the capacity both of couples to live only for each other and of individuals to live in group marriages. Recently, Salsberg (1973) examined nine group marriage units and found the members were white and middle-class, with at least some college. The average group unit had survived 16 months at the time of the study. The ratio of the sexes was balanced, with only one family unit having an excess female. The families were relatively structured, according to Salsberg. Three were rural and six were urban. Three families broke up during the

19-month study. Gender roles within these families tended to follow traditional lines, but failure to assign household tasks contributed to discord among some families. Salsberg concludes that the problems created for individual group-family members taxed them far beyond their ability to solve them, although the group members themselves assessed the outcome of their common marriage as quite positive.

Experimentation with new family forms will and should continue, but I doubt that these forms will be any more successful than monogamous marriage has been. Until socialization away from privacy, exclusiveness, self-centeredness, and similar characteristics occurs, there seems little chance that group intimacy will succeed any better than that between two persons.

SUMMARY

This chapter has attempted to bring together some of the salient factors in marital adjustment. Its focus has been on factors related to formal marriage or marriage-like relationships. It is thus a specific complement to Chapter 6, Psychosexual Partners, and a general one to the rest of the text. Major points have included the following:

1. Increasingly, advice to married couples has aimed at re-establishing or maintaining the vitality of marriage from a humanistic point of view. Self and family actualization, occurring as components of one another, are emphasized.
2. The honeymoon period is the major transitional device for moving the couple from premarital normative behavior to that of the married community. Some theorists feel that much later adjustment depends upon patterns established during the honeymoon.
3. Sexual and marital adjustment is a lifelong process, and success in the sexual aspect depends greatly upon success in nonerotic areas.
4. For many couples, a major factor causing disappointment with marriage is the disparity between idealistic expectations and actual outcomes. Less idealism and a firmer grasp of what can realistically be expected should help reduce disappointment.
5. Sexual adjustment is enhanced in the presence of mutual desire for sex, equality of sex drive, high levels of agreement on most things, a sexually attractive partner, and similar personality traits.
6. Happily married parents, sound sex information gained from parents or teachers, a happy childhood, and learning, within the family of orientation, of the importance of interpersonal communication and responsiveness increase the chances of marital success.
7. Emotional maturity is related to marital success, but it is not clear how much maturity is needed.
8. If sexual responsiveness is defined as the tendency to give a

generally specific response to sexual stimuli sent out by one's mate, it can be said that sexual responsiveness is important to sexual adjustment. Orgasm attainment on the part of the wife is not necessary to the achievement of marital happiness.

9. Critical periods in the adjustment of many couples occur with the arrival of children, (especially the first child), at retirement or in other phases of aging, and during periods when the ego's core privacy is violated.

10. New marriage forms will continue to be tried, but they are unlikely to replace monogamy as the most prevalent marital type. They can, nevertheless, shed light on ways to increase the intimacy of monogamous marriage.

CHAPTER 8

SEXUAL TECHNIQUES

WHY STUDY TECHNIQUES?

Although this book is not primarily concerned with the mechanics of sexual behavior, there are some points that should be made about the techniques of eroticism. Many young readers may not have easy access to technique-oriented books, nor will they have had time to develop their own styles of stimulation. Furthermore, there is a generally high interest in sexual techniques, both among students and among people in general. As women become more liberated, they may wish to improve their knowledge of sexual techniques and their capacity to interact intimately.

Attitudes and techniques are closely related. Poor technique can frustrate the development of positive attitudes by reducing the reward effects of sexual interaction. On the other hand, satisfying erotic methods can change adverse attitudes into more positive ones. Satisfactory sexual techniques combined with favorable attitudes can lead to ever-increasing fulfillment of a couple's potential and at the same time increase that potential itself. Poor attitudes may show up in an individual's inept techniques, and this applies to either sex. Indifferent attitudes on the part of women have long been discussed, but the male who reluctantly continues foreplay may also show his hidden feelings. Neither attitudes nor techniques can stand alone. The strength or weakness of one affects the other.

Good technique can contribute to one's feeling that his or her sexual life is productive and satisfactory. Increased marital happiness and positive sexual adjustment lead to fewer mental and emotional problems. The sexually satisfied person may look and feel years younger than his or her chronological age and may have fewer weight problems. In general, positive attitudes toward sexuality and life itself are highly and positively correlated for most people. Thus anything that adds to one's sexual completeness is worth studying.

PSYCHOLOGICAL FACTORS

Very often the psychological aspects of arousal are more significant than the mechanics of stimulation. In considering the psychology of arousal, background factors, psychological sets, and methods of psychological stimulation are important. In general, psychological factors function in the determination of the efficiency, extent, and direction of satisfaction with one's mate and oneself.

BACKGROUND CONSIDERATIONS

Although females are perhaps becoming more susceptible to psychological forms of arousal, such as viewing or reading erotic material, this is still an area in which the male is most intensely affected. It is usually easier for males to become sexually excited from viewing a woman's nude body than for females to respond by looking at naked men. Thus, a wife may dance unclothed for her husband and arouse him, but he may be chagrined to find that she does not respond to his nudity.

In some instances, wives reject their husband's interest in hard-core pornography and become hostile or dismayed with them. A woman may, on the other hand, acquire an interest in erotic material with a romantic background (witness the popularity of television soap operas, gothic romances, and doctor novels – all of which frequently play upon the sex-romance combination), but her husband may fail to understand the importance of the love-erotic connection to female sexualism. Acceptance of any differences in responsiveness to psychological stimuli is, of course, desirable. More to the point than mere acceptance, however, is the development of appreciation of differences in sexual responding, because appreciation implies the possibility of capitalizing on them. Each sex can make use of the other's psychosexual style of responding to facilitate the mate's enjoyment.

Both men and women enjoy giving pleasure. One partner's ardor and excitement may raise sexual tension and feelings in the other. Very often either mate is simply joyous to know that he or she has pleased the other. It is fun to serve a mate in many ways, and one of these is sexually. An important aspect of that enjoyment is the realization that one is uncritically accepted. Berating a partner either for failure to become fully aroused or because of inadequate techniques can lead to a variety of disappointing outcomes. The good male lover will enjoy giving his partner intense sexual pleasure from time to time without necessarily achieving an orgasm himself. The same is true of his mate.

Both men and women require variation in degrees or types of stimulation, and even long-term sexual partners who have developed their own style of intimacy need to keep open minds in this regard. Variation in techniques may increase the capacity to respond. At other times absolutely no direct stimulation may produce an intense response. Alertness to the responsiveness of the mate is the best gauge of whether or not a change in technique is indicated.

COMMUNICATING ABOUT TECHNIQUES

Communication was discussed in Chapter 6, but it bears repeating that sexual partners are *not* mind readers. Partners should let each other know, both verbally and nonverbally, when they are being satisfied and when they are not. When the partner is not satisfying, patience, modulation of voice, and timing are important. Certainly momentary and occasional dissatisfaction will occur, but only longer periods should be reported. Gentle understanding and a quiet voice often bring results when roughness and harsh demands fail. It is important to get some "sense" of your partner's emotional state before communicating feelings of dissatisfaction. Everyone has moments when his or her self-confidence is lower than at other times, and everyone has periods of special stress. During these periods, complaints are not apt to be well received. Seldom is a sexual technique so badly manipulated that complaints cannot wait until later if necessary. Of course, nonsexual fights should not be carried on as a part of the sexual interaction process. They should be cleared up or temporarily forgotten in order to concentrate on intensely passionate sex.

PSYCHOLOGICAL SETS

A psychological set is a generalized attitude toward a specific objective, fact, or dimension of life. In the sexual arts a psychological set of self-confidence is of vital importance. The individual who is self-confident can instill confidence in a mate, accept constructive criticism, and look forward to fulfilling his or her potential.

A major reason some individuals lack sexual self-confidence is fear of inadequate technical skill. They strongly fear that they are sexually incomplete because they have not gained some mythical level of manipulative ability. Very often a novice remains just that because he or she would not want to be "shamed" in front of others because of lack of know-how. Skills are, of course, acquired through experience, but there are some cases in which one partner will not care enough to try, thereby making it difficult for the other. This can be found in some ocyjacks, occasionally in frigidity, and sometimes in impotency. Clearly, sexual skills are learned and do not occur naturally.

Inhibitions due to sexual phobias may lead to self-depreciation. Failures in sexual responsiveness are often the result of conditioned fears, which themselves are but defenses against anxiety. Anxiety, which arises from strong feelings of personal inadequacy, can devastate any sexual partnership, further reducing ego strength. When increasing effects of anxiety are recognized, psychosexual counseling should be sought.

One important item influencing an individual's sexual self-perception is the manner in which he or she views perversions. It is difficult to engage in an act that one strongly considers a perversion without some degree of self-depreciation. It was mentioned earlier that no particular kind of sexual act between consenting adults need be thought of as perverse. The idea of sexual deviations as pathological is mostly a moral one. In other words, a perversion is primarily what you and your partner agree it is, but even this may vary from time to time.

It is important, then, to build up a psychological set that sex can be good and is enjoyable and that one is indeed a sexual being fully capable of giving and receiving satisfaction and pleasure. No technique can adequately replace realistic confidence in oneself and one's mate.

SENSITIVITY AND EMPATHY

One must learn sensitivity and empathy by practicing them. The greatest enemy of either is indifference to the partner, the situation, or oneself. Empathy is the ability to feel as the other person does. It means the capacity to take the partner's role and to "get into it" as fully as possible. To be sensitive is to be aware of the partner as a whole person, to pick up cues from him, and to understand the kind of interaction that will best meet his needs. Barbara and John were able to practice role-taking quite successfully:

> Barbara's chief complaint was John's habit of leaving his clothes just where he had taken them off, while John's gripe was Barbara's habit of having little things to do when he wanted to lie close to her following their evening meal. They decided to switch roles. John acted like Barbara while she took on his part. As a result, he found himself quite irritated at her for letting her clothes lie around, and she was furious at him for always being "too busy." Needless to say, each developed greater appreciation of the other's needs and more willingness to cooperate.

In sexual interaction, to be sensitive and empathic means that sex will not be used routinely to compensate for other needs that have been incompletely met, nor will it be used to gain competitive advantage over the partner. Sex can and does provide temporary compensation for marital dissatisfaction, but it is seldom a permanent solution. In fact, when partnership relations are generally low, sex which was previously good may turn sour.

SOME PSYCHOLOGICAL METHODS OF STIMULATION

Sexual stimulation usually should begin by setting the mood. Sometimes the development of a sexually receptive state occurs spontaneously, but at others it must be nourished through cooperative interaction. The period of actual sexual participation might be preceded by such mood builders as parties, periods of companionship, or attendance at religious or religious-like ceremonies. Sometimes sensory awareness techniques — such as eye-gazing, yoga exercises, body exploration, or other activities for intimate couples — will enhance an erotic mood. Still other forms of relating include nude meditation, candlelight ceremonies, or periods of silence further enhanced by darkness. Some couples have visited a "haunted house" or engaged in extrasensory perception activities. These and many other general mood builders may be taken seriously or thought of as fun and games. Once a general mood has been achieved, more concentrated effort can be initiated.

One valuable psychological method of stimulation is sexual focusing — keeping attention concentrated on becoming sexually aroused through such activities as observing a partner's body and movements, remembering past activity that was arousing, or any other method whereby nonerotic stimuli are excluded from awareness. Enticing lighting arrangements, stimulating music, and erotic poetry may be helpful.

Pornography. Many couples enjoy pornography in the form of risqué limericks, sexy movies or recordings, romantic stories with erotic undertones, or nude pictures. In some cases the couple themselves pose for their own pornographic pictures, and many wives enjoy nude modeling or dancing for their husbands. Another type of activity is to pose with other couples or to exchange sexy photographs with them.

Novelty. Novelty and experimentation are highly desired by some couples but of little interest to others. Here, of course, a high degree of agreement is essential to satisfactory sexual adjustment. For those who wish novelty, changes in the environment, unusual techniques of stimulation, the placing of mirrors to permit viewing oneself in action, changing partners, and dramatic role-playing may add spice. For the couple who have had long experience with each other in the same place, a night on the beach, coitus in the woods, togetherness in a motel, or other nonroutine atmospheres may intensify passions. Some couples re-enact scenes from books, while others have spent time swimming in the nude. Other changes of pace include engaging in sex in "unusual" places in the home, for example, on the floor or in the bathtub. Novelty may also come from participating in sexual practices that would not usually be favored.

The use of clothing — such as the woman wearing a pair of gloves on occasion or one of the partners dressing in a manner that causes some difficulty in undressing — is erotic to some persons. In the same vein some couples, on rare occasions, like a rape scene in which the man tears the clothes from the woman's body while at the same time stimulating her in a variety of ways. A couple may wish to switch sexual roles and dress in clothes typical of the opposite sex and then proceed from there. Again, some individuals find certain articles of clothing highly stimulating, for example, stockings worn by an otherwise nude female. Body-painting also offers variety.

PHYSICAL METHODS OF STIMULATION

The chief physical methods of bringing about erotic arousal are touching, stroking, caressing, manipulating, massaging, squeezing, pressing, and kissing. The precise kind of stimulation needed to bring about a response is individually determined. It is not known what the factors are that result in preferences for specific types of physical stimulation, but they are probably governed primarily by one's past experiences. There may also be an inheritance factor involved in erotic sensitivity to touch, although this has yet to be convincingly demonstrated.

Satisfying lovers are especially alert to each other's erogenous zones and are keenly aware that there may be some shifting in main zones from time to time. Even though first contacts with a particular area may not be satisfying, later and further contacts may prove very responsive, since it is known that many parts of the body can be conditioned to respond erotically.

JUDGING READINESS FOR COITUS

Sometimes the period of precoital play is either too long or too short. Both men and women may need extended periods of precoital play from time to time, although women are more apt to have this need. Judging a female's readiness for coital contact might include observation of her change in coloring (especially around the breasts and shoulders), erectness of nipples, and degree of vaginal lubrication. A woman's verbalizations, shortness of breath, and generally high muscular tension are other signs of readiness. Except for vaginal lubrication, these same physiological responses apply also to the male, but it is usually assumed that penile erection is his best sign. However, absence of erection even during precoital play does not necessarily indicate lack of readiness for intercourse. Sometimes the man will be busy stimulating his partner, and temporarily his erection will be partly or completely lost. Under most circumstances his erection will be easily regained if he has not recently ejaculated.

Highly experienced females may require less prolonged foreplay than those just beginning sexual activity. The more experienced woman may actually lose sexual interest if coitus is delayed too long. Sometimes prolonged foreplay causes the male to become overly excited, leading to the danger of premature ejaculation. In any case, both partners may benefit from short periods of discontinuance of stimulation. These "cooling off periods" can, however, interfere with the woman's responsiveness if she has reached a high level of excitement.

CARESSING AND STROKING

It may pay to observe each other in masturbation if shyness is not a factor. By observing how each manipulates his or her genitals—noting the amount of pressure used and the changes in technique once climax has been reached—one can gather some insight as to what works best with the partner. Some individuals prefer specific types of manual or oral stroking, such as u-shaped strokes; long, slow, gentle movements; or plucking manipulations. Others desire firmness and roughness, and most will tolerate increased harshness after they have become aroused. Requirements vary from person to person and from time to time within the same individual. Any part of the body can be used to stroke, caress, or manipulate the partner. Feet, toes, buttocks, penis, vulva, breasts, face, or tongue can replace hands and fingers.

THE MOUTH AND LIPS

It is now well known that the mouth and lips are important erogenous zones and that kissing, nipping, sucking, biting, and so forth can be intense aphrodisiacs. Oral-genital relations are highly satisfying to many couples, and not a few consider this as the most sexually intimate relationship possible. Many modern couples try oral-genital relations in a variety of positions, the only limiting factors being the couple's imagination and the outright physical possibilities.

Responses to breast-sucking vary widely among individual women. In my research, one in four college girls reported that they were only minimally aroused from oral stimulation of their breasts, while another fourth stated that they were much to very much aroused by such techniques as sucking, licking, or having the partner place his lips against the nipples in a massaging action. Some men also respond to breast-sucking.

Every part of an individual's anatomy may respond to oral stimulation. For some this will be a kiss on the hand, while others find their tensions increasing from stimulation of the back of the knees, ears, or neck. Still others enjoy oral-anal stimulation.

MASSAGE

Massage of the body, especially of the back and neck, is capable of bringing responsiveness when other forms of stimulation fail. In general, massage should be carried out by stroking toward the heart, should be done in a nonirritating manner, and should be done in a quiet place in which both recipient and masseur or masseuse can find time to enjoy gentleness and closeness. Although the area around the back of the neck is usually a prime location for bringing erotic awareness, massage of the entire body can bring fuller relaxation. Sexual arousal may come naturally through the greater closeness and physical intimacy of massage.

AGGRESSIVENESS

Many couples find an extra measure of stimulation if their sexual interaction is mixed with acceptable forms of aggression.* Aggressiveness may be in the form of strong persuasion, forced submission through physical means, arousal associated with certain forms of physical pain, or various types of subjugation. These activities may be acted out or take place in fantasy only. An act of aggression, such as pinning the partner down, the use of abusive language, squeezing, or biting, may become part of the pleasure derived from sex by experienced couples. Aggressive release must be handled very carefully and should not be a form of angry retaliation. The purpose of mutually agreed upon aggression in intimate relations is to enhance passion by providing two simultaneous forms of stimulation: aggression and eroticism.

Light sadomasochism is a form of communication when used to enhance an erotic situation, but it is important to note that any given individual may wish aggressive behavior with one partner but not with another. The degree to which a man or woman prefers to be handled roughly or gently will vary from time to time and among individuals. Aggressiveness as it is being used here does not refer to the extreme forms of sadomasochism but rather to that which brings a temporary fusion between pain and pleasure to the participants.

MECHANICAL DEVICES

Vibrators and other mechanical devices may be used to stimulate either sex. They may be used before, during, or after sexual intercourse and can be applied to various parts of the body. Some couples enjoy the effects of erotic playfulness while lying on a vibrating mattress. Others have applied powder or lubricants over portions of their bodies, thus making slippery movements easier. Mechanical devices can, of course, become substitutes for human interaction and can be of considerable

---

*Aggression is also discussed on pp. 179–181.

help in some types of disability. They should not be used to replace human interaction but only to enhance it.

DRUGS

Although there appears to be a strong relationship between drug use and willingness to engage in sexual activity (Arafat and Yorburg, 1973; Greaves, 1972), this relationship is probably mediated through the liberal attitudes of those who use drugs and engage in sexual interaction. It is unclear exactly what effects illicit drug usage may have on sexual behavior, but it appears that drugs add little to sexual receptivity for many users. Marijuana is reported to provide extra stimulation by some couples, but others note either no effect or increasing indifference as they become high. Everett (1972) reports that users of amyl nitrite in the San Francisco area claim that orgasms are intensified or prolonged under that drug.

Sometimes tranquilizers will help the especially anxious individual to achieve sexual arousal and release, but illicit drugs, particularly hard drugs, seem more to reduce sexual interests than to increase them. Gay and Sheppard (1973) think their findings may be representative of the psychopharmacological sexual response of the drugs they studied. These researchers discovered that alcohol, the barbiturates, heroin, and psychedelics appear to reduce sexual activity through decreased desire or impotency. They found some evidence that cocaine and the amphetamines may have an aphrodisiac effect, while marijuana appeared to enhance pleasure consistently. They point out, however, that certain personal and social characteristics of their subjects may limit comparisons with other groups.

Considering the dubious benefits of drugs, including excessive amounts of alcohol, it makes little sense to use these artificial stimulants. The individual who is unable to respond to ordinary psychosexual stimulation should probably seek professional help. When drugs are needed, they should be taken only under the direction of a physician. For the most part, sexual disappointment rather than enhancement is to be expected from drugs.

COITUS

Coitus can take place in a wide variety of positions. In addition to the man-over-woman position, there are side positions, sitting positions, crouching positions, and rear entry. All can be used to add variety, but in addition some have functional usefulness at specific times. Those positions in which the woman can rest her legs on a pillow or chair are helpful during the latter phases of pregnancy or when she is especially tired. Sometimes the woman-over-man position is useful when the man has had an especially tiring day. If the female partner is interested, she can hold a mirror while in the rear entry position and watch as she is penetrated. Naturally, the more experienced persons tend to enjoy coitus in a wide variety of positions from time to time, although most come to settle largely on a few favorites.

The majority of experienced lovers seem to prefer movements which are slow and gentle at the beginning of intercourse, but increase in tempo, roughness, and depth of penetration toward the end. From the beginning, in which a generally erotic mood is set, the coitally active couple come to focus increasingly on their genital organs. As the climax of their relationship nears, there is an increasing tendency to think, move, and act in ways that will enhance their own sexual release. More and more the couple lose awareness of the stimuli surrounding them.

Although practically all men achieve an orgasm from their coital activity most of the time, women are not so fortunate. Some females will find orgastic relief beginning with their first coital contact, but the majority need some period of practice before they begin obtaining complete relief. This period may range from a few weeks to a year or more. Even if all conditions are favorable, sexual intercourse must last a minimum of 1 minute before the female partner will achieve orgasm. Most women will require longer times, ranging to a half hour or sometimes more.

If full sexual release is to be achieved, as the peak of sexual tension nears exclusive attention should be focused upon oneself. Concern over the partner's state of arousal is not a part of these last seconds, and when it is, orgastic relief will be interfered with markedly. Attempts at achieving simultaneous orgasm more often detract from levels of sexual intensity and are best avoided. Those who think they must reach orgasm together to prove their love run the risk of failure. When a woman is in the throes of her release, she desires vigorous and deep penetration, but men upon reaching orgasm are most likely to stop all movement or to move only slightly. By assisting his female partner to fuller satisfaction before reaching his own orgasm, the male helps bring the maximum of fulfillment to her. Later she can concentrate on his pleasure.

Orgasm is the release of sexual tension and as such permits a more rapid reduction of erotic tensions; nevertheless, both men and women can enjoy sexual interaction without having obtained this acme of release. Frenzied attempts to reach orgasm as though these were proof of virility ought to be avoided, for the very act of intensely trying can interfere with orgastic attainment. Orgasm is most likely to follow when the individual has developed a psychological set of positiveness toward sexuality and has found a partner who is like-minded, because orgasm is as much a matter of the mind as of the body (see also pp. 216–226).

SUMMARY

The art of sexual stimulation is a psychophysical one in which mutual cooperation pays off highly. Willingness to experiment, freedom from fears and feelings of inadequacy, and the ability to communicate both verbally and nonverbally help maximize the couple's potential to achieve sexual satisfaction.

Those whose personality and temperament permit them to have a psychological set that sexual relations should be fun and can be a source of joy are more apt to be receptive to new or unusual techniques than those who are morally or socially inhibited. The major dimension in the use of techniques is the possession of a psychological makeup that will allow full use of them.

Arrangements can be made to vary the environment and atmosphere in which sexual relations are carried out. The use of sensitivity and of religious or meditation activities can also help increase intimacy and passion.

The entire human body can be an erogenous zone if it is thought of in that way. Techniques such as mutual masturbation, oral-genital relations, or light sadomasochism can be used advantageously over the entire body with final concentration being on the genital area.

Pornography, if acceptable to the couple, can heighten stimulation, provided other techniques are used with it. Photography in which the mates themselves are the models is also an interesting sidelight for some couples. Massage, with its gentle, caring, and self-affirming message, can add real depth to a relationship. The same is true of exotic clothing worn occasionally.

Coitus in a variety of positions is usually attractive to both men and women. In addition to position changes, gadgets such as a vibrator sometimes add zest to coitus.

These are but a few of the sexual methods of stimulation that couples have found satisfactory. There are hundreds (perhaps thousands) of others, but the most important point about their use, I feel, is that they be mutually agreed upon in a free and open exchange of desires in which coercion has little part.

CHAPTER 9

CHILDHOOD SEXUALITY

We will discuss childhood sexuality in terms of three arbitrarily defined periods: birth through early childhood, preadolescence, and early adolescence ending at approximately age 16. This age is about the time parents first permit their children to date with a minimum of adult supervision. Some sexual behavior apparently occurs without the child's awareness of the nature of his acts; consequently, when considering children's sexual behavior, we are sometimes basing our notions on adult interpretations. Reevy (1961, p. 260), in an attempt to objectify adult observations of children, has defined as sexual any response in which tumescence-detumescence of the penis, clitoris, nipples, or other erectile tissue takes place because the child sought that class of stimuli which produces the tension-relaxation syndrome of sex. We will follow his definition in considering childhood sexual behavior.

In addition, we will follow a modified developmental outline of sexuality based on the work of Brown and Lynn (1966) as described in Chapter 3. We will study the development of maleness and femaleness and how each is related to culturally prescribed roles associated with masculinity and femininity. Every individual identifies some roles as part of himself, adapts others without identifying with them, and prefers some roles over others. The significance of genital sex to the developing child will also be explored.

A FEW ASSUMPTIONS

Before discussing the developmental aspects of sexuality, it is necessary to review some prevailing notions about children. These are the beliefs that children have a sexual life, that love and sex fuse naturally, and that childhood is a period of prime importance in the development of personality. Related to this last is the assumption that the bulk of human sexual expression is learned most efficiently during certain maturational stages.

Few persons would dispute the fact that children do experience sexual feelings, but it is not clear to what extent these feelings are similar or identical to those of adults. It is assumed that individuals gradually learn the possibilities of full genital involvement and that much early sexual behavior, although perhaps genitally pleasurable, is only a forerunner of the full implications of adult sexuality.

A second assumption is that love and sex share some common elements and that the interrelationship of these is most easily learned during childhood. It has already been demonstrated (see Chapter 3) that the need for love includes demands for physical contact and that without this contact normal development is unlikely to occur. Some of this contact may be experienced as sexual in nature. The need for human tactile stimulation has been discussed as necessary throughout the life span (Jourard, 1963, pp. 144–145) and as only weakly fulfilled in American mother-child relationships (Clay, 1968). Physical stimulation is an important aspect of human love because it promotes a sense of basic trust and security, and these are assumed essential to optimal sexual functioning. Thus closer physical and psychological relationships during childhood should produce more loving, less inhibited individuals.

We will consider childhood an important, but not necessarily critical, period in the formation of personality and in the development of basic attitudes toward oneself. It is during childhood that one should be helped to understand the nature of both one's own and the opposite sex. A positive regard toward one's body, physiology, and psychosexual responses will do much to enhance one's self concepts. Nonetheless, we will not make the assumption that childhood irreversibly fixes personality for life, for if the conditions giving rise to psychosexual or personality disturbances are interrupted, new ways of learning become possible. The longer poor conditions are maintained, however, the more difficult new learning becomes.

Finally, we will assume that each individual has a given biological potential for sexually responding that is somewhat like the biological basis of intelligence. If this is true, optimal learning conditions should enhance the physiological basis of sex. Since learning is most efficient when begun in a positive manner, it is clear that from the very first children should be taught positive sexual values. Like all humans, they will respond to that which is rewarding, but immediacy of reinforcement is more important in childhood than later, when the capacity to delay gratification will be stronger. Often, however, even well-meaning parents affirm the essential goodness of sexuality in the abstract but belie their own teachings when it comes to the specific sexual acts of their children. The wholeness of personality has as its first setting the healthy family acting in an integrated and responsive manner to the needs of individual members.

INFANCY

Observations of sexual behavior among children have been documented for some time, and even newborn infants have been seen in sexual activity. Just-born males are capable of erections, and infant girls have been observed in coital-like movements of their pelvic areas (Elias and Gebhard, 1970, pp. 16–27; Kinsey et al., 1948, pp. 175–181, and 1953, pp. 101–131).

Among infants, sexual pleasure is self-centered and probably occurs either as a result of accidentally pressing upon some erogenous zones or from biological pressures. Cuddling in mother's arms may produce sexual feelings as well as a sense of security, in which case sexualness is positively rewarded. Such experiences may be the earliest in which love and sexuality simultaneously and naturally occur together. During the early part of infancy, these feelings are apt to be experienced in a more or less diffuse manner. Later some genital focusing takes place, but it is apt to continue randomly until the child learns that certain spots produce pleasurable feelings more intensely than others. However, under the guidance of adults genital focusing may become more clearly established; for example, it has been reported that some nursemaids have fondled their infant charges in order to quiet them.

There are presently few indications that infant sexual responding is dependent upon maleness or femaleness, although some feel that because a penis protrudes it may produce greater sexual awareness in males. Given our current state of knowledge, it is safe to assume that the sexual potential of infant girls differs little from that of boys.

To sum up, infant sexuality seems to be based on a diffuse, accidental response that is pleasurable in nature. Once a satisfactory response is experienced, it is apt to be repeated in a self-stimulatory manner, resulting in the infant becoming his own source of both arousal and relief. In contrast to later periods, when the motives for sexuality are multiple, infancy seems to be characterized almost exclusively by the narcissistic motive of self-pleasure.

EARLY CHILDHOOD

TOILET-TRAINING

During the early part of childhood, toilet-training, with its focus on the genitals, is an important event. If genital attention has not been sharpened up to this time, it will quickly become so, and some of this new awareness will be associated with the pleasure obtained from these organs. It is through toilet-training that the child learns he can manipulate his parents to achieve all sorts of rewards not directly connected with acts of elimination. Thus he learns indirectly that the sexual organs can be used to elicit responses from people, and eventually that sex itself has this power. Not only are sexual responses less diffuse than formerly, but additional motives for sex have been added to that of self-pleasure.

These new motives are the manipulation of others for nonsexual gains and increased curiosity. The child may learn that his parents panic from his activities, thus coming to the knowledge not only that certain sexual acts can be used to gain nonsexual rewards but also that such acts may be punished. Selfishness may become attached to elimination, manipulation of genital organs, or deliberate genital exposure. These naturally occurring responses become sources of fear, uncertainty, and self-doubt if attempts are made to extinguish them too early, too intensely, or without explanation that the child can understand. The story of Benny demonstrates this point clearly:

> Benny's mother began his toilet-training in earnest when he was two years of age. She followed the best advice of child development experts, rewarded him for his successes, was patient with his failures, and generally set a good example for him. She was warm and friendly with her son throughout the training period.
>
> However, on an occasion when Benny's maternal grandmother was visiting the family, Benny slipped out of the house and was discovered playing on the street in the nude. His mother brought him in and set him on her lap while she explained that in our society most people prefer not to be together without wearing clothes and that going out in public in the nude embarrasses others and infringes upon their rights. Grandmother did not agree with her daughter's approach, but having read a smattering of psychoanalytical literature, decided not to discuss the incident in Benny's presence. When she did speak with her daughter, she speculated that holding Benny in the nude was unconsciously seductive.
>
> Although Benny's mother rejected this explanation, she nevertheless began making special efforts to do nothing even remotely suggesting seductiveness on her part. Openness was replaced by more emphasis on privacy, and although a warm, loving, relationship between mother and son continued, an element of distance remained. Years later, when Benny was married and experiencing ambivalence about his sexuality, he thought back through this experience and remembered it as an outstanding event in his early life.

Although this first experience was important, it was the constant fear of erotic connection with her son that led Benny's mother to maintain some psychological distance from him. Thus for most of Benny's life ambivalence about his relationship with his mother persisted. It is only through lifelong positive or negative reinforcements that a particular behavior or defense will be continued.

PRESCHOOL YEARS

Once toilet-training has been mastered, adults pay less attention to the child's genital organs, but it is evident that the following years are fairly active ones. Several events insure this. As the child continues to grow, anatomical differences between the sexes are heightened and some physiological functions, such as erection, become more evident. This growing difference between maleness and femaleness may sharpen curiosity even more. A few children experience orgasm, and as Kinsey et al. (1953, p. 104) have pointed out, these experiences have most of the essential aspects of adult orgasm.

Games involving mutual body exploration or similar activities are sought out. Children may engage in such diverse play activities as "mama and papa," mutual examination of erogenous zones, kissing, necking, petting, self-stimulation, oral-genital relations, and acts in which coitus is either mimicked or actually carried out. Usually the more involved relations follow participation in those that are less complicated, and all are a prelude to adult sexuality.

Another important aspect of development is also occurring: an increase in the ability to communicate verbally. As part of this process, words become attached to various anatomical parts and to certain acts, and new meanings divide sexual motives into many shades and hues. Evidence abounds that sexual communication is now beginning to take place: although much experimentation is on a trial-and-error basis, some little boys mount little girls and engage in coital-like movements. It is evident that they have heard about intercourse and at least one method by which it is carried out. In brief, the rudiments of an important aspect of adult sexuality are being laid down: the ability to experience sexually and to verbalize feelings about those experiences. At this stage the child should be learning to communicate honestly about sex and sexual feelings.

More and more, adults are emphasizing proper sex roles. Masculinity is unfolding as natural to males, and femininity is increasingly associated with females. Thus maleness-masculinity and femaleness-femininity are elaborating and organizing into conceptual wholes, and as the youngster moves through the first years of school, greater differentiation between the sexes is taking place. For a time, only a few roles will be preferred, while others will be adopted because of pressure from parents, peers, and others. The result may be the beginnings of role conflict. For example, the little boy who gets into a fight with his buddy may much prefer some sympathy from his mother but will not accept it because he does not want to feel "sissified." As time goes by, some sex roles will become part of the individual, and those around him will no longer imagine him in any others. Young males will increasingly learn instrumental roles, while females will be oriented toward expressive roles.

Almost from the beginning, action-direction role-taking is encouraged as a sign of masculinity. Greater emphasis on roles of an aggressive-competitive nature prepares the male for his position in adult society, but at the same time he is taught considerateness, courtesy, and other relationship proprieties, so that the stage is set for some of the ambivalences that male adults normally feel.

The expressive-affective roles designated as feminine are still encouraged among the majority of maturing girls. For the most part, girls learn the less rewarding roles traditionally assigned by society to adult women. Home and family preparation through play and school are central. Submission and adherence to social standards are more expected of girls than of boys.

In both sexes, roles are performed within each individual's perception of the requirements of the significant others with whom he or she interacts. Since neither sex is consistently rewarded for performing assigned gender roles, incomplete sex-role identification will occur. If messages sent from parents communicate a basic disagreement between them about the sex roles they prefer for their children, the identity problem will be compounded. Nevertheless, for most children a predonderance of rewards from parents, peers, teachers, and others definitely helps establish a sex-role preference associated with their gender. Most psychologists feel that sex-role identification is best learned during the preschool developmental phase; in fact, John Money (Money, Hampson, and Hampson, 1955), a most knowledgeable researcher in gender identity, feels that from 18 months to three or four years is the critical time for establishing gender identification.

During the child's early years, the sex of playmates does not make much difference, but as the child grows older and gradually adopts the standards of his or her own sex, he or she tends to select playmates on a gender basis. At some point increased consciousness of masculine-feminine differences has come into being, and it is relative to this consciousness that the period of preadolescence will be discussed.

PREADOLESCENCE

Preadolescence is the period of middle and later childhood, possibly beginning as early as age seven or eight. Males still have not developed the capacity to ejaculate, but they may experience orgasms similar to those of females. Kinsey et al. (1948, p. 167; 1953, p. 103) reported that some 57 per cent of their male subjects and 27 per cent of their female subjects recalled some erotic arousal during this period. Orgasms are experienced by one out of 12 girls, and these derive primarily from accidentally discovered self-stimulation (Kinsey et al., 1953, p. 105). Heterosexual erotic contacts are not extensive and are, for the most part, confined to genital exposure. Coitus is practiced by only a few preadolescents, although Kinsey et al. present data suggesting some rather large social-class differences, with the sons of working-class males being the most sexually active. It is evident that genital sex is becoming increasingly important, although it has not reached the intensity that it subsequently will.

DEVELOPING A PSYCHOSOCIAL SET

If preadolescents do not show substantial increases in overt sexual behavior, they have not ceased activity that will prepare them for it in the future. The Freudian notion that this is a "latent period" in which sexual interests are minimal receives little support from more recent studies, such as those of Carlfred Broderick and his associates (1966a, 1966b, 1968).

Social sex roles assist in the preparation of individuals for more direct genital sexual interaction. These pregenital activities have been labeled sociosexual by Broderick and include such heterosexual activities as taking a walk together, going to the movies or on dates, kissing, and "making out." There appears to be a steady and progressive development of cross-sex interests which is fairly predictable and measurable (Broderick and Rowe, 1968; Broderick and Weaver, 1968). Broderick (1966a) has spelled out this focusing process, and the following is a brief summary of it.

Same-sex friendships predominate among 10 and 11 year olds, and there is a clear prejudice against members of the opposite sex. Concurrent with this desire to avoid interaction and friendship with the opposite sex, however, are the developing roots of adult romance. Most of the youngsters in Broderick's group claimed to have fallen in love at some time, although they were not sure that this love was reciprocated:

> George and Tom, both 10 year olds, were quite good friends. They did many things together and sometimes stayed at each other's homes over night. When asked about girls, both could remember when they were "younger and had a girl friend." They stated flatly, however, that they had no such interest now. Nevertheless, Tom confided that George often asked about his sister who was two years older, and on one occasion had gone for a walk with her. Later Tom's sister, after swearing her brother to secrecy forever, confided that George had kissed her on the lips and touched her breasts. She had refused, however, when he had asked her to let him see her pubic hair. At another time George had resisted walking down the street with Tom's sister because "people would think I'm a sissy."

At the age of 12 or 13, the tendency to prefer close friends of one's own gender is still predominant. More willingness to make love interests public and greater expectation that love should be reciprocated are typical. But in general the 13-year-old period seems a plateau in the development of interests in the opposite sex, and indeed some authors have christened this the homosexual period. There is little evidence, however, to support any contention that overt homosexual interests are widespread at this age. Intense friendships in which confidences are exchanged with a member of one's own sex are not unusual, but they may be seen as a part of the preparation for deeper interpersonal heterosexual relationships later on. Physical development and emotional maturity have become important criteria for choosing a date, and the difference between the maturational rates of the sexes is more pronounced. Girls prefer older boys as dates and boys choose younger girls for partners. Budding breasts and sprouting pubic hair sharpen awareness of maleness-femaleness and concomitant sexual potential.

EARLY ADOLESCENCE

Developing maleness and femaleness reach new heights as the secondary sexual characteristics become more prominent. Greater-than-ever identification with adult genitality takes place. For girls, circulating hormones bring on the menarche and the periodicity associated with it sometime between the ages of 11 and 15. Ejaculation, that essential mark of masculinity, also occurs for the first time for nine out of 10 males between their eleventh and fifteenth years. These parallel events produce a new awareness of the genitals as the seat of erotic arousal.

INCREASING EROTIC INTERESTS

An upsurge of sexual interest occurs at both the physical and psychosocial levels between the fourteenth and sixteenth years. As Kinsey et al. have noted, the increase is greater for boys, but girls certainly are not standing still. A study by the author (1964) indicated that almost all his female subjects had engaged at least in breast-fondling before they reached age 17, and that one out of five who had experienced premarital coitus had done so by that age. Males, according to the author's findings, follow a similar pattern.

This evidence seems to parallel that of other research and confirms the extent of genitally focused sex during early adolescence. Offer (1972), for example, studied the sexual attitudes and behavior of 13-to-14-year-old and 16-to-18-year-old teenagers of both sexes. His study was carried out over an eight-year period and at several locations. He concluded that boys were more sexually active than girls and that age was an important determinant of premarital sexual decisions. His principal finding was that there has been no significant increase in adolescent sexual behavior since the Kinsey studies. Adolescent girls felt that they could handle sex with greater ease than adolescent boys. There is no uniform attitude toward adolescent sexual behavior among adolescents themselves. Offer cites other studies that support the thesis of no significant change in adolescent sexual behavior (Gottheil and Freedman, 1970; Simon, Gagnon, and Carns, 1968).

In another major study (Simon, Berger, and Gagnon, 1972), the investigators concluded:

When education and race are held constant there has been little change in the sexual behavior of women [age 17 or under]. Kinsey reported that about one in five of the women in the two highest educational categories had coital experience by age 20. In our two studies, we found that nearly as many college women (17%) reported coitus before age 18 and that among the more age heterogenous sample of Illinois girls, slightly fewer who aspired to at least attend a 4-year college reported coital experiences (p. 206).

The college sample was taken in 1967 and the figures may be somewhat higher now, but the Illinois girls referred to were studied in 1972. This study will be discussed further in Chapter 12.

Thus while there is much speculation about supposed increases in nonmarital adolescent sexual behavior and about greater liberation of attitudes, such speculation is *not* confirmed by most studies. A number of authors have commented that published reports of increased sexual interaction among young people might in fact be self-fulfilling prophecies: they may be cause for increased concern among youth that their sexual proclivities do not meet social expectations (Offer, 1972; Simon, Berger, and Gagnon, 1972).

If they have not tried masturbation before, many girls and most boys will begin practicing it during the 15-to-16-year-old-period (Weikert, 1970, p. 78). Weikert's review of the studies of masturbation indicates that about 90 per cent or more of males have practiced self-stimulation by age 17. For girls the range is between 15 and 35 per cent, depending upon the sample studied, by age 18 (p. 79). Masturbation fantasies are probably less varied among teenagers than among adults, but as young people gain sexual experience and the capacity to accept their own eroticism, the fantasies accompanying self-stimulation may incorporate memories of those experiences as well as varied concepts derived from reading sexual material or sharing experiences with friends. Masturbation, practiced individually or performed mutually with friends, appears to be an important sexual outlet for adolescents, especially for adolescent males.

Montagu (1969, pp. 120–135) presents evidence that for a few years following the onset of menstruation, many girls cannot become pregnant, but with this possible exception, we find both boys and girls truly taking on the physical characteristics of adult sexuality during early adolescence. (Lack of fecundity is discussed further under "Teenagers and Contraception" in Chapter 11.)

HORMONAL INFLUENCES

Although there has been an increase in the flow of hormones, it cannot be assumed that hormones alone are responsible for the heightened sexual desires of adolescents. Money (1961, pp. 1383–1400) studied hormonally precocious children and found that his subjects acted in terms of social stereotypes appropriate to their chronological age rather than in response to hormones. He concluded: "Premature puberty made a difference not in the content and imagery of erotic play, dreams and daydreams, but in the frequency of their occurrence" (p. 1394). Thus Money's study seems to lend support to the thesis that sexuality in children is primarily learned. Hormones add a new stimulus to the desire for sexual experience, but social expectations, explicit or implicit, remain the major motivators of human sexuality.

PSYCHOSOCIAL CHANGES

Side by side with physiological changes go changes of a psychosocial nature. There is increasing heterosexual contact, and this undoubtedly whets sexual appetites further. The fact that virginity is still very much the norm during early adolescence probably inhibits the development of some physical desires, especially for girls. Greater social conformity on the part of girls likely directs their attention to the broader aspects of the heterosexual relationship and results in enhanced social and interpersonal skills. Boys, on the other hand, tend to focus on the physical side of sex. Consequently, they do not gain the degree of interpersonal competence learned by most girls. In other words, females learn to equate their sexuality with their total personality, while males, guided more by peers than by parents or teachers, continue to understand their sexuality as primarily physical. The expression of sensuousness is definitely becoming masculinized and feminized through social-learning processes.

Love and its associated activities have become more serious. Holding hands, hugging, and kissing often symbolize more profound feelings than they did at first. Dating is more regular, and many begin steady dating for the first time. By now the internalization of sex-appropriate roles has deepened, but the preferred method of expressing these roles may follow peer norms. Since focusing has become more complete, it is considerably more important to establish one's identity, and part of this identity is sexual in nature. External controls have shifted from parents to peers, but internal controls are not yet likely to be well established. Throughout this entire developmental phase, individual differences in sexuality are quite apparent, as the contrasting stories of Betsy and Sue demonstrate:

> Sue, age 16, had rarely dated and had never gone steady. Her chief interests were sports and her horses. She had tried "tongue"-kissing but felt no excitement from it. She had also allowed her covered breasts to be fondled, but was only mildly interested. In brief, she currently

preferred lone activities and felt boys would be more important to her in a few years' time. She thus seemed to be in transition between the stage when friendship with a girl was highly significant to her and more advanced heterosexual relationships. She was, nevertheless, sociable and well-adjusted. She felt that she was sexually mature for her age and had no real "hangups." Her upper-middle-class parents, with whom she had excellent communication, felt the same.

Sue's neighbor, Betsy, was brought up under essentially the same conditions. The two girls were close friends, attended the same church, and were about equal in school achievement. They were reared under nearly identical philosophies of child-training, and both felt loved and secure with their parents. Both girls were well thought of by their peers, and Betsy was as self-confident as Sue. Betsy's sexual experiences, however, were quite different from those of Sue:

> Betsy had always shown an interest in boys and seemed to enjoy a sense of excitement. She had begun sexual intercourse shortly after her eleventh birthday, participated in many forms of sexual activity with several males (including a married man more than twice her age), and engaged in self-stimulation several times a week. Erotic stimuli of all types seemed to excite her, including the recounting of her own experiences. She was quite responsive to stimulation of her breasts and began achieving orgasm within a week of her initial coital experience. Betsy enjoyed her responsiveness and took her sexuality in stride. She was aware, however, that adult society would not approve of her behavior, especially since she was only 16 years of age. Interestingly, Betsy never conceived of her activities as sexually precocious and considered herself only sexually mature for her age. Sue was the only person with whom she ever discussed her erotic behavior, and even though she herself was different, Sue accepted Betsy's behavior as quite natural.

In the cases of Sue and Betsy we see quite opposite responses to very similar environments and styles of child-rearing. What accounts for these differences? Perhaps they are partly due to inherited biological potential. However, learning factors cannot be dismissed completely. In the first place, even within almost identical environments, subtle and little-noticed dissimilarities occur and may engender differing responses. Furthermore, behavior that is most intensely rewarded in the time closest to that in which it occurred is most likely to be repeated. Thus Betsy's erotic behavior, initially more satisfactory than Sue's, would be expected to continue and to bring additional rewards. Satisfactory sexual encounters are their own source of reinforcement and once achieved strengthen the tendency to seek further erotic involvement. Time is also an important factor. Even strong parental disapproval would not likely have dissuaded Betsy from a desire for more sexual interaction because it would be too far away from the time of the sexual acts themselves. An intense immediate reward, such as pleasure, is often more powerful than later punishment.

Yet even if they had had an identical environment, Sue and Betsy might still have given attention to different aspects of that environment. *Selective inattention,* to use Harry S. Sullivan's term, helps dispense with awareness of boring or anxiety-arousing material by admitting to consciousness only those experiences that tend to be congruent with the individual's concepts of himself. Adolescents—undergoing rapid body-image changes, seeking to assert their autonomy, eager for adult status but not fully ready to give up childhood, pressured by a variety of new and often to them ambiguous social forces, and unclear about their personal goals—have the important developmental task of finding their identity. Very often they will use selective inattention to "turn off" that which is incongruent with their most immediate needs and self-images. From time to time, this high emotional charging results in considerable portions of experience being relegated to the unconscious without prior consideration. Thus there are no well-worn paths between consciousness and the unconscious, and easy recall of much psychic material is impossible. Warnings that have fallen on "deaf ears" (were not consciously attended to) may have no functional use in the face of strong immediate needs. The same is true of all interpersonal communications, whether positive or negative. Selective inattention may have had some bearing on our subjects' sexuality, since Sue may have attended more to her parents' achievement or other goals while Betsy may have selectively filtered these out as less important than interpersonal attraction.

Nevertheless, the reasons why an individual selectively inattends to various parts of his environment lie only partially within the individual himself. Other reasons can be found in family dynamics. A family situation is a complex of stimuli presented in a variety of configurations, some of which are contradictory. Children, especially as they grow older, are likely to recognize some of these contradictions and automatically choose those alternatives that are most rewarding in terms of either need fulfillment or anxiety reduction. A half century ago, Pavlov (1927) found that only one element of a configuration of stimuli produces virtually all the response to the total configuration. In the course of family dynamics, an individual may do most of his responding at a given time to such stimulus elements as pitch of voice, nonverbal gestures, differences in sibling rearing, perceived unity between parents, or a wide variety of others.

Very often a child will represent to his parents a vicarious reliving of their own imagined youthful experiences. Without verbalizing their wishes, the parents subtly communicate to their child the idea that certain behavior is permissible, even though verbally they may have warned him against it. Sometimes, for example, a dependent childlike mother will nudge her daughter into the mother role, which in some cases may eventuate into the wife role with overt incest occurring between father and daughter. However, one need not go this far. The point is that family dynamics occur in all degrees and that these dynamics, through intentional or unintentional reinforcement, assist in determining what will and what will not be consciously attended.

To summarize: during early adolescence embryonic sexuality unfolds and begins to grow and ripen into the ever-changing sexuality of adulthood. Genital involvement, fusing together a variety of internal symbolic meanings and the demands of the social environment, will henceforth remain a dominant theme of personality development.

HELPING CHILDREN COPE WITH SEX

While adults argue whether or not children truly have a sexual life and really need sex education, children go on with or without their help. Sex has become much more a part of public life since communication has increased so greatly, and the advent of television has meant that children often see heterosexual romance portrayed daily on the screen. Some of this romance has implicit sexual connotations, while other shows are frank discussions of sex. Sexual stimulation abounds, and much of this is at the adult level. All this may increase the thirst for sexual knowledge among children, especially older ones. But although sexual curiosity goes up, insight into what they see and hear is often denied children. Many adults have not changed their basically embarrassed attitudes toward explaining sex, and certain groups have fought against sex education in the schools (Drake, 1968, 1969). The greater public displays of sex have not been accompanied by a corresponding increase in communication between children and adults concerning the place of sex in human life. Prohibition has continued to be the major model of unmarried sex presented to the young.

SOME SOURCES OF LEARNING

Peers have always been the major source of sexual knowledge for the bulk of American youth and continue that way today (Ramsey, 1943; Reevy, 1954; Shope, 1964; Schwartz, 1969). Many sons and daughters find sex education at home unsatisfactory, and thus about 50 per cent of girls and between 75 and 90 per cent of boys learn most about sex from their peers. In 1943 Ramsey found that it was not until age 14 that 100 per cent of his male subjects knew about coitus; the author found that it was not until age 15 that 100 per cent of the present-day males in his group knew about it. Apparently things have not changed much. The prevalence of sexual ignorance is so well established that it needs no further verification.

SEX EDUCATION IN THE HOME

Although children will continue to discuss sex among themselves, it seems clear that increased communication with adults would be welcomed. The home has been and will continue to be a major source of sex education, partly because sexual instruction begins there with the mothering one, regardless of later educational patterns. Much of this training is not direct but comes from examples set by the parents. Mead (1969) says that the couple's feelings about sharing tenderness, physical contact, and other sexual matters with each other determines the attitudes their children are apt to have about sex. Nixon (1962, p. 95) points out in his discussion of children that the discovery-experimentation-mastery sequence includes sexual activity and curiosity, and he goes on to state that if knowledge is insufficient, experimentation becomes dangerous. The earliest sex education is likely to focus upon the child's body, yet this can be a difficult matter for parents to handle if they do not regard their own bodies in a positive light (Johnson and Belzer, 1973).

In the final analysis, more attention to purposeful, conscious, parental teaching of sexual behavior is needed. It is in the atmosphere of the home that sex can best be taught as a total human relationship. Unfortunately, this does not appear to be the usual practice.

Libby and Nass (1971), in a study of parental attitudes toward sex education, found that the overwhelming majority of parents, regardless of their degree of liberalism or conservatism, wished to proscribe sexual activity before marriage. Using a sample of 125 couples living in Manchester, Connecticut, these scientists sought to test three hypotheses: first, that democratic parents would be less restrictive than autocratic parents concerning dating rules; secondly, that democratic parents would evidence significantly less tendency than autocratic parents to support the double standard of morality; and thirdly, that democratic parents would be less stringent than autocratic parents in their courtship rules for girls. None of these hypotheses were confirmed. Both the democratic and autocratic parents in the sample tended to use various fear techniques, such as warnings of pregnancy or venereal disease. The more democratic parents, however, approved of sex education for their children and were more dissatisfied with their own sex education. Seventy-five per cent of the same felt that their children should have contraception information, while one in four of both Catholics and Protestants would deny such information to their children. If the Libby-Nass findings prove generalizable, this general willingness to give contraceptive information while proscribing sexual activity—especially coitus—is evidence of the confusion that exists among parents concerning the sociosexual education of their children.

Gagnon (1965) has postulated some reasons for this ambivalence. He reminds us that only a small portion of sexual information is learned legitimately through parents or school. Furthermore, there is no real community of sexual values among adults and marital coitus has not been the only source of sexuality for the majority of adults, especially males. Because sexual behavior, as an important value, has great secretiveness attached to it, most of the sexual relation is learned by an exchange of gestures and cues—that is, nonverbally. Discussion and direct experimentation are not the ways that the majority of American adults have learned their sexual behavior. As Gagnon points out, no one can be sure of the behavior of others, and any statements about sexual practices may be construed to mean that the individual is speaking from experience. Sexual fantasy is about the only fantasy that cannot be transmitted into reality through interaction with others or through contact with the mass media. Each of these factors becomes a severe restriction for the youngster attempting to check the reality of human sexuality.

Gagnon also believes that many parents invalidly interpret children's behavior as "sexual" by applying to it adult standards and connotations. The result may be negative labeling, mislabeling, or complete absence of labeling, all of which are confusing to the child. For instance, a parent might try to distract a child from what the parent perceives as sexual behavior. This distraction may occur, but the parent may offer no verbalizations about the avoided behavior. This is nonlabeling. In another instance, the parent may simply tell the child that his or her behavior is wrong without further elaboration or specification. This gives the behavior a negative connotation regardless of the situation in which it was performed. At times negative control will extend to sanctions concerning parts of the body. At other times genitals and other body parts may be mislabeled, inculcating a prohibitive attitude toward those parts.

Since children may find it difficult to check the reality of adult labeling, long-term consequences may result from negative labeling practices. When the individual is finally able to test the validity of adult-taught sexual sanctions, the original teacher is not likely to be present, and corrections may be misdirected or incomplete. Thus a residue of childhood-learned sexual prohibitions may continue to plague the adult because of faulty correction outcomes. The context of later relearning may be so vastly different from that of the original learning that inaccuracies occur.

These conditions as practiced in the home—faulty sexual teaching—are apt to remain powerful for some time and to provide a well-ingrained psychological set, especially in those areas that are most prohibited.

Gagnon provides us with the foregoing background to remind us that it is quite difficult (perhaps impossible) to plan a sex education program with highly predictable consequences. According to Gagnon, planning sex education for children is planning the unplannable. He suggests that if sex education is undertaken in the schools, it should be integrated into the regular curriculum. It is more important to prepare the child to receive knowledge than to impart facts to him. The results of negative sociosexual learning during childhood may be quite difficult to eradicate.

Recently it has been suggested that thorough instruction of parents should be the priority of sex education. Such suggestions make sense in light of Gagnon's analysis of parents' training of their children. I would point out, however, that parents face considerable social pressure to rear their children according to social custom. The fact that sociosexual behavior is kept secret in America while sociosexual mores are openly discussed does much to hinder any consensus, for sexual attitudes, beliefs, and values are only imcompletely reflected in sexual activity. This partial reflection makes reality-testing a doubly formidable task for the adult as well as the child. Secretiveness, along with the idea that adults automatically know about sex, has thus made it difficult for parents to accept sex education for themselves.

ASSISTANCE TO PARENTS

From the material just discussed and other studies (Reeve, 1963; Libby, 1970; SIECUS, 1971), it appears (1) that a majority of parents do favor public school sex education (however the parents define this term), (2) that liberal individuals would include a wider variety of topics than conservatives, but (3) that the general tenor of all such public education should be conservative. It is also clear that many parents are confused and bewildered about their own values concerning their children's sex education. On the one hand, parents understand the need to teach their children about human sexuality. On the other hand, parents attempt to protect their children from the consequences of sexuality by framing sex education in ideal terms rather than in realistic ones.

For those parents who wish to help their children gain insight into human sexuality within the context of parental values, a number of useful books are available. Some of these emphasize the application of traditional models of sexual morality to present-day society (Driver, 1965; Duvall, 1968; Filas, 1966; Narramore, 1956). Others employ less traditional viewpoints (Calderone, 1966; Johnson and Belzer, 1973, Pomeroy, 1968, 1969). Some theorists have surveyed special aspects of sexual development. W. R. Johnson (1969) and Kempton, Bass, and Gordon (1971) discuss sex education for the mentally retarded. Andry and Schepp (1968) have written an animated account of sexuality for small children that includes drawings of dogs copulating.

ANSWERING QUESTIONS

Certain specifics are believed to be important in answering the sexual questions of children. Most important, perhaps, is the question of values, for human sexuality cannot be divorced from them. Eventually, children will acquire a set of their own values, based partly on early learning but to a considerable extent the product of several other sources. It seems vital that parents, teachers, ministers, and other trainers of youth define their own values as accurately as possible. Scarvelis (1968) discusses the need to place all sexual education within a framework of values relevant to the general background and development of the child. He asks: "How can children intelligently and rationally discuss relationships with others and 'right and wrong' acts without being aware of what they themselves hold as values?" Thus, at the time when it seems most clear to the parents that the child can understand them, sexual values should be taught right along with other information.

Lieberman (1969), a psychiatrist, has written concerning mistakes adults sometimes make when assisting their children to explore the sexual world. There may be a tendency to explain more than the child is ready to grasp intellectually and emotionally. Lieberman points out that the child should not be overwhelmed with sex information he might not want. He explains that a simple diagram or the use of a doll is often the best way to discuss anatomy. Three circles drawn in a vertical line to represent the urethra, vagina, and anus are all that is needed to first explain female anatomy. Lieberman says that if the child is old enough for this anatomy lesson, he is old enough to learn the proper words, but aimed at his conceptual level. If the child seems satisfied with what he is told, he is likely being told enough for the time being.

The question may arise as to how much the child already knows. Lieberman suggests asking children for this information in an indirect manner, perhaps by saying: "Tell me what you think first, and then I'll tell you what I think." If the child does not speak up, answer his question anyway but try to get some feedback that will give you a clue as to whether you are on the right track.

Many adults will not answer sex questions because they are afraid they may answer incorrectly, but it is probably more harmful not to answer at all or to rebuff the child for asking. Do not try to bluff the child, for sooner or later he might find out. Most children can accept the fact that adults do not always have the last word on the subject, and they are more likely to respect your truthfulness.

If the goal is to rear a child who will develop stable self-control, Lieberman continues, he or she should not be punished, ridiculed, or embarrassed because of faulty sex knowledge or lack of certainty about emotions. Overreaction from an adult can shut off further communication.

All these suggestions require an adult who understands himself, does not overreact to the child's sexual exploring, has some final outcome he desires for the child, and is knowledgeable about sexual matters.

SUMMARY

The following are some conclusions that may be derived from our current knowledge of childhood sexuality.

1. Sexual reactivity exists almost from the moment of birth.
2. There are wide differences in degree of reactivity among children.
3. The child's capacity to function fully in all types of intimate relations may be interfered with by negative sexual conditioning.
4. Children need tactile stimulation—to be held, fondled, and touched—if they are to learn to trust themselves and others.
5. The child's attitudes toward his body are related to his self concepts, and some of these can be expected to carry into adulthood.
6. Sexuality and related interpersonal acts, including kissing, dating, and romance, follow a fairly predictable sequence until adolescence, when greater genital awareness comes about.
7. The so-called latent period is characterized by more direct and indirect sexual behavior and interest than was previously understood.
8. Parents are the most potent influence on the child's early sexual

attitudes, especially through their approaches to each other.
9. Open discussion with feedback from the child, simple approaches at the child's level, and an attitude that sex is naturally good can be expected to help the child achieve sexual stability.
10. Often much of the joy that could be obtained from adult sexual interaction is destroyed during childhood.

CHAPTER 10

MALE SEXUALITY

It is often easier to predict a man's response to a given sexual relationship than to estimate a woman's reactions to the same situation. An understanding of male sexuality may, however, provide some of the insights needed to bring the genders closer together in their erotic needs. As needs become more alike, interpersonal attractiveness can be expected to increase, since similarity of needs has been found to be a significant factor in interpersonal attraction (Poe and Mills, 1972).

THE SOCIAL MODEL

The social model of masculine sexuality focuses primarily on physical aspects and only secondarily on sensuousness. Like the general model of masculinity presented in Chapter 5, male sexuality is expected to be aggressive, dominant, voyeuristic, free from guilt, uninhibited, and less sensitive than female sexuality. Applied to the individual male's sexual life, each of these expectations has a special meaning.

AGGRESSIVENESS

Whether or not he feels like it, the male is usually expected to be the sexual aggressor. This is not to infer that a biological tendency for males to be more aggressive has definitely been established. (At this point, the reader may wish to refer to the section on hormones, beginning on page 14). In fact, theorists differ about the source of aggressive tendencies, many agreeing that such tendencies have a complex origin and manifest themselves nonuniformly in both sexes.

Although he is primarily a learning and developmental theorist, Mischel (1970, pp. 3–72) has also reviewed the literature on masculinity and femininity and has concluded that from the earliest moments of life human males are more aggressive than females. Indeed, he sees aggressiveness as somewhat unique in that it seems to be the only personality characteristic that derives at least partially from physiological differences between men and women. In support of this hypothesis, he (p. 5) cites Wagman, who discovered that in general males fantasize more aggressive, assertive, sexual, heroic, and other self-aggrandizing themes, while women's fantasies typically involve passive, narcissistic, affiliative, and physical attractiveness themes.

Mischel, in brief, presents evidence supporting a biological basis for male aggressive tendencies, but he recognizes also that aggressive behavior is not simply a masculine personality trait. Other theorists (e.g., Roger Johnson, 1972) suggest that both the development and manifestations of aggression are tied to sociocultural conditioning. McCord, McCord, and Howard (1961) discovered that aggressive boys frequently come from homes in which the parents are rejecting or inconsistent in their guidance, constantly fighting themselves and undermining each other's values. Feshbach (1970) found physical punishment to be the variable most strongly related to the development of aggressive behavior.

An important function of conditioning is to direct aggression toward socially rationalized goals. The intention of this process may be to reinforce differences between the sexes—boys may be taught to channel their aggression into self-protection or armed combat, whereas girls may be instructed to value verbal aggression above the physical kind—but the results are not always clear-cut. Individual differences in aggressive behavior are evident in both sexes. As Roger Johnson (1972) has demonstrated, women are not necessarily nonaggressive; 46 per cent of spouse-killing is the wife killing the husband, and women may also be responsible for lesser degrees of violence, such as child-beating or vehement family quarrels.

The question of the class basis of aggression has also engendered considerable discussion. Although physical aggressiveness is more typical of the working-class male (Rainwater, 1966), Kanin (1967, 1969) has noted some facets of the sexual aggressiveness of college males by comparing a group who reported they had been erotically assaultive with another group who had not been as aggressive. He found that his aggressive subjects were more likely to seek "pickups" who were educationally and socially beneath them, to misunderstand the intentions of these girls, to have unfavorable sentiments toward their own mothers, and to be slightly less religiously devout. He also found that various degrees of sexual aggression took place through all phases of their dating relationships except engagement. The sexually aggressive males tended to rate their sexual drives higher than the less aggressive males. Perhaps the most important of Kanin's findings, however, was that sexual assaultiveness on the part of an individual male is but one aspect of his general tendency toward strongly aggressive behavior.

Many of Kanin's less sexually aggressive males suffered psychologically painful experiences at the hands of girls with whom they sought meaningful relationships. They also professed unusually strong love for their mothers. Kanin attributes the painful experiences to the fact that less sexually aggressive males usually become more quickly involved in meaningful relationships.

Kanin's studies implicitly demonstrate both that male sexual aggressiveness can transcend class and educational barriers and that males are not of necessity sexually aggressive. Kanin also discovered that when male aggressiveness and female receptivity occur together, they frequently operate in a complementary relationship. Many of the girls who had sexual relations with his aggressive males willingly engaged in tongue-kissing, genital petting, and other stimulative acts. Most men are likely to interpret such participation as an invitation.

Finally, it is important to remember that competition — especially competition for the most desired females — may be tied to a male's sexual aggressiveness and also to his sense of self-worth. Men with the highest self concepts are most apt to seek desirable women (Murstein, 1971). Men with low self concepts usually cannot compete successfully for such women, and indeed they may prefer less attractive wives or girlfriends because they are afraid of losing more attractive ones.

SADISM AND DOMINANCE

The desire to dominate and subdue a female during the sexual encounter is another facet of masculinity that is strongly felt by many men. In the man-woman relationship, society traditionally expected the male to do most of the pursuing. The modern male, of course, can only sexually dominate a woman if he convinces her that she wants to be dominated by him, for this same woman may categorically refuse to allow other men to control her. The competitive male, however, may still "win" his girl's affection and thus her willingness to be dominated, pursued, and even playfully subdued by him.

Some couples play at sexual sadism, with definite limitations established on the extent to which one partner or the other may go. If the couple play sexual games involving light paddling or temporary subjugation, it is most often the woman who is expected to play the submissive role. Many women "feel more feminine" if they relate sexually to a reasonably (in their view) dominant male.

Certainly it is true that some women are more dominating than men, but others are apt to consider them somewhat masculine. Even if a woman is dominant in nonsexual matters, she is unlikely to have a desire to dominate most of her sexual liaisons. Men are still generally regarded as the masters of sexual interaction — as knowing the proper moves, techniques, and timing to bring out the erotic best in their mates.

VOYEURISM

There is little doubt that men are expected to enjoy looking at women. To be voyeuristic in a nonpathological manner is to want to look, to become sexually excited by looking, to notice the physical attributes of a woman, to enjoy sex vicariously through pictures and other images. Much group sex caters to the voyeuristic desire of the participants to watch others in sexual interaction.

Voyeurism is related to the competitive strivings of the male through the oft-implied axiom that others may look at and admire the beauty of one's mate but they may not touch or ogle too much. This is the male's basic dilemma: having sought out the most attractive girl and convinced her to accept him as husband or lover, he is now in danger of losing her because of the very beauty that initially attracted him. A high level of voyeurism toward his wife by other men is a two-edged sword. His ego is both raised and reminded of its vulnerability to threat.

ADVENTURESOMENESS

Generally, males are more socially rewarded than women for being bold, daring, rash, and impulsive, or at least they are less frequently censured for engaging in adventuresome behavior. The man's sense of adventure is so highly instilled by the culture that some women accept their mate's searches for other sexual partners as "natural to men." It is very often the husband who must introduce new varieties of sexual behavior into the marriage, and it is usually the man who persuades his wife to join nudist colonies or mate-exchanging clubs.

The female sexual adventuress, while more acceptable than formerly, is still likely to be pictured in many quarters as wicked and immoral, while her male counterpart is accepted as normal and healthy. A man's presumed need for sexual variety is seen as one aspect of his adventuresome nature. That many women support this sociocultural definition of maleness is evidence of the strength of social conditioning. The fact that a larger percentage of modern women are accepting the notion that they too should enjoy sex with more than one partner in no way negates the view of the mainstream of American womanhood that sexual variation is primarily an interest and prerogative of men.

FREEDOM FROM GUILT

Supposedly, men are freer than women of the restraints imposed by anticipated guilt. It is clear, nevertheless, that men are not entirely free of sexual conscience (Bell, 1966; Ellis, 1961). Shortly we will look at the author's finding that personal moral scruples (and thus anticipated guilt) are one of the most important reasons why males avoid premarital coitus. One source of guilt is religion, since the more devout males tend to avoid all unapproved sexual relationships. For men, guilt is an effective inhibiter of sexual responding and is often a factor in impotence. Certainly there is much variety in the depth and intensity of all guilt, but for many males guilt drops in effectiveness with sexual arousal and returns in greater intensity after sexual release. It is the anticipated fear of the aftereffects of sexual participation that keeps many men and women from engaging in sexual interaction.

A word about the nature of modern guilt is in order at this time. In days past, guilt was related to the transgression of moral codes and to some extent, it continues to be, but today guilt is connected more with shame. In both sexes, guilt, shame, and related feelings are products largely of feared sexual inadequacy. Inadequacy of technique, failure to arouse one's partner to orgasm, and the inability to respond fully can all contribute to the male's sense of sexual failure and thus to his concept of himself as a less than worthy partner. Yet although many males tie their inability to arouse their sexual partners to faulty technique, a man's attitudes toward women in general and to his sexual partner in particular (as well as the general quality of their relationship) are probably more important. Modern sexual guilt, in other words, is often the result of incorrectly understanding the sexual nature of women.

SELF-CONTROL

Two cultural myths surround the question of the male's sexual self-control. According to one paradigm, men (and especially younger men) become so sexually excited that they are unable to control themselves. Mothers warn their daughters not to enter compromising situations, emphasizing that men may deliberately seek to place girls in such positions and that under sexual tension neither partner may be able to control the emotions adequately. The second stereotype is often seen on television: just after the star attracts a pretty young woman to his bed, a sudden emergency or solution to a problem confronts him. The gallant man turns his attention to the emergency or solution, tenderly kisses the girl goodby, extends his apologies, and then leaves her waiting longingly. Although the hero is very capable of seducing the admiring female, he is such a cool person sexually that he can turn off his ardor in favor of duty. Of course, neither of these extremes generally fits the facts.

As our knowledge of the male's sexual needs has increased, it has become apparent that erotic needs are well within the control of most men. In a laboratory experiment, Laws and Rubin (1969) discovered that their male subjects could exert considerable control over their sexual responses when specifically instructed to do so. The subjects were required to control their erections upon demand, even in the presence of normally stimulating pornographic movies. The four subjects who comprised the major portion of the experiment were able to restrain their erections with minimal difficulty. A repeated experiment with other subjects produced similar results (Henson and Rubin, 1971).

Kirkendall (1967) studied the kinds of sexual decisions made by college men. He discovered that 42 per cent of his male subjects had on at least one occasion rejected intercourse, even though the women involved were apparently willing. In turn, 45 per cent of the subjects stated that they had been rejected in their approach for coitus, while an equal number reported that the decision-making process had at least once led them actually to engage in sexual relations. At one time or another, 57 per cent had made a mutual decision with the girl to avoid intercourse. Thirteen per cent of Kirkendall's subjects had never been in a situation requiring them to make a decision about coitus.

In all, 348 decisions out of 558 possibilities were made in which Kirkendall's male subjects renounced (often mutually with their partners) chances for sexual intercourse. Thus although there was considerable sexual activity among these subjects, much of it was short of coitus. The study clearly demonstrates that men have substantial control over their sexual behavior, if not necessarily over their desires.

SENSITIVITY

Men are expected to have a moderate amount of sensitivity to the sexual needs of both themselves and their partners. In this case, to be sensitive to another is to be aware of her needs and desires, to appreciate her because she does have needs, to be empathic to those needs in a positive manner, and to help her fulfill her needs and desires in such a way that she will be rewarded. Sensitivity, of course, is not simply a social demand on males but applies equally to women. Men, however, are called upon to be more controlled in their emotional responses and thus their sensitivity is reduced accordingly. Balswick and Peek (1971) comment on the inexpressive male. The male in our society, they believe, is specifically taught to stifle his emotions. Inexpressive males are of two types: those who have developed positive feelings toward women and those who relate without any special positive feelings. A man may learn through a series of increasingly involved relationships to become situationally expressive. Consequently, he may learn to be emotionally open to his wife but not to other women. Balswick and Peek see the ability to be expressive only to one's wife as functional in maintaining marriage, but they remind us that the inexpressive male must go through a period of unlearning his inexpressiveness if he is to relate to his wife in a mean-

ingful way. At any rate, because many men have not learned to be emotionally expressive, they often interact sexually with reduced passion.

THE MALE SEXUAL SELF

Clearly, much of the male's self-image is based on his own assessment of his sexual prowess. Little scientific evidence exists regarding
the male's image of his sexual self, partly because males have traditionally been thought to exaggerate their sexual accomplishments and
partly because men are more guarded than women in their general self-
expressiveness.

Nevertheless, clinicians are well acquainted with problems of impotency based on feelings of inadequacy and are quick to point out to wives
the importance of helping their husbands feel secure during such
periods of impotency. Much of the male's self-image depends upon his
ability to live up to the expectations he has of himself. These expectations are correlated with his ability to evaluate correctly his capacities to
relate to others intimately and to bring into dynamic equilibrium his
own needs, the demands of others, and the requirements of living in his
society.

FACTORS ENHANCING A MAN'S SEXUAL
SELF-IMAGE

A man builds his sexual self-image on his perception of the quality
and quantity of his past sexual experiences, on his value systems, on ratings by dating partners and male peers, and on his success in the nonsexual spheres of his life. It is apparent that those things which any particular male will find rewarding are closely related to his ideas of
masculinity. His capacity to excite his mate, the intensity of her sexual
desire for him, his ability to introduce and participate in sexual variety,
his position of leadership in the sexual encounter, and his ability to bring
about conception are some of the important factors that may contribute to
his concept of his sexual self.

FACTORS LIMITING A MAN'S SEXUAL
SELF-IMAGE

Any of the factors that are capable of enhancing a man's concept of
his sexual self are also capable of reducing that image. For many men,
the failure of their wives to reach orgasm at least part of the time is a sign
of their own masculine failure. The male who responds with high levels

of emotion and sensuousness may, especially if his mate is impatient for coitus, feel insecure about himself. The major influence on a man's sexual self-image is undoubtedly the type of feedback he receives from his partner. He is most vulnerable to negative feedback when he is in love with her.

THE MALE'S EXPERIENCE OF THE SOCIAL MODEL OF HIS SEXUALITY

Most men have assimilated the social model of male sexuality to a high degree, and living up to that model is an important aspect of their sexual adjustment. They find it particularly difficult to cope with needs — such as those for dependency — that do not fit this model. Some males fight off dreaded feelings of dependency to such a degree that they fail in one interpersonal relationship after another.

Another aspect of the social model of male sexuality is that after midlife men experience a marked reduction in their sexual powers. While it is true that the older male's sexual responsiveness is reduced, evidence will shortly be presented that indicates sexual activity can continue well into the later years of life. Despite this evidence, however, many men follow the social model of declining sex with advancing age and in effect give up their sexual lives and the contributions that these lives have made to their self-images.

MALE DEFENSES

If anything threatens the male's self-image, he may employ a variety of measures to defend himself against undue anxiety or feelings of rejection. In general, men are most likely to use force and power, withdrawal, and denial as methods of controlling themselves and their mates sexually. A man may simply shrug off threats to himself as untrue. Or he may withdraw from the relationship, either by developing an attitude of not caring or by actually leaving physically. Another favorite defense is to project personal inadequacies onto his mate or onto the circumstances surrounding their relationship. Again, he might use aging as a means of denying or devaluing his sexual feelings. Some men react to their unacceptable sexual impulses by a reaction-formation in which harshness, insensitivity, and even brutality replace their usual levels of interaction. Others defend themselves against their inability to meet the sexual demands of women by attempting to keep them in subjection, convincing them that they are "bad" if they are more sexy than men.

MALE SEXUAL RESPONSIVENESS

There appears to be a greater consistency of sexual needs among males than among females. Because of this consistency, men are said to have "stronger sex drives" than women (Dengrove, 1961; Kinsey et al., 1948, p. 543). There also appears to be greater uniformity of sexual impulses among males. The wider variation for women has been noted by the Kinsey group (1953, p. 681) and by other researchers as well. Nevertheless, the suspicion is growing that the supposedly stronger sex drive of the male is an artifact of culture.

ATTITUDES AND RESPONSIVENESS TO WOMEN

A major erotic stimulant for men is women. Very often a man is first attracted to a woman by her physical beauty; only later do intelligence, personality, and other factors come into play. Despite all the emphasis on power, masculinity, and other barriers to the man-woman relationship, it is clear that many men are quite considerate of their mates or sexual partners. The mutual sharing of feelings, companionship, and similar interpersonal growth factors is the aim of most (perhaps the majority) of men, and this desire for mutual sharing may last a lifetime (Stinnet, Carter, and Montgomery, 1972).

Although most permanent and semi-permanent relationships seem to have many desirable qualities, a number of authors have noted that women are often treated as objects instead of as persons. As an offshoot of this recognition, the need for individuals to relate to each other more sensitively has become widely acknowledged (Jourard, 1971; Zehv, 1970a). One of the ways in which men tend to treat women as objects is through the use of power. Brenton (1966) has pointed out that the double standard, with its effect of depersonalization, is one of the male's major power tools in his relationships with women. When a man overuses his power (in his mate's estimation), the sexual aspects of the relationship may suffer.

Men often expect an emotional response from their sexual partners that they themselves would be unable to exhibit. Greater sensuousness and passion in erotic encounters is more feminine than masculine; consequently, many males appear either unable or unwilling to give themselves up to full sexual-sensuous release. Furthermore, there is evidence that men are not as playful about their sexual encounters as some women can be. Carolyn Symonds (1971) reports that in the nude "touchy-feely" groups she and her husband operate to train individuals to appreciate their own sensuousness, the women are more apt to be playful than the men. The greater reluctance of men to expose what they consider weakness seems well established. The possibility that many men resent the greater ability of women to communicate their sexual-emotional selves needs to be investigated. Symonds and others have reported the apparent enjoyment that many men feel while watching women relate to each other in a sensuous manner. Could it be that males vicariously experience the deeper emotions of women by watching them relate intimately?

The ambivalent attitudes of men toward women should also be mentioned. Men may place their mates on pedestals at one time and demote them at another. The major religions have emphasized the superiority of men and at the same time have made women responsible for many of the male's difficulties. It was Eve, not Adam, who first sinned, and this concept of woman as temptress of man has continued to be reinforced by both pornography and religion, two strange bedmates indeed. Females are at the same time desirable and undesirable, and while single college males feel that other men's daughters ought to be sexually liberated, they have a much more conservative attitude about their own future daughters. This is another facet of the double standard: men may view women as objects to be loved at a male's whim or as oversexed temptresses, but they have difficulty believing that a woman may simply enjoy sex for itself alone. Greenwald (1968) comments on the male's apparent inability to accept as fact the notion that women can enjoy sex: ". . . many of them are not convinced that women are really interested in sex" (p. 653).

The old idea that women cause men to "fall" has not gone out of existence as much as it has gone underground, hidden by social convention or subconscious thinking. As long as sexual interaction involves guilt, a need for someone to project that guilt onto will remain, and women have fit the bill from time immemorial. The history of the man-woman relationship is blighted with many instances of vindictive attitudes, and modern education does precious little to alter this unhappy heritage. Part of the education of men, I believe, should be aimed at teaching them the art of appreciating women's humanness. The approval of a woman just because she is a woman and not because she fits some norm or has accomplished some feat or has achieved in the occupational world should do much to bring the return of real passion to heterosexual relationships.

RESPONSES TO OTHER STIMULI

Men are responsive to a wider variety of sexual stimulants than women. They are more likely to become aroused from observing others in sexual interaction, from fantasy, from observing animals in coitus, and from viewing all forms of pornography. Males are more likely to produce frankly sexual literature or other artistic productions. One out of four males will make some response to sadomasochistic stories, while only one out of eight females will respond. Females do react more to romantic stories and movies and to being bitten during sexual arousal. The preceding data are from Kinsey et al. (1953, pp. 642–689).

The greater interest in sexual matters which the male professes is often turned into action. The men in our society are more likely than women to seek sexual relationships, are apt to engage in a broader spectrum of sexual behavior, and are likely to have had erotic relationships with a larger number of partners. It is common knowledge that, in our society, men are more sexually oriented than women.

Rosen and Turner (1969) discovered that exposure to the mildly pornographic book *Candy* was greater among men than among women. These researchers found that older males were less likely to have read *Candy* than younger ones, and that among religious groups Catholic males were more likely to have read the novel than Protestants or Jews. Depth of religious sincerity did not significantly deter males from reading *Candy*, although it was an important deterrent for females.

Schmidt, Sigusch, and Meyberg (1969) studied the emotional and behavioral reactions of German men to viewing photographs of sexual interaction, including pictures of coitus and oral-genital relations. They found that viewing pornography, even hard-core pornography, did not result in any significant amount of sexual disinhibition, that their subjects' degree of sexual arousal depended upon their general degree of liberality or conservatism, and that the only significant increase in reported sexual behavior after viewing the pictures was an increase in masturbation. Only a very slight increase in heterosexual activity was encountered.

In another German study (Sigusch, Schmidt, Reinfeld, and Wiedemann-Suttor, 1970), men and women were compared on their responses to pornographic slides. All these men and women were coitally experienced. The slides depicted 24 themes (from simple nudity through kissing, petting, oral-genital relations, and coitus) and were rated by the subjects on the degree of erotic responsiveness the slides aroused and on the favorableness-unfavorableness of the subjects' attitudes toward each depicted scene. Seventeen of the slides were rated significantly more arousing by the men. Female subjects tended to consider male nudes somewhat less than exciting, but the men found female nudes quite stimulating. Although the men gave higher arousal and favorableness ratings to slides of petting, oral-genital contact, and coitus than the women, there were far fewer sex-specific differences than for the lone nudes. In fact, in their ordering of the slides' erotically stimulating effects, women gave the first five ranks to petting and coital scenes.

Men, then, have responded for some time to a wide variety of sexual stimulants, including women as sexual beings, pornographic material of all types, couples in sexual interaction, and themselves.

FANTASY

A man's fantasy about sexual interaction is often greater than his actual behavior. Some men will resort to fantasies rather than seek the same activity with a partner. In their masturbation fantasies, men picture every sort of sexual scene possible and some that are impossible from a physical point of view. Many a man's sexual fantasies add to his passion and increase his enjoyment, especially with a sexual partner with whom he has had considerable experience. Fantasy assists a man in reducing boredom when he finds his mate less stimulating than he desires. Some men dream of homosexual activity, sometimes envisioning themselves as the participants and sometimes fantasizing their wives or girl-friends in lesbian relationships. Many men have taken flight into fantasy while engaging in extramarital affairs.

What specific sexual fantasies have men been known to have? Men masturbating have reported thinking of every sexual trick imaginable, including sex with animals, intercourse in impossible positions, self-fellation, cunnilingus, anal coitus, whipping or otherwise bringing pain to a partner, or being whipped or tortured by someone else. Also reported are fantasies of masturbating or orally stimulating another man or woman, incestuous scenes, or mind-pictures of lesbian relationships. Some males imagine themselves in the woman's sexual role, and some who have a particular fetish see themselves interacting with it.

The author asked men and women college students to write a brief account of what they considered a superior night of intimacy. Here is a typical male result:

> As I stepped into her living room, I noticed she lived alone. That meant one of two things. Either she wants to get away from it all or she wants to get "it." I found out a short time later as she let her robe fall to the floor while guiding me toward the bedroom. Emotion triumphed over circumstance when finally she insisted that I take off her pants — and in a hurry. The game was over. I pulled her roughly to the floor and took her body.

The direct, aggressive approach of many men is well depicted in this story, as are certain assumptions about women. For many men, fantasized sexual relationships are more physical and impersonal than in reality these same men would admit to or engage in. Such is the powerful influence of social conditioning on male sexuality.

SOCIAL APPROVAL

Men, of course, vary in their needs for social approval, but almost all men modify their sexual behavior in accordance with the type of reinforcement provided by the significant members of their segment of society. Some men have strong needs for such social approval and thus limit their sexual responses, although not necessarily their sexual arousal. Schill and his associates (1970) found that men with a high need for social approval inhibited their responses to double-entendre words regardless of the sex of the experimenter, but men with low social-approval needs gave significantly more sexual responses when the sex of the experimenter was male. Schill suggests that men with strong social-approval needs may be operating on a generalized expectancy that sexual responses are never publicly appropriate and are largely disapproved. Low-social-approval-need (nondefensive) males may operate from expectancies based mainly on specific cues in the situation. This hypothesis will need more research before it can be accepted or rejected, however.

Although the correlation between religiosity and social conformity is probably high and positive, the Schill et al. findings and other similar studies (Byrne and Sheffield, 1965; Galbraith, 1968; Galbraith and Mosher, 1970) suggest that social disapproval may be as strong a force as introjected religious codes in controlling the male's sexual behavior. Many men, then, do suffer inhibitions to a high degree, and some may have more difficulty giving up these inhibitions than any woman.

VIRGIN AND NONVIRGIN MALES

Clearly, men are not a homogeneous group in regard to their sexual interests, attitudes, and activities. It was pointed out earlier that biological sex impulses vary, with some individuals having considerable push while others have almost no biological spark impelling them to focus on sexual stimuli. This certainly must be true for men as well as women, and indeed we find many sex researchers stating that some of their women subjects were more erotically oriented than the average man. In spite of differences in biology, however, I suspect that learning is what makes men differ as widely as they do.

Recently, Wallace and Wehmer (1972) compared the attitudes toward visual pornography of generally conservative men and men who were more liberal on a number of nonsexual factors. The more liberal men accepted and intellectually evaluated the pornography, while the conservatives reacted quite negatively and considered it unacceptable. In another study, Glassberg (1970) discusses the quandary of a male virgin who came for counseling after being rejected by his girl-friend because he would not engage in coitus with her. Glassberg defends the male's right to be different and to be conservative without being made to feel unmanly. In an analysis of Glassberg's article, Ard (1970) raises the question of whether or not the average male has thought out the values by which he guides his life and pleads for more introspection on the part of males as to what personally constitutes manhood for them. I am reminded at this point of Barbara and Steve:

> Steve was well known on campus for his sexual prowess. An
> athlete of some renown, he was considered quite desirable and had
> dated a large number of girls. Eventually he met Barbara and they
> began going steady. Barbara, however, refused to have coitus with
> Steve and in spite of his reputation allowed him only light petting.
> Eventually they married. After two weeks of marriage, they were al-
> most at the breakup point, since both were very dissatisfied with their
> sexual relationship. Barbara had married because she thought that a
> man with Steve's reputation would make an excellent sexual partner.
> But because she had made him wait for sex until after marriage, he had
> inferred that she would not make sexual demands upon him and that
> by marrying her he could free himself from having to live up to a repu-
> tation he did not want. Their basic problem was failure of com-
> munication: Barbara hoping for a satisfying sex life, was dismayed to
> discover that Steve's desire for coitus was not nearly as great as her
> own.

Clearly, many men are pushed into being more or less sexual than
they wish. Like the gunfighters of the Old West, some maintain their
reputations regardless of personal cost. What are the differences and
similarities between coitally experienced males and those without such
experience?

A RECENT STUDY

In 1972, the author completed a study comparing coitally inexperienced males (virgins) with others who reported in a personal, structured
interview that they had experienced coitus. This latter group I labeled
male nonvirgins (MNV). The MNV group was compared with the virgin
(MV) group in regard to their experiences, responses, and attitudes on a
number of variables. The 40 MV and 50 MNV subjects were asked to estimate their responses to the best of their ability. Repeat interviews and
cross-checks with girl-friends served to indicate that the data collected
were highly reliable and reasonably valid. No claim is made that these
are reports of actual responses and feelings during sexual interaction.
Indeed, most subjects were aware of considerable variation in their sexual feelings, responses, and pleasure from time to time, but each subject
was able to make some estimate of what he considered his "average"
responses. Reports were categorized by the number of subjects placing
themselves in each dimension and were statistically compared using
chi-square.

All subjects were from a large Eastern university or a small state
college, with the sample about evenly divided between the two schools.
No differences were found between subjects from the university and
those from the state college. The age range of these white males was
from 18 to 24 years.

While these reports emphasize the self-experiences of particular
males, generalizations to the larger population must await further study

with more representative samples. This study, then, is exploratory and suggestive but not definitive.

In Chapter 4 the attitudes of these virgin and nonvirgin males toward premarital sex, extramarital sex, homosexual relationships, pornography, and sex research were presented. In this section we will discuss dating, petting, attitudes, and experiential dimensions as reported by these men.

Dating

Reference to Table 10-1 reveals that virginal men dated significantly fewer girls, began steady dating at a later age, and had fewer girl friends they considered as steady dates than the coitally experienced males. Casual dating was not significantly related to coital experience. Although more of the MV group reported that they began steady dating below age 14, it was the number of virginal men who were 19 or more before they began steady dating that contributed most to the reported differences.

These data suggest that for males both the breadth and intensity of dating experience are significantly related to the probability of engaging in coital activity. (Parellel studies of women showed a *tendency* for dating characteristics to be related to the probability of coital experience,

TABLE 10-1. SOME DATING CHARACTERISTICS OF MALE VIRGINS AND NONVIRGINS

Dimension	Percent of Group in Each Dimension*		Significance
	MV†	MNV†	
Percent of group who had ever			
dated 10 or fewer girls	48	26	
dated 21 or more girls	8	52	.01
Number of steady girl-friends			
none	8	4	
one	33	10	
two	33	34	.01
three	23	16	
four or more	5	36	
Age began steady dating			
14 or less	15	10	
15–16	28	42	
17–18	25	44	.01
19 or more	33	4	
Age began casual dating			
14 or less	12	32	
15–16	68	52	NS‡
17 or more	20	16	

*Percentage errors due to rounding.
†MV = male virgins; MNV = male nonvirgins.
‡Not statistically significant.
Ns were as follows: MV = 40; MNV = 50.

but the female data did *not* reach statistical significance.) Both the male and female data are in agreement with the findings of Simon, Berger, and Gagnon (1972).

Four possible explanations for the differences in dating patterns (and thus in coital experience) of the virgin and nonvirgin males suggest themselves to this author. First, men from more liberal backgrounds may participate more frequently in dating and similar social activities and thus may have more opportunity to find cooperative coital partners. A second possibility is that those men with the strongest sexual urges date most extensively in quest of potential sexual liaisons. Two other potential factors may be inferred from Ira Reiss' hypotheses (1967, pp. 160–164): (3) men who are more attached to their parents or who have had greater responsibility for the maintenance of the home may date less extensively; and (4) those men most intensely devoted to their careers and studies perhaps date less widely. Only future research can ascertain the accuracy of these four possibilities.

Petting

Coitally experienced men were significantly more active in a variety of petting behaviors, ranging from fondling of clothed breasts to such activities as oral-genital relations and interfemoral intercourse. Table 10–2 indicates some of the erotic behaviors that differentiated the MV from the MNV group.

Coitally experienced males reported a greater number of petting partners, more petting experiences per month, and a greater likelihood of achieving orgasm from petting. On the average, MNV subjects began petting a year earlier than the virginal males, were more highly aroused at the sight of a live, nude female, and had less difficulty in becoming satisfactorily aroused.

Other items not included in Table 10–2 are the number of men in each group who had experienced fellatio (66 per cent of MNV males, 5 per cent of MV group); cunnilingus (70 per cent of MNV males, 13 per cent of MV group); and interfemoral intercourse (78 per cent of MNV group, 40 per cent of MV men). Among the coitally experienced, 54 per cent had played sex games, such as musical chairs, strip poker, and so forth. Only 18 per cent of the virginal males had played sex games.

Taken as a whole, these data indicate that intense experiences with erotic petting are highly correlated with the probability of engaging in coitus. Two points need further consideration, however. One of these is the nonsignificant differences between the groups, and we shall return to this shortly. The other concerns the extent to which the males used "strong psychological persuasion" or physical force to obtain coitus. Forty-eight per cent of the MNV group reported that they had deliberately employed "strong psychological persuasion" to convince their partners that they should engage in coitus. Such persuasion included threats to tell others about any intimacies that had taken place and

TABLE 10–2. A COMPARISON OF MALE VIRGINS AND NONVIRGINS
ON SEVERAL DIMENSIONS IN A STUDY BY SHOPE (1972)

Dimension	Group MV°	MNV°	Level of Significance
Median number of petting partners	1.75	3.25	.01
Per cent of group reporting four or more petting partners	23	76	.01
Median age began petting	17.2	16.1	.05
Per cent who first petted at age 18 or later	53	26	.01
Estimated number of times petted per month within past two years	63%: 4 or fewer times; 37%: 5 or more times	28%: 4 or fewer times 72%: 5 or more times	.01
Ever climax from petting? Yes	38%	60%	.05
Degree of arousal from looking at live, nude female Much to very much	58%	80%	.05
Reported level of difficulty in becoming satisfactorily aroused Some Much	28% 10%	10% 4%	.05

°MV = male virgins; MNV = males with coital experience.

threats to elaborate such intimacies. Other tactics consisted of refusal to
continue to date the girl unless she provided coitus and implications that
she was not coitally responsive because she was frigid or immature.
Only 13 per cent of the virgin group had tried such tactics, and all had
failed. How many coital decisions were mutual was not ascertained, but
apparently quite a few coital contacts were made on an accommodation
basis rather than through consensual agreement.

The men themselves accounted for their successes and failures in
terms of their personal persuasive powers, the types of girls they were
apt to try to coerce, and their estimation of the likelihood that the girls
would report them or make their aggressive qualities known.

Some Similarities

An emphasis on the differences between the MV and MNV groups
should not overshadow the many similarities. Perhaps most importantly,
the degree of pleasure and enjoyment that the men received from those
activities in which they had engaged was nearly identical. Thus virgin
men were not refraining from coitus because they received less pleasure
from petting. Furthermore, the level of arousal from petting was the
same in both groups. The men in the two groups daydreamed about sexual activity to the same extent, began masturbation at nearly the same
median age (MNV group 12.8 years, MV group 13.5 years), stimulated
themselves an average of one and one-half times per week, and had not

changed their rate of petting within the past year. Slightly more of the MNV subjects desired sexual experiences with older, more erotically adroit women, but the difference between the groups was statistically nonsignificant.

Predicted marital happiness and sexual adjustment, as measured by the Adams Marital Happiness Prediction Inventory, were the same for both groups. On the basis of these limited data, then, coital experience before marriage seems unrelated to marital happiness and sexual adjustment for men.

It is obvious that large numbers of men without coital experience are quite sexually active in other domains and that lack of coital experience does not mean inability to enjoy many facets of erotic life. Male virgins, like female virgins, may be less sexually active, but they are by no means sexually inactive by any criteria other than coitus.

It should be strongly emphasized that male sexual interests, attitudes, responses, and pleasures are not constant. Male sexual proclivities are on a continuum, varying from individual to individual and within the same person from time to time. Categorizing provides a picture of discrete steps, but the actual situation is one of ebb and flow of erotic desires.

Premarital Coital Decisions

In this section we will examine the reasons why the men in the author's study began or avoided coitus by looking at the most important reason that each gave. We can then make some comparisons with other studies. Decision-making processes between unmarried pairs will be discussed in Chapter 12, Nonmarital Sex.

The probability of engaging in or refraining from premarital coitus depends upon many variables, some of which may be fortuitous, but we are concerned here with conscious decisions arrived at through rational or irrational means. Table 10–3 surveys each subject's single most important reason for beginning coitus or remaining virginal up to the time of the study. Almost half of the MV group stated that love and respect for the girls they were dating was the most important reason why they had not engaged in sexual intercourse. "Personal moral scruples" are the beliefs held by the male concerning the right or wrong of premarital sexual intercourse. Two men had avoided coitus because of respect for their parents' wishes. Taking the three reasons—love for the girl, personal moral scruples, and respect for parents' wishes—it is clear that person-centered reasons for avoiding premarital coitus were significant in these men's decisions. Although some of the men might have been refused had they asked for coitus, not all the women were unwilling, as the following remark to the author by the girl friend of one of the MV men testifies:

> We had progressed to the point where I had nothing on but my underpants when he asked me if it would be all right to continue. That disgusted me, and I immediately cooled off.

TABLE 10-3. MALE'S MOST IMPORTANT REASON FOR REFRAINING
FROM OR ENGAGING IN COITUS

Reason for Refraining from Coitus (MV Group)	Number of Subjects Giving Reason
Love and respect for girl	17 (43%)
Personal moral scruples	11 (28%)
Girl refused	5 (13%)
Fear of pregnancy	5 (13%)
Respect for parents' wishes	2 (05%)

Reason for First Engaging in Coitus (MNV Group)	Number of Subjects Giving Reason
Curiosity	23 (46%)
Because male wanted coitus	10 (20%)
Just seemed natural	8 (16%)
Love for girl	7 (14%)
Girl asked for coitus	2 (04%)

Driscoll and Davis (1971) found that among their virgin men, not being in love and personal moral scruples were exceeded as restraints on premarital coitus only by the fear of causing pregnancy. About 11 per cent of Driscoll and Davis' virgin males were unable to talk a girl into coitus — a figure about equivalent to that for my "girl refused" category. Driscoll and Davis found that as a restraint on premarital coitus, the necessity of love before engaging in intercourse was closely associated with moral scruples, postcoital shame, and fear or ruined reputation. For men as well as for women, the feeling of being in love is a powerful force in reducing guilt and anxiety about coital activity.

Curiosity is also an important reason for beginning coitus for both men and women. One in five men felt they had such an intense need for coitus that their dates accommodated them. Others felt that an evening with a girl had just naturally led to their first coital encounter. Apparently, it is rare for a man to have his first coital experience because a female asks for it, yet two MNV men claimed this was how they began their coital activity. The sexual partners of both these men were experienced while the men themselves were sexually naive, reminding us that some experienced women will openly let the man know when they are interested in coitus.

In summary, the preceding evidence clearly demonstrates that virginity is not so much a specific category, except when arbitrarily defined, as it is a continuum. Virginity may be defined as the state of not having engaged in sexual intercourse, but intercourse is but one aspect of the sexual responsiveness continuum. Thus for both men and women the dichotomy of virginity-nonvirginity, like so many operationally defined terms, does not do justice to reality if it blinds us to the fact that there are many degrees of sexual involvement.

OTHER ASPECTS OF MALE SEXUALITY

UNMARRIED MEN

Some males remain unmarried because they wish to be free to pursue their occupations, some because they wish to avoid the responsibilities of marriage, some because they prefer sexual relationships without commitment, and some because they prefer exclusively homosexual relationships. According to Kinsey (1948, p. 626), half the men among his subjects who remained unmarried until age 39 had engaged in homosexual relationships. Many of these would never marry.

Rallings (1966) investigated the backgrounds of married and never-married men. She concluded that on the whole sociological variables were unable to differentiate her groups. She found no differences between married and never-married men in regard to their parent-child affectionate relationships, type of home discipline, religion, or educational level attained. Rallings did find that never-married males were more likely to come from homes in which the father worked at odd hours compared to other men in the neighborhood or from homes in which the parents were in "disgrace" because they were unmarried.

The reasons why males never marry appear to be quite personal and idiosyncratic. It is certain that those who remain single hoping for greater sexual variety stand a high chance of being disappointed, since all studies indicate that the married male has greater access to all forms of sex than the unmarried male. One additional reason some males may remain unmarried is that they have low sexual needs. John was one such individual:

> A factory worker with no strong ambitions, John lived alone. He did not care for pornography or other sexual stimulants, nor was he repelled by them. He was not religious. None of the usual reasons for engaging or being interested in sex seemed to apply to John. He claimed to have no more homosexual than heterosexual interest, and there was no reason to disbelieve him. He never condemned the sexuality of others; on the contrary, he seemed to understand their needs. Perhaps the most significant erotic relationship John had ever engaged in was with an attractive, neighborhood prostitute who had been hired by his friends to "teach" him how to respond sexually. Because of his professed desire to gain some sexual feelings, John went along with this scheme, but according to the girl, he became neither erotically nor emotionally involved, despite her best efforts.

Some men desire both homosexual and heterosexual relationships, and many of these bisexual males marry. While the exclusive homosexual sometimes marries a female as a cover for his activities, the bisexual may make an excellent sexual partner. Matthews (1969) has written of her sexual relationships with bisexual males. She finds them to be very satisfactory partners and feels that if the wives of these men are adequately counseled, no disasters need result from their bisexual interests.

AGING AND MALE SEXUALITY

The variability of male sexual interests has been pointed out previously, but one additional facet of this variability needs to be emphasized. The male who has a low sexual interest in his youth is very apt to continue to have low interest throughout his life span. He will also begin sexual interaction later and forgo it earlier than those who are sexually active right from the beginning.

Although there is some slowing down in a man's sexual activities as he grows older, the change is less among more sexually active males. Rubin (1965) indicates that seven out of ten healthy married couples over 60 engage in coitus at least once a month. Masters and Johnson (1966) make the point that it is difficult to reawaken sexual interests in the older person once they have been allowed to wane. The older male's sexual interests may be enhanced by a deeper esthetic appreciation and more willingness to explore sensually rather than simply seek immediate physical release.

The older male, then, does have one distinct advantage: he has had a longer time to free himself from undesirable restraints upon his eroticism. He may permit more of what Bruce (1967) has described as femininity in the male. These feminine traits that Bruce feels every man should possess include an urge to self-adornment and the personality projection that goes with increased self-care; reduction of the aggressive role; a love of and feeling for women which implies that the man wants to partake of what he reveres; and the needs to acquire virtue, to experience beauty, attractiveness, and goodness, and to evaluate these for himself by the same criteria used to evaluate them for others. In a word, older men can be more tender and gentle and less directly demanding in their sexual relationships, but there seems little reason for one to wait for the mellowing effects of age to achieve these ends.

As we have seen, the male, throughout his life span, is apt to have a greater interest in sexual matters than his wife. At every stage men are likely to set the pace for sexual encounters, while women simply follow their lead. Aging does not seem to affect this pattern. Pfeiffer, Verwoerdt, and Davis (1972) found that the men among their 45- to 69-year-old subjects had more interest and activity on all sexual indicators than their wives, and that any decline in sexual activity was attributed to the men by the women and by the men to themselves.

In brief, the older male may be slower, more mellow, and more tolerant in his sexuality than when he was younger. He will likely continue to have a greater interest in sex than women of the same age, and he will probably be more sexy as an older man if he has had an active and continuous interest in sex throughout his life span. Though he must accept a slowdown in his physiological reactions to sexual stimuli, there seems little reason for him to suppress his sexual interests in old age just because "that is what men are supposed to do."

MALE ATTITUDES TO BIRTH CONTROL

Unwed Fathers. Robbins and Lynn (1973) found that certain attitudes contributing to unwed fatherhood may occur in several generations of males. Although this hypothesis needs further exploration in a variety of populations, Robbins and Lynn did discover significant factors in their group of California Youth Authority wards. The subjects were all unwed fathers. Robbins and Lynn found that a significant number were themselves illegitimate children and had illegitimate siblings. These unwed fathers approved of their own children becoming unwed parents, approved of extramarital sex, and disapproved of the use of contraceptives, although they felt responsible for the pregnancies they caused.

The uniform rate of illegitimacy often found in families (especially lower-class ones) suggests that family attitudes toward contraception and unwed pregnancies are frequently handed down from generation to generation. This transmittal of attitudes may come more from example than from specific training, but in either case, realistic education about contraception and greater sensitivity to the needs of the mother and unborn child might be useful in breaking anticontraceptive attitudinal linkages.

Inner-City Youth. After distributing free condoms to a group of inner-city adolescents, Arnold (1972) followed up their reactions. Most of his subjects were still in secondary school, and 92 per cent were single. Their average age was 18.2 years. Arnold found that these young men used condoms in three out of four of their coital contacts, but only 17 per cent had ever discussed birth control with the girl. Only 15 per cent of the girls had ever discussed the use of condoms with the boy involved. The first source of condoms was a "friend," further attesting to the sociosexual relationships that occur among young people. Ninety-three per cent of these young men had used condoms prior to the beginning of the study. Half said they would marry a girl they made pregnant, 85 per cent were concerned with the specific problems that an illegitimate child might face and 60 per cent stated that the principal reason they used condoms was for the prevention of pregnancy. Arnold concludes that the stereotype of the exploitative inner-city male may lack validity, at least with regard to heterosexual coitus.

College Undergraduates. Bauman (1971) found that the condom was the most widely used contraceptive among a group of never-married undergraduates at a large southeastern university. Even though newer forms of birth control were available, students did not seem prone to use them. In fact, 60 per cent of men and women used no form or an unreliable form of contraception during first coitus, and about 40 per cent continued to use nothing or an unreliable form.

Coitus Interruptus. Cherniak and Feingold (1973) discuss coitus interruptus as well as other methods of birth control. The objection that coitus interruptus will prove physically harmful is absolutely unfounded they report. The psychological side effects are much more important, they believe, and include fear that the man will be unable to withdraw in time, apprehension of possible interruption before the woman reaches orgasm, and reduction of enjoyment associated with fear of pregnancy.

Sterilization. Nag (1973) found that sterilization has had a somewhat unexpected success, particularly in the United States. He reports that as many as 750,000 American men and women were sterilized in 1970. Of these 70 per cent were men. (In 1960, in contrast, 60 per cent of sterilizations were performed on women.) Thus as education concerning the effects of vasectomy increases, more men appear to be accepting the operation. Nag concludes that suspicion about oral contraceptives, fresh awareness of population growth problems, more willingness to talk openly about sexual matters, opposition from women's liberation groups to female-only methods, and greater awareness that vasectomy does not interfere with sexual activity all account for the increased number of vasectomized males.

In a follow-up study of 31 married couples in which the husband had had a vasectomy one to two years previously, Freund and Davis (1973) found no negative effects on sexual behavior or attitudes from the procedure. Vasectomy did not inhibit an early return to coitus or other sexual activity, and frequencies were either the same or increased. Eleven of the group had pain during the first coital contact following vasectomy, while 21 men experienced discomfort at other times, such as during urination or exercise. Only one man returned to the physician requesting relief from this discomfort, although 13 of the 21 who had such discomfort reported it to the physician. Ease and strength of erection were unaffected by the operation; neither were time from intromission to ejaculation, duration of ejaculation, and strength of ejaculation. Wives felt increases in feelings of sexual freedom, in ease of reaching orgasm, and in willingness to initiate coitus and to play an active role during erotic encounters. For the most part, Freund and Davis found that their subjects reported either no change or increased desire for sexual pleasure during coitus and orgasm. (Compare these findings with those of Ziegler and Rodgers, given in Chapter 11 under Female Attitudes to Birth Control.

Summary. Although the onus remains on women to protect themselves from unwanted pregnancies, the evidence suggests that many men are also quite concerned. The attitudes of men toward the newer contraceptive techniques are not constant. About half of college and working-class males resist such contraceptive forms as the Pill, vasectomy, and the as-yet-to-be-developed male oral contraceptive. Condoms appear more acceptable to males but have the inherent problem of irregular or careless use. Among those men who have had vasectomies, the overwhelming majority have found their sexual lives improved, and their sexual partners have likewise enjoyed the freedom from fear of pregnancy.

It would seem that the male who has produced the number of

children he desires would be more accepting of all forms of contraception, especially the more permanent ones. This assumption is tempered, however, by the fact that some males still rate their masculinity partially by their ability to beget offspring.

ABILITY TO BRING ABOUT CONCEPTION

The ability to bring about conception is a factor of paramount importance in many a male's self-estimation, and lower-class males are apt to be especially guarded about acceptance of contraceptives. Balswick (1972) found that 47 per cent of his male subjects objected to the use of a potential male contraceptive pill, that 51 per cent objected to the female Pill, and that 59 per cent would refuse a vasectomy. These lower-class males, 41 per cent white and 59 per cent black, indicated that the possible harmful effects of the Pill and the fact that contraceptive pills are "against nature" were their chief reasons for rejecting them as birth-control devices.

The commonest reason for rejecting a vasectomy is the desire "not to be cut on." Bauman and Udry (1972) found that black men who feel powerless to control major life problems, such as the future of their children, or who feel that the future looks dreary are apt *not* to use contraceptives. Some men fear contraceptives will reduce their sexual activity or pleasure, but Ziegler and Rodgers (1968) note that among their contraceptive-using subjects, sexual behavior either remained constant or advanced to higher levels.

Those males who have not conceived the number of children they want are most apt to reject contraception.

FATHERHOOD

The effects of fatherhood can be quite varied and equivocal. After the arrival of a child, the wife must divide her time and attention, and jealousy may become a greater problem if it existed before, as can the feeling of entrapment. If religion has been a quiescent issue between the couple, the arrival of a child may bring that problem to an acute and dramatic head. If money has been a problem and the couple have been dependent upon the wife's income, the loss of her earnings can be quite frustrating. In short, whatever difficulties existed for the couple previously, the arrival of a child is not likely to ease them. Often a new baby brings to light both spouses' dependency needs, frustrated achievement needs, feelings of isolation, or other personally damaging factors, and when this occurs the sexual relationship between the parents may be impaired.

When fatherhood seriously interferes with the male's erotic needs, he can be expected to fantasize sexual relations, temporarily sublimate his desires (perhaps by taking a stronger interest in work or sports), or seek a sexual partner outside of marriage. Because his children sometimes symbolize various threats to him, a husband may prefer sex with another woman.

It is equally important to recognize that fatherhood is an inherent source of pride for the majority of men. Some men become more interested in their children than in their mates. When the idea of fatherhood is positive, the man will often be willing to participate in household tasks, assume partial care of the baby, and engage in many roles he may before have shared only reluctantly. This closer working together can provide a couple harmony that enhances the sexual relationship. The male who has not felt his masculinity threatened by sharing roles with his wife before the arrival of children is likely to be the one who will provide the kind of help she needs once they have a family.

SUMMARY

The following generalizations concerning male sexuality were discussed in this chapter:

1. The sexual characteristics governing male sexuality are determined primarily by the culture, and this sociocultural image of male sexuality, like the one for masculinity, applies more universally than the social image of female sexuality applies to women.
2. Much of the male's sexual image of himself is dependent upon feedback he receives from his sexual partners.
3. The ability to bring about conception is very important to many males, especially those of the lower socioeconomic classes. This importance theoretically diminishes after the male has produced the number of children he desires.
4. Men utilize all of the usual defenses to fight off anxiety about their sexual prowess, but denial, projection, and the use of power seem especially important.
5. There seems to be a greater consistency and uniformity of sexual needs among men than among women.
6. Usually, men cannot respond as emotionally to sexual desires as women can.
7. Although males are in general more responsive to erotic stimuli than women, there are large numbers of men who are not very responsive to such stimuli, and some are less responsive than the average woman.
8. Fatherhood requires an adjustment in a couple's sexual life, with at least temporary reduction in the amount of sexual activity — a reduction some men do not tolerate well.
9. Growing older reduces the quantity and perhaps the intensity of the male's sexual interaction, but most males are active well into advanced age.
10. The chances of virgin males for marital happiness and sexual adjustment are neither better not worse than the chances of those who are sexually experienced.
11. The sexual behavior of virginal males is quantitatively lower and less intense than that of nonvirginal males, but there is no significant difference in the virginal male's reported arousal or pleasure from petting activities.

CHAPTER 11

FEMALE SEXUALITY

Any discussion of female sexuality must begin with recognition of the wide differences among women themselves. The sex-role attitudes of women range from almost total rejection of any overtly masculine expression to the nearly complete refusal of anything suggestive of femininity. Among the latter women one may find cases of confused gender identity, while many of the former have been subjected to especially strong traditionally feminine conditioning.

Despite the blurring of sex roles within recent years, the sexuality of the human female shows some striking differences from that of the male, and it is partially for this reason that feminist movements have failed to detour large numbers of women from the psychosocial roles traditionally identified with their gender (W. L. O'Neill, 1969). It is clear, nevertheless, that more and more women are demanding freedom of opportunity and self-determination in all spheres, including the emotional-sexual one. Female sexuality is growing, dynamic, and increasingly self-fulfilling. The traditional roles have not been abandoned, but slavery to those roles is less prevalent now than formerly.

SOME STEREOTYPES OF FEMALE SEXUALITY

In general, women are more receptive to social conditioning than men, and much of the conditioning of a woman's sexual nature comes from the culture in which she is reared (Bernard, 1968). Cohen (1955), for instance, found that almost all the adolescent girls in the Jamaican community that he studied claimed to have attained an orgasm from coital experience. He reports that the particular subculture of these young people permits them considerable sexual freedom. They feel little need for an affectionate relationship before engaging in sexual intercourse, and most early adolescent liaisons are begun for the physical satisfaction of the participants. The sexuality of these Jamaican adolescents thus reflects the rearing practices of their subculture.

The very religious girl usually behaves quite differently from her more liberal sister. However, women tend to a considerable extent to modify their behavior to fit the norms of the particular group with whom

205

they are in contact. Hence, a sexually promiscuous girl may respond quite modestly in the presence of certain groups, such as her family, whereas a girl who is normally less active sexually may be more liberal than usual when group norms call for it. There is, nevertheless, a socially stereotyped female sexuality with a long cultural history. These traditionally defined stereotypes of femininity include submissiveness, masochism, narcissism-exhibitionism, and guilt-inhibition complex.

Before examining some examples of behavior associated with each female stereotype, we should be aware that although the concepts traditionally associated with female sexuality remain, they have taken on some qualitative differences from the past. The same words do not necessarily refer to the same behavior as formerly. Nor should we assume that the components we are about to study are exclusively female: although they are more characteristic of women than of men, we shall see that they are, like aggressiveness, manifested in varying degrees by both sexes.

SUBMISSIVENESS

This complementary of male sexual aggressiveness and dominance refers more to a willingness to follow than to a humble acquiescence in any sexual behavior the male chooses. Most women will accept the leadership, pursuit, and suggestions of men they admire. The act of sexual submission, except in the face of physical force, is thus mostly a matter of willing surrender and of giving oneself to another. It is a cooperative event in which neither the male's aggressiveness nor the female's submissiveness is considered negative. In fact, the majority of men prefer on some occasions to switch roles and submit to their sexual partners.

Modern women are often as desirous of sexual relations as men, but even when they are not they may surrender to persuasion and pursuit. Sometimes women prefer to initiate sexual relationships and to dominate entire erotic encounters. Like all human traits, submissiveness is usually only partially expressed and is found mixed with dominance to varying degrees. In one sense, women have a subtle form of control over men during their sexual relationships, since they can react in ways that either enhance or retard the male's intensity of arousal.

MASOCHISM

Masochism, the receiving of pleasure and satisfaction from physical or psychological pain, was thought by Freud to be an aspect of female biology. Recently, however, others have expressed doubt that women are more biologically prone to need pain (Horney, 1967; Robertiello, 1970).

Like its complement sadism, masochism may be expressed in different intensities by both sexes, from such normal needs as being bitten to the point at which sexual pleasure is impossible in the the absence of physical pain. The latter instance is usually considered pathological, but masochism in its milder forms is often very sexually arousing and to some extent is part of many sexual encounters. There is, of course, another type of sadomasochism that does not involve conscious sexual intent, but we are considering only that which is part of sexual interplay.

Discipline, in which one partner voluntarily submits to the control of another for brief periods of sexual play, is another facet of masochism. As temporary play in erotic relationships, masochism is normal and does not necessarily represent punishment of a degrading nature. On the other hand, compulsive or extreme acts that produce permanent or serious physical or psychological pain cannot be other than pathological. Whatever its ramifications, masochism is traditionally considered an aspect of female sexuality.

NARCISSISM-EXHIBITIONISM

Nonpathological narcissism is the desire to be physically and psychologically attractive; exhibitionism is the willingness to be looked at and admired for one's beauty, personality, intelligence, and other personal attributes. Although males also wish to be admired and enjoy being told they are attractive, it is considered more a feminine trait to want to be thought of as pretty and sexually alluring because of this physical beauty. The normally narcissistic girl has a positive regard for herself both physically and psychologically. She is alert to sociocultural conditions and keeps herself posted on events of special importance to her particular mate. Only when the concentration on herself is overemphasized or becomes obnoxious to those around her can it be considered abnormal. The woman who thinks well of her body, intellect, behavior, and spirit is apt to make a better sexual partner.

The tendency to show off one's charms to the best advantage I have labeled "feminine exhibitionism." In our society feminine beauty is considered esthetically desirable, but although moral prejudices against displaying the human body have lessened, little has been done to enhance the nonerotic aspects of feminine beauty.

The shy, bashful girl of yesteryear is no longer in vogue, but moderate degrees of charm and coyness are still generally accepted as an aspect of femininity. Too much boldness too quickly can destroy the romantic and sexual interests of many men. Coyness demands special expertise, which comes only with increased experience.

THE GUILT-INHIBITION COMPLEX

Fearfulness in erotic situations was more expected in times past, and it was pointed out earlier in this text that modern men expect their female partners to be nearly as sexually skillful as they are themselves. Guilt—which arises from many sources, including moral anxiety due to strict parental and religious training, fear that one's partner will be displeased or inadequately satisfied, and anxiety about one's intensity of arousal—may give rise to inhibitions. While modern women are not expected to conform to the inhibited image usually associated with the Victorian age, most females are expected to focus their arousal on one man and to restrict their sexual relationships with others. The guilt-inhibition complex is thus a two-edged sword for many women. Taught to inhibit their sexual desires except in socially approved situations with socially acceptable male partners, they must nevertheless meet the demand to turn on sexually during these approved situations. Many times a wife will be expected to give an exquisite erotic performance with the very man who limits her personal growth and who would be absolutely dismayed if he found her more sexually excited by someone else. Little wonder, then, that many women inhibit themselves and follow the sexual leads of men, for not to do so may result in guilt and even greater attempts to orientate themselves in socially approved and personally acceptable directions.

A growing phenomenon noticed by the author among his counselees (and also reported by other counselors) is the consternation some women exhibit because they do not feel guilty about their violations of the sexual mores. It is as though they intellectually knew that they were supposed to feel guilt but actually felt none. Many women have experienced what they once considered forbidden behavior only to find themselves without the intense and enduring self-recrimination they expected. When this happens, the individual may find herself "feeling guilty about not feeling guilty."

Our brief review of some of the stereotypes of feminine sexuality has been based on the assumption that such stereotypes are learned and that this explanation is all that is needed for the purposes of this book. The learned nature of masculinity and femininity is so well established that upon demand most students can produce highly accurate stereotypes of these socially ordered phenomena (Lunneborg, 1970).

THE FEMALE SEXUAL SELF

A woman's view of herself is less related to sexual prowess than is a man's self-image; nevertheless, sex and sexual strivings can have a profound effect upon her ego strength. Many of the factors influencing female self concepts have been described in Chapter 5 and earlier in this chapter, but several other elements are also involved. Like her male counterpart, a woman is controlled in the formation of her sexual self primarily by her phenomenological experience of her own sexuality and sexual relationships. The level at which she prizes or detests her sexual experiences, desires, and behavior sets much of the tone for her identity as a sexual being.

SOME ADDITIONAL FACTORS

In addition to the factors that influence her general femininity, there are other considerations that profoundly affect a female's evaluation of her sexuality. These include the ability to integrate certain preferred male roles, freedom to grow as an individual, attitudes toward children and child-bearing, and the degree to which her sexual responsiveness fits her desire to respond. In addition, success or failure in relationships with males directly influences most women's self-images.

Just as men must learn to accept some of the femininity that they possess, so women must integrate certain roles that they prefer but which are socially described as masculine. The desires to initiate sexual relationships, to play the "masculine role," or to ask for some form of "forbidden sex" must be accepted as wholesome and positive if the female's sexual self-image is to grow and develop. Furthermore, from time to time every woman needs to be freed from the constant tyranny of fulfilling feminine roles and to engage in activities she considers self-enhancing. When her husband agrees, the wife finds self-enhancing roles even more desirable (Arnott, 1972). All mothers need some freedom from their children in order to engage in adult contacts. While most women do take leave of stereotyped feminine roles at least occasionally, many feel guilty or less than acceptable because of this. Self-destructive guilt is not likely to enhance anyone's erotic responsiveness.

When women are required against their wishes to meet the criteria of acceptability set by another person or by society, they are likely to think less well of themselves than they could. Thus if women, like men, feel that their sexual impulses are an integral part of their physiology and believe that their control of these impulses is internal rather than external, they have a greater probability of positive self-regard. Internal locus of control* was found to be more strongly related to personal adjustment for women than for men (Warehime and Foulds, 1971).

---

*The term "locus of control" refers to whether or not the individual feels he has control over his fate. If one believes one's reinforcements are the consequences of one's own behavior, one's locus of control is internal; if one believes that one's reinforcements are controlled by luck, chance, fate, divinity, or powerful others, one's locus of control is external.

FEMALE SEXUAL PERSONALITY

Elsewhere (Shope, 1968) I have proposed that women modify their usual behavioral reactions during their erotic relationships with men. I have called this "the female special sexual personality." The idea I wish to suggest by this term is that in most of her sexual interactions with a male, the average woman reorders her output of behavioral characteristics to fit both the social model of femininity and the desires of her partner. A generally aggressive, dominant woman may react with greater submissiveness in the erotic situation than in her other relationships. For example, the career girl, quite self-sufficient on the job, may become considerably more dependent during her sexual encounters. This proposition has yet to be examined further, but the reader is invited to think about it in relation to his or her own sexual experiences.

A woman's sexual experience of herself is many-faceted, with connections, loops, bypasses, and detours characterizing almost every phase of her life. This greater influence of the nonsexual phases on her sexual life probably brings the average woman closer than most men to achieving a unity between sexuality and total being. When a man forces a woman into a secondary role, however, or when she devalues her own eroticism, the need for adaptive psychological defenses arises.

FEMALE DEFENSES

Although some women directly confront a short-term sexual partner with negative feelings about that person, it appears that many more, perhaps subconsciously, undermine the man in subtler ways. If the male has failed to relate to her in a manner of which she approves, if he is inconsistent with her needs or values, or if his responses are incongruent with her ideas of how a man should relate to a woman, a female partner may fail to respond sexually, thus wounding the male's ego. Sometimes a woman will become more responsive to or pay more attention to another man, hoping to create jealousy in order to get more attention from her partner. Very often such jealousy results only in increased control by the partner, and this in turn can lead to a downward spiraling of the relationship.

Some women, perhaps preoccupied with society's resistance to equality between the sexes, choose homosexual relationships in preference to heterosexual ones. For some lesbians, interpersonal relationships are exclusively homosexual, whereas others relate to men in noninterpersonal matters but reserve intimacies, including affection and sexuality, for other women. Some females accept the bisexual approach to their interpersonal erotic needs, believing that the only way to comprehend heterosexual love is first to experience love for another woman. Many of these women marry. Lesbianism, of course, does not always or even usually occur because the woman wishes to avoid intimate relationships with the opposite sex, but this is certainly one reason for both male and female homosexuality.

Females, of course, also employ non-sex-specific defenses against the anxiety engendered by the demands of intimacy upon them. Withdrawal, denial, sublimation, and projection are common adaptive mechanisms of women as well as men. Some women have as little to do with eroticism as possible. Others have formulated negative evaluations of their bodies or physiological functions, and by maintaining these negative feelings, give feedback via their own nervous systems to the original depreciating attitudes. In this way the body becomes a boundary between the individual and the very external sources of erotic pleasure and relief that could eliminate the basic faulty self perceptions. Women, then, may act irrationally to defend themselves against sexual feelings and the men who remind them of those feelings.

FEMALE SEXUAL RESPONSIVENESS

We have already seen that historically women have often been believed to have lower sexual needs than men. That this concept may need future revision will become more evident as both individual men and society at large permit women increased sexual self-determination. Modern women are apt to engage in a greater range of sexual behavior than was customery in nineteenth- and early twentieth-century America. When her need for variety is acceptable—neither demanded nor suppressed—a woman's attitudes toward her own sexuality are enhanced. When variety cannot be accepted even though it is strongly desired, self concepts suffer. Successful (from the woman's phenomenal viewpoint) sexual encounters are likely to lead to increased interest in and greater potential for erotic arousal.

Certainly, females have engaged in every type of sexual behavior known possible. Since the Kinsey (1953) studies, we have recognized that the greatest changes in female sexual behavior began in the 1920's. Since then, there has been a gradual but somewhat slower trend toward increased female liberality.

PATTERNS OF SEXUAL ACTIVITY

Any woman's degree and pattern of sexual activity are partly dependent upon her particular social status—that is, whether she is a casual date, steady girl-friend, fiancée, wife, or mistress—and also on whether she is heterosexually or homosexually inclined. Other factors affecting a woman's erotic patterns are her idiosyncratic needs, cultural conditioning, age, access to a partner, and rhythmic changes occurring in conjunction with her menstrual cycle.

There is considerable variation among women in their need for sexual activity. Some seem to have low sexual desires while others have needs that exceed any man's. An inconsistent pattern of sexual behavior is not unusual for women, and even among the experienced some will abstain from sexual activity for months or years while others find it intolerable to do without sexual relief for more than a few days. Sometimes this greater desire is linked to nonsexual psychological needs, such as a desire for male companionship, but often it is the result of genuine physical needs. The more arousable women are likely to need the most steady outlets. Sexual desires may also vary with physical illness, fatigue and overwork, periods of unusual psychological stress, and absorption in nonsexual activities, such as studying, housework, or a variety of other interests.

As she grows through adolescence into young adulthood, the average woman increases her interest in sexual activity until this interest reaches a peak somewhere between the ages of 25 and 40. Thereafter, she will maintain her interest level well into old age. As they grow older and lose some of their inhibitions, most women react accordingly.

For some women, a rhythmic patterning of sexual needs is associated with the menstrual cycle, but there is no substantial evidence linking particular phases (pre-, during, or post-) of the cycle with sexual arousal. In a study to be presented shortly, the author found 24 per cent of his subjects reporting the time of greatest sexual arousal approximately one week before their periods, 11 per cent after their periods, 16 per cent immediately before and after their periods, and 49 per cent reported no awareness of increased sexual arousal in association with menstruation.

RESPONSIVENESS TO MEN

For most couples, the male will set much of the tone for both the frequency and type of sexual relationships in which the partners are involved. A woman is apt to have more interest in a man who shows considerable motivation in having her as a sexual partner and who is *consistently* desirous of her as a total person. She is desirable to him; he needs her and his behavior is congruent with his needs. P. Rossi (1955) found considerateness, personality stability, tranquility, and the capacity to be realistic associated with men's sexual adjustment. These factors represent desirable traits in men that most women seem to favor.

Rejection by a desired male can be one of the most devastating things that can happen to a woman. Rejection can be outright refusal to interact with her, or it can occur in more subtle ways. Among the more common of these subtle forms are making fun of a female partner, ridiculing her, placing her on a pedestal, or ignoring her once the sexual encounter is over. Another type of rejection shown by some males is a display of guilt and remorse following a sexual relationship with a woman. A woman may interpret any of these rejection forms as a sign that her partner's only interest in her was sexual, and therefore she may feel "used." If she feels she is being continually exploited, she may react with anger and self-recrimination, not because of the sexual interaction itself but rather because she feels "unintelligent" for letting herself "be taken advantage of."

Some women are so dependent upon a man for their self-esteem that they react to his every mood change, becoming happy when he is happy and depressed when he is sad. Such a high degree of dependency is not likely to serve a relationship for very long, and the resultant breakup only adds further to feelings of unworthiness.

There is evidence that females tend to fall in love less quickly than men (Kanin, Davidson, and Scheck, 1970). In this sense they are more realistic than males, for this delay in falling in love serves to protect them from overly strong ego insults by permitting a more gradual intensity of involvement. Once they do become involved in love affairs, however, females tend to be more idealistic in a romantic sense and are more apt to look upon their mates favorably, whether or not such accolades are warranted. Thus once committed to involvement, women have more chance of being hurt than men.

In their sexual relationships with men, women are, for the most part, dependent upon the male to initiate and facilitate the majority of the erotic aspects. The Pfeiffer and Davis (1972) study confirms what others have found—that the presence of a sexually capable, socially sanctioned partner is a crucial determining influence on women's sexual responsiveness and behavior. Thus women are frequently quite dependent upon men for their erotic responsiveness, intensity of arousal, sexual behavior, and acceptance of their own sexuality. Once they can be certain that their mates will accept, appreciate, and respect a given type of behavior or level of responsiveness, most women will find it easier to accept that level of sexuality themselves.

Erotic dependency is one aspect of feminine sexuality that in many cases is clearly related to the "female special sexual personality" described earlier in this chapter. Concerning such erotic dependency, Luquet-Parat (1970) had this to say:

> One could say that erotic dependence never really ceases for women because of their anatomical and physiological makeup. But this search for a position of dependence often reaches beyond sexual behavior. . . . Women take on a certain "role" in an eroticized adaption to the role the other person has, maintaining it according to the pleasure thereby derived from it. I believe that one must distinguish this from

actual dependence with which one might easily confuse it. The latter behavior, including the taking of secondary and subordinate positions, is due to inhibitions, regression, and guilt and is based on a feeling of obligation or represents a defense rather than a preference according to pleasure (p. 93).

Thus Luquet-Parat emphasizes that erotic dependence originates freely in the pleasure received from such a role, but erotic dependence need not result in a more generalized dependence upon the male. Generalized dependency has causes other than sexual pleasure.

RESPONSIVENESS TO EROTIC STIMULI

Previously it was pointed out that men are responsive to a wider variety of sexual stimuli than women. While it is true that *more* men respond to *more types* of sexual stimuli, it should not be assumed that women are *never* aroused by such stimuli. Several studies have demonstrated that about one in three women can be as aroused as the average man by pornography. A few women can be more aroused than almost any man. What erotic subjects tend to arouse women, then, and what factors are important in their responses to these subjects?

In the study by Sigusch and his associates (1970), cited in Chapter 10, women were found to rate erotic slides containing romantic themes (e.g., mouth-kissing and embracing) more sexually stimulating than men rated these same slides. However, in a study by the author, only 22 out of 96 female subjects of college age and background who had seen pictures depicting specific sexual action were from *much* to *very much* aroused. Thirty-three girls were *somewhat* aroused, but 41 reported *no arousal* from viewing pornography. Nor was level of sexual experience a factor, since virgins, women coitally experienced to orgasm, and those coitally experienced without orgasm reported almost exactly the same levels of arousal. In another study, Mosher and Greenberg (1969) had college females evaluate their own responsiveness after reading a passage of erotic literature. They concluded that imaginative productions helped both in the formation of erotic feelings and in the assessment of those feelings.

In these three studies, an element of romantic content in erotic portrayals was found to be important. When the author generally compared virgins with nonvirgins, he found no significant differences in responsiveness to romantic movies or stories, but when the coitally experienced women were further classified on the basis of whether or not they had achieved orgasm, significantly more of the nonorgastic girls were *much* to *very much* aroused by such movies and stories. This generates the speculation that overemphasis on romanticism may actually inhibit a woman's sexual responsiveness, whereas an optimum amount of romantic content in conjunction with erotic material may add to her arousal. A second interpretation of these same data is that the nonorgastic girls were confusing romantic-affectional feelings with sexual excitement. Still another interpretation is related to the phenomenon of anticipation and experience: the nonorgastic girls perhaps idealized orgasm because their personal concepts of it had yet to meet the test of reality. In any event, the female in our society seems less likely than the male to become aroused by overtly sexual themes.

When the Sigusch female subjects were asked to rate the favorableness of the same slides they had rated for arousableness, the frankly sexual scenes were not ranked as favorably as the less arousing solitary nude figures. Furthermore, the women also ranked these specifically sexual scenes lower in favorableness than the men. These results, of course, are predictable, since overt sexual behavior is less socially acceptable for women. However, Sigusch and his associates found that their women subjects reported almost as often as the men that they had experienced genital responses and increased activation of sexual behavior after viewing the slides. This introduces the possibility, which these researchers recognized, that many women may actually respond physiologically to sexual stimuli but be unaware of these responses unless asked about them specifically. The women's emotional rejection of sexuality, Sigusch and his associates speculate, could be responsible for this finding.

One out of three subjects in the author's female sample reported never having viewed scenes explicitly depicting sexual encounters. This result is perhaps due to the subjects' relative youth: Rosen and Turner (1969) found that older women and those who have been married for several years are more likely than single girls to have seen erotic films and photographs.

FANTASY

The erotic fantasies of women, especially those of young women, are apt to be highly colored with romantic interludes, and daydreams are often accompanied by images of tender, loving care. Here is a typical female fantasy of a superior erotic relationship, written by a 20-year-old coed:

> The bedside table light was on as I entered the room. Its dimmed light cast lavender shadows on my soft, pink, nylon negligée, which revealed just a hint of my body beneath. He smiled as he lay in bed with his naked body half concealed by covers. With only a motion, he picked up the covers for me to join him. As I slipped beneath the covers I felt his warm body surround me. Our lips met, and our embraces grew tighter. A short time later he loosened my bow, and the nightgown fell away. Crazy, wonderful shivers went through my

body, and we kissed for quite some time. Perhaps with the fear that his body weight might hurt me or perhaps with satisfaction, he moved and once again lay beside me on the bed very calmly.

From this beginning, the story proceeds with increasing eroticism until coitus is finished, when once again the romantic aspects dominate.

Comparison of this feminine fantasy with the typical fantasy of a college male (see p. 190) demonstrates that the coed's story is not only less direct and aggressive but also highlights romanticism as a functional aspect of erotic interaction. All the stories the male college students wrote contained elements of the romantic, while each female fantasized some initiation and aggressiveness on her part. In general, however, the fantasies of these men and women appear to reflect sociocultural expectations about the manner in which the sexes are to interact erotically. Males are aggressors, and females submit. Consequently, it is less possible for many women to admit that direct sexual stimuli are effective, except in a socially approved situation.

RESPONSE-ENHANCING ATTITUDES: A RECENT STUDY

While orgasm is neither a necessary nor sufficient condition for the satisfaction of a woman's sexual desires, those who reach it are most likely to be completely satisfied (Gebhard, 1966). Masters and Johnson (1966) have demonstrated that blood engorgement may continue as long as 24 hours (and in some cases even longer) if the sexually excited woman has not reached orgasm. Wallin (1960) believes that orgasm may be a physiological relief process, but sexual satisfaction is social or psychological in nature.

Maslow (1942) concluded that females with moderate masochistic tendencies are most likely to achieve orgasm. He believed that the feeling of having been subdued had positive psychological effects upon the women in his study and was related to their orgastic ability. On the other hand, those subjects who were dominant and wanted to feel superior to their male partners seemed least likely to achieve orgasm.

Burgess and Wallin (1953) raised the question of whether or not women who expect to attain an orgasm but do not are more frustrated than those who do not expect orgasm. It seems likely that if the female expects to achieve an orgasm and then does not, she will report considerably less sexual satisfaction and adjustment than otherwise.

Studies by the author (Shope, 1968, 1971; Shope and Broderick, 1967), including one unpublished study, show that certain attitudes toward sex are more typical of unmarried college women reaching coital orgasm than of those who do not. Women who reported during interviews that they were able to attain an orgasm from coitus were more likely to be free of conflict with their parents (especially their fathers) and did not feel that they would rear their daughters more restrictively than their sons. Orgastic girls more often rated themselves free of sexual inhibitions, became more aroused from petting, and were more satisfied with their capacity to become sexually excited.

Adjustment and Orgasm

In their attitudes toward their male partners, the orgastic women tended to feel their sex drives were about equal to those of their lovers, found it easier to discuss sex with them, and were more likely to initiate sexual activity. Their general as well as their sexual adjustment to their mates, as they rated it, was significantly better than that of the nonorgastic girls. Importantly, the general adjustment of most of these orgastic girls was good before they began sexual intercourse. About half the nonorgastic girls felt that their relationships needed some improvement, while another 20 per cent felt that their relationships with their coital partners were poor.

Thus in many cases good general adjustment seems to be a prelude to coital orgastic responsiveness, although it is not an absolute necessity. Perhaps, however, the relationship between responsiveness and adjustment operates conversely as well: how much did orgasm contribute to the orgastic subjects' general adjustment? Gebhard (1966) found that only high incidences of coital orgasm are significantly related to adjustment. Adams (1953) saw the relationship between orgasm and marital adjustment as present but indirect: orgasm contributes to sexual adjustment, which in turn positively affects marital happiness and thus by extension the wife's happiness (see p. 137). For Adams' subjects, the mediating factor among orgastic responsiveness, sexual adjustment, and personal happiness appeared to be the male partner's acceptance of and attitude toward the woman's sexuality. In brief, then, orgasm does indeed seem to contribute to general relationship adjustment, but less directly than good general adjustment contributes to coital orgastic capacity.

Orgastic and Nonorgastic Females: Similarities and Differences

Some response factors significantly differentiating the coitally orgastic from the nonorgastic women in the author's latest (1972) study are presented in Table 11-1. In addition to the data in Table 11-1, the groups had about equal sexual experience, including number of coital partners (median two), age at which coitus was first begun (median 17 years, 8 months), number of male petting partners (median three) and age at which petting was begun (median 16 years). Additionally, no differences were found in age at menarche, length of menstrual cycle, or physical distress during menstruation. In total number of males dated, age at which dating was begun, and number of steady boy friends the

TABLE 11–1. SOME CORRELATES OF COITAL ORGASM ADEQUACY AMONG UNMARRIED WOMEN OF COLLEGE AGE AND BACKGROUND (SHOPE 1972)

Dimension	Response Category	Number of Subjects		Level of Significance
		Org.*	Nonorg.†	
Number of times subject estimated she had engaged in coitus	15—	10 (20%)	2 (05%)	
	16–40	7 (14%)	16 (40%)	
	41–80	10 (20%)	11 (27½%)	.02
	81–130	7 (14%)	3 (07½%)	
	131+	16 (32%)	8 (20%)	
Usual degree of arousal from coitus	None/little	0 (00%)	1 (02½%)	
	Some	1 (02%)	5 (12½%)	.01
	Much	8 (16%)	19 (47½%)	
	Very much	41 (82%)	15 (37½%)	
Usual enjoyment of coitus	None/little	0 (00%)	4 (10%)	
	Some	1 (02%)	6 (15%)	.01
	Much	5 (10%)	14 (35%)	
	Very much	44 (88%)	16 (40%)	
Amount of time woman felt that she must "give in" to male pressure for coitus	Never	37 (74%)	13 (32½%)	
	Sometimes	12 (24%)	8 (20%)	.01
	Often	0 (00%)	10 (25%)	
	Usually	1 (02%)	9 (22½%)	

		Org.*	Nonorg.†	
Desire for a continuation of sexual activity following coitus	Never	4 (08%)	14 (35%)	.01
	Sometimes	16 (32%)	15 (37½%)	
	Often	18 (36%)	2 (05%)	
	Usually	12 (24%)	9 (22½%)	
Amount subject is disturbed by outside noises	None/little	31 (62%)	6 (15%)	.01
	Some	11 (22%)	12 (30%)	
	Much/very much	8 (16%)	22 (55%)	
Subject's rating of her degree of sexual inhibition	None/little	31 (62%)	7 (18%)	.01
	Some	16 (32%)	16 (40%)	
	Much/very much	3 (06%)	17 (42%)	
Best coital position	Man over woman	17 (34%)	25 (62½%)	.05
	Woman over man	1 (02%)	2 (05%)	
	All equal	22 (44%)	8 (20%)	
	Other	5 (10%)	1 (02½%)	
	Only tried one	5 (10%)	4 (10%)	

*Coitally orgastic subjects.
†Coitally nonorgastic subjects.
Ns were as follows: Org. = 50; Nonorg. = 40.

groups were again alike. About half the women reported engaging in fellatio and slightly more than half reported experiencing cunnilingus. These oral-genital relations figures were nearly identical for the two groups. Neither arousal from nor enjoyment of oral stimulation of their breasts differentiated these groups. Both orgastic and nonorgastic women had begun self-stimulation by a median age of 15, and group differences in the number of subjects who had ever participated in self-stimulation were not significant. Forty-two per cent of the orgastic and 30 per cent of the nonorgastic females reported that they had engaged in self-stimulation. All these figures are surprisingly similar to those presented by Kinsey and his associates (1953) for females of college age and background.

Differences between the orgastic and nonorgastic subjects in the 1972 study reflect the importance of attitudes as mediators of coital orgastic responsiveness. Notice that the attitudes of the orgastic women indicate a degree of willingness to *focus* on sexual involvement, which may be related to a fuller acceptance of sexuality as good in and of itself. Concerning the number of times each subject estimated she had engaged in coitus, it is clear that this experience might account for the greater capacity of some girls to achieve orgasm. However, in the 1966 group orgastic and nonorgastic women had had nearly equal amounts of coital activity. Furthermore, the number of orgastic females in the 1972 group who reported 41 or more coital contacts was not highly different from the number of nonorgastic subjects who placed themselves in the same above 41 category. Experience certainly appears to count, but experience in the presence of negative attitudes toward sexual participation is probably less response-enhancing than experience that occurs in the presence of positive sexual attitudes.

Coital orgasm and enjoyment are highly correlated for both sexes, but a high level of enjoyment, even in the absence of orgasm, was evident among most of these females. For women, coitus is often an activity to be enjoyed regardless of orgastic arousal and relief. After orgasm the male needs varying periods of rest before he can continue sexual intercourse, but women can repeat both the plateau and orgasmic phases of erotic arousal before entering a resolution period. The plateau phase of arousal is apparently very rewarding to many women, and they may be satisfied on occasion to go no further.

Postorgastic Sexual Activity

A phenomenon familiar to sexually experienced women is the often-felt desire for sexual activity to continue even after orgasm. Pleasurable sexual feelings and a need for closeness and intimacy probably account for much of this desire. Between 15 and 20 per cent of women are capable of multiple orgasms during a single erotic encounter, and this adds much to the intensity of their pleasure. Once again attitudes are important: among the women in the author's study who reported no desire for coitus to continue, the four orgastic subjects each stated that sexual activity, especially coitus, was a period of such high intensity that they usually felt too tired to keep going. Several of the nonorgastic females, on the other hand, felt that coitus was an activity to be "gotten over with."

Distractions

As expected, the orgastic females were less annoyed by ordinary outside noises, such as passing trucks or playing children, and some reported that friends moving about even in the same room did not disturb them. Nevertheless, some orgastic subjects were occasionally more disturbed by outside noises than a few of the nonorgastic women. Clearly, the situation in which coitus takes place can have an important influence on an individual's sexual responsiveness.

That more of the nonorgastic females considered themselves sexually inhibited does not tell us whether failure to reach orgasm was caused by such inhibitions or whether the subjects considered themselves inhibited because of their orgastic failure. Clinically, both types of women may be found, and thus it is very likely that inhibitions do reduce orgastic capacity, which in turn further convinces one that she is indeed not free of sexual fears.

A Willing, Experimental Attitude

Apparently, the attitude that sex is something personally wanted and needed which one would go out of her way to get is conducive to higher levels of sexual responsiveness. This is somewhat like the positive male attitude toward sexual interaction. Sex for the sake of sex alone appears highly correlated with female orgastic capacity. One finds a greater number of orgastic females satisfied by a variety of coital positions. Again, 86 per cent of the orgastic women enjoyed sexual experimentation *much to very much*, whereas only 52 per cent of the nonorgastic women fell into this category. An experimental and searching attitude toward things erotic seems related to feminine orgastic capacity.

Mutuality of Desire

Giving in to male pressure for coitus is highly and negatively correlated with women's likelihood of experiencing coital orgasm. Mutuality of desire for coitus, along with the previously described feeling that one's sex drive about equals that of one's partner, is important to the achievement of orgasm. The nonorgastic subjects more frequently regarded coitus as an act of forced submission, necessitated by a desire either to please the male or to gain certain nonsexual goals from him. To them, sex for fun was a male prerogative. Very often nonorgastic girls engaged in sexual relations because they wanted to make their mates

TABLE 11–2. SOME DIMENSIONS OF PURPOSEFUL CONTROL DURING COITUS REPORTED BY COLLEGE FEMALES (SHOPE 1972)

Dimension	Response Category	Number of Subjects		Level of Significance‡
		Org.°	Nonorg.†	
Type of coital stroking subject reported liking best	Begin easy, become a little rough, deep penetration	26 (52%)	7 (18%)	
	Begin easy, become quite rough, deep penetration	16 (32%)	7 (18%)	.01
	Easy throughout, deep penetration	7 (14%)	14 (35%)	
	Rough throughout, deep penetration	1 (02%)	8 (20%)	
	Easy throughout, partial penetration	0 (00%)	4 (10%)	
Type of self-control over thinking during coitus	1. Begin by controlling to enhance responsiveness, gradually lose control	31 (62%)	7 (18%)	
	2. Begin by controlling to enhance responsiveness, partially maintain	16 (32%)	2 (05%)	.01

3. Begin by controlling so as not to get "carried away," gradually lose	2 (04%)	6 (15%)	
4. Begin by controlling so as not to get "carried away," partially maintain	1 (02%)	17 (43%)	
5. Control so as not to get "carried away" throughout coitus	0 (00%)	8 (20%)	
Type of self-control over movements during coitus			.01
1§	32 (64%)	5 (12%)	
2	15 (30%)	7 (18%)	
3	2 (04%)	7 (18%)	
4	1 (02%)	12 (30%)	
5	0 (00%)	9 (22%)	

*Org. = women who reported orgasm from coitus.
†Nonorg. = women who reported no orgasm from coitus.
‡Level of significance based on chi-square.
§Numbers 1 to 5 same description as type of self-control over thinking, above.
Ns were as follows: Org. = 50; Nonorg. = 40.

happy, even though they were under no threat of losing them if they did not allow intercourse. Evidently this noble motive did not provide the quality of involvement necessary to their own orgastic satisfaction. Simply permitting coitus without becoming a full participant in it does not seem to result in orgasm for women.

Repeatedly, evidence has demonstrated the need for women to become personally and meaningfully involved in their own erotic arousal and to experience and evaluate themselves as positive because of this involvement if high intensities of responsiveness are desired. This process of getting lost in oneself means focusing more and more throughout sexual intercourse, until at last one either loses or voluntarily surrenders self-control. For a few moments consciousness is blurred. Self-control, often used in the sense of inhibiting oneself, also means the ability to become as purposely involved and aroused as one wishes. Table 11–2 presents the effects of cooperation and of intentional acts meant to be either stimulating or inhibiting.

In earlier studies, orgastic women were found to rate themselves as significantly more cooperative in their movements and thinking, but the studies did not specifically define the details of this cooperativeness. In the author's 1972 study, the questions were refined to disclose the details of cooperativeness more explicitly. The results may be found in Table 11–2. Women who had attained an orgasm during coitus were unanimous in their desire for deep penile penetration. The overwhelming majority of orgastic women also preferred easy coital movements at the beginning, with these movements gradually increasing in roughness as coitus proceeded. The intensity of roughness desired is individually determined, and most girls reported that, despite a general desire, their individual wishes concerning roughness, fastness, and so on varied from time to time. This emphasizes the importance of clear, uninhibited communication concerning the state of one's arousal.

There is little doubt about the differing effects of inhibitory and excitatory self-control on the potential for coital orgasm. No woman who consciously maintained inhibitory control throughout coitus, whether this control was over her thinking, movements, or experiencing of her partner's stroking, was able to achieve orgasm. Furthermore, even beginning coitus with the intention of conscious inhibitory control is almost certain to cancel orgasm, despite the fact that some intentional control is invariably lost during coital activity. It is thus evident that orgasm is highly associated with either the inability or the refusal to maintain conscious inhibitory control over one's movements or thinking. For both men and women, awareness and orgasm do *not* go together.

Fantasy and Orgasm

Fantasy appears helpful in stimulating a woman to orgasm. Ninety-eight per cent of the orgastic girls in the author's study reported experiencing sexually oriented fantasies during periods when they were not engaging in sexual activity. In contrast, only 80 per cent of the nonorgastic girls fantasized during nonsexual periods. The nature of these female fantasies has been described earlier in this chapter. S. Fisher (1973, p. 207) found that the average woman in his samples thought about sex often. Some therapists, when conditions are appropriate, encourage their counselees to live out their sexual fantasies so that they may experience both intellectually and emotionally their inner psychic feelings about sexuality (Robertiello, 1969).

Other Factors Influencing Orgastic Capacity

After reviewing the literature on female sexual responsiveness, S. Fisher (1973) found the majority of studies supporting the following facts:

1. There is no significant relationship between physical maturation, as measured by a number of indices, and orgastic responsiveness.
2. Number of children borne was unrelated to the capacity of a woman to achieve orgasm, nor was her relationship with her own mother a significant factor.
3. As measured by current psychological tests, personality factors neither of the woman nor of her husband accounted for levels of orgastic response.
4. Extent of religious practice and devoutness did not significantly influence orgastic capacity in women.
5. Neither ordinal position in the family nor age seems to affect a woman's orgastic capacity.

However, some sociological variables, such as higher levels of education, middle or upper social class, and being an only child, *are* positively related to orgastic capacity. Experience, Fisher notes, seems to have only a limited effect on increasing feminine orgastic capacity. Fisher postulates that those women who feel secure that their love relationships will not fail are most likely to achieve orgasm. Conversely, fear of the loss of one's love object, he believes, is a major factor in inhibiting orgastic responsiveness in women. Thus a father who is moderately demanding and indicates that he has expectations of his daughter may do much to instill in her an orgasmic attitude, because the expectations may themselves communicate to her his sense of personal concern. Very permissive or extrapunitive fathers would be less likely to communicate a personal concern for their daughters. I would suspect that a daughter's perception of her father's concern *for* her rather than *about* her or her behavior would be a significant factor in her orgastic capacity. If the effects of having being reared by a dependable father and mother are later reinforced and intensified by a loving and dependable (in the wife's perception) husband, orgasm capacity should be enhanced. If Fisher's formulations are correct, whenever the loss of a love object is seriously understood, orgasm capacity can be expected to suffer.

Some Conclusions

Orgastic females appear to enjoy and become aroused from all sexual activities much more than those who are less responsive. Orgastic women are more likely purposely to increase their state of arousal, feel less inhibited, and either give up or lose awareness of their surroundings as sexual excitement intensifies. The deliberate attempt to inhibit oneself sexually has a high probability of success, but intentional control to enhance one's responsiveness to the point of orgasm may not be successful. One must suspect that subconscious inhibitions and conditioning account for this.

SUMMARY OF FEMALE SEXUAL
RESPONSIVENESS

Despite the obvious physical differences, many of the variations in sexual responsiveness between men and women seem the result of learned social and interpersonal processes. Many women respond to erotic stimulation to a greater degree than the average man, and some men are much less sexually responsive than the average woman. Social conditioning is effective in focusing gender differences in erotic responding to the extent that many individuals become convinced that their masculinity or femininity depends upon making the "correct" sexual response.

FEMALE VIRGINS AND NONVIRGINS

Although virginity (inexperience of actual coitus) may be less important than formerly, large numbers of women prefer to remain virgins until marriage, and even among the coitally experienced, virginal attitudes, as manifested in self-restrictions and inhibitions, may continue to prevail. Only a few females are proud of a wide variety of sexual experiences with several partners. In recent studies by the author, women who reported that they had never experienced coitus (virgins) were compared with those who reported during personal interviews that they had had coital experience (nonvirgins). The subjects were all women of college age and background and were equally distributed among the dating statuses of casual, pinned, or engaged. They were matched on religious affiliation, socioeconomic background, and year in college. Data were obtained from two study periods, one of which was previously reported (Shope, 1964). The latest data were completed in 1972. In addition to answering the interview questions, each subject completed the Adams Marital Happiness Prediction Inventory (MHP)—a personality inventory that measures a number of attributes found to be predictive of marital happiness and sexual adjustment (see also p. 132). These attributes have been named sociability, agreeableness, realism, fearfulness, normalcy of mental processes, touchiness, flexibility, prejudice, emotional stability, standards and ideals, family and background, and philosophy toward marriage.

No differences were found between the groups in their rankings on sociability, agreeableness, touchiness, realism, fearfulness, normalcy of mental processes, flexibility, and philosophy toward marriage. In the 1964 group prejudice toward conservative attitudes was found to be significantly more likely for the virgins, but in the latest study (1972 group) no significant differences were found between virgins and nonvirgins on this dimension, although there was a definite but nonsignificant trend for the virgins to rank higher. In the 1972 study the factor of emotional stability fell just short of significance (chi-square = 7.189; three degrees of freedom; P = .10), whereas in the 1964 group differences between virgins and nonvirgins were significant at the .01 level. While both the emotional stability factor and the prejudice factor can be accounted for as statistical artifacts, it would not be unreasonable to assume that bias favoring conservative outlooks has lessened among women since 1964.

Slight but statistically significant differences between virgins and nonvirgins in family and background and overall predictions for marital happiness and sexual adjustment were found in both the 1964 and 1972 studies. Virgins have the family relationships and background most conducive to marital happiness. Virginity continues to be significantly and positively related to higher predictions for marital happiness and sexual adjustment. Liberality of attitudes toward interpersonal relationships was not statistically significant in 1964 but was significant in the 1972 study. The trend toward greater conservatism among virgins reminds us that moderately conservative individuals are more likely to find happiness and satisfactory sexual adjustment, since marriage norms remain relatively stable.

Although personality factors as measured by the MHP were not directly related to virginity, certain specific sexual attitudes and behavioral responses were more likely among virgins than nonvirgins. Religious devoutness was greater among the virgins. Virgins estimated that they dated fewer men (median 15) than nonvirgins (median 20), had fewer steady boy-friends (median 1.5, nonvirgins median 2.4), and petted with fewer men (median 1.3 versus a median of 3.2 petting partners for the nonvirgins).

Nonvirgins were more aroused from petting and more likely to enjoy petting. Nonvirgins were also involved in a wider variety of petting activities and were more likely to initiate petting. For the nonvirgins, petting usually took place in the man's apartment; otherwise, there were no differences between the groups. Other petting locations were the woman's home, a car, a motel, and the man's home, in that order.

Nonvirgins were more likely to allow a man to deep kiss and pet with them on a first date and were more likely to have had an orgasm from some source. Nonvirgins were more sexually oriented on most dimensions. On the other hand, the groups could not be differentiated by their responses to romantic stories or to pictures of nude males and sexual activity. Nor were there significant differences in the number of subjects who wished to become more responsive, had difficulty in achieving a satisfactory level of arousal, or reported a particular time of the month they were most easily aroused.

Although 14 out of 80 virgin women reported they had never engaged in covered breast-fondling (the starting point in petting), those who had petted did not seem unusually troubled by guilt. In the 1964 study, 14 per cent of the virgins and 10 per cent of the nonvirgins reported much to very much guilt following petting; the comparable 1972 figures were 12 per cent and 7 per cent.

Recently, Athanasiou and Sarkin (1974) have provided evidence supporting the conclusion of Shope and Broderick (1967) that women with moderately conservative attitudes are most likely to report the happiest marriages. Investigating the hypothesis that levels of pre- / marital sexual activity are associated with mate-swapping, adultery, and degree of marital unhappiness, they found that their married subjects who reported the highest levels of premarital sexual intercourse were also most likely to report the highest levels of extramarital activity. Those who were happiest with their premarital experiences and who had had these experiences with the most partners were most apt to desire extramarital sexual relationships. In brief, Athanasiou and Sarkin found that among their subjects a generally conservative attitude was positively—but not highly—correlated with marital stability.

Virgins, then, who are less sexually active than nonvirgins but by no means sexually inactive, can anticipate slightly greater marital happiness and sexual adjustment. In personality traits measured by the MHP, they are more like nonvirgins than different from them. Specific sexual attitudes and a willingness to become involved are more important determinants of sexual involvement than personality, neurotic thinking, or frustrating loneliness. Virginity falls toward the more conservative end of the sexual involvement continuum, but even within virginity wide differences in erotic receptivity can be found.

OTHER ASPECTS OF FEMALE SEXUALITY

UNMARRIED WOMEN

Stereotypes of the unmarried woman run the gamut from the miserable spinster to the beautiful, popular, and successful bachelorette. None of these stereotypes, of course, accurately describes the majority of single women. Today unmarried women enjoy less encumbered sexuality than they did in the past, but many prefer erotic interaction with only one or two men. Some have marriage in mind, even though they do not openly pursue this course. Others, however, find that when they are given the chance to be creative in society, they can find adequate personality expression and personal fulfillment without the benefit of husband or children (Baker, 1968).

There are many reasons why some women do not marry, including a high interest in a career, poor attitudes toward marriage or sex, religious values which teach that virginity is the highest state of "purity," failure to find a man whom they wish to marry or who will marry them, and severe physical disability or disfigurement. Some women are overly particular, and no man could ever suit them. Their attitudes toward men are distorted, or their daydreams are so idealistic that they insist on finding the "one right man," and if they cannot have him they will have no one. Janice Glover (1963), writing for single girls, says this: ". . . if a maiden doesn't meet her man here, maybe she will meet him in the hereafter" (p. 213).

The unequal social yokes (Kelly, 1972) borne by men and women have caused some women not only to dismiss marriage but also to exclude men from their relationships. In many ways, the dynamics of the lesbian dyad are similar to those of heterosexual relationships (Bass-Hass, 1968). Undoubtedly, many lesbians have also engaged in heterosexual contacts and are bisexual, but others prefer the softer, more tender touch of another woman. They seek female contacts not out of defensiveness against men but out of positiveness toward women. In the final analysis, there is little reason to believe that the sexuality of unmarried women is fundamentally different, except in its direction, from that of their married sisters.

AGING AND FEMALE SEXUALITY

Kinsey and his coworkers (1953) found that women reach a peak of sexual responsiveness in their late twenties and maintain this rate until quite late in life, with an occasional female remaining active to age 90 or more. He (p. 353) discovered, in addition, that by the time many of his female subjects had reached higher levels of sexual responsiveness, their husbands had tapered off in their sexual ardor. Thus by the time the wife has reduced her sexual inhibitions to the point at which she is as desirous of sexual contact as her mate, much of the potential of sexual activity to contribute to marital happiness has been lost.

One method of coping with unmet sexual needs is masturbation, and as women grow older, they may gain a larger portion of their total sexual outlet through self-stimulatory techniques. Recently books teaching the art of female masturbation and the self-acceptance of one's sensuality have appeared on the market. One such book is *The Yes Book of Sex* (Vandervoort and McIlvenna, 1972).

Masturbation, however, is not the only source of sexual gratification for older women. Kinsey (1953, p. 532) found that although marital sex was the most important source of orgasm for married women at all ages, extramarital petting and extramarital coitus were the second most important sources for married women past age 40, replacing masturbation, which was second until that age was reached.

Menopause.   One of the most important changes to take place in a woman's life is menopause, the period that marks the cessation of menstrual activity. According to a United States Government report (*Age at Menopause*, 1966), about 10 per cent of women reach menopause by age 38, 20 per cent by age 43, 50 per cent by age 49, 90 per cent by age 54, and 100 per cent by age 58. Those who begin menstruation earliest are apt to continue it longest. The stoppage of menstruation usually begins gradually with some missed or late periods, followed by active menstruation for a time. Eventually the time between periods becomes longer, and after some cyclic episodes, they stop altogether. For this reason it is unwise to assume that pregnancy cannot occur until after at least a full year without menstruation.

Menopause is not always the disturbing phenomenon it is reputed to be; nevertheless, for a few the time is one of considerable discomfort. Hot and cold flashes due to vasoconstriction can occur, fatigue, dizziness, insomnia, depression, a desire for excess sleep, and headaches are other widely known symptoms. If such symptoms do occur, modern hormonal treatment, tranquilizers, or other medications (perhaps accompanied by short-term psychotherapy) may be useful in alleviating them.

Estrogen replacement therapy, in which the bodily supply of the female hormone estrogen is maintained despite the decline in production due to ovarian slowdown, may prevent menopause from occurring altogether. R. A. Wilson (1966) argues the benefits of estrogen therapy and urges women to seek it beginning in their late thirties. By the use of a "Femininity Index," the amount of estrogen present in the body is determined, and when the concentration falls below that necessary to maintain sound health, replacement therapy provides the proper amount. Wilson lists eight reasons why women should seek estrogen replacement therapy: (1) menopause can be prevented; (2) treatment begun in the thirties may forestall the physical changes associated with menopause; (3) continuance of menstruation keeps the uterus cleansed and healthy; (4) menopausal symptoms, such as weakening of bones and muscles, dowager's hump, and atrophy of the breasts and sexual organs, may be reduced or prevented entirely; (5) menopausal depression can be avoided by early treatment; (6) sexual competence and enjoyment can be more assured; (7) appearance is kept more youthful, and vigorous energy can be retained; and (8) estrogen-progestin therapy will *not* prolong fertility for a single day. An important thing hormonal therapy *may* do is prevent withering and cracking of the vaginal walls, which often makes intercourse painful and thus less enjoyable.

Aging, then, need not destroy a woman's sexuality, erotic responsiveness, or capacity to arouse others. Old age does not necessarily nor even usually bring about a cessation of sexual activity (Oman, 1969). Early in life the individual woman needs to rid herself of the illusion that as an automatic function of aging sex will become either less important or less meaningful. The fact is that older women, like older men, are often less sexually functional than they desire because society has mistakenly taught them that sexual interaction is only for the young.

FEMALE ATTITUDES TO BIRTH CONTROL

Little research has been done concerning the specific attitudes of women toward the many available methods of birth control. What has been done indicates that the use of contraceptives is based on several factors, including personality, need for freedom from fear of pregnancy, partner's attitudes, socioeconomic class, and educational level. Of these factors, personality seems to have the weakest relationship to contraceptive choice and acceptance. More clearly related are degree of liberality-conservatism, desire for a particular number of children, agreement between spouses concerning sexual behavior, and wish to augment coital pleasure.

Contraception and Pleasure. Hawkins (1970) found that some couples augment sexual pleasure through the use of contraceptive jells, foams, or creams to reduce abrasion. He further discovered that all contraceptive methods have some element of erotic significance for such couples. For example, oral and intrauterine devices permit concentration on the arousing aspects of sex without interference. On the other hand, helping the man slip a condom onto his penis can be very exciting for both partners. Hawkins reached the conclusion that contraceptives have erotic significance because many of his respondents sought a balance between erotic interests and contraceptive interests in choosing a birth control method. Certainly, for most couples the effectiveness of the contraceptive is as important as added erotic pleasure.

One might conclude that there is a high correlation between the expectation of erotic pleasure and the safety one feels about being free of possible pregnancy, but this correlation is not perfect. Ziegler and Rodgers (1968) compared the outcomes of the oral pill and vasectomy. They state:

> The rather inconsistent and somewhat contradictory results from the two groups suggest that sweeping generalizations cannot accu-

rately be made about the relationships between coitus and the likelihood of conception and between sexual satisfaction and sexual behavior (p. 186).

Ziegler and Rodgers found that for a few months after the initiation
of contraception the rate of coital activity was up, but later it leveled off
to the same as the period before contraception was begun. Vasectomized
husbands were more dissatisfied with the rate of coitus than they were
before the operation. Ziegler and Rodgers believe that this dissatisfaction might be attributable to masculinity problems.

Ziegler and Rodgers also found that the rate of noncoital techniques
did not change and conclude that couples use sex play more for the fun
of it than for contraceptive purposes. They further conclude that effective contraception removes the fear of pregnancy both as an inhibitory
device and as a bargaining tool within marriage. Furthermore, the level
of frigidity of the wives in this study did not significantly decrease after
the initiation of these types of contraception, nor were there increases in
extramarital activity.

The Temperature-Rhythm Method. Tolar, Rice, and Lanctot
(1973) studied couples using the temperature-rhythm method of birth
control. They found that women who generally considered their successes or failures a function of their own behavior tended to accept this
method more readily. Also, conservative couples were usually more successful with the method. Stresses emphasized by these couples included
the fact that 56 per cent of the women and 43 per cent of the men felt that
sexual abstinence was relatively difficult, while 45 per cent of the men
and 24 per cent of the women felt that such restraint was almost always
difficult. The researchers also found 63 per cent of their women reporting the fertile period as the period of highest sexual desire — a contrast to
other research, which shows no relationship between menstrual cycle
and period of greatest arousal. Most of the respondents who were willing
to use the rhythm method were Catholics.

Femininity and Contraception. Kapor-Stanulovic and Lynn (1972)
investigated the relationship between feminine identification and feminine preference as these relate to problems in the use of contraceptives.
They classified their female subjects into four categories according to
their tested level of femininity (feminine identification) and their level
of desire to adopt behavior associated with one sex or the other. These
categories were average feminine identification — average feminine preference (AA), high feminine identification — low feminine preference
(HL), low feminine identification — high feminine preference (LH), and
high feminine identification — high feminine preference (HH).

The study revealed mild uneasiness concerning contraception in all
four types of women. Problems tended to increase among HH and LH
women, and women with high feminine identification but low feminine

preference reported less difficulty with contraception. Kapor-Stanulovic and Lynn suggest that HH women may regard the activity associated with contraceptive practice as an intrusion upon their feminine passivity and dependency. LH women likely find contraceptive practice an unpleasant and conflict-laden activity. HL women seem to find their use of contraceptives a more carefree experience. Thus these researchers have given us a set of useful dimensions that may be related to personality constructs, contraceptive acceptance, and the efficiency of contraceptive usage. In the future, expanded studies in this area may provide us with needed insights. In the meantime, however, the relationship of femininity preference and feminine identification to each other and to contraceptive usage remains tentative.

Teenagers and Contraception. Cutright (1972) reminds us that since teenagers (from 14 to 19 years of age) have always been quite sexually active, the increased number of illegitimate children born to teenage girls over the past several decades may be accounted for ultimately by advances in health rather than by an increase in coital activity among the young. Society's restrictive attitude toward providing contraceptives to the unmarried is perhaps traceable to the fact that fewer young girls were able to become pregnant when the average age of menarche was greater (e.g., 16.5 years in Europe in 1870). Currently, the median age of menarche in the United States is 12.5 for both whites and nonwhites. It is estimated to take from two to three years after the onset of menstruation before the majority of young women can easily become pregnant. Cutright states that one consequence of earlier menstruation is the estimate that 94 per cent of girls age 17.5 are fully fecund. Fecundity is sporadic during the first two or three years after menarche, he states, with pregnancy being possible in some months but not in others. Two factors increase the need for teenagers to employ contraceptives in their coital activities: the greater likelihood of becoming pregnant earlier and the decreased probability of spontaneous abortion. Both of these factors are due, in large measure, to better health and nutrition. The same two factors, Cutright thinks, may also account for much of the increase in teenage illegitimacy.

In a study comparing the different attitudes toward sexual behavior and contraception among a group of girls aged 13 to 17, Goldsmith, Gabrielson, Gabrielson, Mathews, and Potts (1972) found that most of these sexually active girls did not want to become pregnant but that 85 to 94 per cent found sex enjoyable. Goldsmith and her associates divided their subjects into three categories: those who sought contraceptive information, those who sought abortions, and those who were continuing their pregnancies but were living in maternity homes. The members of the contraceptive-seeking group were significantly more oriented toward higher education and the postponement of marriage, more accepting of their sexuality, and more willing to acknowledge the need for contraceptives. Two out of five girls in the maternity-home group stated that they would say "no" to a boy, in a hypothetical case, who asked a girl who really liked him for coitus. Presented with the same situation, those seeking contraceptive devices or information were more likely to answer that they would start using the Pill just in case. This and other evidence suggests that those girls likely to use contraceptives are also more likely to admit the possibility of coitus than those who seek abortions or are in maternity homes; that is, they are more realistic concerning their sexual potential and impulse control.

Abortion. Reviewing the effects of abortion for the Joint Program for the Study of Abortion (JPSA), Tietze and Lewit (1972) found (1) that among JPSA patients 71 per cent of the abortions were performed at or before 12 weeks of gestation, (2) that about 49 per cent of the women at or below age 19 waited until 13 weeks of pregnancy or more before seeking abortion, and (3) that no deaths were reported among the 30,000 women who had had abortions during the first trimester. Only four deaths occurred among the 42,598 patients in the study, and each of these patients had other pre-existing medical complications. Complications occurred in about six persons per 100 when the gestation period was 12 weeks or less at time of abortion and rose to 21 per 100 patients at 13 weeks or more of gestation. Of all these patients, one or two women per 100 developed what Tietze and Lewit call major complications.

Tietze and Lewit speculate that younger girls seeking abortions wait until 13 weeks or more of gestation because they do not have the money, because they are unwilling to accept the reality of their predicament, because they are reluctant to seek advice, or because they are unable to recognize the symptoms of pregnancy. One possible reason for the higher risk of complication among these younger women, in addition to the lateness of their abortions, is the likelihood that they are too immature to cope with pregnancy and the extensive physiological changes that accompany it. Teenage mothers generally have more difficulty completing their pregnancies successfully.

Fischer and Caudle (1973) found that nurses' attitudes toward abortion are affected not only by the reasons for each particular abortion but also by their own generalized attitudes toward the procedure itself. The nurses' personal beliefs had a firm influence on their specific impressions of a particular case, regardless of the circumstances surrounding that case.

The literature on abortion indicates that there are few serious or long-lasting psychological consequences for most women who have experienced the procedure (Osofsky and Osofsky, 1972). Among the Osofsky subjects, affect, predominant mood, physical emotionality,* atti-

---

*Physical emotionality refers to facial expressions (crying, neutral expression, smiling, etc.) during interviews following the abortion.

tudes toward self, and feelings about abortion were not seriously damaged or hampered. Those under age 18, however, more frequently showed the stress involved in an unwanted pregnancy and had greater psychological difficulties in dealing with their situation.

In a discussion of the need for abortion counseling, Brashear (1973) notes that a study she conducted in 1971 revealed that less than 50 per cent of her college level, sexually active girls were using reliable contraceptive methods. Her most sexually active subjects were most apt to use the more reliable contraceptives. Consequently, if this finding can be generalized, the less sexually active woman may run greater risk of pregnancy.

Summary. Attitudes toward birth control are determined by a number of sociocultural factors in combination with personality and situational influences. Factors guiding attitudes toward birth control and the choice of a contraceptive method appear to include degree of liberality or conservatism, congruence between one's preference for femininity and one's actual level of femininity, rate of sexual activity, and the extent to which the individual accepts her sexuality. Other factors are effectiveness of the contraceptive, influences from male partners, and parental pressures.

MOTHERHOOD

Pregnancy and childbirth can be expected to have varying effects on female sexual responsiveness. When the pregnancy and child are wanted, mutually agreed upon, and looked forward to with anticipation, and when the birth process is not overly difficult, the erotic functions of living are likely to be enhanced. Very often, however, the advent of parenthood, especially for the mother, brings with it additional role strain and unanticipated effects. If the pregnancy was unplanned even greater strain may result, especially for black women (Presser, 1971). If the father is willing to share the burdens and pleasures of child-rearing, he probably can expect his wife to be more responsive than if he regards the child-rearing tasks as primarily her responsibility. Although modern contraceptives have successfully separated erotic interactional functions from reproduction, the act of producing children cannot be divorced from family task assignment and cooperation.

It has long been known that the second trimester of pregnancy is often a period of highly erotic sensitivity for women. By the third or fourth month, the woman's physiological adjustment to pregnancy has usually stabilized, and this greater feeling of good health, combined with freedom from fear of pregnancy, may result in increased interest in sexual activity, especially when it is met with greater attentiveness on the part of the husband. Many (perhaps most) men are more aware of and responsive to their wives' needs during pregnancy, and this lends a feeling of intensified romanticism to the marriage. An unwanted pregnancy, of course, can spoil all this.

The birth process may be planned so that the mother and sometimes the father can watch. Plotsky and Shereshefsky (1969) studied the psychological reasons women gave for preferring to watch the birth of their own children. Studying 57 primigravidas, they found that many women desired to participate in this significant aspect of their lives and to achieve a feeling of completion. Other reasons given for watching the birth process included (1) distrust of their own conduct and a wish to maintain control over it, (2) unwillingness to submit passively to the control of the obstetrician, (3) need to use the experience for its counterphobic qualities, (4) voyeuristic tendencies, and (5) a need to detach the child-bearing experience from its emotional aspects. For some women, watching the birth process was experienced as an anatomical assault, further intensifying fears about body intactness deriving from earlier periods in the pregnancy. When delivery is seen as an aspect of marital relationship fulfillment, however, greater family solidarity may result, and this in turn enhances the woman's positive evaluation of her own sexuality.

Newton (1971) describes a phenomenon well recognized but often ignored: women can derive sexual satisfaction from the birth process and from breast-feeding as well as from coitus, and he argues, this could be a conscious part of sexuality. Awareness and acceptance of these pleasurable aspects of childbirth and child-rearing might enhance both motherhood and sexuality for women.

SUMMARY

Much more needs to be learned about female sexuality than is now known; nevertheless, we are not in total ignorance concerning the sexuality of women. A few points made in this chapter follow.

1. The sexual needs and responses of women are more closely tied to other emotional needs and are more likely to be socially conditioned than in the case of men.
2. A feminine sexual personality based on specific sexual attitudes can be described, but personality traits as measured by a standard personality test were unrelated to feminine sexual proclivities.
3. Females are very likely to control their sexual output in response to the demands of their partners.
4. As a group, women are more variable than men in their responses to erotic stimuli and seem more affected by physical forms of arousal than by fantasy.

5. Some women are much more sexually responsive than the average man, and a few are more responsive than any but the most unusual man.

6. Women likely to experience a coital orgasm are apt to feel that their sexual needs are about equal to those of their mates and to report that they are seldom coerced into coitus by their mates. Orgastic women have more generally positive attitudes and feelings toward sexual behavior than those unable to reach orgasm.

7. Virgins are not unresponsive to sexual stimuli but control the type and extent of their erotic outputs to fit personal and cultural norms. Personal and cultural norms are more likely to be congruent for virgins than for nonvirgins.

CHAPTER 12

NONMARITAL SEX

Although marriage is likely to remain a chief cornerstone of long-lasting, viable sexual relationships, it is clear that nonmarital relationships are becoming acceptable to a steadily growing number of people. Liberalized attitudes prevail in many segments of society, and thus nonmarital sex — premarital, comarital, and extramarital — may increase in incidence until the point of saturation is reached.

SEX APART FROM MARRIAGE

It has been suggested that human sexuality be considered a separate social institution, divorced from its traditional ties to marriage and procreation, and that a normative system be developed for this "institution of sexuality" (Sprey, 1969). This new normative system could provide a more useful basis for the analysis of sexuality and would give sex, as a human trait, social recognition. Norms for socially institutionalized sex could derive from such considerations as the pleasurable aspects of erotica, the private nature of sexuality, reciprocity of need satisfaction, and sex-role assignment based on classes of sexuality (wife, husband, prostitute, casual date, steady girl-friend, and the like). In the final analysis, the quality of that sexual behavior proceeding from inherent norms of human sexualness would be the basis for judging the fitness of a relationship. The norms of sexuality would apply to both marital and nonmarital sexual activity, but the marital-nonmarital (or procreative-nonprocreative) dichotomy would not be the basis for evaluations. Society would consider phenomena such as pornography, deviancy, and sexual crime by means of intrinsic rules of sexual interaction. Thus sexual theory would become one means of establishing a sociological analysis of the institution of sexuality.

Regardless of the desirability of establishing sex as an entity in itself, the changes necessary to do so are not likely to take place soon. Established social and religious norms, like all ingrained social facts, can be expected to continue for some time as important determinants of human sexual behavior. About the best we can hope for is that by comprehending the demonstrable facts about our sexual nature, we will be able to interpret and apply existing sociosexual structures more realistically until desirable changes take place.

PREMARITAL SEX

PREMARITAL SEXUAL ATTITUDES

Among the young and unmarried, attitudes toward premarital sexual relationships are becoming increasing liberal. (This is not as true for the parents of sexually active teenagers.) Despite the fact that several studies bear out the theory of liberalizing attitudes, however, any "sexual revolution" is in great doubt (Offer, 1972).

Two studies reported in 1970 indicate that increases in premarital coital activity are occurring primarily among women, or more specifically, among women attending college. Christensen and Gregg (1970) found that their male and female subjects from the Midwest, the Mormon culture, and Denmark all reported that more women were experiencing coitus. Nevertheless, while there was a significant increase in both the approval and actual experience of coitus among the women in the study, the men exhibited approximately the attitudes and behavior they had demonstrated in an early study (1958) completed by Christensen. This suggests a convergence of attitudes, bringing equality of the sexes closer to social reality. Significantly, it was in the Danish culture — the most liberal of the three — that equality between the genders was most in evidence. Christensen and Gregg believe this finding indicates that permissive sexual norms can induce a leveling of gender differences.

Bell and Chaskes (1970) also concluded that premarital coital permissiveness increased over the 10-year period from 1958 to 1968. Comparing well-matched samples of coeds from the same school (a large urban university), they found that the sample of 1968 coeds was more liberal than a sample Bell had studied in 1958. The 1968 women were less likely than the earlier group to have the level of their sexual intimacy influenced by their dating status. Only one in five girls had limited her coital experience to the engagement period. In the courtship statuses of both casual dating and going steady, the proportion of girls engaging in coitus was higher in the 1968 group than in the 1958 study. Guilt following participation in coitus was less a factor in the later group, but those girls with the most religious experience were still least likely to participate in premarital intercourse and most apt to report feelings of guilt if they had had coital experience.

Although the samples in the Bell and Chaskes research were in general well matched, there were more girls who had been engaged at one time or another in the 1968 group (37 per cent versus 22 per cent for the 1958 group). The average number of men dated by the 1958 girls was 53, whereas women in the 1968 study had dated only an average of 25. In combination, these two factors may indicate that women in the 1968 group had more intense relationships than those in the 1958 study. This intensity might have occurred with or without engagement and may partially account for the increased incidence of coital activity.

Although differences in methodology, questionnaires, sampling techniques, and geographic areas tested limit comparisons among the many studies of premarital sexual activity, other research does tend to confirm the results of the two studies just summarized. As noted in Chapter 4, two trends seem clear: (1) American women are both liberalizing their sexual attitudes and increasing their premarital sexual involvement, while American men maintain approximately the same attitudes and activities as 15 or 20 years ago (Robinson, King, and Balswick, 1972; Hunt, 1973; Simon, Berger, and Gagnon, 1972). (2) The average man, nevertheless, still engages in considerably more sexual activity than the majority of women. Schmidt and Sigusch (1972) noted similar trends among their West German subjects.

When increases in sexual behavior do occur among the young, they may comprise not only a greater incidence of intercourse but also more willingness to engage in intense petting experiences, such as oral-genital relations and sexual games (Hunt, 1973; Schmidt and Sigusch, 1972). Although this varied sexual experience usually takes place with only a slightly greater number of sexual partners than in the past, Schmidt and Sigusch noted among their West German subjects few *attitudinal* restrictions upon number of coital partners. Ninety per cent of their respondents did not require virginity of their future spouses, and this finding held regardless of educational level. Furthermore, of their 1970 subjects, 28 per cent of the males and 63 per cent of the females preferred a coitally experienced partner.

It is doubtful that such high percentages could be reproduced in an American population; indeed, Simon, Berger, and Gagnon discovered that among their teenage and college-age subjects, attitudes exerted a more direct influence upon premarital sexual expression than in the West German study. In the first place, permissiveness with affection was the prevalent standard. Secondly, there was considerable adherence to traditional sexual commitments (e.g., no sex with another while going steady, emotional ties to first coital partner, especially for women, and restriction in number of sexual partners). Premarital coital activity, in short, was not approached casually by the vast majority of the individuals in this study. Simon, Berger, and Gagnon state: ". . . the use of sex as a part of traditional patterns of courtship in our society (the exchange of progressive amounts of sexual intimacy for greater amounts of emotional commitment) still appeared as the predominant character — particularly for females" (p. 220). Liberality did not appear to be divorced from monogamous courtship processes. The Schmidt and Sigusch findings parallel those of Simon, Berger, and Gagnon in many ways, but the West Germans placed less emphasis on premarital sex as preparation for marriage.

It would seem, then, that for a considerable number of young people no particular sequence of sexual experiences with a specific individual necessarily leads to marriage; rather, the relationship between strong emotion and coital activity may follow the opposite course. Young people are not apt to seek out a wide variety of sexual experiences or a large number of sexual partners on the assumption that a permanent relationship with one individual will be the ultimate outcome of their behavior. Instead, they will convert their sexually free attitudes to behavior only with selected individuals who meet personally and emotionally meaningful criteria. Until such an individual is found, their sexual experiences will be somewhat sporadic, not organized into a demonstrable sequential pattern. This preferential sexual freedom I call *selective liberality*.

Once the attitudinal decision is made to engage in coitus, selection continues to operate, but the quality of the coital activity and the couple's shared participation in it are now the important factors. Murstein (1974) confirmed this hypothesis—and also the conclusions of many earlier studies already reported in this text—when he studied the relationship between a couple's sex drive and their courtship progress.

In general, Murstein found that: (1) perceived equality of sex drive was associated with good courtship progress as the couple themselves evaluated it; (2) couples in which the male's orgasm rate was far in excess of the female's orgasm rate showed slower courtship progress; (3) orgasms associated with the partner are related to good courtship progress for women, but are unrelated to courtship progress for men; (4) rate of orgasm for women is significantly associated with good courtship progress for women; and (5) a low discrepancy in the source of orgasm (mutual coitus, coitus with another, masturbation) is predictive of better courtship progress.

Yet selective though it may be, liberality today is greater and more widespread than it was in the past. In general, increased premarital sexual permissiveness, more openness and candor in discussing sex, greater freedom from guilt, and more realistic knowledge about erotic relationships prevail among the young and especially among the college-educated young. Furthermore, a good deal of implicit (and some explicit) support comes from certain members of the older generation through the various media, through training programs emphasizing openness, through public discussions about all forms of sex (including premarital and extramarital), and even through public and private education.

PROS AND CONS OF PREMARITAL SEX

When Kinsey (1953, pp. 307–309) listed the pros and cons of premarital sex, he gleaned his information from a number of marital texts. Some of the cons (such as guilt, possible pregnancy, and danger from abortions) have since diminished in importance. Others (such as the contracting of venereal disease, overemphasis on the physical aspects of sex, and the undesirability of marriage forced on one by pregnancy) may be increasing in significance. Still others have been refuted by new research data. For example, the marital texts discussed the possibility that females might be inhibited in their marital responses if they had been exposed to the more traumatic effects of premarital experience. However, most studies indicate that those with premarital coital experience are actually more apt to be responsive in marriage. As society becomes increasingly permissive, it is difficult to find reasons other than those based on a moral perspective for abstaining from nonmarital coitus.

Regardless of the arguments to the contrary, the chief reason given in the past for engaging in premarital intercourse was that the experienced person is a more responsive sexual partner within marriage. Several studies tended to confirm this viewpoint (Burgess and Wallin, 1953; Terman, 1938; Wallin, 1960). Actually, of course, many individuals engaged in premarital sexual relationships simply because they were fun and exciting. A response to feelings of love and desire to cement a relationship were other reasons for accepting premarital coitus.

Kinsey found the marital texts gave several additional reasons: premarital sexual behavior might test a couple's ability to make satisfactory sexual adjustments to each other; it might prevent homosexual patterns from developing; failure in premarital relations is less disastrous than failure in marriage; and sexual activity might enhance one's ability to function satisfactorily in nonsexual fields. There is no more evidence to support these positive reasons than there is to refute the negative ones.

Parental Influences

Parents continue to be a major influence upon many young persons' decisions about premarital coitus. Most parents, however, are more restrictive about their children's sexual behavior before marriage than they were about their own (Grater, 1958; Reiss, 1967; Wake, 1969). Reiss, as we have seen (p. 29), found that liberal college students frequently revert to their original family standards once they marry and have children. Wake (1969) discovered that both fathers and mothers decrease their permissiveness toward their children's sexual intimacies as sex acts increase in seriousness (move closer to coitus). In his study, significantly more fathers and mothers were more permissive about their own premarital sexual behavior than about the possible behavior of their children. Wake also found that the fathers in his group were more permissive than the mothers and would permit sexual intimacies at an earlier age. Interestingly, parents were no more permissive with their sons than with their daughters.

Apparently, the observation of some young persons that their parents implicitly follow a policy of "do as I say and not as I do" has some validity. This factor may partially account for the failure of parents and children to communicate with one another about sexual behavior and attitudes. It may also be one reason why peer groups, in the absence of strong family ties or deep religious convictions, may have such a high influence upon sexual decisions.

The generally conservative attitude of parents toward their children's sexual behavior was also noted by Libby and Nass (1971), whose study was discussed in Chapter 9.

Some Personality Considerations

Generally, the correlations between specific personality traits and premarital sexual attitudes have not been found to be high. This could be expected, since in America the dating system of the young and un-married is relatively independent of traditional restraints, while those within the never-married group are increasingly homogeneous in their acceptance of a single standard: permissiveness with affection. Personality variability exists in many otherwise homogeneous groups (religions, for example), and thus many different types of persons could fit within the large categories of "liberal" or "conservative," as these terms are usually defined.

Nevertheless, some significant correlations have been found between certain personality characteristics and attitudes about premarital sex among those who have never been married. For instance, in view of the fact that sexual interaction is an interpersonal event of a psychosocial nature (Reiss, 1970; Simon, Berger, and Gagon, 1972), one might expect extroverts to engage more frequently than introverts in a wider range of sexual activities. As we noted in Chapter 4 (p. 65), Eysenck (1972) studied unmarried students and found evidence to support this hypothesis.

In another study, Sutker and Kilpatrick (1973) had 11 white men, 33 white women, 15 black men, and 14 black women attending three southern universities complete the Minnesota Multiphase Personality Inventory (MMPI) and a Sexual Attitude Survey (SAS). They found that the highly permissive men attended church at a significantly lower rate than the more sexually conservative men, that the black men were significantly more sexually active than the white men, and that the black men began their sexual activities at an earlier age (mean age of 12.07 versus a mean age of 15.60 for the white men). For the men, *behavioral* predictions were best made on the basis of race alone, but *attitudes* of liberality or conservatism were best predicted on the basis of church attendance. There were no significant differences in MMPI scores for the men. In general, all male subjects were within the normal limits on the MMPI scales.

Like their highly permissive men, Sutker and Kilpatrick's highly permissive women attended church less frequently than the more conservative women. They also scored higher on Scales 3 and 4 of the MMPI. Nonvirgins scored significantly higher than virgins on the MMPI Scale 9.* In brief, Sutker and Kilpatrick found that regardless of gender, religion was positively and highly correlated with conservative sexual attitudes among both blacks and whites, that racial identity was the best predictor of sexual behavior for the men but not for the women, and that sexual attitudes were more liberal than sexual activity, especially for most of the women. When considered alone, none of the factors measured (including religiosity) was significant in predicting liberal sexual behavior.

In a third study of the influence of personality traits upon premarital sexual activity, DeMartino (1963, pp. 113–143) compared 30 females between the ages of 22 and 50 and concluded that those who scored highest on his dominance scale were more experimentally minded, assumed a more active role in the expression of sexual behavior, and were less annoyed at being seen nude by their partners. He found, nevertheless, only a slight difference in sexual desire between high and low dominant women.

In summary, then, current personality trait tests have failed to establish a strong relationship between personality characteristics and premarital sexual attitudes. Tentative evidence suggests that those with freer attitudes toward sexual interaction are not very different in their personality characteristics from those with a more conservative orientation. Those who are most apt to carry their sexual attitudes into action *may* be more adventuresome, sociable, and independence-seeking, or they may be more independent, frank, and worrying. They also tend to be more questioning of social standards and may score slightly higher on dominance scales.

Comparability among these studies is limited by such factors as the manner in which personality is construed, the wording and sequencing of questions, the population sampled (usually college volunteers), and the statistical procedures employed in data analysis. Nevertheless, within these limits the implication that the more sexually active among the unmarried are more experimental, daring, questioning, and so forth seems to hold. Only future research can establish the general applicability of this hypothesis. As one extends current findings concerning the relationship between personality traits and sexual behavior to popula-

---

*Scale 3 ascertains the degree of hysteria in an individual by measuring somatic complaints and a tendency to overcompensate for possible neurotic feelings (Good and Brantner, 1961). Normal subjects who score above average are said to be frank, talkative, enthusiastic, sociable, adventuresome, affectionate, and worrying. Scale 4 is believed to measure, in normal subjects, many of the same characteristics as Scale 3, but also indicates attempts to achieve independence from family and other authority figures, a tendency to be individualistic, and questioning of social and moral standards. When the results are within the normal score range, Scale 9 notes in addition to these components a marked tendency to be curious.

tions increasingly different from the study subjects, one must be increasingly cautious about applying them.

A THEORY OF PREMARITAL
DECISION-MAKING

Libby and Carlson (1973) have given us a general theory concerning the manner in which a couple make premarital sexual decisions. In Chapter 10, we saw that today a good many unmarried couples decide mutually to engage in sexual interaction, and I suspect that the mutuality of these premarital sexual decisions is often greater than that of many so-called "agreements" within marriage. Regardless of marital status, however, Kirkendall and Libby (1966) believe that focus on the consequences of an act rather than only on the act itself negates the view that simple participation is equivalent to liberality. Consideration of consequences, both positive and negative, may be more moral in many individuals' thinking than mere abstinence.

Libby and Carlson consider two major types of decisions that might be made by the premarital dyad. A decision is *accommodative* if the couple reach a resolution through compromise, bargaining, or coercion. In the *consensual* decision, in contrast, all involved feel equally committed and give equal assent to the agreement. As Libby and Carlson point out, decision-making is a process and as such the type of decision made is subject to change. Nevertheless, the symbolic meaning of the commitment and any accompanying acts is functional in shaping the decision-making process. The more closely both participants agree upon their mutual symbolic exchanges, the less likely it will be that their decisions will be governed by force and coercion. The man who espouses love only to win a woman's sexual favors is apt to consider the sexual encounter a mere ego trip, and if he happens to bring her to orgasm, that just makes him a better man in his own eyes. On the other hand, the man and woman who wish to have a sexual relationship simply for the pleasure of it and without further commitment may make a decision as fully consensual as that made by those in love.

Obviously, honest communication is an essential ingredient of consensual decisions. So is the capacity to know oneself and one's abilities and limitations in the erotic area. If decision-making is to be continuously consensual throughout a long-term relationship, a high degree of personality flexibility will be required when backgrounds and philosophies are significantly different. Unless one partner or the other is consistently willing to be the weaker, it is difficult to imagine such an incompatible relationship lasting more than briefly.

The Libby-Carlson theory recognizes this need for agreeable and similar backgrounds if consensual decisions are to be made. Here the extent of the agreement concerning values is highly important. Those with very similar values have a greater probability of reaching a large number of consensual decisions. The values brought into a sexual relationship may be those more conservative ones learned from parents and other adults and continuously reinforced by selection of a like-minded peer group. Women are especially prone to be influenced by conservative values, since they often have less emotional autonomy from their parents. On the other hand, the individual who is independent of his or her parental values may select or be attracted to more liberal peer group values. Whatever the case may be, values are apt to shape symbolic expectations, and recognition of differences in desires is likely to produce some degree of accommodative decision-making.

In brief, the three major factors involved in the accomodative-consensual continuum (can a decision ever be purely one or the other?) are type of socialization, significant reference groups, and nature and intensity of values. Libby and Carlson provide two major hypotheses based on similarities between sexual partners. These are:

> The more common elements found in the value systems of the participants, the more consensual the decisions made in the relationship (p. 373).
> The more congruent the reward cost outcome as perceived by the two participants in the dating relationship, the more likely that consensual decisions will be made (p. 375).

It is important to emphasize that while the Libby-Carlson theory predicts the *type* of decision to be made, it does not necessarily predict whether or not the couple will engage in coitus. Libby and Carlson provide little information about reliable or valid methods of determining which values the individual brings into play when making a sexual decision. Their theory also fails to predict the degree or intensity of similarity needed to provide high levels of consensual agreement. Within both groups and single individuals, there is usually some degree of ambivalence concerning general values and specific sexual philosophy.

Yet although the Libby-Carlson theory is still in need of further refinement (a limitation which they themselves recognize), it promises to shed light on many interpersonal decision-making processes, sexual and nonsexual. However a particular sexual dyad or group makes a decision, it is evident that the decision and its consequences can be a learning experience for the individuals involved.

EFFECTS OF PREMARITAL EXPERIENCE

Although, as we have seen (p. 242), Kinsey and his associates included in their 1953 study the standard arguments against premarital sex presented in contemporary marriage manuals, they themselves concluded that any premarital physical contacts positively experienced are correlated with the ability to achieve sexual responsiveness after marriage and thus with satisfactory marital adjustment:

> When there are long years of abstinence and restraint, and an avoidance of physical contacts and emotional responses before marriage, acquired inhibitions may do such damage to the capacity to respond that it may take some years to get rid of them after marriage, if indeed they are ever dissipated (1953, p. 330).

Recently, Ard (1974) conducted a longitudinal study to determine more definitively the effects of premarital coital experience upon subsequent marital adjustment. His results seem to reinforce those of earlier post-Kinsey research: among 161 couples still married to each other after 20 years, no significant relationship was found between premarital sexual interaction and adjustment after marriage. Of those with premarital experience, only 15 per cent of the husbands and 11 per cent of the wives reported negative effects on their marriages from such experience with each other. These figures increased by 3 to 4 per cent when the couple had engaged in coitus with other partners.

In evaluating the effects of premarital coitus on Ard's couples, however, it is necessary to bear in mind that these couples experienced their relationships during a time when society was much more negative about premarital sex than it is today. Quite possibly, both the premaritally experienced couples and those without such experience were expressing personal moral opinions rather than objective facts about their relationships, or perhaps after 20 years they had discovered that other factors were more important to marital adjustment than any type of premarital activity. At any rate, their responses tended to justify their own past behavior: most of those with premarital experience felt that such experience had contributed to their marital adjustment, while most of the couples without premarital experience thought their avoidance of sex before marriage had contributed to their adjustment. The study would also have been more precise had all those in the original sample responded. Those who might have been separated or divorced were not included; from an original sample of 300 engaged to be married couples, 227 marriages were still in force after 20 years. Nevertheless, Ard correctly points out that the popular belief that premarital coitus is harmful to later marital adjustment is not substantiated by his evidence.

Readiness for sexual experience is most pertinent, whether that experience is within marriage or outside it and whether it is coital or noncoital in nature. The following section offers some suggestions for maximizing the learning aspects of premarital sexual relationships which I have found useful with counselees across a wide variety of value systems.

SOME IDEAS FOR PREMARITAL TRAINING

Achieving a climax is usually not a problem for males, but it may represent something of an enigma for the woman who becomes passionately aroused yet is unable to achieve full release. As we noted in the preceding chapter, there is much evidence that psychological factors are of supreme importance in the female climax. It may take some time before a woman begins to reach orgasm from her coital activity, and few females achieve this release in every sexual contact. Patience, along with an attitude of desire, is often needed. For many women, the greatest obstacle to achievement of orgasm is discouragement because they have not reached it as quickly as they expected. Low key but persistent expectations are better than panicky attempts to force an immediate response. Nevertheless, climax is the aim of most males, and many are discontented if their partners do not reach this acme of sexual release. Furthermore, most females also wish as much relief from sexual tension as possible. It therefore makes sense to try to bring each other to climax in as many sexual contacts as possible. This can well be one of the most important of premarital sexual goals, since failure to obtain orgasm can condition a woman to fall short of full release. Men, on the other hand, may have difficulty delaying their climaxes, and thus working through premature ejaculation may be another important task before marriage as well as after it.

If they plan a continuing association, sexual partners should provide each other with frequent nonerotic physical contacts in which warmth, security, and love are emphasized. Such contacts can also test one's ability to abstain from sexual intimacy while maintaining the other aspects of the relationship. Stopping short can be very trying for both sexes, but it provides a realistic preparation for future periods of enforced abstinence.

It is quite clear that today almost 100 per cent of both men and women engage in some erotic behavior with their future spouses and with others. The importance of noncoital sexual activity in assessing one's sexual potential has been discussed by Eleanor Hamilton (1969), who points out that coitus is not necessary to learning about human sexuality. General petting, oral-genital contacts, mutual or self-masturbation, and interfemoral intercourse can all be fulfilling and in addition provide important experience based learning.

Another way to enrich premarital sexual experience is to read and view erotic material. This enables one not only to check one's degree of arousal, disgust, or disdain at such material but also to condition oneself to enjoy much of what was previously uninteresting, especially if the material is viewed with a desirable partner or is followed by satisfying sexual interaction. In addition, the *type* of material capable of providing arousal can be ascertained. One can also make some educated guesses about the kind of sexual interests a partner might have by noting the type of material that he or she finds most interesting.

The premarital period can be a most useful time for developing both an experimental attitude toward sexuality and curiosity concerning human passions generally. The period is one of high natural excitement, since few engaged couples have become as accustomed to each other as most marrieds, and if mutual exploration is encouraged both sexually and emotionally, marriage may be served well later when new ideas must be introduced to invigorate a sagging relationship. Furthermore, as we have seen, the experimental attitude is an important attribute of orgastically responding women. Actual sexual contact is not necessary to developing an experimental attitude. Kissing, game-playing, or the light petting that most engage in can all help one consider the extent of one's curiosity and attitudes toward intimate physical contact. In this area, some of the activities of sensitivity groups, such as microlabs, can be very useful.

MATURITY OF PREMARITAL SEXUAL BEHAVIOR

Earlier it was suggested that premarital sexual behavior was conducive to learning when it was free from excess guilt, could be combined with other life goals, was free from coercion, and was acted upon responsibly. These same criteria provide us with one means of judging the level of maturity of premarital sexual relations. Lester Kirkendall (1961a) has given us other criteria.

According to Kirkendall, when a sexual relationship tends to dissolve barriers and to build greater integrity into the partnership, when it enhances the self-respect of the participants, increases their cooperative attitudes and general trust in people, and adds to the fulfillment of their individual potentials, it may be considered mature. Obviously, these are outcome criteria and after the fact unless considerable care is taken to assess the relationship before coital contact is begun. A mature friend, pastor, counselor, or other third person can assist the young person to understand his or her attitudes toward sexual behavior outside the marital bond. Care must be taken to guard against rationalizing one's capacities because of a strong need for sexual involvement. Gradually developed erotic interaction can safeguard against immature impulsiveness.

If internally mediated self-control rather than control by outside forces is a sign of maturity, then those with the highest degree of self-control must be considered the most mature. Self-control includes the capacity to choose whether to engage in or refrain from erotic activity. Very often self-control is associated only with avoidance of erotic contacts, but willfully entering into sexual liaisons with as much understanding as possible is as much a part of self-control as abstinence. When the choice of time, place, and partner is freely made, internalized self-control is maximized. For some, this means waiting until marriage, but for others more permissive conditions are the criteria.

EXTRAMARITAL SEX

Extramarital sex (EMS) comprises both one-to-one relationships and collective sexual encounters, such as wife-sharing and group sexual activity. It includes petting and may or may not involve coitus. The petting may encompass fondling, mutual masturbation, oral-genital contacts, or any combination of these. While it is suspected that considerably more petting (especially breast-fondling) than coital contact takes place, it is difficult to gather reliable information on this subject. Neubeck and Schletzer (1969, p. 150) believe that among those low in marital satisfaction, EMS is usually sought through fantasy rather than actual involvement.

Kinsey and his associates (1953) pointed out that those who engage in premarital coitus are twice as likely as those who were virgins at marriage to try extramarital intercourse. If this trend has continued, one would expect an increase in extramarital coital behavior. Furthermore, greater freedom for females and the Christensen finding that liberality may be associated with a lessening of the double standard support the notion that extramarital sexual relations are on the rise. The waning importance of marriage as a permanent and exclusive source of sexual satisfaction also predicts increased extramarital sexual activity.

Mitigating against any rise in the rate of EMS are the strong social forces and teachings favoring monogamy. Many of the dimensions of EMS are similar to those of premarital eroticism, but the counterforces may be much stronger in their control of extramarital contacts. As with premarital activity, religion, family and clan expectations, personal moral scruples, fear of pregnancy, and failure to find a willing partner may all hinder extramarital expectancies. In the final analysis, the simple truth is that EMS is more difficult to arrange than premarital relations and the effects of public exposure are generally more severe.

REASONS FOR EMS

Until recently, EMS was viewed as a problem by most writers, but the fact that some couples have consistently engaged in it without dire consequences to their marriages has been known for some time. Bell (1966, pp. 151–153) has discussed a few of the reasons why marital partners may participate in EMS. Some individuals have not assimilated the monogamous norm as deeply as others and thus seek sexual variation as a release from marital monotony. As satisfactory as marriage is for some, it is unlikely to provide mutual erotic fulfillment to the degree many would like or need over an entire lifetime. Sometimes EMS is sought because one partner discovers the other has been having an affair and seeks revenge through retaliatory action. In such cases, getting even is a more important motive than real sexual interest in the nonmarital partner. Others wish to demonstrate their independence of what they feel are the unwarranted restrictions placed upon them by marriage. Rebellion against the unreasonable nature of marriage is their primary reason for seeking a nonmarital outlet.

Emotional involvement with a person other than one's marital partner, especially for women, is another important reason for seeking nonmarital attachments. EMS may grow out of mutual friendship. Making friends with those of the opposite (indeed the same) sex can lead to both emotional and sexual interests.

EMS may also occur in response to aging. As women become older they may develop their sexual capacities more fully and become freer of inhibitions. At the same time their aging husbands may be losing sexual interest. Whitehurst (1969, p. 141) found that the needs to "certify masculinity and assert vitality" were motives for EMS among his male subjects. Thus both partners may seek EMS as a means of proving their sexuality and desirability. For some older persons, EMS offers a connecting link to the youth culture much flaunted in our society.

Both general and sexual dissatisfaction within marriage are often postulated as major reasons for engaging in EMS. Neubeck and Schletzer (1969, p. 150) concluded that strength of conscience was unrelated to the need for satisfaction, but R.E. Johnson (1970) found dissatisfaction to be of much greater significance for the men than for the women in his study. Johnson also noted that the *opportunity* for EMS was an important intervening variable. Those with the greatest opportunity were the most likely to engage in EMS, although it is not clear how these opportunities came about or whether those involved deliberately sought them. It seems unlikely that all opportunities were merely the result of chance. Among Johnson's subjects who had not recognized an acceptable possibility for EMS, half the men but only 5 per cent of the women wished for such an opportunity. Johnson concluded that 50 or 60 per cent of the husbands in his sample had positive attitudes toward EMS. Thus, for men the combination of dissatisfaction and opportunity may play an important role in determining whether or not they will engage in EMS.

Women, on the other hand, seem to engage in EMS for complex and multifaceted reasons. Although one out of three of Johnson's subjects reported sexual dissatisfaction within marriage as a reason for seeking EMS, two-thirds of those with EMS experience were satisfied with their marital sexual relations. Opportunity was important for the women but did not have nearly the significance that it did for the men. Furthermore, although common sense seems to indicate that employment outside the home would increase a woman's chances of becoming involved in EMS, Johnson found that neither work nor college education were significantly associated with opportunity for nonmarital sex. The complex of reasons why women engage in EMS has yet to be untangled, but it certainly must include the emerging concept that females can and should enjoy erotica as fully as males and the lowering of the double standard. Like much evidence concerning EMS, Johnson's information comes primarily from counseling files and thus may be biased by this sampling limitation.

Hunt (1973) found an increase in extramarital sex only among his married women age 25 or less. Since his sample was largely urban and volunteer, it may represent the more liberal strata of Americans, but even among his subjects above age 25, extramarital sexual relationships did not increase beyond the levels noted by Kinsey (16 per cent of women by age 30; 26 per cent of women by age 40; 50 per cent of males by age 40). Kinsey (1948, p. 587) found that his noncollege males engaged in extramarital coitus more during the early years of marriage than after age 40 (45 per cent early compared with 19 per cent actively engaged in EMS at age 40). His college-level males reversed this trend, with only 15 to 20 per cent involved in the youngest age groups, and the active incidence at age 40 increasing to 50 per cent.

From our sampling of the literature it is evident that the motives for engaging in EMS are many and varied, ranging from a simple desire for pleasure to highly complex, subconscious drives. More often than not, a combination of reasons best explains the desire for extramarital contacts of all kinds, sexual and asexual. Recently, there has been an increased emphasis in the literature upon comarital sexual relationships, and it is these that we will now examine in greater detail.

COMARITAL SEXUALITY

Mate-swapping, swinging, and comarital sex are terms that have been applied to the activities of those who engage in sexual interaction outside the marriage with the approval and encouragement of their spouses.

Denfeld and Gordon (1970) studied comarital behavior and concluded that it may actually support rather than disrupt monogamous relationships. They suggest that certain "rules of the game" not only facilitate the successful operation of swingers' groups but also contribute to marriage. Many groups insist that each participant's marriage command paramount loyalty, proscribe all nonphysical attachments, and prohibit singles from joining. Other rules are designed to discourage cheating and lying. Seeking partners outside the swinger's own group is often forbidden. Telephone contact is sometimes discouraged. Control of pregnancy through enforced contraception is required by most groups. Denfeld and Gordon assert that discretion is of major importance and a common by-word among swingers. Swingers want to protect their jobs, community status, and children from undue criticism.

George and Nena O'Neill (1970) noted four phases in the swinging activity of their respondents. Phase 1 finds the average group sex participant highly interested, curious, enthusiastic, and very frequently involved. Phase 2 begins at the peak of involvement and ends with participation dropping from 30 to 50 per cent. The O'Neills believe that this reflects disillusionment, boredom, and reaction to negative experiences. The third phase, a leveling off, finds the swingee more selective about the groups in which he or she participates. Phase 4 represents an extension of the plateau of Phase 3 and is characterized by an attitude of "take it or leave it" on the part of many swingers. Sexual activity in groups becomes intermittent or infrequent, with those who no longer wish to participate finally dropping out.

Group sexual activity may be sought as a means of enhancing one's feelings of masculinity or femininity, as a method of overcoming a sense of alienation, to achieve greater contact with humanity, or to reawaken jaded sexual interests (Greenwald, 1968). Thus some positive consequences may indeed result from mate-sharing, especially if these activities are an adjunct to marriage rather than a replacement for it and if those involved have acquired a psychological set that makes positive outcomes possible.

Sometimes comarital eroticism is encouraged by a spouse as an excuse for his or her own desire to engage in extramarital sex, but often it is a genuine attempt to help the mate find increased sexual satisfaction and personal growth. Comarital sex with mutual approbation can lead to greater marital satisfaction for the pair, since the element of deceit is eliminated. Spouse encouragement may come simply as part of a hedonistic pattern of interests. At any rate, many individuals seek comarital, as well as extramarital, sexual relationships simply for the fun of it. A new partner may mean increased excitement and passion. No deep or hidden psychological motives need be involved.

When both partners agree, comarital sex offers one possible solution to the boredom that may occur in marriage, especially among those who have been married for several years. The two biggest dangers seem to be immoderate jealousy and possible affectionate exchanges that could disrupt the marital bond. To date, well-controlled empirical studies using control groups and other scientific safeguards are lacking. However, what empirical evidence there is receives support from clinical evidence. Most of my counselees who have tried comarital sex have, in my opinion, appraised their relationships quite realistically, recognizing the dangers yet evaluating their experiences as worthwhile and happy overall. What is not clear is whether comarital sexual liaisons indeed contribute to marriage or whether the marriages are maintained in spite of outside sexual alliances. Among my marriage counseling couples, at least, those who have developed a generally intimate friendship with their comarital partners have realized the fullest potential from their relationships as they themselves evaluate them. Karen and David explain their comarital sexual activity:

> "We had been married for about nine years when one evening we sat down and talked. Both of us felt that we were happy with each other, and satisfied with our sexual adjustment, but that despite our love, new experiences with others would give us new ideas, help us gain a deeper appreciation of each other, and promote greater communication between us," Karen stated.
>
> David nodded his assent and added: "We never had disapproved of the idea for others, but we had not considered it a need of our own. Now understand that our marriage was not failing. We simply had read a few swingers' magazines and talked with some friends we suspected of swinging. After a couple of months we decided to try swinging with some others with whom we knew we could develop deep nonsexual friendships. This may be a rationalization, but we think the total friendly relationship was helpful to our erotic get-togethers. This is our sixteenth year of marriage, and we believe that our life style is the ideal one, for while neither Karen nor I wishes for casual, uninvolved sex, we have learned to understand the needs of those who do and the feelings of those who totally reject swinging."
>
> Karen agreed: "Our marriage has been better because of our willingness to let others become part of it when those others were supportive of the marriage. Couples we felt might disrupt our marriage we did not participate with. Both David and I believe that the basis for our success is the high level of agreement we both feel." David concurred.

Mate-Sharing and Family Stability

Cole and Spanier (1974) have reviewed the literature on comarital sexual relationships and have also presented evidence from their own sample of 579 married respondents from a Midwestern university community of 40,000. This latter sample was not exclusively a sample of swingers, although about 2 per cent indicated that they had engaged in comarital relationships at least once and another 6.7 per cent stated that they would try swinging if the opportunity were available. From their review and their own research group, Cole and Spanier found the following facts to be significantly related to couples engaging in comarital sex: (1) It is usually the husband who initiates swinging activity, although many wives are satisfied to continue it even after the husband has lost his interest. (2) Swinging females tend to report that their marriages have become more equalitarian. (3) Mate-sharing couples are generally conservative in almost everything but their swinging activities. Most of the subjects studied by Cole and Spanier were middle class and placed considerable value upon material comforts.

Couples engaging in comarital relationships tend to validate their self-images through friends rather than family and are not likely to desire participation with extended kin, but according to Cole and Spanier, swingers are often as willing as nonswingers to provide financial support for parents. Thus among swingers strong emotional ties with parents may exist, even though a high value is placed on autonomy.

Cole and Spanier offer the hypothesis that value consensus between the husband and wife is the crucial factor in determining whether mate-sharing will be detrimental or supportive of the husband-wife relationship. They conclude that no available evidence suggests that comarital sexual liaisons are necessarily harmful to marriage. However, some comarital relationships do fail, and it is to a recent study of these that we now turn.

Swinging Failures

Successful swingers have been studied most because they are generally more available, but Duane Denfeld (1974) asks: "What of those who dropped out of comarital relationships?" Denfeld studied such a group by sending to members of the American Association of Marriage Counselors and the California Association of Marriage Counselors questionnaires about drop-outs from swinging. A total of 1175 couples who had abandoned swinging were included in the returns from the counselors. About half the counselors queried returned the questionnaire. Thus the results reported here are confined to those drop-outs who had seen a marriage counselor, are restricted to the sample of counselors who returned questionnaires, and are limited by the fact that many of the counselees may exaggerate swinging as the cause of their difficulties.

With the preceding qualifications in mind, let us look at Denfeld's results. Jealousy was cited as a reason for dropping out of swinging by 109 couples. Several husbands were concerned that their wives were having more fun than they or were envious of their popularity. Wives were often fearful of losing their husbands and thus gave up their comarital sexual capers. Other reasons, along with the number of subjects reporting them as most important, follow: guilt (68), threat to marriage (68), development of attachments outside of marriage (53), boredom and loss of interest (49), disappointment because anticipated benefits did not materialize (32), and separation (29). The wife's inability to "take it" accounted for another 29 couples giving up swinging.

Denfeld also found that 58.7 per cent of the time the husband initiated swinging, while wives initiated comarital sex only 12 per cent of the time. Mutual decisions accounted for the remaining 29.3 per cent. Dropping out of swinging was initiated by the wives 54 per cent of the time and by the husbands 34 per cent of the time. The enthusiasm of the men, Denfeld reports, was not matched by the women. Many of these wives felt that they had been forced into swinging activities by the desires of their husbands. Denfeld believes that this finding is evidence of sexism.

Nevertheless, the assumption that swinging is a sexist activity because it is usually initiated by men can be no more generalized from this sample than from other data. Regardless of their feelings after the fact, women must consent before swinging can occur. Inherent in the definition of comarital sexuality is *agreement* through a couple philosophy: each partner seeks to enhance his own sexual knowledge through relationships in which shared equality is a goal.

SUMMARY

All forms of nonmarital sexual activity appear to be increasing. Noncoital premarital sexual interaction is so widespread that it involves virtually 100 per cent of the population. On the other hand, premarital coitus is not now practiced by all Americans, nor is it likely to be in the near future. Nevertheless, in looking toward the future, Athanasiou and Sarkin (1974) envision an extensive polarization of postmarital sexual ethics: some individuals will continue to hold to the traditional notion of fidelity in marriage, while large numbers of others will embrace a comarital or extramarital ethic. Both ethics, of course, now exist, but the latter is still held by only a tiny minority of married couples.

The following points have been discussed in this chapter:

1. Both nonmarital sex itself and society in general would benefit if a workable set of norms could be established for sexual activity outside the marital bond.
2. Attitudes toward premarital sexual activity are becoming increasingly liberal, and there is a concomitant increase among females in the frequency of premarital coital contacts.
3. The rate of premarital intercourse among males has remained relatively constant over the past several years.
4. More females are willing to accept premarital coitus with casual or steady dates than previously, and engagement is less a necessary condition for intimate relations then in the past.
5. Premarital sexual activity may be regarded as an educational venture in which a humanistic approach to intimacy along with individual readiness for such relationships can be tested. As education, the idiosyncratic patterns of interaction and responding can be focused upon, while sexual techniques can receive less emphasis.
6. It is not necessary to engage in coitus or even heavy petting in order to learn something about one's individual responsiveness.
7. Several techniques for and goals of premarital training have been presented, but it should be noted that these activities can just as easily be tested and used during marriage.
8. Extramarital and group sex may be on the increase, and both have been found beneficial by some couples who are psychologically ready for such experiences or whose interest in sex has been waning.
9. Marriages in which the partners seek extramarital sexual activity are not necessarily in trouble, since many marital pairs seek sex outside the marriage bond simply for the pleasure of it.
10. During comarital relations, jealousy and possessiveness must be carefully controlled if difficulties are to be avoided.

CHAPTER 13

SEXUAL MORALITY

A brief review of the many published works reveals that sexual morality is spread over a continuum of permissiveness bounded at each end by an extreme of thought. One of these extremes sees sex as a human good separate from any traditional or nonhuman values. If no one is being harmed or exploited, any mutually agreed upon sexual act is a right one. The rightfulness of sexual relationships is determined by their outcome to the participants, and traditionalists do more harm than good by imposing codes of conduct irrelevant to modern society. At the other end of the scale are those who feel any sexual act outside of marriage is immoral and against God's will. Abstinence from all non-marital sex is proof of individual purity and goodness, and some among this group would even limit sexual expression within marriage.

Between these two extremes can be found an almost infinite number of variations. For example, a small group of writers has sought to combine personal faith in an affectionate Supreme Being with sexual-emotional functioning, regardless of marital status. They seek to combine faith with humanness, hoping to find greater mystery and satisfaction within the sexual relationship. For them sex is good because God made it that way, and when understood as part of His creation, it is morally sound with or without marriage. This group forms one of the branches of the new morality.

There is little possibility that these various views will ever be brought into a single monolithic one. Albert Ellis (1968, pp. 29–30), a leading spokesman for the liberal outlook, sums up his analysis of American sexual attitudes by suggesting three possible courses of action: (1) more democratic toleration of each individual's right to hold either liberal or conservative views; (2) movement toward a standard of liberalism; or (3) return to the conservative sexual standards of the past.

Since there seems little likelihood of widespread agreement concerning sexual ethics, the individual attempting to find satisfactory values will often continue to be faced with muddled confusion. Arbitrary decisions about right and wrong will, of course, be sought by some who will then attempt to enforce their codes on others. But resistances will come in the future just as they have in the past, and from these resistances will arise new systems of sexual ethics. Rationality, logic, humanism, existentialism, and religion will continue as the bases of moral

259

decision-making, but more and more the individual will seek his own values with little or no regard for formal considerations.

Nevertheless, personal decisions do not come from out of the clear blue sky. There must be some reason for them, whether or not it is recognized. Although we shall not delve into the formal propositions of moral logic, we will focus on a few definitive points that hopefully will assist the individual in developing his personal moral code. These points derive principally from those described by Harold Christensen (1969b), one of the leading writers and researchers in the field of sexual values.

THREE MORAL PATTERNS

Christensen has labeled the first of his three points on the moral continuum around which moral judgments orbit the *Absolutistic Position*. This is the traditional moral system of total prohibition of sex outside of marriage. Christensen states that the unyielding dogmatism of this position leads to morality by commandment. On the pleasure end of the continuum is Christensen's *Hedonistic Position*. He points out that this has been called the "fun morality" but quickly reminds us that equating hedonism with irresponsibility may be erroneous, since responsibility is a matter of accountability. According to Christensen, "The responsible hedonist, while using pleasure as his central value criterion, is most interested in lasting pleasures and the ultimate fulfillment of human potentials" (p. 10). Thus we are reminded that pleasure-seekers are not necessarily indifferent to other values.

THE RELATIVISTIC POSITION

Christensen's third category, the *Relativistic Position,* is currently in ascendency in many parts of the United States. This system of morality emphasizes the importance of judging each situation on its own merits. There are few universals that can be applied to all human sexual relationships; consequently, it is more ethical and more logical to consider each action in relation to the time, place, participants, and circumstances under which it took place. Christensen calls this position "a morality of circumstances." In an informal sense, the Relativistic Position is similar to situation ethics, although it often goes a step further in depending upon empirical happenings for its moral validation. The scientific method of data-gathering, analysis, hypothesis-making, and prediction can be used to ascertain the degree of morality within a given situation as well as to formulate public sexual policies when needed. Since there are few universal absolutes, relativists usually consider morality a matter of degree; thus every situation has within it the quality of more or

less. Traditional moralists do not recognize the shades of gray understood by relativists, whereas hedonists deal with these moral variations
by focusing primarily on the pleasure principle.

One of the most important characteristics of the relative position is
the fact that individual circumstances decide the ethics of any situation.
Morality becomes personalized in a manner not possible with either the
absolute or the hedonistic position. Concern for the individual is paramount. Rather than consider moral imperatives for their own sake or
pleasure for pleasure's sake, relativists regard the ethical outcome of a
sexual relationship as partly dependent upon the fulfillment of the individual needs and values of each participant. Those uninvolved cannot
correctly judge the rightness or wrongness of the situation, since the
worth of the relationship must be ascertained according to the phenomenal experience of the sexual partners. Of course, when others have been
affected by sexual acts, they become part of this phenomenal experience
and enter into the moral judgments of the partners. To ignore or deliberately hurt others when it can be avoided is considered immoral by most
systems and for all practical purposes may be seen as a universal moral
imperative. Jane's problem revolved around just this type of consideration as she discussed the pros and cons of her relationship with Bob.
This was the gist of her conversation:

> "I was brought up to believe that sex before marriage is wrong,
> and I know it would hurt my parents if they knew I had sex with Bob,
> yet I love him so. I was almost tempted to tell my father, but Bob says it
> is more immoral to hurt my father than anything else we could do. We
> aren't doing anything now that we are ashamed of, so why should we
> turn our relationship into pain for someone else? This is Bob's reason-
> ing, but I was taught that deceit is wrong, and I don't want to deceive
> my parents. Which is worse—to hurt them by telling them about Bob
> and me, or to deceive them by keeping quiet?"

Jane must find her own answer to this question, of course, and it is
one that many other young people must also face. If she tells her parents,
she will be deliberately hurting them (or so she thinks). Her question,
then, is one of deciding whether to follow a moral absolute that she has
learned (thou shalt not deceive) or whether to consider the pertinent
factors in her particular case. Note, however, that the moral imperative
not to deceive is only one facet of the situation. This is typical of most
practical experiences in that all three moral systems—the absolute, the
relativistic, and the hedonistic—are involved. Rarely, if ever, would an
individual follow any system in its purely abstract form.

Sex is often considered the ultimate expression of one's inner self,
and when the values one lives by have been individually determined,
this self-expression is even more highly personalized. Setting up one's
own standards and meeting them is an essential aspect of gaining identity. In some cases individuals engage in sexual relationships just because they have the opportunity to choose to do so without interference

or advice from others. This gives them the ultimate experience of privacy and affirms their individuality. If personal values have been thought through before such encounters, they may be further enhanced. All this personal choosing, whatever the final outcome, is an aspect of the Relativistic Position, which assumes that those involved are capable of thinking through their own moral judgments.

TRADITIONAL RESERVATIONS

Traditionalists argue that the very act of permitting each individual to choose his own moral code leads eventually to selfishness and to utter disregard for the welfare of others and the good of society. Ultimately, if society is destroyed, the individual is the loser. Furthermore, the traditionalists point out, human behavior is essentially unpredictable; therefore, no individual can accurately anticipate the consequences of his acts. Traditional values that have stood the test of time are best, since they guide the individual along surer paths. In turn, the experience of successful self-discipline leads to greater self-acceptance; thus living up to traditional values really serves the individual as well as society at large.

It has also been argued that the acceptance of dogmatic values can spare us the necessity of making difficult personal decisions, for much of our life is lived on the basis of judgments already made. If we were forced to judge every situation that arises on its own merits, the daily activities of living would quickly bog down. On the other hand, relativists argue that stereotypes retard social progress and discriminate against the person by failing to recognize individual differences.

INTERWORKING OF THE THREE MORAL SYSTEMS

It is obvious that no pure system of morality exists, for even the traditional code allows some personal discrimination as to right and wrong, and the relativists operate out of certain moral imperatives in spite of their denials. All systems claim to be interested in the individual, and only the extreme hedonists would ignore social considerations. Few if any individuals want to identify themselves as deeply immoral, and most find ways of rationalizing their sexual values to meet their personal needs. In fact, fitting values to needs can be considered a prime developmental task, especially as one approaches late adolescence and early adulthood. In the final analysis, then, the three systems lend themselves well to individual interpretation. It is the extensive overlap among them that makes possible the flexibility needed when personality dynamics change. The three systems are not entirely antagonistic to one another, regardless of the claims of their most vehement adherents.

RELIGION AND MORALITY

Until recently, the Judeo-Christian religion was the almost exclusive interpreter of sexual morality and has generally tended to support the Absolutistic Position. Studies over the past several years have demonstrated that the religiously devout are still less sexually active, least likely to achieve sexual freedom, and least apt to engage in prohibited sexual acts (Kinsey et al., 1953, pp. 686–687; Kanin and Howard, 1958, pp. 556–562; Ehrmann, 1959, p. 94; Shope, 1964, pp. 74–79; Reiss, 1967, pp. 42–45). Very often those who are sexually inhibited are the same persons who criticize the more liberated. Females are more affected by religious demands, and Reiss (1967) found that whites were more responsive to religious pressures than blacks. Once a forbidden sexual activity is begun, the rate of that activity remains lower among the more devout males than among the not-so-devout. This is not true of females, however, for once a very devout female begins a morally prohibited sexual act, her rate of activity is about the same as that of those less devout (Kinsey et al., 1953, p. 687). Christensen (1966, 1967) found sexual attitudes highly correlated with the permissiveness of the society in which one lives. He studied the sexual norms of Denmark, Midwest America, and the Mormon culture of Utah and found that Utah was the most conservative of the three groups. Thus religion still exerts considerable influence: even when this influence is not direct, it is still felt, since American mores and laws are founded on the Judeo-Christian tradition.

Most religious groups have modified their positions slightly in the direction of increased sexual liberality, and a few rabbis, priests, and ministers have become considerably more modern in their views. Mostly their ideas have encompassed situation ethics within a religious framework or have acknowledged the permissibility of premarital sex for couples in love. This is an aspect of the "new morality" and fits into the Relativistic framework. Few religionists, however, are likely to espouse the right of married people to seek sex outside the marital bond, and even fewer are apt to contend that sex should be fun without some sort of additional commitment.

THE NEW MORALITY

If formal religion has failed to meet the demands of modern erotic life, interest in sexual morality has not waned as seriously as some claim. The number of books, pamphlets, and articles published on the subject is legion, to say nothing of the other sources of information. Among the young (and indeed among many of their elders), concern with change in sociosexual conduct is high. A considerable portion of this interest is focused upon the "new morality," which often as not is merely some variation on the "old morality." The idea of picking one sexual partner and giving complete sexual loyalty to that individual underlies both the morality of marriage and the morality of approval of sexual intercourse between those in love but unmarried. Both espouse the notion that sex is good, pure, and joyful, but with only one partner at a time.

FOUR CODES OF BEHAVIOR

Borowitz (1969) has described four codes of behavior, which he has labeled the *ethics of healthy orgasm*, the *ethics of mutual consent*, the *ethics of love*, and the *ethics of marriage*. The last ethic is a view that sex can be best practiced in marriage, but the other three are aspects of the new morality.

According to the ethics of healthy orgasm, everyone needs sexual relief and the experience of orgasm or near-orgasm. Orgasm can be nothing more than physiological release or it can lead to greater self-expression and mysticism. The expression of our deepest, most human powers is denied us when we are denied orgasm, according to this view. We must all look out for ourselves in seeing that we have a satisfying sexual life, for although it may seem basically selfish, each individual is interested in seeking pleasure and avoiding pain when it comes right down to the fundamentals of living. Intercourse and orgasm that are sought for social or other reasons may not be true expressions of the individual self, and therefore according to this ethic are immoral. This concept applies also to those who deny themselves access to intercourse as a form of self-punishment. Freedom to express oneself sexually is a major criterion for assessing the moral worth of any interaction.

No specific commitment is made or implied for those following the ethics of healthy orgasm, since the focus of this ethic is exclusively on sexual relations. Concerns for the partner are not, according to Borowitz's description, genuinely considered in deciding upon the ethics of a situation. This puts the ethics of healthy orgasm in the category of self-interest.

In mutual consent, each partner fully agrees to the acts involved in the relationship. Each receives equal dignity and respect and enters into the relationship of his or her own volition. No form of coercion or exploitation takes place, and only those capable of giving honest consent can be part of the alliance. Mutuality of consent requires the individual to be skillful enough to assess the future consequences of his or her own acts and to be willing to abide by those consequences. Thus mutual consent adds the dignity and worth of the individual to the unqualified self-interest of the ethics of healthy orgasm.

The ethics of love maintains that love is more than mutual consent; it is the sharing of one's inner self. Since love by definition exalts and fulfills, sexual intercourse for those in love cannot be wrong. It must be the honest affirmation of oneself in relation to the beloved. It must be freely and genuinely communicated. For those who follow the love ethic, the relationship is the important consideration, and no amount of formal ritual will increase the morality of the sexual interaction as long as true love exists. Love, not marriage, justifies the sexual relationship. Winston Ehrmann (1959) found that males who are in love do not pressure their partners and are often willing to wait until marriage for intercourse, while females in love often willingly engage in premarital coitus with their sweethearts. The ethic of love adds to the criteria of mutual consent and healthy orgasm.

Borowitz goes on to point out the problems inherent in each of these ethics. It is difficult to assess the presence of true love. The erratic nature of human emotions is well known, and the attainment of personal honesty is often obstructed by social conditions. Borowitz seems to finalize his approach by suggesting that healthy orgasm, mutual consent, and love can best be carried out under the aegis of the marriage contract. In other words, the positive aspects of each ethical system may also be found in marriage, while the relationship is safeguarded from temporary and rampant emotional upsurges.

Although marriage can be based on love, honesty, freedom from exploitation, relations by mutual consent, and a variety of other positive considerations, it is clear that a good many are not and that few, if any, could operate at this ideal level for any length of time. Thus the dilemma of the old morality, which insists that marriage is the only proper institution within which sexual relations may take place. It is clear that from the standpoint of the individuals involved, marital relationships may themselves become immoral from time to time, as when one partner exploits the other or when sex is used as a bartering mechanism.

Wood (1968) notes this travesty and comments: "In a time when we should know better from the data of divorce statistics and various clinical studies, we persist in the belief that the moral dilemma of sexuality is dissolved by tying the marriage knot" (p. 11). He goes on to discuss what he terms a "person-centered morality." The essence of person-centered morality is its insistence that any evaluation of moral issues must have as its focus the persons involved. Individual personalities, transcendence, other-centeredness, mutually agreed on use of each other's bodies, and the personification of the partner through sex are central considerations in person-centered morality. The most moral position within this system is supreme concern for the other(s) involved in the sexual relationship. Concern for one's partner before considering oneself is the criterion of moral behavior. This position definitely fits the Relativistic view.

The person-centered morality of Wood can be found either in or out of marriage, for the true test of a meaningful relationship lies principally in its person-centeredness. Person-centered morality encompasses Christianity by insisting that we refer to what Wood calls the "personhood of Jesus." Christ is seen from the standpoint of his loving characteristics, and these, not absolute laws, are the measure of moral decisions. The spirit of love as exemplified in a positive, overall concern for the partner, not the emotion of love, is the guiding force by which true morality may be judged.

ATTITUDES OF THE NEW MORALITY

The new morality and sexual liberalism are not confined to the United States. Luckey and Nass (1969) studied the attitudes of German, English, Norwegian, Canadian, and American students. Here are some of their findings. North American women (United States and Canada) were more conservative in their sexual permissiveness, whereas English and Norwegian students were most liberal. Young people in the United States and Canada desired more guidelines and limits than those in the other countries, and only the English felt that their peers were the preferred source of guidelines. Marriage was highly favored by students from every country, with the preferred age of marriage being somewhere between 21 and 25. Canadian and Norwegian females gave strongest support to the idea that their first full sexual experience should come with the individual they intended to marry. About half the American females felt that coitus should wait until after marriage, and their male partners were more satisfied to wait than the European men. The double standard was poorly supported in all countries, although more women than men agreed it was acceptable for a man to expect his wife to be a virgin even though he was not. Many students in all countries felt that numerous affairs before marriage would not be a serious deterrent to the marital relationship, but Norwegian women were more inclined than the others to think that such affairs would negatively affect marriage.

German students were the most conservative among the Europeans, while the English were the most liberal. Luckey and Nass draw the conclusion that both male and female European students tend to have a greater acceptance of sexual equality, although women students, even in the most liberal countries, were more conservative than men. Canadian and United States students expressed ideas indicating that preparation for marriage and marital roles was a major motivation for much of their sexual behavior.

The threads of the old morality are deeply interwoven in the fabric of newer thinking even among the very liberal, and this tie with the past is an important social and personal security base. Christensen has pointed out that when a considerable discrepancy exists between values and behavior, many negative results can accrue to the individual. It is clear that those who relinquish older values without firm new ones to take their place may be heading for all sorts of personal difficulties. When older values are dropped before new ones have become established, the individual is in a sort of psychological limbo and is subject to confusion, misjudgments, misdirected behavior, and other personally disturbing phenomena.

INDIVIDUAL DECISION-MAKING

In the final analysis, everyone must decide for himself or herself the place, meaning, and importance of sex within his or her life. This placing of sexuality in juxtaposition with the other facets of life and attaching a value to it determines its goodness or badness for the individual. This is sexual morality. The individual must select from among a variety of social standards and norms those which will best meet his personal needs and must from time to time reselect and revalue certain personal positions in regard to sex, for the attaining of sexual morality is a dynamic concept that cannot be achieved once and for all time. Ellis (1968, p. 19) believes the average American is confused and knows that he "does not know right from wrong" about sex. Thus he continually changes his mind and often engages in sexual acts that make him uncomfortable, although not engaging in them would make him even more uncomfortable.

The process of gaining a moral stance is one of increasingly personal decision-making, accompanied by the responsibility that is concomitant with individuality. Some will accept institutionalized social norms, but to others such norms will seem overly explicit and concrete. Since personal morality is a matter of individual decision-making based on private experiences, ready-made values can do no more than set the general tone for ethical considerations. Perhaps, then, comparisons of the old and new moralities along certain dimensions would be helpful.

COMPARISON OF ISSUES

In arriving at any personal ethical system, certain considerations must be taken into account in regard to which aspects will be embraced and which will not. Some important issues in comparing the old morality with the new are the following: legalism versus idealism, internal versus external control, preoccupation with past errors versus the opportunity to take new risks, exploitation versus increased realization of one's sexual potential, control of passions versus full self-giving, and symbolism (e.g., marriage) versus actuality (e.g., the relationship).

Both legalism and idealism have important merits. Legal codes, such as the Ten Commandments or the established laws and social mores of a society, provide a solid basis for decision-making. Ambiguity is not so great. It is not necessary to make up one's mind about right and wrong; these are already spelled out, often quite explicitly. For those who prefer the comfort of "knowing for sure," the established codes reduce individual decision-making to a minimum. Furthermore, it is easier to institute a relationship with another if he also accepts the fixed code. Ready-made standards assist in evaluating behavior already engaged in and help the individual predetermine whether or not such behavior should be repeated.

Idealistic standards are less rigid and require that each situation and each relationship be considered on its own merits. The very best ideals would prohibit the comparison of one relationship with another, because each would be recognized as too unique and individual to be measured by any standards outside the alliance itself. Furthermore, there should be a marked fluidity of meaningfulness among situations within a given relationship. Each act and every individual is personified when ideal goals are the aims of the participants. The very nature of idealism is dynamic and intrinsically subjective. As such it is quite insubstantial and offers nothing concrete beyond the personal competencies of the involved individuals correctly to assess themselves and others.

Another facet of the old-new morality dichotomy is whether the major aspects of control should be external or internal. Those who espouse the necessity of external control usually point out that all societies have some form of control over sex and that sexual acts, even those done in private, may affect the public good. Thus, since society has a stake in every sexual relation, it should exercise control over the participants. More humans are needed in the world so it is wrong to prevent conception, or less humans are needed in the world and all unnecessary conceptions should be prevented. Some individuals are too young, some insufficiently experienced, and some just not bright enough to make their own sexual decisions; consequently, society should protect these innocents.

External control can derive from either of two sources. Not only is there the social manipulation of the individual just noted; there is also the direction of one person by another, often without mutual consent. Parents remind their children that they will be disappointed in them if they engage in sexual relations outside of marriage; husbands pressure their wives into some sexual act they do not desire; or boys refuse to date girls without some sort of sexual involvement. In each of these cases the pressure is from individuals, and in each a position of greater power is used to bring conformity to a standard of conduct set by the powerful one.

In contrast, internal control means that sexual relations are engaged in or refrained from only after one has studied the possibilities, alternatives, and consequences. The desirability of erotic activity is essentially individually determined, and the responsibility for actions is assumed by the actor. Internal controls, in adulthood, are acts of the will and demand that the individual making the self-determination be prepared to cope with every facet of his decision, whether or not these facets are predictable. The instability of human emotions and the multifaceted society in which we live make full internal control without some external pressure an impossible goal. Recent evidence indicates that college students strongly believe that sex is a private matter, not a religious or community affair (Robinson, King, Dudley, and Clune, 1968). External controls, then, are rejected as acceptable moral guides, but this idealistic outlook fails to point to specific, external-reference sources from which individual moral codes may be derived. To refuse external control is one thing, but this should not be stretched to denial of moral assistance from others.

A major complaint against older moral standards has been that many of them have concentrated too heavily on past errors. Preoccupation with past errors versus the opportunity to take risks is a dimension of some importance in deciding upon a moral position. For those persons with a desire to minimize the risk of being hurt, considerable investment in dealing with past mistakes is a must. In this sense, the old morality emphasizes past sins so highly that looking forward is a difficult task. Behavior that has been detrimental to another in a significant way, of course, needs to be thought about and modified, but dwelling on guilt feelings does not add to the possibility of change until after such pondering ceases. If one adopts idealistic standards, prefers internal controls, and seeks the maximum benefits from human intercourse, sexual or otherwise, one must take risks with the self, the other person or persons, and particular situations and acts. To avoid taking a chance with a new partner, approach, or type of sexual behavior because former situations did not work well is to limit one's personal growth.

Many individuals adopt external controls uncritically and then find themselves unable or unwilling to live up to them. But because they accepted a particular code that was not met, they reflect time and time again on their failure to live up to their chosen standards. They do all they can to avoid relationships and behavior forbidden by the code and frequently go out of their way to avoid activity that is even similar to the banned conduct. As a result, they not only spend a good deal of their time feeling miserable and self-pitying, but they also fail to seek ways out of their dilemma.

Another determinant of morality related to the risk-taking attitude is that of exploitation versus achievement of full sexual potential. Few persons like to be exploited and not many would argue that those who deliberately misuse another's trust are morally justified. When danger from exploitation is of primary concern, there is less possibility that the full potential of sexuality will be realized. This fear of exploitation is partly a matter of attitude and partly a matter of standards. One can feel that almost everything others do has some element of abuse associated with it. This lack of basic trust inhibits the abilities to love, care for another, and take chances with intimate relations. To achieve one's *full* sexual potential is only a goal, and one that cannot be reached. For this reason, many feel that it is not worth going out of one's way to obtain better sexual involvement and satisfaction. Yet one way of deriving the most from sex is to be willing to reach out for new methods, feelings, and involvements, even though purposely working toward increased gratification for all concerned runs the risk both of failure and of misused trust.

The inhibition of raw human passion is a major aim of the old morality. Yet if sexual passions are held back too tightly, other human qualities may not reach the peak of their potential. Thus one of the moral decisions that each individual must make relates to the amount of control that he or she wishes to exert over personal passions. Showing the full depth of feeling and passion one has toward another is one way of achieving the maximum potential inherent in the relationship. But self-giving with no holds barred is not easily accomplished, since open passion continues to be viewed so negatively in many parts of our society. The revelation of unusually strong passionate desires may be misinterpreted or devalued even by one's mate, especially if it is a female who is uncontrollably aroused. Many persons still do not believe that "nice girls" would let themselves become sexually over-zealous.

The new morality tends to regard the richness of powerful inner passions affirmatively and to see emotionally flat sexual relationships as unhealthy if not immoral. Practices aimed at helping the individual to "let go" are viewed as positive attempts to assist him in reaching his fullest potential. The unleashing of strong inner currents of eroticism, when mutually accomplished with an accepting partner, is a moral good because it is expected to have a beneficial effect on other aspects of the relationship. One is not reduced to animalism but is raised above the beasts, for animals are incapable of achieving a sense of passion beyond the mechanics provided by instinct. When released with an appreciative partner, powerful affectional-sexual emotions are among the greatest symbols of individual freedom, especially when the social system prohibits them. The passion of the new morality is not mere sexual arousal but rather the emotional gestalt of the whole person. When sexual activity is involved, it is merely the vehicle for full deliverance of one's total self to one's mate.

Status symbols signifying certain morally approved positions are most important in the old morality. In addition to rings, beads, tokens, and other gadgetry, the crucial symbol of morality in the past has been marriage—a ceremony binding two persons of the opposite sex together in a lifelong unity and personal commitment. It is the *institution* of marriage that is most important and that takes precedence over all other considerations. This state of social and religious acceptability (marriage) constitutes the only genuine moral atmosphere in which sex (and quite often love) may be personally communicated. Yet while they acknowledge that each marriage should be based on "love," traditionalists do little to intensify love relationships. Involvement of the marital pair with others outside the marriage is expected to be largely impersonal or secondary. First loyalties are to the institutionalized mores, life routines, and organizations that have surrounded marriage, including the church, vocations, children, or other socially desirable considerations. Seldom is one's first allegiance to one's mate as a person. It is better to be true to the values of the church, for example, than to acquiesce in a mate's requests when these are at variance with religious dogma. The traditionalists neatly handle deviations from their code by insisting that a spouse who really loves his or her partner will not seek morally prohibited relations.

The new morality is less concerned with socially or religiously approved statuses. Newer sexual codes stress the *quality* of the relationship as more important than other considerations. The word "quality" refers to reaching for the maximum potential inherent in the relationship—to freedom from exploitation, openness to risk-taking, internal acceptance of the relationship, and a committed, personal involvement. Other aspects of the quality sexual relationship include willingness to seek ways of improving it and the capacity to respond appropriately to shifting demands. Under these conditions any mutually agreed upon sexual interaction is optimally moral, whether or not those involved are married. It is the interpersonal context, as Kirkendall (1961a) has pointed out, that provides the basis for judging the ethical soundness of any sexual alliance. Jeffreys (1962) agrees when he states: "The respect of persons for one another, which is implied in fellowship and formulated in Kant's principle that we should treat people as ends in themselves and never as means to our own ends, is the basis of morality" (p. 16). The new morality by no means rejects marriage but insists that nuptial ties be based on a desire for quality within the relationship. Marriage adds to interpersonal quality by announcing publicly that those involved intend to make a total life together and seek social approval of their commitment.

Obviously, few of us would care to exist at the extremes of either the old or the new morality. If impersonal, legalistic codes were to rule every aspect of our lives, we would be depersonalized and robbed of the important autonomous feeling of having set our own standards. On the other hand, to be forced to decide the ethics of every situation on its own merits would seriously interfere with our daily, ongoing relationships. It is simply more efficient to accept some socially made rules and live by them. To the extent that established concepts of morality assist us in living fruitfully and in achieving our goals, they serve a purpose similar to the dynamics of the new morality.

PERSONAL ASSESSMENT

The extent to which each individual fuses past moral codes with more recent thinking depends upon many factors. How willing am I to accept the consequences of my behavior? What kind of a risk-taker am I, and what type of risks do I want to take? How depersonalizing do the codes of my ancestors appear to me? How much do I desire personal involvement of a dynamic nature? Can I best meet my real potential through ready-made codes, or might I actually increase my potential through making my own standards? What does sex symbolize to me? What really makes a marriage morally right? Are there genuine moral imperatives for me which are absolutes, regardless of situations? These and a variety of other questions bring to the forefront the underlying dynamics by which decision-making is determined.

In one sense every man is an island. Moral individuality demands that the final decision to include or exclude behavior be the responsibility of the behaving person. The mechanical absorption of others' ethics cannot be considered an act of moral decision-making. Following the crowd in any direction cannot produce moral behavior, but open, honest dialogue among people can assist all to arrive at their own conclusions. Many times, discussing rather than sermonizing opens the door to new understanding.

SUMMARY

Our brief look at the ethics of human sexuality has left us with no well-spelled-out conclusions about the specifics of erotic life. A few tentative generalizations are possible, however. These include the following:

1. Even among relatively homogeneous groups there is imperfect consensus concerning the right and wrong of sexuality.
2. Many of our legal and social codes are the direct results of Judeo-Christian thinking of an earlier era.
3. Traditional moral systems are quite concrete and specific about what they do not condone. Permissible behavior is less clearly defined.
4. Liberal sexual attitudes are not necessarily incompatible with a belief in a Supreme Being or other religiomystical experiences.

In fact, such experiences can often add to the fullness of sexual interaction.

5. The new morality is a many-faceted concept and is to a considerable extent nothing more than older outlooks modified to meet modern demands.

6. Central moral issues include the right of the individual to choose his own ethics, preoccupation with past errors, the control of passion, freedom from exploration, and the place of marriage or other symbols in determining the propriety of sexual relations.

7. A quality sexual relationship is one based on a person-centered ethic in which a high degree of personal regard for self and other is held by the participants. Love, honesty, freedom from exploitation, mutual consent, openness, and considerateness are qualities of a morally sound relationship.

8. If marriage contains these qualities of moral soundness, the marital state will add to them by bringing a sense of stability to the relationship.

CHAPTER 14

ATYPICAL SEXUAL BEHAVIOR

VALUES AND DEVIANCE

Tolerance for sexual behavior that deviates from social norms is, perhaps, greater today than ever before. Nevertheless, much pressure still exists to maintain traditional standards and to impress upon the public the "fact" that non-normative sex acts are pathological. A few years ago many of these same acts would have been prohibited because they were regarded as immoral, but today they are considered unacceptable because they represent behavioral aberrations.

The definition of pathology once stemmed from moral interpretations based on Judeo-Christian principles. This is still true to some extent, but other values of a more "scientific" nature are now the chief cornerstones of behavioral evaluative processes. The importance of our biological nature, the welfare of society, the uniqueness of our human attributes, and the wholeness of the individual are among the rock-bed considerations. Very often the critical issue has been the competition among various factors as they tug and pull at each of us. Clearly, all concepts of behavioral pathology are based on particular value systems, although those related to sex are most closely tied to traditional morality. The individual who prefers unconventional sexual relations is often considered to be manifesting some obscure personality quirk and may be treated as possessing a serious character flaw. Many persons suffer from irrational guilt because they have occasional desires to engage in socially condemned behavior. Their fears reflect the sociomoral basis of sexual pathology, for the desire to be socially acceptable is itself fundamentally a value.

Attempts to define and describe abnormal human behavior are punctuated by the "proper" goals for man and society. Those who believe that individual happiness, satisfaction, integrity, dependability, and personal growth are most important emphasize these values in their descriptions, while those who feel that social solidarity, cultural expansion, and ideological foundations should have top priority use these values as the nucleus of their definitions. Almost all professionals, however, view a balance between personal needs and social desirability as integrative when the individual finds and gives satisfaction within the interpersonal context while avoiding disruption of the social scene. In the final analysis, it does not seem possible to describe human behavior as abnormal without reference to beliefs, attitudes, and assumptions. Despite its desirability, there is no objective science of abnormal human sexual behavior.

DEFINITIONS OF ABNORMALITY

Lack of objectivity notwithstanding, considerable interest in describing pathological sexual behavior continues among professionals and lay persons, and much effort has gone into the task. A major difficulty lies in finding widespread agreement on the criteria of abnormality. Part of this lack of consensual validation stems from the fact that every definition of behavioral aberration is based on a set of assumptions that have been valued by the definer more than the other possibilities. These assumptions frequently include those concerning the "natural state of man," the importance of social learning in modifying biological drives, and the relationship of mechanisms to functions in achieving sexual satisfaction. (*Mechanism* refers to overt sexual acts, while *function* is the psychological purpose or consequence of sexual behavior.) The place of normative data versus intensity in sexual arousal is also of importance.

SOME POINTS OF VIEW

THE SOCIOSTATISTICAL VIEW

Some people feel that sexual acts which occur infrequently or in only a small percentage of the population should be labeled as deviant. It is reasoned that the society has been built on a set of social mores which have proved invaluable during its rise and that serious deviation from these values should come slowly if at all. New modes of sexual expression are not entirely prohibited, but the net effect of this sociostatistical approach is to curtail drastically the introduction of new sexual folkways. The assumption underlying the sociostatistical view is that certain types of sexual behavior, especially permissiveness, would be detrimental to social well-being. Those who prefer this frame of reference cite considerable evidence concerning the rise and fall of civilizations (Zimmerman, 1947, 1972; Queen and Habenstein, 1967). They note that sexual freedom is often one of the first freedoms to be lost under despotic rulers, for it is here that highly personal agreement may be strongest, giving rise to the thought that agreement in other areas is possible. Anything that smacks of a potential coalition cannot be tolerated by dictators.

In addition to the inhibition of large-scale sexual innovations, some disadvantages of a purely sociostatistical basis for evaluation of behavioral normalcy are lack of agreement about the cut-off point at which deviancy begins, the fact that all definitions must be considered in the context of the culture to which they apply, and a relatively high disregard for offending individuals. In a heterogeneous society such as ours, the individual may have more than one reference group from which his personal code of conduct is derived. One consequence of this multireference source is the limits it places on any generalizations about sexual behavior. Behavior cannot be defined as abnormal simply by reference to some presumed cultural code, since it is necessary to consider the basic background and major reference groups of the individual. Groups themselves might be defined as abnormal on a sociological basis or in terms of the goals of a given society, but this is definition by opinion. At any rate, the view currently prevailing in America finds public control of private sexual behavior distasteful, and as long as the individual does not impose on another's rights or violate public propriety, many consider private sexual behavior a matter of personal choice. Where this rule prevails, sociostatistical criteria are less important than psychopathology.

THE MORAL-LEGALISTIC VIEW

Legal and moral definitions of abnormal sexual behavior tend to reinforce the sociostatistical viewpoint: each seems to lend support to the other. Thus the legal and moral issues involved in defining behavioral pathology suffer from the same limitations as the sociostatistical position.

The legal notion of abnormality often hinges on the supposed ability of the offender to know right from wrong and on his or her capacity to deal with reality. Very often the legal code is little more than a set of outdated moral precepts designed to maintain the status quo. For example, many states define certain sexual acts as crimes against nature and as abnormal. Kinsey and his coworkers (1970, pp. 11–32) have asked whether any behavior typical of a species' ancestors should be considered a crime against nature. Furthermore, modern scientific and philosophical concepts question the precise meanings of the words "nature" and "natural." In addition to these limitations, legal definitions often assist further crime and exploitation, as when a wife wins a divorce from her husband because of his "animal nature" or when homosexuals are beaten and robbed.

Moral descriptions of abnormal behavior are essentially theological concepts biased toward the promoter's interpretation of God's will. The variety of religious beliefs concerning sexual sin scarcely need be mentioned, except to make clear the considerable ambiguity that prevails when theology is the basis for interpreting behavioral pathology.

Much anxiety exists among large segments of the population about both the normalcy and rightness of their sexual behavior. This anxiety has been described as the "ecclesiogenic neurosis," and its origins have been located in faulty religious teaching. The symptoms of ecclesiogenic neurosis include fears, guilt feelings, chronic depression, and unremitting tensions. Other symptoms are insomnia, early awakening, extreme irritability, neurotic dependency, and loneliness. This type of neurosis is highly prevalent among members of the clergy and religious zealots. Many of the symptoms may be expressed as gynecological complaints or in men as inordinate guilt over "strong sex drives." It is suggested that even today a high percentage of sexual problems stem from faulty religious teachings, and that consequently reinterpretation of the scriptures to fit sexual dynamics more correctly should be considered (Kroger, 1969, pp. 2–11). Obviously, religious definitions of perversion not only define pathology but also add to it many times. Unfortunately, theology can only tentatively redefine its position on behavioral pathology, since the dynamics of sex have not yet been clarified in a generally acceptable manner. It might be of some usefulness, however, to distinguish concepts of sin from those of behavioral deviancy. In order to make this distinction, we must turn to the behavioral sciences for help.

THE PSYCHOLOGICAL VIEW

The major responsibility for defining and treating abnormal sexual behavior lies with the psychological sciences. Within psychology there are several major points of view, each reflecting a particular theoretical orientation. Dynamic psychologists are interested in internal pressures upon the individual, whether these be from biological propensity, physiological cause, or social conditions. They may relate malfunctioning sexual behavior to unsatisfactory or incomplete psychosexual development or to psychic regression. The actual sex acts are nothing more than symbolic representations of internal dynamics that have as their base disparity between libidinal instincts and social demands. Deviant behaviors are a disguise hiding the real source of conflict and reflect the inability of the individual to face himself. The blocked flow of sexual energy finds outlet through various detours, and the major task of the therapist is to assist the individual in restoring this energy to its biologically intended outcome with the least disruption of his or her social life.

Existentialists take a somewhat different view of human psychodynamics. C. Wilson (1963) has related one of these existential positions to the functions of human sex and the place of sexual deviancy. He feels the very attribute of humanness has forced us into an awareness that while we are part of nature, we are also essentially alienated and separated from it. The fundamental human longing to be permanently incorporated into the scheme of things and to have a sense of attachment with nature and one's fellow men can never be fully gratified. In spite of the presence of beloved others, we are aware of an apartness from them and recognize that we must walk some paths alone. This feeling of alienation can be heightened or decreased depending upon whether or not we exist in a loving atmosphere, but it can never be completely eliminated.

During sexual intercourse, and especially during orgasm, we are about as close to nature (and thus to our fellow men) as we can possibly be. Consequently, Wilson speculates, one of the major functions of human sexual relations is to reduce feelings of aloneness and alienation. But since the most that sexual interaction can accomplish is to bring us temporarily into contact with basic nature, sexual relations and particularly coitus must be continually re-enacted. When the feelings of alienation have been dispelled, a sexual cycle has been completed. Yet we can never learn anything from sex in and of itself, because biology has a sort of cutoff point in the human that prevents our ever attaining a state of full and permanent satisfaction. This *damper mechanism*, as Wilson terms it, not only limits what we can learn from sexual activity but also keeps us from achieving a lasting identification with our own basic nature.

If a sense of contact with nature is to come about through sexual relations, sexual partners must have a partial but permanent air of strangeness. When this sense of the unfamiliar is lost, one's partner cannot bring one into a feeling of having verified one's individual uniqueness through communication with the unknown of human existence. One relates only to that which is familiar. To counteract this loss of essential strangeness, one must seek a new sexual partner or engage in some sexual acts that society considers perversions. These may be what Wilson calls the minor perversions, such as oral-genital relations or homosexuality. In other cases, major deviations are carried out in the subconscious expectation of achieving greater contact with nature through the heightened passion that these acts will bring. Thus sexual perversions are ultimately attempts to validate the self and to bind that self permanently with nature.

Those who follow the behavioral tradition in psychology take a third view of abnormal sexual acts. Behaviorists are more concerned with schedules of reinforcement as they affect habit patterns than with internal dynamics. Variant acts are learned and persist because they have reinforcing value for the individual. Unacceptable sexual responses are acquired through conditioning or through contiguity with others who perform similar acts. Any unwanted sexual responses are eliminated by the use of a variety of counterconditioning techniques.

The major theories of psychopathology tend to emphasize constructs that are particular to the general orientations underlying them, but they agree that social learning plays a crucial role in the production of anomalies and that many deviant acts are carried out because doing so reduces neurotic anxiety. All would agree that behavior which has the highest reward value is most apt to persist. Most would agree that normal behavior could be defined in terms of achieving personal fulfillment while meeting the requirements for living in society. The concept of sin implies violation of a presumed rule of a divine deity. Sin is most closely tied to behavioral pathology when the individual engages in acts that reduce personal fulfillment because he considers them morally reprehensible.

THE HEALTHY PERSONALITY

In an attempt to avoid the complexities inherent in describing abnormal behavior, Shoben (1964, pp. 12–21) has suggested concentration on definitions of normalcy. Normalcy, according to Shoben, exists when man's special attributes are used in a manner that integrates his life style and personality into a satisfying wholeness. The uniqueness of our symbolic processes is our major asset, because through them we can learn from our own and others' experience, gain self-control by anticipating behavioral consequences, and set goals beyond our immediate needs. Our second major asset, our long period of dependency, allows us the opportunity to grow through the dependent period to independence and finally to adult dependability (Mowrer and Kluckhohn, 1944).

Through this developmental sequence, the normal individual learns to accept behavioral limits out of concern for others, forms and maintains intimate relationships, acquires the ability to acknowledge a need for others, and comes to act in accordance with democratic principles. Shoben lists as democratic principles not only a concern for others but also a valuing of persons above things and a willingness to participate in mutually gratifying relationships with many types of individuals, regardless of personal knowledge of them. He further suggests that our capacity to form idealistic attitudes beyond our capabilities is a normal attribute: "an integrative adjustment does not consist in the attainment of perfection but in striving to act in accordance with the best principles of conduct that one can conceive. Operationally, this notion implies that there is an optimum discrepancy between one's self concept and one's ego ideal" (p. 19).

Shoben's normal person is able to delay gratification, to maintain intimate relationships, to be dependable and therefore relatively predictable, to exert self-control, to understand the human need for others, to think and act democratically, and to strive to meet a set of individually formulated idealistic standards. Most importantly, he or she is able to integrate these elements into a personal life style so that each blends smoothly with all the others. In all this the normal one exercises a certain freedom of choice. Harry and Jean are representative of a well-organized couple:

> After several years of marriage, Harry decided that he wanted greater sexual variety than he had been accustomed to with his wife

Jean. He pondered the possibility of initiating new types of activities with Jean, and considered both extramarital relations and the vicarious enjoyment of sex (substituting pornographic reading for direct sexual expression). Since he wanted to include his wife in his activities, he told her of his desire for greater variety and shared his feelings about it with her. Because Jean was usually a congenial person, they worked out a plan involving all three of the possibilities that Harry had originally considered.

Although this couple engaged in a variety of sexual acts often considered "abnormal," indulged in occasional nonmarital sex through joint participation in group activity, and found pleasure in viewing pornography together, to a remarkable degree they meet Shoben's criteria for judging normalcy. Harry was prepared to face the consequences of telling his wife about his desires. Fortunately, she was like-minded. As a couple they understood and acknowledged their need for each other and on some occasions for others outside their marriage. Because of their joint decision, they were able to heighten the intimacy of their relationship while continuing to act dependably. Each could exert greater self-control with the help of the other. Absence of the double standard attested to the democratic basis of their marriage. As a couple they knew that there could be undesirable outcomes from their behavior, but they were prepared to accept them. Each believed that in the long run their activities would lead to their fuller functioning as individuals and to their greater integration as a couple.

Shoben's criteria of normalcy are obviously value judgmental and idealistic, and as such they are seldom, if ever, met. He did not intend them as absolute standards of judgment but rather as goals to be sought. His criteria emphasize the fact that normalcy is always a matter of degree. It is this more or less aspect that makes possible the wide range of behavior accepted as free from pathology. The values set forth by Shoben are, of course, subject to individual interpretation. The length of time that gratification should be delayed is itself an individual problem and subject to debate. Yet in spite of these limitations, the Shoben criteria will, for large segments of American society, prove to be useful generalizations.

PERSONALITY GROWTH

Recently a number of writers, recognizing that the ideals of adjustment and stability reflect only a normative view, have argued that personal growth that allows the healthy person to maximize his or her potential is more suited to the needs of most individuals (Chiang and Maslow, 1969; Otto, 1969; Stoller, 1970b; Rogers, 1970). As a consequence of this new theory, a number of "growth centers" have arisen around the country, and much small-group activity, aimed at personal development rather than readjustment, is taking place. The family is also a small group, and some aspects of small-group theory certainly apply to the family or even to a couple. Thus personal effectiveness, couple effectiveness, and family effectiveness in terms of interpersonal functioning are widely accepted goals in today's society. Such increased ability to relate effectively to others implies nothing more than increased use of latent potential. In other words, personal growth does not mean psychological recovery but rather a reaching out to oneself and to one's fellow men. Growth is moving toward the self-actualizing personality so well described by Maslow (1954).

Self-actualizing people, Maslow discovered, are realistically oriented, accept themselves and others, focus their attention on specific problems, resist useless conformity, are creative, democratic, autonomous, and independent, have an air of detachment and a need for privacy, and have profound and mystical experiences, although these are not necessarily religious.

There are exceedingly few persons who approach the ideal self-actualizing personality. Basic biological and psychological needs must be met before higher values can be sought. Trust can be learned (Stoller, 1970b) and usually precedes spontaneity. Furthermore, as White (1966, Chap. 9) reminds us, there is no set of traits that applies universally to all adults under all conditions. As one moves from adolescence toward adulthood, specialization increasingly takes place in such areas as occupation, family life styles, and role-taking. To White, then, growth is both directional and process. One needs to be aware of the direction of growth and of the forces that impel one in that direction, but one must also be aware of the processes of growth: inner dynamics, one's philosophy about the nature of man, interpersonal exchanges, levels of communication, and so forth. An awareness of growth processes is conducive to self-direction and a reminder that one does indeed have a certain degree of power to shape one's destiny.

The healthy individual, in brief, is not merely free of crippling habits, degrading self-attitudes, contempt for mankind, lack of trust, or other negative functions; he or she is one who can reach out to others, enjoy the mysteries of life, and turn on to himself or herself. Such a person is able to engage in normal relationships as he or she defines normal and is the fully functioning person in the self-actualizing family described by Olim (1968).

SEX AS A RELATIONSHIP

NORMAL RELATIONSHIPS

Most sexuality is carried out with another person or persons, and the exclusive loner is seldom considered normal. Thus relationship criteria of normal sexuality loom as most significant. Personal limitations, whatever their source, are important primarily because they impair one's ability to relate satisfactorily to others. It is within the relationship context that sexual pathology becomes most manifest.

If personal enhancement, pleasurable feelings, psychological satisfaction, adjustment to one's group, and a sense of achievement are sound goals of sexual interaction, it is clear that one measure of normalcy is the extent to which these ends are met in an enduring manner. Chronic dissatisfaction with oneself or with significant others lessens the possibility of establishing or maintaining a relationship based on meaningfulness. The long-term consequences of sexual interaction are important bases for judging the normalcy of sexual acts. When these outcomes are characterized by increased self-fulfillment, the enhancement of a satisfactory self concept, and adequate interpersonal competence without stressful social ostracism, normal interpersonal behavior has occurred.

The idea of a normal relationship implies a certain freedom of will, an inherent purposefulness, and limited predictability. The notion that we are capable of exerting some degree of conscious control over our environment (including, most importantly, those other humans with whom we interact) and over our own behavior underlies these propositions. It is assumed that those partners most able to handle knowledgeably and insightfully the factors of freedom of choice, purposefulness, and predictability will be in the best position to judge the normalcy of their own acts. Neither those driven by uncontrollable needs nor those stifled by irrational fears are fully capable of choosing.

Normal sexual behavior carries with it the implicit notion that the activity was chosen on a rational basis and was fairly free from unconscious needs or strivings. The more we know of ourselves and of the reasons for our choices, the more likely we are to choose self-enhancing behavior and to rid ourselves of personally unacceptable actions. This statement assumes not only intellectually based insight but also the emotional capacity to accept one's self or to change that which is unacceptable. Self-acceptance is a developmental task lasting throughout the life span of each individual. Stagnation of self-acceptance at any developmental level is itself a form of psychopathology.

The idea of freedom of will and intentionality suggests planfulness based on free choice. Coercion, defensiveness, and the like are signs that freedom of choice is being compromised and that the intended outcomes, for one or all, are apt to be distorted. When sexual partners willingly give themselves up to one another, intentionality has been an integral part of their relationship.

The concept of purposefulness is based on two attributes of a viable relationship: a state of agreement concerning the many facets of togetherness, and an intrinsic reason for grouping together into a human alliance. The existential notion of searching for a basic identity with nature and man's instinctive gregariousness are important motives for grouping.

Every group has many purposes for banding together, and purposefulness, in this context, is a label for this conglomerate of purposes. A purpose is a goal, a desired outcome or reason for engaging in singular acts. For example, the purposefulness of a relationship might be to find and create love with another person, but in order to do this, many everyday purposes must also be carried out. The everyday purposes either contribute to or detract from the total purposefulness of the relationship. When the daily dynamics of relating are primarily negative, relationship purposefulness is apt to suffer. Either a single highly devastating act or a cluster of many less drastic ones can be responsible for the failure to fulfill purposefulness.

Sometimes failure to achieve perceived goals is clearly evident, and the individual consciously senses a broken agreement. Understanding at the level of awareness has dissipated. At other times, however, a vague sense of dissatisfaction exists even though many consciously expected outcomes have been realized. In this case, either the need for fulfillment of the gregarious instinct (through greater intensity or through increased diversity) or the search for existential communion with nature has been frustrated. Satisfaction is present, but the fundamental joy of communing with oneself through association with others is absent. Purposefulness is being only partially fulfilled.

In a normal relationship the participants expect to be able to predict, in a broad sense, the reactions each might expect of the other. It is this relative predictability that makes the continued existence of the relationship possible. Predictability makes for stability. Highly erratic behavior is abnormal because those within the relationship are unable to guess the moves, responses, or requests that might occur next. Planning is dependent upon predictability, and relationships are usually begun and continued on a basis of planned satisfaction. In addition, the use of human foresight is also partly dependent upon predictability; thus one of our most human characteristics may be denied expression when many predictions about ourselves and others are unreliable. Although a considerable amount of precise predictability is desirable, however, a limited degree of uncertainty, determined by the personal desires of those within the relationship, adds a sense of excitement. The exact point at which accurate foreknowledge of anticipated responses becomes threatening is a matter to be decided within each alliance.

Normally, then, the determinants of sexual acts should be a high degree of freedom of choice, a fulfilling and expanding purposefulness, and enough predictability of response that a sense of reliability is engendered.

BEHAVIORAL CRITERIA

Freedom of choice, purposefulness, and predictability may be viewed as motivational constructs whose effectiveness is best judged by the behavior they bring about. The existence of all three is inferred from the consequences of actions. In the final analysis, it is through overt behavioral acts (including verbalizations) that motivation, integration, humanness, and transcendental movement are best communicated to self and others. Abnormal processes are maladaptive behavioral acts that interfere with this communication. By focusing on overt behavior, we obtain clearly visible criteria that can be evaluated in terms of both personal and social values. When conscious intentions are transformed into behavioral acts that are free from severe public censure, normal relationships may be maintained. In addition to high visibility, behavioral criteria emphasize conscious control, cooperation, freedom from irrational fears or guilt, and functional outcomes.

ATYPICAL SEXUALITY

The word "atypical" can be used to denote the fact that certain forms of sexual behavior result in disequilibrium between the idealized self (ego ideals) and the real self. The idealized self comprises several factors, including individually perceived social ideals and standards, insights into the self of significant others, ideologies of major reference groups, and personal moral scruples. Atypical behavior is usually unacceptable to oneself, to those with whom one interacts, to one's personal reference groups, and in extreme cases to the larger society. Perhaps the most important consequences of atypical behavior are the distorting, clouding, and lowering of one's self picture and the serious disruption of interpersonal relationships. The word "atypical" emphasizes an incongruity between demands and outcomes and points out the psychosocial nature of personal dynamics.

An individual might regularly engage in specific atypical acts that supply immediate satisfaction but interfere with long-term goals. Other persons develop a sexual life style that has the same, although more intense, effects. Sexual behavior is atypical of that which ordinarily engenders personal and social satisfaction, when guilt is overwhelming or unusually persistent, when the behavior is obsessive or compulsive, or when it produces prolonged or serious psychological disequilibrium. Other relational criteria include a considerable loss of happiness to one or both partners over an extended period of time, irresponsibility, discovery that one is purposely misusing the other, and agreement that their behavior is wrong for them.

Guilt and shame are two of the greatest inhibitors of full sexual release. A good deal of sexual interaction carries with it a degree of guilt, either because the individual has learned that certain acts are "bad" and "sinful" or because he or she cannot perform up to specific standards. The mere presence of guilt in initial contacts is no sign that the behavior should be stopped or that attitudes should be changed. Similarly, feelings of shame about particular sexual activities do not necessarily indicate that such activities should be excluded. In modern society many individuals feel little moral inhibition but avoid certain sexual behaviors because they are ashamed of their lack of know-how. The point is that whether guilt or shame is confined to particular sexual acts or is generalized as overall sexual inhibition, discovery that it is interfering with desirable relationships is a sign that changes should be made.

When irrelevant thoughts persistently flood one's mind or when the exact same acts must be repeated in detail over and over again, we have obsessive or compulsive behavior. Often as not the two operate simultaneously within the same person. Obsessive thoughts help separate action from feelings about that action, while compulsions assist in avoiding behavior that might result in recognition of unresolved psychological needs. Both the thoughts and the actions tend to isolate the individual from real sources of anxiety and thus are disassociating mechanisms. Ritualistic behavior, sequences of compulsion, and recurrent thought processes are especially tormenting during sexual encounters, since they are often indirect methods of expressing forbidden impulses. The obsessions and compulsions themselves may be experienced with considerable horror, disgust, or guilt. Unfortunately, they may be of such magnitude or so completely divorced from deeper needs that no real relief is found.

SPECIFIC SEXUAL VARIANTS

FETISHISM

A fetish is a particular kind of compulsion in which sexual arousal and behavior can occur only in the presence of a specific stimulus. The function of a fetish is to detour direct but unacceptable sexual expression into more psychologically subtle routes, thus relieving overwhelming anxiety. The fetish must be an article or other stimulus which is nearly the exclusive determinant of sexual expression. Locks of hair, articles of clothing, or other mementoes of romantic origin and intent are not fetishes, even though they may arouse vicarious sexual memories.

A fetish is an essential part of some relationships, and as long as the fetish is available and all the participants are agreeable, no major problems need result. However, dependence upon a fetish limits the effectiveness of other sexual stimulants, and among some fetishists no human contact occurs. All that is needed for a complete cycle of arousal, action, and satisfaction is some inanimate object. From the standpoint of relationship criteria, then, it is the *exclusiveness* of the fetish that assigns it to the atypical category. Fetishism of such a strong pathological nature is almost exclusively a male problem and is likely tied to fears concerning masculinity or to other phobias.

PRESSURING

Certain types of behavior may be engaged in by one partner in a relationship because they are demanded by the other. Such actions may cause severe or prolonged psychological stress, and their final outcome is apt to be a breakup of the relationship, either through a change in equilibrium or because of increasingly heightened defense barriers. The compliant partner may be fighting desperately (although perhaps subconsciously) to maintain the partnership, but because of dependency needs rather than by free choice.

A good deal of the time the stresses produced by pressuring are hidden beneath a variety of defense mechanisms, but from time to time they will burst forth clearly into consciousness, producing a flood of guilt, anxiety, self-doubt, and other negative reactions. In some persons these anxieties are handled by projecting onto the partner the doubts that one has about oneself. In others even greater internalization of negative self-evaluation occurs. Both the relationship itself and the psychological health of the individuals involved in it suffer. Continual doubts about oneself or one's mate should be confronted realistically and not allowed to exist in smothered silence. Often professional assistance in working through the needs of all within the relationship is required.

Sometimes one individual, recognizing that he is deliberately being taken advantage of, feels resentful. Such resentment may have little foundation in concrete evidence, but it may also be based on behavioral and motivational knowledge of a partner. In either case psychological distress, with its accompanying guilt, anxiety, and defense mechanisms, is apt to ensue. Facing one's partner with one's feelings or with the facts often helps to clear the air. Feelings without real evidence may be projections of an attitude of indifference toward oneself that one feels but cannot face. Whenever there is persistent antagonism toward a desirable partner, efforts must be made to reduce the antagonism before indifference sets in.

MORAL GUILT

Occasionally, both partners agree with those outside their alliance that certain behavior they are engaging in is morally wrong. Often the partners will simply stop the action in question, but the behavior may produce such immediate satisfaction that strong habits have been formed which are not subject to rational control. Help from a therapist, who can assist the couple to develop their own values based on self-understanding and mutual agreement, may be needed. If the couple do not desire to change their values, they may wish to seek a therapist or counselor whose convictions are similar to their own. Others may agree that certain forms of behavior are desirable or undesirable but have no deep convictions. In this case, if outside help is sought, a nondirective counselor in either a private or group setting may allow for more self-exploration.

SEX-DRIVEN PERSONS

Many times a high concentration on sexual matters is part of freedom of choice, but at others sexual needs hold a higher position in the need hierarchy than the individual desires. Such all-powerful urges for sex may be hiding a subconscious fear of other types of personal interaction. Men, for example, may have a distaste for affectional relations that stir up their emotions in unfamiliar ways. They can engage in specific kinds of loving responses but have trouble with others — often, no doubt, because repressed memories are brought nearer to the surface of consciousness. Thus they find it safer (psychologically) to concentrate on sex, since this is understood as a male prerogative. The important point is that whenever sexual needs interfere with other life goals to a greater extent than the individual wishes, one or the other must change so that an equilibrium comes about between them. A consuming concentration on sex may limit growth possibilities. If one or both members of a pair are dissatisfied with the degree of their sexual needs and experiences, an atypical situation has developed.

In cases of persistent sexual dissatisfaction and uncontrollable desire, the female is said to be *nymphomaniac* and the male to be suffering from *satyriasis*. These states are obviously extreme ends of a continuum and as such are quite rare. More significant is the fact that some persons are led to feel guilty because of their high sexual interest and are invested with terms denoting abnormality or animal-like drives. This is more a moral judgment than anything else. When sexual needs manifest themselves in unabated, overt accusations, internalized dissatisfaction with self or mate, or other relational breakdowns, the help of a professional person qualified in the area of sexual counseling should be sought.

SEXUAL IRRESPONSIBILITY

Irresponsible behavior is typified by unreliability, incongruency between demands and acceptance, indifference to consequences or to the rights of others, and inability to accept the outcome of one's personal actions. A representative instance of sexual irresponsibility is failure to provide adequate protection against unwanted pregnancies. Another is taking advantage of certain power positions, the father in an incestuous relationship being one example. The consequences of irresponsible behavior are often unpredictable, and it is this lack of predictability that results in the downfall of many otherwise successful partnerships.

In certain cases, the individual will act without concern for those involved as only one aspect of a general indifference to the rules of society. This is the *sociopathic* personality whose traits include a neutral conscience, exploitative attitudes, deception, and a narcissistic orientation that is almost completely self-centered.

As often as not, the sociopath's indifference and exploitation are neither hostile nor malicious in content. Much of the sociopathic attitudinal dimension arises from the highly ingrained expectation that one ought to be catered to and have every whim met because of one's superiority. Since much of this is at the unconscious level, it is very difficult to deal with such persons. They simply do not feel the kind of regret or self-recrimination that motivates much psychotherapeutic change. Moreover, sociopaths are often very pleasant and enticing and consequently are quite capable of repeatedly deceiving those with whom they interact. The husband who leaves his wife over and over again, only to return with promises of doing better, may be such a person. Like all traits, sociopathy is found on a continuum and ranges from a very low to a very high intensity. Seeking the advice of a trusted therapist may be the best way of dealing with a sociopathic personality.

LOSS OF HAPPINESS

Personal satisfaction is a major incentive for establishing erotic liaisons, and although it is difficult to define the precise meaning of the word "happiness," few would deny its importance in motivating intimate interaction. Thus it is axiomatic that any time the happiness of the individual is seriously threatened, the entire relationship is apt to suffer. This truth may be a self-fulfilling prophecy, but its importance lies in the fact that even short periods of less than optimal happiness cannot be tolerated by some persons. Those who are easily threatened by temporary disruption, unhappiness, or anger are most likely victims of some form of maladjustment or lowered self concept. Such individuals are often of a moody temperament and expect to control others with their mood changes.

When the loss of happiness is protracted over a long period of time, especially if it was preceded by happy and fulfilling interaction, a condition pathological to the relationship prevails. In America, long-standing relationships are expected to produce a reasonable amount of happiness, and it is no longer assumed that an unhappy partnership will endure merely for the sake of law or custom. Furthermore, long periods of unhappiness are likely to result in disillusionment, which in turn may develop into indifference. Intolerable losses of happiness should be dealt with directly and forthrightly, for if real joy is to be found in a relationship, happiness must be there first.

The point of view has been set forth that anything which tends to produce negative results in a desirable relationship is pathological. The term "atypical" has been used to describe these pathological behaviors, since many of them are socially determined even though it is the individual who is most affected. Loss of happiness, irresponsibility, intentional misuse and exploitation, obsessive-compulsive behavior, acts that produce prolonged psychological disequilibrium, and unrelenting guilt and shame are among the chief culprits that destroy relationships.

SOME SOCIAL EXTREMES

Thus far, dysfunctional sexual behavior has been discussed from the standpoint of a relationship. The nature of this relationship does not matter. It can be heterosexual, homosexual, mixed race, or any other. As long as the atypical criteria just described do not prevail, that relationship may have a desirable outcome from the point of view of the participants. However, a few forms of sexual interaction are so highly condemned by society that the condemnation alone places them in an abnormal category, although each of them usually inhibits satisfactory relationships as well.

Necrophilia.   One such type of sexual behavior is necrophilia, or sexual relations with a dead body. Necrophiliacs cannot (or are afraid they cannot) meet the criteria for establishing a normal relationship, and thus they find it less frightening to obtain sexual gratification with a corpse. Obviously, necrophilia is primarily if not exclusively a male problem and is high on the list of behavior considered extremely pathological.

Incest.   Incest is tabooed in almost every culture, including our own, although the exact reasons for such disapproval have never been satisfactorily explained. Weinberg (1968, pp. 167–202) includes among the causes of incest heavy overcrowding, with many incestuous families living in one or two rooms; modeling after parents who were seen in coital acts; and sexual familiarity of siblings, as exemplified in the telling of dirty jokes or in seeing one another nude. Weinberg found that in father-daughter incest the father was usually a manual laborer, ordinarily selected the oldest daughter for his first affair, and was of dull normal or less intelligence in the majority of instances. Very often excessive drinking contributed to all the forms of incest studied. Sisters were more aggressive in enticing their brothers than daughters were in seducing their fathers; nevertheless, in many cases the females involved were willing partners and the incestuous acts were not discovered until a pregnancy occurred or until a daughter or sister decided to seek revenge, usually for some nonsexual wrong. Incest, even when mutually agreed upon, is considered atypical because of the strong social condemnation that not only makes a satisfactory relationship difficult to establish but also makes antirelationship acts such as revenge more possible.

Rape. Forced rape is by definition an abnormal sexual act, since no mutually sought relationship can occur. Statutory rape, on the other hand, may be a mutually agreed upon adjunct to a more broadly based relationship. If the girl involved is of sound intelligence and able to distinguish right from wrong, there is no reason to label such encounters abnormal. On the contrary, the law that interferes with the relationship might be considered "abnormal." The exact age at which a female is unable to give her informed consent to sexual participation is difficult to establish by law, but many believe that the age of consent should be lowered to 13 to 15 years.

Child Molestation. Child molestation is also regarded very negatively in our society and should be considered abnormal even though other cultures permit or encourage adult-child sexual relations. It is assumed that children are unable to give informed consent and cannot be aware of the consequences of sexual acts to the extent that adults can. Gebhard and his associates (1968, pp. 241–267) have described the male who is likely to be accused of child molestation. He tends to be slightly older than other sex offenders (the average age of Gebhard's child molesters was 35 years). About ten per cent are psychotic or severely neurotic, and among Gebhard's subjects, a third were under the influence of alcohol at the time of the offense. About 60 per cent are friends or acquaintances of the girls involved. Most of the physical contact is some form of petting, with very little attempted coitus. Gebhard's men were mostly of a nonaggressive nature and tended to be quite moralistic and guilt-ridden about their acts.

Pedophiles—those sexually interested in young children—may be either heterosexual or homosexual. Psychodynamically, pedophilia is a return to childhood sexual experiences that proved to be satisfactory (Millon, 1969, p. 481). Either adult heterosexual relations have not developed fully or the individual has been receiving much negative feedback from his current adult activities.

Exhibitionism. Exposure of one's genitals to an unsuspecting public, especially when a man exposes himself to women or young children, is called exhibitionism. Like pedophilia, this form of behavior is a consequence of one's fear of ridicule, doubts about masculinity, or other developmental failures. Most exhibitionists are considered harmless, but they may become public nuisances. When there is a mutual desire among consenting adults for body exposure, the normal wish to see and be seen is operating. In private circumstances in which all involved are agreed to exposure or nudity, it may be considered atypical not to be able to reveal oneself. Obviously, moderately exhibitionistic tendencies are quite normal.

Voyeurism.   The voyeurist or "Peeping Tom" has psychodynamics similar to those of the exhibitionist in that he is unable to seek open adult sexual relations. He fears the consequences of approaching a potential sexual partner and must react as a child might — by stealing his sexual excitement in a nonthreatening manner. Just as it is normal to want to be seen in the nude under certain circumstances, so it is normal to want to look at the sexual organs of others, especially those of the opposite sex. It is not the desire to look that is abnormal but rather the devious manner in which sight is used. The peeper and the peeped upon are unlikely to establish personal contact.

Bestiality.   Bestiality, or sexual contact with animals, was found by Kinsey and his associates to be more prevalent among rural males, but when these same males had access to humans, they tended to drop their animal contacts (1948, pp. 670–671). The Kinsey group (1953, pp. 505–507) found only 3.6 per cent of their female subjects admitting to animal contacts, and these contacts were often mere body hugging, lesser amounts of animal masturbation, and oral stimulation. Coitus with animals was very rare. Bestiality, of course, fails to meet the human relationship criteria discussed earlier in this chapter and is illegal in every state.

Each of the strongly antisocial sexual behaviors described in this section is considered especially repugnant or childlike within our society. The very strength of the attitudes against these behaviors frustrates the establishment of a successful relationship. Other clearly deviant behaviors such as murders or mutilations with sexual overtones, have not been discussed because they are characterized less by the sexual intent of the offenders than by other pathology. Acts such as sadomasochism, oral-genital relations, transvestism, anal intercourse, and bondage and discipline also have not been considered separately because they are part of many successful relationships. These behaviors can be regarded as atypical only when they reach threatening proportions, and then the criteria suggested for relationship satisfaction will apply.

In the final analysis, it is the *relationship* aspects of sexuality that have the most important consequences, both for individual participants and for society at large. The range of sexual behavior practiced and permitted in our society is constantly being broadened despite antiquated laws and traditional mores, but the fundamental value of affectional relationships as a necessary condition of survival has not waned. Although the forms of human interaction are changing and may continue to change, the basic criteria of relationship normalcy will remain fairly constant.

SUMMARY

In this chapter, I have concentrated on the relationship aspects of normal and abnormal sexuality. No effort has been made to explain atypical sexual behavior from such varied approaches as psychoanalytic theory, self theory, learning theory, or social theory. Failure to cope adequately within an interpersonal context has been defined as atypical, both for the individual himself and for the relationships in which he or she may be involved. Among the chief points that have been made are the following:

1. Today deviancy is explained on a moral basis less frequently than in the past.
2. Widespread disagreement exists among professionals concerning the criteria of abnormalcy.
3. Legal, sociological, statistical, and psychological models of abnormalcy tend to support the older codes or to reflect the theoretical biases of those who define pathology.
4. One way to avoid the complexities of defining abnormal behavior is to concentrate on definitions of the normal. Shoben has proposed that integration of the unique attributes of humans into a satisfactory life style be the model of normalcy.
5. I have suggested that freedom from coercion, purposefulness, and predictability be considered attributes of the normal sexual relationship. Overwhelming guilt or shame, obsessive-compulsive behavior, irresponsibility, prolonged loss of happiness, agreement that certain behavior by a given couple is morally wrong for them even though they continue to engage in it, and intense or prolonged psychological disequilibrium are all signs of an atypical relationship.
6. Regardless of the relationship outcomes, a few highly condemned sexual acts have been considered abnormal. These include, among others, forced rape, incest, necrophilia, and pedophilia.

CHAPTER 15

EPILOGUE

The search for answers to the many dilemmas of human sexuality will continue, but it seems unlikely that any real agreement or substantial progress in this aspect of human relationships is near. A variety of social institutions (including religion, education, and the family) as well as scientific research compete for favorable reaction and funding from the public. This competition, along with lack of definitive approaches, low-quality interdisciplinary communication, and inability of the social sciences to develop a common vocabulary, seems certain to keep many mysteries of the human relationship shrouded in the fog of ignorance.

Yet despite this unfavorable prognosis for the future study of man, progress *has* occurred in our understanding of ourselves, and the very institutions that have hampered growth have also contributed to it. This ambivalence has not added to the security that one would wish for in seeking to answer his or her life problems. However, a new breed of Americans has appeared — one that will not be content with answers from any one source and one which demands that answers supplied by others be congruent with the experiences of the questioning one. Questioning of the answers supplied by religious institutions came first, but it has been followed by a questioning of science, education, and government. Recently, I believe, there has been a tendency among many persons to combine the answers to life supplied by our various institutions. Once answers have been found by the individual, it is up to him or her to practice them.

One may have discovered from reading this text that certain areas of psychological privacy are important to maintain, or that long-term relationships usually cannot occur among persons who do not know themselves or who refuse to change in needed directions. Women may have gained awareness that orgastic responsiveness is more likely among those who can enjoy sex in and of itself. Male readers, likewise, may have noted that they might best tell their wives that they love them from time to time, not simply assume that marriage insures that a woman will sense this message automatically.

Whatever new information or rekindling of knowledge already acquired has occurred, it will all be in vain unless the applicable (to the individual) contents are experienced and acted upon. There is very little point in knowing every available fact and fancy concerning human sexuality if they are to be allowed to settle into oblivion in the human brain. To be useful, knowledge learned must be experienced, thought through, and re-evaluated as one goes through life. As a marriage counselor and college teacher, I have encountered many persons and couples who had more than sufficient know-how to develop and enhance the relationships in which they were engaging but who were failing because they were not practicing what they already knew.

In the final analysis, warmth, accurate empathy, enlightened communication, sharing, accepting, and loving are characteristics of those actively involved in life. Active, not passive, human sexuality can lead one closer to self-understanding and to a broad, general interest in mankind when the sensuous base of that sexuality has branched both to genital interests and to love in its broadest sense. Current studies, such as Eysenck's (1970, 1971, 1972) personality explorations and Bancroft's 1971) research into the measurement of sexual behavior, will add further to our sexual knowledge, while others, such as Figley's (1973) focus on child density or Ridley's (1973) study of the effect of work satisfaction on marital pairs, will help us gain insight into marital satisfaction. It remains for the experiencing individual, however, to put all this into the context of his or her own life. It is the responsibility of each person to be a student of his or her own existence, no matter to what sources of outside help he or she may turn.

APPENDIX A

Anatomy and Physiology

This brief review of gross sexual anatomy and physiology is intended to give the reader only a glimpse of the most elementary aspects of sex organ structure and function.

MALE ANATOMY

Gross male sexual anatomy comprises the penis, testicles, scrotum, vas deferens, seminal vesicles, and prostate gland. Their respective locations can be found by referring to Figure A–1.

The penis consists of the shaft and glans or head. Tumescence (erection) occurs when hollow spaces within the shaft fill with blood, and detumescence takes place when blood flows from these spaces faster than it flows in. The glans, especially the undersurface, is highly sensitive and quite responsive to stimulation. Smegma, a smelly, cheese-like substance, is produced by the small Tyson's glands located on the undersurface of the glans.

Sperm and testosterone, an androgen partly responsible for erotic sensitivity in both sexes, are produced by the testicles. Sperm are transported by ciliary action through the sperm duct (vas deferens) to the seminal vesicles. Here they are stored until ejaculation. At this stage the matured sperm, only about 1/500 of an inch long, are quite lethargic.

Semen, the male ejaculate, is manufactured primarily by the seminal vesicles and the prostate. On the average, 3.5 cc. of semen are produced by the healthy male between the ages of 20 and 50 after two or three days of continence. The buffered semen and a fluid—the small amount of clear liquid that can be seen oozing from the penis during sexual excitement—provide the alkaline environment essential to the life of sperm.

Ejaculation occurs in two steps (Fig. A–2). During the first phase the seminal fluid is forced from the prostate and other accessory organs into the urethra. The impending ejaculation can be felt at this time, and for two or three seconds the male can sense the process before the second stage begins. During the second stage semen is propelled through the

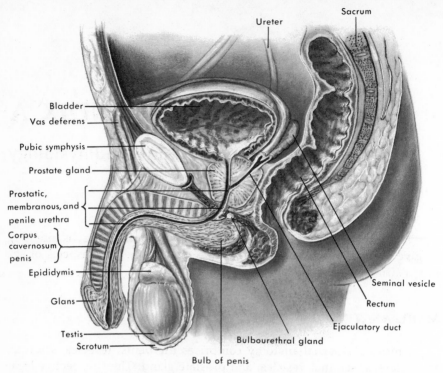

Figure A–1. The male reproductive system. (From Dienhart, C. M. *Basic Human Anatomy and Physiology,* 2nd ed. Philadelphia: W. B. Saunders Co., 1973.)

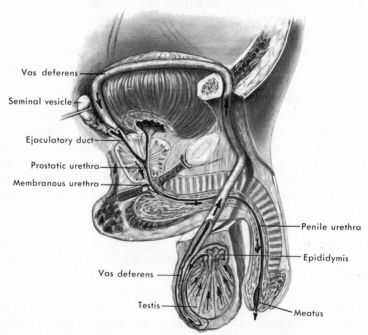

Figure A–2. Passage of spermatozoa. (From Dienhart, C. M. *Basic Human Anatomy and Physiology,* 2nd ed. Philadelphia: W. B. Saunders Co., 1973.)

urethra by a series of muscular contractions. In the adult male, orgasm and ejaculation usually occur together, although some males experience orgasm without ejaculation from time to time. Younger males may experience orgasm before they have developed the capacity to ejaculate. It should also be pointed out that it is possible to ejaculate without having achieved an erection.

Here are a few facts about male anatomy and physiology.

1. There is no reliable relationship between body dimension and penis size.
2. Except for the possible psychological effects, penis size makes no difference in how effectively a woman will be stimulated by penetration, except in cases of unusual vaginal or penile hypertrophy.
3. Erections can occur from causes other than sexual arousal. A few of these are penile irritation, heavy lifting or other stressing of muscles in the perineum, and unusual emotionality.
4. Once the period of normal growth is past, nothing is likely to increase the size of the penis. If treated with hormones early enough, male children with unusually small penises may be assisted toward normal growth.
5. Sexually active persons are believed to have less loss of size due to the atrophy of aging than those less active. In this way regular sexual indulgence helps prevent loss of size.
6. Men do not undergo a change of life similar to that of women. There may be a few men who experience a male climacteric owing to hormone deficiency, but such changes can hardly be equated with menopause, which is a normal physiological event. Some middle-aged men go through an "emotional change of life" during which they try to regain their youthful vigor. This, if severe, may call for psychological counseling or at least reassurance, support, and understanding from their wives.
7. The majority of young men experience nocturnal emission (wet dreans), and some do so fairly frequently. Lowered inhibitions during sleep are usually considered the important cause.
8. Castration does not necessarily destroy the sex drive. Once a male has matured, his sex drive is related to many factors, such as good health and proper nutrition, the kind of learning he has had, the availability of erotic stimuli, and so forth. Since the male's sex drive is not entirely dependent upon the testicles, it is no surprise to find that their removal will not necessarily destroy it, especially if hormones (androgen) are regularly administered. Younger castrates may demonstrate signs of lack of sexual interest, such as the inability to achieve an erection, but this does not mean that they will not show a psychological interest in sex, although the lower the age at which an individual is castrated, the more likely he is to be disinterested. Castration, in brief, does not dispel the need for sensual expression.

FEMALE ANATOMY

The gross sexual anatomy of the human female may be divided into sexual and reproductive aspects (Figs. A–3 and A–4). Most of the parts we will label as sexual are also involved in reproductive functions, but these are secondary to the erotic sphere. The reproductive organs are only secondarily involved in sexual relations.

The major female organs are the mons pubis, major and minor labia, vestibule, and clitoris, which collectively make up the vulva or external sex organs. The organs of the vulva along with the vagina I have termed sexual organs because they serve most importantly in erotic arousal and responsiveness, regardless of whether pregnancy ensues. The uterus (womb), fallopian tubes, and ovaries are more strictly reproductive in function.

The mons pubis (also called mons veneris) is the rise caused by the female pubic bone. Because it is erotically and esthetically pleasing, it is

Female External Genitalia

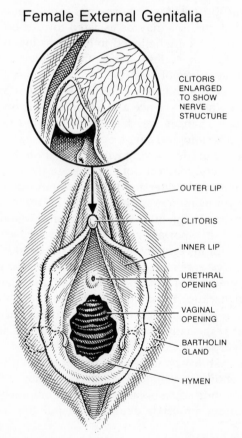

CLITORIS
ENLARGED
TO SHOW
NERVE
STRUCTURE

OUTER LIP

CLITORIS

INNER LIP

URETHRAL
OPENING

VAGINAL
OPENING

BARTHOLIN
GLAND

HYMEN

Figure A-3.   (From Burt, J. J., and Meeks, L. B. *Education for Sexuality*, 2nd ed. Philadelphia: W. B. Saunders Co., 1975.)

Female Reproductive System
Side View

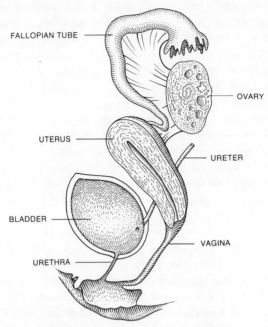

FALLOPIAN TUBE

OVARY

UTERUS

URETER

BLADDER

VAGINA

URETHRA

Figure A-4. (From Burt, J. J., and Meeks, L. B. *Education for Sexuality*, 2nd ed. Philadelphia: W. B. Saunders Co., 1975.)

also known as the "fount of love" or the "mount of Venus." The major and minor labia serve to protect the entrance to the vagina. In addition, the minor labia are quite erotically sensitive and may change in color from bright red to burgundy for the woman who is about to reach climax.

The clitoris, the homologue of the penis, is the major organ of female sexual responsiveness and has no other known function than to serve as the seat of erotic sensitivity. It too engorges with blood upon excitement and the shaft increases in diameter. Although clitoral erection does not occur, a tumescent glans may leave this impression. During periods of high sexual excitement, the clitoris withdraws into the labial hood, making direct contact with it virtually impossible.

A nontraditional way of conceptualizing the clitoris has been suggested (Sherfey, 1966). The clitoris comprises not only the organ we have labeled as such but internal sections of the "clitoral system" as well. These unseen aspects have their counterparts in the penis, including nerve and blood supplies and hollow areas that fill with blood, simulating erection. The inward extension of the clitoris is continuous with the part that protrudes and may provide the basis for so-called vaginal orgasms.

The vagina is lined with a membrane famous for its accordian-like capacity to expand. The vagina produces the sticky fluid that serves to lubricate its surface during periods of sexual arousal. Since there are very few sensory cells within the vagina itself, it cannot be a major source of physical arousal, although it is often of considerable psychological importance.

The area between the edge of the vagina and the beginning of the anus is known as the perineum. It is composed of several underlying structures, but from the standpoint of sexual stimulation, the muscles seem most important. When the perineum of either sex is appropriately stimulated, these muscles can be felt as stiff and rigid, and the entire area can be a source of considerable eroticism. The perineum is important in childbirth, as it can be severely stretched or torn.

The uterus or womb is about three inches long and two inches wide and is divided into the fundus and cervix. The uterine blood supply is especially rich and the entire area is laden with blood vessels and nerves. The body or fundus is intertwined with many heavy muscles that contract to expel the child during the birth process, and the outside is covered with peritoneum. The structure of the endometrium or lining of the uterus varies with the time of life, day of the month, whether or not one is using oral contraceptives, and whether or not one is pregnant. The major function of the uterus is to house and protect the unborn child.

The cervix, or neck of the uterus, extends partially into the vagina. It is rounded or conical in shape and has a central canal through which the fetus and menstrual flow may pass. Normally it is held tightly closed by strong muscles. During sexual intercourse, however, the cervix withdraws into the pelvic cavity; consequently, it is no longer regarded as a major source of sexual excitement.

The fallopian tubes lead from the fundus to the ovaries but have no direct connection with the latter. The ends closest to the ovaries have fimbria that assist in capturing the ovum. It is through the fallopian tubes that the sperm must make their way, and it is within them that conception occurs.

In addition to ova production, the ovaries excrete the hormones responsible for the appearance of female secondary sexual characteristics.

MENSTRUATION

Follicle Stimulating Hormone (FSH) incites the ovaries to begin ova production within the small sacs in which each ovum is contained. These sacs, the graafian follicles, also grow under the influence of FSH. Simultaneously, estrogen is produced from cells within the graafian follicles. This initiates the build-up of this important female hormone in the bloodstream. When an ovum has matured and ruptured its graafian follicle, the estrogen level is at its peak and inhibits further production of FSH, but the pituitary gland begins secretion of the luteinizing hormone (LH), whose function is to bring about the development of the corpus luteum. The corpus luteum is formed in the crater left by the rupture of the graafian follicle. The corpus luteum produces a little estrogen but mainly progesterone, another important female hormone. Progesterone causes the endometrium to thicken and increase in vascularity. If the ovum is impregnated, the corpus luteum continues to produce progesterone, as does a new source of this hormone, the endometrium.

If the ovum is not fertilized, the progesterone level falls owing to regression of the corpus luteum. This lowering of the progesterone level begins on approximately the twenty-second day after the beginning of the last menstrual period, and by the twenty-eighth day progesterone is below the level needed to keep the endometrium intact. Menstruation, the shedding of the lining of the uterus, begins. Although the 28-day cycle is typical, it is well known that normal variations range from 22 to 35 days, and that whatever its duration, the cycle is brought about by the same hormonal physiology.

At some point the lowered level of estrogen and progesterone induces renewed production of FSH, and the process of ovulation begins anew. Usually the ovaries alternate monthly in ovum production, and within 12 to 14 days after the beginning of the last period, a new ovum will be released. Although it is possible to menstruate without the ovulatory process, such anovulatory cycles are unusual.

The following are a few facts about female anatomy and physiology.

1. During sexual arousal, the cervix draws well up into the false pelvis and discharges nothing even remotely resembling ejaculate, nor does it "suck" sperm into itself.

2. Masturbation does not produce acne or smaller breasts, nor does it "show up" in one's facial expression nor have any other known relationship to body size or functioning.

3. There is no known relationship between the size of any normal anatomical part and sexual responsiveness. The ability to become passionate is shaped largely by learning.

4. Orgasm is believed to occur only rarely or not at all among female animals. Some 10 to 15 per cent of American women never reach it, and it has been shown that among women rate of orgasm varies in response to cultural conditioning.

5. Menopause does not engender severe physical or psychological stress in most women. There may be slight distress for many women and considerable discomfort for a few, but the stories surrounding menopause are often exaggerated.

Readers interested in more detailed information than that provided here may consult one of the following: Dickinson: *Human Sex Anatomy* (1949), Masters and Johnson: *Human Sexual Response* (1966), Raboch: Penis size: An important new study (1970), or Sherfey: The evolution and nature of female sexuality in relation to psychoanalytic theory (1966).

APPENDIX B
Contraceptives

It is the intention of this Appendix to list briefly a number of popular contraceptive procedures along with their rated efficiency. It should be pointed out first, however, that 9 out of 10 Americans believe that birth control information should be made available to men and women (Lipson and Wolman, 1972). Lipson and Wolman also found that half of those they surveyed thought that decisions about abortion should be made between the individuals concerned and their doctor, that 60 per cent supported birth control education in public schools, that 8 out of 10 favored voluntary sterilization, and that two-thirds felt that population growth was a serious problem. While this is only one of many studies on popular attitudes toward contraception, there is little doubt that the overwhelming majority of Americans favor the dissemination of birth control information. Fischer (1972) suggests that attitudes toward contraception could be related to concern about overpopulation and that those most concerned intend to restrict their family size. He found that his highly authoritarian subjects seemed to view birth control as necessary to role fulfillment, while those who were high in his measures of trust were less concerned about population growth and intended larger families. He concludes that significant correlations between personality and birth control attitudes hold, regardless of the religious affiliation or class background. In brief, American men and women are willing to educate themselves about contraception, but differ in their attitudes toward putting this information into practice.

The following discussion owes much to Ramsy (1973) and to Cherniak and Feingold (1973). Students interested in more detail might consult these sources or the many fine publications of Planned Parenthood of New York, Optimum Population Incorporated, and similar organizations.

Oral contraceptives contain synthetic estrogens and/or progestogens. The combination Pill, containing both estrogen and progesterone substitutes, is virtually 100 per cent effective in preventing pregnancy when taken as directed. The Pill can be legally obtained only by a physician's prescription, and periodic checkups should occur routinely. Cherniak and Feingold report a British study which discovered that there were 1.5

deaths per 100,000 nonpregnant women between 20 and 34 years of age who were on oral contraceptives. These deaths were from pulmonary cerebral thromboembolism. Deaths from this condition among non-Pill-users were 0.2 per 100,000. For women beyond age 35, the rates were 3.9 for the oral contraceptive users and 0.5 for the nonusers. Thus the Pill has some risks, but so does pregnancy. The same authors report 1.3 deaths per 100,000 maternities for the 20-to-34-year age group and 4.6 for the older women. Thromboembolism is the most serious risk in taking the Pill. Other possible risks lacking convincing evidence include increased susceptibility to cancer and vascular disease. Breakthrough bleeding, fluid retention, and nausea are among the unpleasant but asymptomatic side-effects. As experience is gained with oral contraceptives, many scientists have increased their confidence in the Pill.

Intrauterine devices (IUDs) are made to be inserted into the uterus by a physician. These mostly plastic devices come in a variety of shapes. They differ in effectiveness, but from 3 to 8 per cent of users have become pregnant, according to various studies. It is not known exactly how the IUD works, although there are a number of theories on the subject. The rate of acceptability of the device generally decreases with time, but the IUD is acceptable to only about 75 per cent of users during the first year. The most serious complication of the IUD is pelvic inflammation, which occurs in 2 to 4 per cent of users. Although one in about 2500 women suffers perforation of the uterine wall, the open-type loops are seldom removed, since the body will not react to them. Uterine bleeding, nevertheless, was responsible for the recent recall of one intrauterine device, the Dalkon shield, by the United States Food and Drug Administration. Expulsion of an IUD sometimes occurs, and one may risk pregnancy if she is unaware of this possibility. Generally, however, the IUD may be adopted if one cannot use or fears to use oral contraceptives.

Condoms are reported to be anywhere from 85 to 95 per cent effective in preventing unwanted pregnancies. They would be practically 100 per cent effective if used all the time and properly. Condoms should not be carried around in a manner that will abrade them and produce holes. Spermicidal jelly spread over the condom and placed within the sheath adds to its contraceptive effectiveness.

A *diaphragm* and spermicidal jelly provide an effective mechanical and chemical barrier to sperm. The diaphragm is fitted around the cervix by a physician and usually must be refitted following a pregnancy. The woman must learn to insert the diaphragm and place it in proper position before intercourse is begun. The chief reason diaphragms fail is that they are laid away and not used. Sometimes, however, they can slip out of position or lose their fit for one reason or another. A good deal of the diaphragm's effectiveness depends upon the liberal use of spermicidal cream or jelly. Women who dislike handling their genital organs may find the placing of the diaphragm distasteful.

The oral Pill, IUD, diaphragm, and condom are considered the most effective contraceptive devices according to a pamphlet, *Birth Control*, published by Planned Parenthood of New York in 1971.

Sterilization through tubal ligation or vasectomy is another very successful method of preventing unwanted pregnancies. Tubal ligation—cutting the fallopian tubes and stapling or stitching the ends—can be done within 12 hours after a normal delivery as well as at other times. The laparoscopic method uses a tiny light bulb passed through a small tube in the abdominal wall. Carbon dioxide is pumped into the abdominal cavity to bloat it. This permits the pelvic organs to be easily seen. The surgeon then passes special instruments through the lighted tube, "burns" the fallopian tubes until they have hardened, and cuts through them. This procedure is less traumatic than ordinary tubal ligation. However, it is even easier to do a vasectomy on the male, since it is necessary only to make a small incision in the scrotum, cut the vas deferens, and suture the ends. For three to four weeks following a vasectomy, tests should be made periodically to determine if any sperm are present, since these will have been stored in the seminal vesicles prior to the operation. Other contraceptives must be used until no sperm are found in the ejaculate. In about 1 per cent of patients, the ends of the vas deferens grow together again, and thus for a six-month period a checkup for sperm count should be made from time to time as a precaution. About 50 per cent of vasectomies can be reversed. Reversible methods are being studied but are not yet in popular use.

The *"morning-after pill"* contains potent estrogens as the major active ingredient. Taken within 24 to 48 hours after intercourse, it will probably halt conception. Because its possible side-effects have not yet been clearly determined, the morning-after pill should be considered an emergency measure and not a regular form of contraception.

Abortion may also be used as a birth control method. With the legalization of abortions in the United States, more freedom to choose for oneself has come about. Abortion methods include dilatation and curettage, vacuum aspiration, hysterotomy, and intra-amniotic saline injection. Details of these methods may be found in a number of places, but the reader should be thoroughly warned that only a legally licensed physician should induce an abortion. The safety of abortion and its possible psychological consequences have been discussed in Chapter 11.

There are other methods of contraception, but these are less reliable. *Spermicidal jellies, creams,* and *foams* may be used, but they have too high a failure rate for the woman who must not become pregnant. The foams are the most effective of the three, and there is little reason to use the jellies or creams except in combination with a condom or diaphragm. These contraceptives can be obtained at most drug stores and require no prescription. Some men and women find themselves allergic to particular spermicides and need to switch brands, but for the most part none of these contraceptives have noticeable side-effects. Sometimes leakage from the vagina can be annoying. The foams can be safely applied half an hour before coitus.

The *rhythm* or *"safe period" method* of contraception is used by some persons because of their religious beliefs or because they refuse to use other methods for a variety of reasons. This technique requires that no intercourse take place during the woman's fertile period, which for a 28-day menstrual cycle begins on day 10 and ends on day 18. Because of the variation in cycle length, a record should be kept of the beginning and last day of each period. The reader might wish to consult a family planning center to determine her fertile days, especially if her period varies more than a day or two. At best, the rhythm method has a 7 per cent failure rate, probably because there are quite a few unsafe days and sexual desire cannot necessarily be controlled to fit around those days. The rhythm method is thus considered a family spacing method rather than absolute zero birth control.

Some women also use the temperature method. In this method the body temperature is recorded each morning before rising with a special thermometer. A slight rise in temperature occurs following ovulation, and a drop in temperature precedes ovulation by about 48 hours. These temperature variations, once a woman has acquired her basal body temperature, are helpful in predicting the time of ovulation. Of course, there are many things that may cause temperature variation, and the method is at best a family spacing technique for couples who would not be too upset if the woman happened to conceive.

Withdrawal or coitus interruptus, the oldest form of contraception, is the technique of the man retracting his penis just before he ejaculates. This requires timing, a sensitivity to oneself, and cooperation on the part of the male sexual partner. He should ejaculate away from the vaginal entrance. Although there are no known physical side-effects from withdrawal, the method may produce some negative psychological effects. These are discussed in Chapter 10 under the heading Male Attitudes to Birth Control. If a couple wish to prevent conception, they should consider coitus interruptus an emergency method only.

Other methods of "contraception" might include a variety of noncoital sexual techniques, although strictly speaking such techniques are not contraceptive because conception cannot take place when they are used. Anal intercourse, oral-genital contacts, masturbation, and any other forms of sexual play that keep sperm from coming into contact with ova will result in zero births. Celibacy and homosexuality, obviously, are also forms of zero birth control.

The most important consideration concerning any birth control method is that it be used regularly, completely, and in the manner in which it was intended.

APPENDIX C

The Venereal Diseases

It is not the purpose of this text to emphasize the unhealthy aspects of human sexual relationships, whether these aspects be of a medical or psychological nature. Nevertheless, the venereal diseases can be an unwelcome outcome of sexual activity and need to be dealt with forthrightly.

The two major diseases spread through sexual contact are syphilis and gonorrhea. Other venereal diseases include lymphogranuloma venereum (found almost exclusively in blacks) and granuloma inguinale, classed as a venereal disease because it affects the anogenital area, but not spread by sexual contact. The major problem diseases, syphilis and gonorrhea, are sometimes spoken of as epidemics, but this label may be more appropriate to gonorrhea than to syphilis. Incidence rates of reported cases, according to the *Statistical Abstract of the United States 1973*, are presented for various years in Table C–1.

The figures in the table must be interpreted with caution, since they comprise only data reported to the United States Center for Health Statistics. It is believed that there are many more cases than are actually reported, although it would be difficult to obtain reliable estimates of just how many more venereal disease cases do exist. Furthermore, data from Alaska and Hawaii are not included in the statistics prior to 1960. The most important use of Table C–1 and others like it is in indicating trends.

The increased incidence of venereal disease has been attributed to a variety of causative factors. Hilleboe and Larimore (1965) report that a diminished fear of such diseases, a decrease in the percentage of diagnosed cases reported, and higher rates of sexual activity account for the increases. Another possible factor is the substitution of oral contraceptives

TABLE C-1. INCIDENCE OF REPORTED CASES OF SYPHILIS AND GONORRHEA IN THE UNITED STATES (CIVILIAN CASES)

	1950	1960	1965	1969	1970	1971
Gonorrhea	286,746	258,933	324,925	534,872	600,072	670,268
Syphilis	217,558	122,003	112,842	92,162	91,382	95,997
Other	8,187	2,811	2,015	1,778	2,152	2,101

for condoms, which of course provide protection from venereal diseases as well as from conception. Although the number of cases of gonorrhea increased approximately two and one-half times between 1960 and 1971, it should be remembered that during the same period urban populations grew faster than rural populations (in fact, the rural population of the United States dropped 0.3 per cent between 1960 and 1970) and that there was also a substantial growth in the number of persons between the ages of 14 and 34 (26.7 per cent in 1960 versus 31.7 per cent in 1970) — significant factors, since venereal disease is more likely to be found in an urban and sexually active population.

Population changes, however, do not nearly account for the increases in gonorrhea and only insufficiently account for recent upsurges in syphilis. *The major reason for the increases in both gonorrhea and syphilis is complacency.* Effective medical treatment is available, but it is not being used, especially by those in their teens and early adult years, among whom the highest incidence of the venereal diseases is found (*Newsweek,* Jan. 24, 1972, pp. 46–50). Until a vaccine is developed for syphilis and gonorrhea, it is up to the individual to take the responsibility for obtaining treatment once he or she has had sexual contact with an infected person. It bears repeating: indifference and a false feeling of security are the chief culprits in the spread of syphilis and gonorrhea. Let us now turn to an examination of the symptoms of these two venereal diseases, but with the understanding that one should not wait until the symptoms appear to seek medical treatment. Mere exposure to a known infected individual calls for prompt medical attention.

SYPHILIS

This discussion of syphilis, like the following one of gonorrhea, derives from *Preventive Medicine* by Hilleboe and Larimore (1965) and Conn's *Current Therapy 1974.*

Syphilis is caused by a spirochete, *Treponema pallidum,* which can live and multiply only within its host, the human. *Treponema pallidum* must be deposited by direct contact, preferably on moist skin or mucous membranes. In addition to the mouth, the penis, vagina, and anal areas are ideal locations for the growth of syphilis spirochetes.

Once deposted, the organisms quickly begin to reproduce and within hours may be carried by the bloodstream to other parts of the body. After about three weeks of incubation, sores develop around the primary site of infection. These sores may be minimal or misdiagnosed, possibly because of the widespread use of antibiotics. The primary lesion will heal without treatment, as will the other lesions that appear at various places on the body. This very self-healing may fool the exposed individual into thinking that he or she has had a spontaneous cure, but this is not the case, because without treatment the spirochetes remain alive and well, even though for periods no evidence of their presence is seen.

Syphilis may be divided into primary (or early), secondary (or late), and latent stages. During the primary stage syphilis is communicable, and an untreated pregnant woman may infect the fetus she is carrying after the fourth month of pregnancy. If left untreated, a mother may infect her fetus even ten years after initial exposure. As the untreated disease progresses into the secondary stage, the body lesions usually disappear, and the condition is not communicable as long as no lesions are present. The latent period, which begins two to four years following infection, may be subdivided into two stages. In the early latent stage, which lasts about two years, no physical symptoms are seen. Both the early and late phases may respond to treatment, preventing the recurrence of other symptoms of untreated syphilis. These latter symptoms may not appear until 15 to 20 years after the initial exposure and are quite lethal, involving the cardiovascular system, the spinal cord, the brain, and the optic nerve. The result may be general paresis (a form of mental illness that cannot do other than get worse), locomotor ataxia, blindness, and eventually death.

Despite rumors that strains of syphilis exist which are resistant to penicillin, such resistant strains appear to be limited to a very few specific geographical areas of the world and may actually be disappearing. At any rate, penicillin is the treatment of choice and is effective in almost all patients when the physician's advice is followed. If penicillin cannot be used, the physician has other effective drugs at his disposal. In the case of the venereal diseases, as with all treatment, the full course of therapy must be completed if success is to be expected.

GONORRHEA

Gonorrhea is an acute venereal disease that incubates in from one to ten days. The gonococcus must usually be deposited directly on the body, since it is unable to live outside its natural host, the human. In the male, gonorrhea causes inflammation of the anterior urethra and a smelly discharge. Urination is accompanied by a burning sensation. If the infection continues, the posterior urethra, prostate, and epididymis may become involved. Urethral strictures may occur in poorly treated or chronic cases. Women often show no symptoms of the disease and may be unaware of it until a partner is infected. The female infection starts in the urethra or the cervix and may or may not show a discharge. If it is allowed to persist, it may involve the fallopian tubes and the peritoneum, causing low abdominal pain and possible sterility.

The gonococcus can usually be controlled by antibiotics, and a single injection of penicillin will effect a cure in most males. However, some strains of gonococci show resistance to antibiotics and longer treatment may be required in these cases.

SUMMARY

It is evident that venereal diseases are on the rise, but this increase need not continue if those exposed accept the services of a physician, The medical cure and prophylactic measures necessary to control the venereal diseases already exist. Sex education aimed at eliminating ignorance, fear, guilt, and mistrust may be helpful in reducing the anxieties of exposed individuals who should be seeking medical help.

GLOSSARY

Aberration: often considered to be any deviation from the broadly acceptable sexual practices of a given culture. See also *Atypical*.

Abortifacient: a drug that causes abortions.

Abortion: premature expulsion of the products of conception.

Amenorrhea: absence or abnormal stoppage of menstruation.

Analingus (Analinctus): oral stimulation of the anus.

Androgen: substances capable of producing masculine characteristics, very often the male sex hormone. See testosterone.

Anus: outlet of the rectum, lying between the buttocks.

Aphrodisiac: anything used to enhance sexual arousal. Often refers to foods, drugs, etc. taken internally to increase sexual excitement. The substances used are primarily the outcome of folkways, since no true aphrodisiacs to be taken internally have been found.

Areola: the pigmented ring of tissue surrounding the nipple.

Asexual: not sexual.

Atypical: behavior not characteristically found in a given status-role position.

Autoeroticism: masturbation, deriving sexual pleasure from oneself.

Axillism: sexual gratification through the use of the armpit (axilla) either actively or passively.

Bestiality: human sexual relations with an animal. Can be actual intercourse or simply stimulation of the animal.

Bisexual: sexual preferences for either gender.

Buggery: anal-genital intercourse.

Castration: removal of the testicles in men or the ovaries in women.

Cervix: mouth of the uterus, at the lower end; extends into the upper portion of the vagina.

Circumcision: removal of the end of the prepuce by a circular incision.

Clitoridectomy: removal of the clitoris.

Clitoris: the small, highly sensitive penile homologue, located in the upper triangle of the vulva. Highly sensitive to erotic stimulation.

Coitus (Sexual intercourse): insertion of the male penis into the female vagina,

313

followed by a variety of types of movement depending upon individual desires and intended to stimulate.

Coitus interruptus: withdrawal of the penis just before ejaculation, usually as a method of birth control.

Comarital sex: sexual relationships by marital partners with others outside the marriage, but agreed to and encouraged by the spouses.

Conception: penetration of an ovum by a sperm, the beginning of life.

Condom: a snug-fitting sheath or covering over the penis to prevent contraction of venereal disease; also used as a contraceptive.

Continence: self-restraint, used especially in regard to refraining from coitus.

Contraceptive: any device, chemical, or substance that has the purpose of preventing conception.

Coprophilia: obscene language used as a sexual stimulant.

Cunnilingus (Cunnilinctus): oral stimulation of the female genitals, legally forbidden in most states.

Detumescence: ceasing or loss of erection in erectile tissue, especially the penis.

Dysmenorrhea: painful menstruation.

Dyspareunia: painful coitus in the female.

Ejaculatio precox: premature ejaculation.

Ejaculation: ejection of the seminal fluids from the male urethra.

Endometrium: lining of the uterus.

Epididymis: the network of very small tubes in the male that connects the testicles with the vas deferens.

Episiotomy: small cuts made in the perineum to prevent tearing during delivery of a child.

Erection: stiffening and hardening of erectile tissue, due to blood engorgement.

Erogenous zones: areas of the body particularly sensitive to erotic stimulation.

Erotic: refers to sexual stimuli, sensations, attitudes, and feelings.

Estrogen: a hormone secreted by the ovaries which aids in normal growth of such female features as uterus, breasts, and vagina, and which functions to regulate part of the menstrual cycle.

Exhibitionism: deriving sexual pleasure from exhibiting one's body to others. This is normal to a limited extent in most people.

Fallopian tubes: the tubes or ducts which connect the uterus to the ovaries and through which sperm and ova pass.

Fellatio: oral stimulation of the penis. Illegal in most states but rarely enforced when a couple are married.

Fellator: male who performs fellatio.

Fellatrix: female who performs fellatio.

Femaleness: refers to the physical characteristics associated with the feminine gender.

Femininity: refers to those social and psychological characteristics associated with the feminine gender.

Fetishism: fixation on an object or part of a person's body.

Frigidity: indifference or insensitivity on the part of a woman to sexual stimuli and coitus; the inability to gain pleasure from sexual experience.

Frottage: sexual compulsion to rub against some part of another's body. Often occurs in crowds or similar situations.

Genitals: the sex or reproductive organs.

Gestation: pregnancy.

Glans: head of the penis or the clitoris.

Graafian follicle: one of the small sacs or vesicles of the ovaries which contain and discharge ova.

Hermaphrodite: person with sexual organs of both sexes. Various combinations can occur.

Heterosexual: preferring a sexual partner of the opposite gender.

Homologous: an anatomical structure that corresponds in origin, structure, or position with another anatomical structure. The penis and the clitoris are homologous.

Homosexuality: sexual preference for persons of one's own gender. There is no fixed point on the heterosexual-homosexual continuum at which it can be said that one is entirely heterosexual or entirely homosexual.

Hormone: a chemical substance originating in an organ, gland, or part which is conveyed through the blood to another part, stimulating it to increased functional activity and increased secretion.

Hypothalamus: region of the forebrain beneath the thalamus, believed responsible for many of the involuntary motor components of emotions. The hypothalamus has close ties with the pituitary gland, thus the possible connection between certain emotional states and hormonal output.

Impotence: the inability to get or maintain an erection; the inability to achieve coitus in either sex.

Incest: sexual relations with close relatives; may be variously defined under the laws of each state or in other cultures.

Interfemoral coitus: coital movement by a couple without penetration.

Interpersonal: relationships and relationship processes occurring between persons.

Intrapersonal: processes—mental, emotional, or physical—within the individual.

Irrumation: fellatio.

Labia majora: the outer lips surrounding the vaginal opening.

Labia minora: inner lips lying within and between the labia majora, an important part of a woman's sexual excitatory anatomy.

Lesbianism: female homosexuality.

Libido: the energy of the sex impulse, in common use to refer to the sex drive of a person.

Maleness: refers to physical characteristics of the male.

Masculinity: the social and psychological characteristics usually associated with the male gender.

Masochism: desire for pain, especially when the pain is needed to bring on sexual arousal.

Masturbation (Autoeroticism):   self-stimulation to bring about sexual arousal and relief.

Menarche: first menstrual period.

Menopause: period during which regular monthly menstrual cycles slacken off until they finally stop altogether.

Menstruation: the female monthly shedding of the endometrium which occurs in women between menarche and menopause.

Mons Veneris (Mons pubis):   the triangular mount of fatty tissue at the symphysis pubis in females, located just above the vulva.

Multipara (Multiparous):   woman who has given birth to more than one child. Compare *Nullipara.*

Narcissism: self-love, may be expressed in varying degrees.

Necrophilia: the trait of becoming sexually aroused at the sight or thought of a corpse.

Nocturnal emission (Wet dream):   ejaculation during sleep.

Nullipara (Nulliparous):   woman who has never borne children. Compare *Multipara.*

Nymphomania: a very rare condition in which a woman lacks control of her sexual desires, has an unquenchable urge for sexual intercourse, and is compulsively driven to activities even though these may be self-defeating and may lead to self-contempt. Ellis (1965) states that most nymphomaniacs achieve one or more orgasms per night. Nymphomania should not be confused with promiscuity. Compare *Satyriasis.*

Ocyjack: a male who ejaculates almost upon vaginal entry.

Orgasm (Climax):   the more or less sudden release of sexual tensions resulting in physiological and psychological relief and usually accompanied by a sense of well-being and achievement. Ordinarily occurs in conjunction with ejaculation in the male.

Ova (Ovum, singular):   reproductive cell produced by females.

Ovary: one of the two glands in the female that produce ova and certain hormones.

Penis (Phallus): the male sex organ.

Perineum: the space lying between the vulva and the anus in the female and between the scrotum and the anus in the male. May be very erotically stimulating.

Phimosis: tightness of the prepuce so that it cannot be drawn back over the glans.

Prepuce: penile foreskin.

Priapism: abnormal, painful, and continued erection of the penis due to disease or trauma, usually without sexual desire.

Progesterone: hormone produced in the corpus luteum (in the ovaries) which prepares the endometrium to receive the fertilized ovum.

Promiscuity: casual sexual relations with many persons.

Prostate gland: gland in the male that surrounds the urethra and neck of the bladder.

Prostatic fluid: the part of the male ejaculate produced by the prostate gland; fluids produced by the prostate.

Role (Sex role): the behavior expected of or associated with a particular social status (such as husband, wife, child) or with one's gender.

Sadism: gaining pleasure, particularly sexual pleasure, from inflicting pain on others. See also *Masochism*.

Satyriasis: an unquenchable need by a male for sexual excitement and relief. A form of male nymphomania and very rarely found.

Scrotum: pouch which holds the male testicles and accessory organs.

Seminal fluid (Semen): male ejaculate.

Seminal vesicle: sac on either side in the male, connected with the vas deferens and serving to store temporarily seminal fluid and sperm.

Sensuousness: a general awareness and state of excitability; a sense of needing physical contact that may or may not culminate in sexual interaction.

Sex flush: the pinkish, measle-like rash that may be found on the skin over abdomen, breasts, shoulders, neck, and face during high levels of sexual arousal.

Sexuality: the total social, personality, and emotional characteristics of an individual that are manifest in his or her relations with others and that reflect his or her gender-genital orientation.

Smegma: a cheesy, ill-smelling accumulation of secretions under the prepuce or around the clitoris.

Sodomy: anal copulation. Legal definition may vary from state to state but usually includes all sexual acts except penile-vaginal intercourse.

Soixante-neuf: French for 69, 69 being simultaneous oral-genital relations.

Sperm (Spermatozoa): the male germ cell.

Testes (Testicle, singular): the ovoid male gonads located in the scrotum which produce sperm and some of the liquid elements of the seminal fluid.

Testosterone: the male sex hormone that brings about and maintains the male secondary sexual characteristics.

Transsexual: one who desires physically to become the opposite sex through surgery.

Transvestite: a person (usually male) who prefers to dress in clothes of the opposite sex and who may obtain sexual pleasure from such dressing.

Tubal ligation: cutting or tying of the fallopian tubes as a method of birth control.

Tumescence: the process of swelling or the condition of being swelled.

Uterus (Womb): hollow, pear-shaped organ in the female within which the fetus develops.

Vagina: tunnel-shaped opening between the female's legs which serves as a sheath for the penis during coitus and as the birth canal. The vagina extends from the vulva to the cervix of the uterus.

Vaginismus: strong contractions of the vaginal muscles preventing entrance of the penis.

Vas deferens: sperm ducts in the male through which sperm pass from the epididymis to the seminal vesicles.

Vasectomy: cutting or tying of the vas deferens as a method of birth control.

Vasocongestion: congestion of blood in the veins around the genital area.

Venereal disease: collective name for diseases such as syphillis and gonorrhea which are transmitted through sexual intercourse.

Vestibule: the cleft between the labia minora and behind the clitoris which serves as the opening to the vagina.

Voyeurism: the trait whereby an individual receives primary sexual satisfaction from observing nude or seminude persons of the opposite sex. Common in most people in minor degrees.

Vulva: collective name for the external female genitalia; includes the vestibule, major and minor labia, and the mons pubis.

REFERENCES

Adams, C. R. An informal preliminary report on some factors relating to sexual responsiveness of certain college wives. Thesis, mimeographed, Pennsylvania State University, 1953. *Also in* DeMartino, M. F., ed. *Sexual Behavior and Personality Characteristics.* New York: Grove Press, 1963, 208–226.

Adams, W. J. How hidden feelings spoil the sex act. *Sexology, 35* (Nov., 1968), pp. 220–222.

Allport, G. W. The psychologist's frame of reference. *Psychol. Bull., 37* (1940), 1–28.

Amelar, R. D., and Dublin, L. Sex after major urologic surgery. *J. Sex Res., 4* (Nov., 1968), 265–274.

Andry, A. C., and Schepp, S. *How Babies Are Made.* New York: Time-Life Books, 1968.

Arafat, I., and Yorburg, B. Drug use and sexual behavior of college women. *J. Sex Res., 9* (Feb., 1973), 21–29.

Ard, B. N., Jr. Seven ways to enjoy sex more. *Sexology, 35* (March, 1969), 508–510.

Ard, B. N., Jr. Commentary. *Fam. Coord., 19* (Jan., 1970), 86–87.

Ard, B. N., Jr. Premarital sexual experience: A longitudinal study. *J. Sex Res., 10* (Feb., 1974), 32–39.

Arnold, C. B. The sexual behavior of inner city adolescent condom users. *J. Sex Res., 8* (Nov., 1972), 298–309.

Arnott, C. C. Husbands' attitude and wives' commitment to employment. *J. Marriage and Fam., 34* (Nov., 1972), 673–684.

Athanasiou, R., and Sarkin, R. Premarital sexual behavior and postmarital adjustment. *Arch. Sex. Behav., 3* (May, 1974), 207–225.

Baker, L. G., Jr. The personal and social adjustment of the never-married woman. *J. Marriage and Fam., 30* (Aug., 1968), 473–479.

Balswick, J. Attitudes of lower class males toward taking a male birth control pill. *Fam. Coord., 21* (April, 1972), 195–199.

Balswick, J., and Peek, C. The inexpressive male: A tragedy of American society. *Fam. Coord., 20* (Oct., 1971), 363–368.

Bancroft, J. The application of psychophysiological measures in the assessment and modification of sexual behavior. *Behav. Res. Ther., 9* (1971), 119–130.

Bandura, A. *Principles of Behavior Modification.* New York: Holt, Rinehart and Winston, 1969.

Barclay, A. G., and Cusumano, D. R. Father absence, cross-sex identity, and field-dependent behavior in male adolescents. *Child Dev., 38* (March, 1967), 243–250.

Bass-Hass, R. The lesbian dyad. *J. Sex Res., 4* (May, 1968), 108–126.

Bauman, K. E. Selected aspects of the contraceptive practices of unmarried university students. *Med. Aspects Hum. Sex., 5* (Aug., 1971), 76–89.

Bauman, K. E., and Udry, J. R. Powerlessness and regularity of contraception in an urban Negro male sample. *J. Marriage and Fam., 34* (Feb., 1972), 112–114.

Beigel, H. G., ed. *Advances in Sex Research.* New York: Harper and Row, 1963.

Beigel, H. G. Sex pleasure in pain. *Sexology, 34* (July, 1968), 851–853.

Beigel, H. G. Let yourself go and really enjoy sex. *Sexology, 35* (July, 1969), 796–798.

Bell, R. R. *Premarital Sex in a Changing Society.* Englewood Cliffs, N.J.: Prentice-Hall, 1966.

Bell, R. R., and Chaskes, J. B. Premarital sexual experience among coeds, 1958 and 1968. *J. Marriage and Fam., 32* (Feb., 1970), 81–84.

Berger, A. S., Simon, W., and Gagnon, J. H. Youth and pornography in social context. *Arch. Sex. Behav., 2* (1973), 279–308.

Berlyne, D. E. Conflict, Arousal, and Curiosity. New York: McGraw-Hill, 1960.

Bernard, J. *Marriage and Family Among Negroes*. Englewood Cliffs, N.J.: Prentice-Hall, 1966.

Bernard, J. *The Sex Game*. Englewood Cliffs, N.J.: Prentice-Hall, 1968.

Bieber, I., et al. *Homosexuality: A Psychoanalytic Study of Male Homosexuals*. New York: Basic Books, 1962.

Blinder, M. G. Married couple group therapy. Tape no. 75508. Hightstown, N.J.: McGraw-Hill Sound Seminar Series.

Borowitz, E. B. *Choosing a Sex Ethic*. New York: Shocken Books, 1969.

Boxer, L. Mate selection and emotional disorder. *Fam. Coord., 19* (April, 1970), 173–179.

Boyd, H. Love versus omnipotence: The narcissistic dilemma. *Psychotherapy, 4* (Dec., 1968), 272–277.

Brashear, D. B. Abortion counseling. *Fam. Coord., 22* (Oct., 1973), 429–435.

Brecher, E. M. *The Sex Researchers*. Boston: Little, Brown & Co., 1969.

Brenton, M. *The American Male*. New York: Coward-McCann, 1966.

Brim, O. G., Jr. Family structure and sex role learning by children: A further analysis of Helen Koch's data. *In* Heiss, J., ed. *Family Roles and Interaction: An Anthology*. Chicago: Rand McNally, 1968, 341–357.

Brissett, D., and Lewis, L. S. Guidelines for marital sex: An analysis of fifteen popular manuals. *Fam. Coord., 19* (Jan., 1970), 41–48.

Broderick, C. B. Sexual behavior among preadolescents. *J. Soc. Issues, XXII* (April, 1966a), 6–21.

Broderick, C. B. Socio-sexual development in a suburban community. *J. Sex Res., 2* (April, 1966b), 1–24.

Broderick, C. B. Beyond the five conceptual frameworks: A decade of development in family theory. *J. Marriage and Fam., 33* (Feb., 1971), 139–159.

Broderick, C. B., and Bernard, J., eds. *The Individual, Sex and Society*. Baltimore: Johns Hopkins Press, 1969.

Broderick, C. B., and Rowe, G. P. A scale of preadolescent heterosexual development. *J. Marriage and Fam., 30* (Feb., 1968), 97–101.

Broderick, C. B., and Weaver, J. The perceptual context of boy-girl communication. *J. Marriage and Fam., 30* (Nov., 1968), 618–627.

Broverman, I. K., et al. Sex-role stereotypes: A current appraisal. *J. Soc. Issues, 28,* 2 (1972), 59–78.

Brown, D. G., and Lynn, D. B. Human sexual development: An outline of components and concepts. *J. Marriage and Fam., 28* (May, 1966), 155–162.

Brown, M. The new body psychotherapies. *Psychotherapy, 10* (Summer, 1973), 98–116.

Bruce, V. The expression of femininity in the male. *J. Sex Res., 3* (May, 1967), 129–139.

Burchinal, L. G. Adolescent role deprivation and high school marriage. *Marriage and Fam. Living, 21* (Nov., 1959), 378–394.

Burgess, E., and Cottrell, L., Jr. *Predicting Success or Failure in Marriage*. Englewood Cliffs, N.J.: Prentice-Hall, 1939.

Burgess, E., and Wallin, P. *Engagement and Marriage*. Philadelphia: J. B. Lippincott Co., 1953.

Byrne, D., and Sheffield, J. Responses to sexually arousing stimuli as a function of repressing and sensitizing defenses. *J. Abnorm. Psychol., 70* (April, 1965), 114–118.

Calderone, M. S. An approach. *Am. Educ., 11* (1966), 17–18.

California Department of Public Health. *Divorce in California, 1966*. Berkeley: California Bureau of Vital Statistics, 1967.

Calonico, J. M., and Thomas, D. L. Role-taking as a function of value similarity and affect in the nuclear family. *J. Marriage and Fam., 35* (Nov., 1973), 655–665.

Caprio, F. S. Anything goes in lovemaking. *Sexology, 35* (May, 1969), 652–655.

Centers, R. Evaluating the loved one. *J. Pers., 39* (June, 1971), 303–318.

Chapman, J. D. *The Feminine Mind and Body*. New York: Philosophical Library, 1967.

Cherniak, D., and Feingold, A. *Birth Control Handbook*. Montreal: Montreal Health Press, 1973.

Chiang, H. -M., and Maslow, A. H., eds. *The Healthy Personality*. New York: Van Nostrand Reinhold, 1969.

Christensen, H. T. Scandinavian and American sex norms: Some comparisons with sociological implications. *J. Soc. Issues, XXII* (April, 1966), 60–75.

Christensen, H. T. The new morality: Research bases for decision in today's world. *Brigham Young University Studies, 8* (1967), 23–25.

Christensen, H. T. Children in the family: Relationship of number and spacing to marital success. *J. Marriage and Fam.*, 30 (May, 1968), 283–289.

Christensen, H. T. Normative theory derived from cross-cultural research. *J. Marriage and Fam.*, 31 (May, 1969a), 209–222.

Christensen, H. T. *Sex, Science and Values.* SIECUS Study Guide No. 9. New York: SIECUS, 1969b.

Christensen, H. T. Scandinavian vs. American sex patterns. *Sex. Behav.*, 1 (Dec., 1971), 4–10.

Christensen, H. T., and Gregg, C. Changing sex norms in America and Scandinavia. *J. Marriage and Fam.*, 32 (Nov., 1970), 616–627.

Clark, L. Is there a difference between clitoral and vaginal orgasm? *J. Sex Res.*, 6 (Feb., 1970), 25–28.

Clay, V. S. The effect of culture on mother-child tactile communication. *Fam. Coord.*, 17 (July, 1968), 204–210.

Clayton, R. R. Premarital sexual intercourse: A substantive test of the contingent consistency model. *J. Marriage and Fam.*, 34 (May, 1972), 273–281.

Cohen, Y. A. Adolescent conflict in a Jamaican community. *J. Indian Psychoanal. Instit.*, 9 (1955), 139–172. *Also in* Cohen, Y. A., ed. *Social Structure and Personality.* New York: Holt, Rinehart and Winston, 1961.

Cole, C. L., and Spanier, G. B. Comarital mate-sharing and family stability. *J. Sex Res.*, 10 (Feb., 1974), 21–31.

Commission on Obscenity and Pornography. *The Report of the Commission on Obscenity and Pornography.* Washington: Superintendent of Documents, United States Government Printing Office, 1970.

Conn, H. F., ed. *Current Therapy 1974.* Philadelphia: W. B. Saunders Co., 1974.

Coombs, L. C., and Zumeta, Z. Correlates of marital dissolution in a prospective fertility study: A research note. *Soc. Probl.*, 18 (Summer, 1970), 92–102.

Cutright, P. The teenage sexual revolution and the myth of the abstinent past. *Fam. Plan Perspect.*, 4 (Jan., 1972), 24–31.

Davis, K. *Factors in the Sex Life of Twenty-two Hundred Women.* New York: Harper and Bros., 1929.

Dean, D. G. Emotional maturity and marital adjustment. *J. Marriage and Fam.*, 28 (Nov., 1966), 454–457.

DeMartino, M. F. Dominance-feeling, security-insecurity, and sexuality in women. *In* DeMartino, D. F., ed. *Sexual Behavior and Personality Characteristics.* New York: Grove Press, 1963.

Denfeld, D. Dropouts from swinging. *Fam. Coord.*, 23 (Jan., 1974), 45–49.

Denfeld, D., and Gordon, M. The sociology of mate swapping: Or the family that swings together clings together. *J. Sex Res.*, 6 (May, 1970), 85–100.

Dengrove, E. Sex differences. *In* Ellis, A., and Abarbanel, A., eds. *The Encyclopedia of Sexual Behavior.* New York: Hawthorn Books, 1961 (rev. ed., 1973).

Dengrove, E. Sexual responses to disease processes. *J. Sex Res.*, 4 (Nov., 1968), 257–264.

Dengrove, E. Twelve ways to improve your sex manners. *Sexology*, 36 (Oct., 1969), 4–7.

DeRopp, R. S. *Sex Energy.* New York: Delacorte Press, 1969.

Dickinson, R. L. *Human Sex Anatomy.* Baltimore: Williams & Wilkins Co., 1949.

Dollard, J., and Miller, N. E. *Personality and Psychotherapy: An Analysis in Terms of Learning, Thinking, and Culture.* New York: McGraw-Hill, 1950.

Drake, G. V. *Is the Schoolhouse the Proper Place to Teach Raw Sex?* Tulsa, Okla: Christian Crusade, 1968.

Drake, G. V. *SIECUS: Corrupter of Youth.* Tulsa, Okla.: Christian Crusade, 1969.

Driscoll, R. H., and Davis, K. E. Sexual restraints: A comparison of perceived and self-reported reasons for college students. *J. Sex Res.*, 7 (Nov., 1971), 253–262.

Driver, H. *Sex Guidance for Your Child.* Madison, Wis.: Monona Publications, 1965.

Drury, M. *Advice to a Young Wife from an Old Mistress.* New York: Doubleday and Co., 1968.

Duvall, E. M. *About Sex and Growing Up.* New York: Association Press, 1968.

Edwards, J. N. Extramarital involvement: Fact and theory. *J. Sex Res.*, 9 (Aug., 1973), 210–224.

Ehrmann, W. *Premarital Dating Behavior.* New York: Holt, Rinehart and Winston, 1959.

Eichenlaub, J. E. *New Approaches to Sex in Marriage.* New York: Delacorte Press, 1967.

Elias, J., and Gebhard, P. Sexuality and sexual learning in childhood. *In* Taylor,

D., ed. *Human Sexual Development.* Philadelphia: F. A. Davis, 1970.

Ellis, A. *The Folklore of Sex.* New York: Grove Press, 1961.

Ellis, A. *The American Sexual Tragedy.* New York: Lyle Stuart, 1962.

Ellis, A. The ambiguity of contemporary sex attitudes. *In* Sagarin, E., and MacNamara, D., eds. *Problems of Sex Behavior.* New York: T. Y. Crowell, 1968.

Ellis, A., and Sagarin, E. *Nymphomania: A Study of the Oversexed Woman.* New York: Manor Books, 1965.

Evans, R. B. Sixteen personality factor questionnaire scores of homosexual men. *J. Consult. Clin. Psychol., 34* (April, 1970), 212–215.

Everett, G. M. Effects of amyl nitrite ("poppers") on sexual experience. *Med. Aspects Hum. Sex., 6* (Dec., 1972), 146–151.

Eysenck, H. J. Personality and attitudes to sex: A factoral study. *Personality, 4* (1970), 355–376.

Eysenck, H. J. Introverts, extraverts and sex. *Psychol. Today,* (Jan., 1971a), 49–52.

Eysenck, H. J. Masculinity-femininity, personality and sexual attitudes. *J. Sex Res., 7* (May, 1971b), 83–88.

Eysenck, H. J. Hysterical personality and sexual adjustment, attitudes and behaviour. *J. Sex Res., 7* (Nov., 1971c), 274–281.

Eysenck, H. J. Personality and sexual behavior. *J. Psychosom. Res., 16* (1972), 141–152.

Fast, J. *Body Language.* New York: M. Evans, 1970.

Ferenczi, S. *Thalassa: A Theory of Genitality.* New York: W. W. Norton and Co., 1968.

Feshbach, S. Aggression. *In* Mussen, P. H., ed. *Carmichael's Manual of Child Psychology,* Vol. II. New York: John Wiley and Sons, 1970.

Figley, C. R. Child density and the marital relationship. *J. Marriage and Fam., 35* (May, 1973), 272–282.

Filas, F. L. *Sex Education in the Family.* Englewood Cliffs, N.J.: Prentice-Hall, 1966.

Fischer, E. H. Birth planning of youth: Concern about overpopulation and intention to limit family size. *Am. Psychol., 27* (Oct., 1972), 951–958.

Fischer, E. H., and Caudle, J. Outsiders' reaction to abortion: Personal beliefs and situational influences. *Proceedings of the 81st Annual Convention of the American Psychological Association, 8* (1973), 339–340.

Fisher, P. R. *The Gay Mystique.* New York: Stein and Day, 1972.

Fisher, S. *The Female Orgasm.* New York: Basic Books, 1973.

Ford, C. S., and Beach, F. A. *Patterns of Sexual Behavior.* New York: Harper and Row, 1951.

Ford, D. H., and Urban, H. B. *Systems of Psychotherapy.* New York: John Wiley and Sons, 1963.

Frank, S. *The Sexually Active Man Past Forty.* New York: The Macmillan Co., 1968.

Freud, S. *The Sexual Enlightenment of Children.* New York: Collier Books, 1963.

Freud, S. *Three Contributions to the Theory of Sex.* New York: E. P. Dutton, 1962.

Freund, M., and Davis, J. E. A follow-up study of the effects of vasectomy on sexual behavior. *J. Sex Res., 9* (Aug., 1973), 241–268.

Friedan, B. *The Feminine Mystique.* New York: W. W. Norton and Co., 1963.

Fromm, E. *The Art of Loving.* New York: Harper and Row, 1956.

Gagnon, J. H. Sexuality and sexual learning in the child. *Psychiatry, 28* (Aug., 1965), 212–228.

Galbraith, G. G. Effects of sexual arousal and guilt upon free associative sexual responses. *J. Consult. Clin. Psychol., 32* (1968), 707–711.

Galbraith, G. G., and Mosher, D. L. Effects of sex guilt and sexual stimulation on the recall of word associations. *J. Consult. Clin. Psychol., 34* (Feb., 1970), 67–71.

Garai, J. E. Five ways to get more sex pleasure. *Sexology, 35* (June, 1969), 724–728.

Gaughan, E. J., and Gaynor, M. W. College student ratings of arousal value of pornographic photographs. *Proceedings of the 81st Annual Convention of the American Psychological Association, 8* (1973), 411–412.

Gay, G. R., and Sheppard, C. W. "Sex-crazed dope fiends": Myth or reality? *Drug Forum, 2* (Winter, 1973), 125–140.

Gebhard, P. Factors in marital orgasm. *J. Soc. Issues, XXII* (April, 1966), 88–95.

Gebhard, P., Gagnon, J., Pomeroy, W., and Christensen, C. Child molestation. *In* Sagarin, E., and MacNamara, D., eds. *Problems of Sex Behavior.* New York: T. Y. Crowell, 1968.

Gersuny, C. The honeymoon industry: Rhetoric and bureaucratization of status passage. *Fam. Coord., 19* (July, 1970), 260–266.

Glassberg, B. Y. The quandary of a virginal male. *Fam. Coord., 19* (Jan., 1970), 82–85.

Glick, P. C., and Norton, A. J. Frequency, duration, and probability of marriage and divorce. *J. Marriage and Fam., 33* (May, 1971), 307–317.

Glover, J. *Sense and Sensibility for Single Women.* New York: Doubleday and Co., 1963.

Goldsmith, S., Gabrielson, M., Gabrielson, I., Mathews, V., and Potts, L. Teenagers, sex and contraception. *Fam. Plan. Perspect., 4* (Jan., 1972), 32–38.

Good, P. K., and Brantner, J. P. *The Physician's Guide to the MMPI.* Minneapolis: University of Minneapolis Press, 1961.

Goode, W. J. The theoretical importance of love. *Am. Sociol. Rev., 24* (Feb., 1959), 38–47.

Gottheil, E., and Freedman, A. Sexual beliefs and behavior of single, male medical students. *J.A.M.A., 212* (May, 1970), 1327–1332.

Grater, H. A. The underlearning and overlearning of maternal standards in the etiology of neurosis. Unpublished doctoral dissertation, Pennsylvania State University, 1958.

Greaves, G. Sexual disturbances among chronic amphetamine users. *J. Nerv. Ment. Dis., 155* (Nov., 1972), 363–365.

Greenwald, H. Group sex orgies. *Sexology, XXXIV* (May, 1968), 652–655.

Greer, G. *The Female Eunuch.* New York: McGraw-Hill, 1970.

Grummon, D. L., and Barclay, A. M. *Sexuality: A Search for Perspective.* New York: Van Nostrand Reinhold, 1971.

Hamilton, E. *Sex Before Marriage: Guidance for Young Adults.* New York: Hawthorn Books, 1969.

Harlow, H. The nature of love. *Am. Psychol., 13* (Dec., 1958), 673–685.

Harlow, H. *Learning to Love.* New York: Ballantine Books, 1973.

Harlow, H., and Suomi, S. Nature of love — simplified. *Am. Psychol., 25* (Feb., 1970), 161–168.

Harlow, H., and Zimmerman, R. Affectional responses in the infant monkey. *Science, 130* (Aug., 1959), 421–432.

Harrison, D. E., Bennett, W. H., and Globetti, G. Attitudes of rural youth toward premarital sexual permissiveness. *J. Marriage and Fam., 31* (Nov., 1969), 783–787.

Hawkins, C. H. The erotic significance of contraceptive methods. *J. Sex Res., 6* (May, 1970), 143–157.

Hazo, R. *The Idea of Love.* New York: Praeger, 1967.

Heath, R. G. Pleasure and brain activity in man: Deep and surface electroencephalograms during orgasm. *J. Nerv. Ment. Dis., 154* (Jan., 1972), 3–18.

Hedblom, J. H. Dimensions of lesbian sexual experience. *Arch. Sex. Behav., 2, 4* (1973), 329–341.

Heltsley, M. E., and Broderick, C. B. Religiosity and premarital sexual permissiveness: A reexamination of Reiss' traditionalism proposition. *J. Marriage and Fam., 31* (Aug., 1969), 441–443.

Henson, D., and Rubin, H. B. Voluntary control of eroticism. *J. Appl. Behav. Anal., 4* (Spring, 1971), 37–44.

Hilleboe, H. E., and Larimore, G. W. *Preventive Medicine,* 2nd ed. Philadelphia: W. B. Saunders Co., 1965.

Hoffman, M. Homosexuals and the law. *In* McCaffrey, J., ed. *The Homosexual Dialectic.* Englewood Cliffs, N.J.: Prentice-Hall, 1972, 121–136.

Hooker, E. *Final Report of the Task Force on Homosexuality: National Institute of Mental Health.* Bethesda, Md.: N.I.M.H., 1969.

Horney, K. *Feminine Psychology.* New York: W. W. Norton and Co., 1967.

Hunt, M. Sexual behavior in the 1970s. *Playboy,* Oct., Nov., Dec., 1973.

Inselberg, R. M. Marital problems and satisfactions in high school marriages. *Marriage and Fam. Living, 24* (Feb., 1962), 74–77.

Janeway, E. *Man's World, Woman's Place.* New York: William Morrow Company, 1971.

Jastrow, J. *Freud: His Dream and Sex Theories.* New York: Chilton Book Company, 1960.

Jeffreys, M. V. C. *Personal Values in the*

Modern World. Baltimore: Penguin Books, 1962.

Johnson, M. M. Sex role learning in the nuclear family. *Child Dev.*, *34* (June, 1963), 319–333.

Johnson, R. E. Some correlates of extramarital coitus. *J. Marriage and Fam.*, *32* (Aug., 1970), 449–456.

Johnson, R. N. *Aggression in Man and Animals*. Philadelphia: W. B. Saunders Co., 1972.

Johnson, W. R. Muscular performance following coitus. *J. Sex Res.*, *4* (Aug., 1968), 247–248.

Johnson, W. R. Sex education and the mentally retarded. *J. Sex Res.*, *5* (Aug., 1969), 179–185.

Johnson, W. R., and Belzer, E. G., Jr. *Human Sexual Behavior and Sex Education*. Philadelphia: Lea and Febiger, 1973.

Jones, H. K. *Toward a Christian Understanding of the Homosexual*. New York: Association Press, 1966.

Jourard, S. *Personal Adjustment*, 2nd ed. New York: The Macmillan Co., 1963.

Jourard, S. *The Transparent Self*, 2nd ed. New York: Van Nostrand Reinhold, 1971.

Kaats, G. R., and Davis, K. E. Effects of volunteer biases in studies of sexual behavior and attitudes. *J. Sex Res.*, *7* (Feb., 1971), 26–34.

Kanin, E. J. An examination of sexual aggression as a response to sexual frustration. *J. Marriage and Fam.*, *29* (Aug., 1967), 428–433.

Kanin, E. J. Selected dyadic aspects of male sex aggression. *J. Sex Res.*, *5* (Feb., 1969), 12–28.

Kanin, E. J., Davidson, K. R., and Scheck, S. R. A research note on male-female differentials in the experience of heterosexual love. *J. Sex Res.*, *6* (Feb., 1970), 64–72.

Kanin, E. J., and Howard, D. Postmarital consequences of premarital sexual adjustments. *Am. Sociol. Rev.*, *23* (Oct., 1958), 556–562.

Kanter, R. M. Communes. *Psychol. Today*, *4* (July, 1970), 53–57, 78.

Kanter, R. M. *Commitment and Community*. Cambridge, Mass: Harvard University Press, 1972.

Kapor-Stanulovic, N., and Lynn, D. Femininity and family planning. *J. Sex Res.*, *8* (Nov., 1972), 286–297.

Kaufman, S. *The Ageless Woman: Menopause, Hormones, and the Quest for Youth*. Englewood Cliffs, N.J.: Prentice-Hall, 1967.

Kelly, J. Sister love: An exploration of the need for homosexual experience. *Fam. Coord.*, *21* (Oct., 1972), 473–475.

Kempton, W., Bass, M. S., and Gordon, S. *Love, Sex and Birth Control for the Mentally Retarded: A Guide for Parents*. Philadelphia: Planned Parenthood, 1971.

Kenny, J. A. Sexuality of pregnant and breastfeeding women. *Arch. Sex. Behav.*, *2*, 3 (1973), 215–229.

Kinch, J. W. A formalized theory of the self-concept. *In* Manis, J. G., and Meltzer, B. N., eds. *Symbolic Interaction*. Boston: Allyn and Bacon, 1967, 232–240.

Kinsey, A., Pomeroy, W., and Martin, C. *Sexual Behavior in the Human Male*. Philadelphia: W. B. Saunders Co., 1948.

Kinsey, A., Pomeroy, W., Martin, C., and Gebhard, P. H. Concepts of normality and abnormality in sexual behavior. *In* Taylor, D., ed. *Human Sexual Development*. Philadelphia: F. A. Davis Co., 1970, 181–193.

Kinsey, A., Pomeroy, W., Martin, C., and Gebhard, P. H. *Sexual Behavior in the Human Female*. Philadelphia: W. B. Saunders Co., 1953.

Kirkendall, L. A. *Premarital Intercourse and Interpersonal Relations*. New York: Julian Press, 1961a.

Kirkendall, L. A. Sex drive. *In* Ellis, A., and Abarbanel, A., eds. *The Encyclopedia of Sexual Behavior*, Vol. 2. New York: Hawthorn Books, 1961b, 939–948.

Kirkendall, L. A. Characteristics of sexual decision-making. *J. Sex Res.*, *3* (Aug., 1967), 201–211.

Kirkendall, L. A., and Libby, R. W. Interpersonal relationships — crux of the sexual renaissance. *J. Soc. Issues*, *XXII* (April, 1966), 45–59.

Kirkendall, L. A., and Rubin, I. *Sexuality and the Life Cycle*. SIECUS Study Guide no. 8. New York: SIECUS, 1969.

Komarovsky, M. *Blue Collar Marriage*. New York: Random House, 1964.

Komisar, L. *The New Feminism*. New York: Franklin Watts, 1971.

Kroger, W. S. Comprehensive approach to ecclesiogenic neuroses. *J. Sex Res.*, *5* (Feb., 1969), 2–11.

Kupperman, H. S. Sex hormones. *In* Ellis, A., and Abarbanel, A., eds. *The Encyclopedia of Sexual Behavior*. New York: Hawthorn Books, 1961, 494–502.

Kupperman, H. S. *Human Endocrinology*.

San Francisco: Davis Publishing Co., 1963.

Ladner, J. A. *Tomorrow's Tomorrow*. New York: Doubleday and Co., 1971.

LaTorre, R. A. Sexual stimulation and displaced aggression. *Psychol. Rep., 33* (1973), 123–125.

Laws, D. R., and Rubin, H. B. Instructional control of an autonomic sexual response. *J. Appl. Behav. Anal., 2* (Summer, 1969), 93–99.

LeMasters, E. *Modern Courtship and Marriage*. New York: The Macmillan Co., 1957.

Libby, R. W. Parental attitudes toward high school sex education programs. *Fam. Coord., 19* (July, 1970), 234–247.

Libby, R. W., and Carlson, J. E. A theoretical framework for premarital sexual decisions in the dyad. *Arch. Sex. Behav., 4, 2* (1973), 365–377.

Libby, R. W., and Nass, G. D. Parental views on teenage sexual behavior. *J. Sex Res., 7* (Nov., 1971), 226–236.

Libby, R. W., and Whitehurst, R. *Renovating Marriage*. Danville, Calif. Consensus Publishers, 1973.

Lieberman, J. How *not* to teach children about sex. *Sexology, 35* (Feb., 1969), 494–497.

Lipson, G., and Wolman, D. Polling Americans on birth control and population. *Fam. Plan. Perspect., 4* (Jan., 1972), 39–42.

Loney, J. Family dynamics in homosexual women. *Arch. Sex. Behav., 2, 4* (1973), 343–350.

Luckey, E. B., and Nass, G. D. A comparison of sexual attitudes and behavior in an international sample. *J. Marriage and Fam., 31* (May, 1969), 364–379.

Lunneborg, P. W. Stereotypic aspect of masculinity-femininity measurement. *J. Consult. Clin. Psychol., 34* (Feb., 1970), 113–118.

Luquet-Parat, C. The change of object. *In* Chasseguet-Smirgel, J., ed. *Female Sexuality*. Ann Arbor: University of Michigan Press, 1970, 84–93.

Luttge, W. G. The role of gonadal hormones in the sexual behavior of the rhesus monkey and the human: A literature survey. *Arch. Sex. Behav., 1, 1* (1971), 61–88.

Lyness, J. L., Lipetz, M. E., and Davis, K. E. Living together: An alternative to marriage. *J. Marriage and Fam., 34* (May, 1972), 305–311.

Lynn, D. B. Sex role and parental identification. *Child Dev., 33* (Sept., 1962), 555–564.

Lynn, D. B. The process of learning parental and sex-role identification. *J. Marriage and Fam., 28* (Nov., 1966), 466–470.

Maddock, J. W. Mortality and individual development: A basis for value education. *Fam. Coord., 21* (July, 1972), 291–302.

Mailer, N. *The Prisoner of Sex*. Boston: Little, Brown and Co., 1971.

Manosevitz, M. Early sexual behavior in adult homosexual and heterosexual males. *J. Abnorm. Psychol., 76*:3 (1970), 396–402.

Martin, D., and Lyon, P. *Lesbian/Woman*. San Francisco: Glide Publications, 1972.

Maslow, A. H. Self-esteem (dominance-feeling) and sexuality in women. *J. Soc. Psychol., 16* (1942), 259–294.

Maslow, A. H. *Motivation and Personality*. New York: Harper and Row, 1954.

Maslow, A. H. A theory of metamotivation: The biological rooting of the value life. *In* Chiang, H., and Maslow, A. H., eds. *The Healthy Personality*. New York: Van Nostrand Reinhold, 1969, 35–56.

Masters, W., and Johnson, V. *Human Sexual Response*. Boston: Little, Brown and Co., 1966.

Matthews, J. Bisexuality in the male. *J. Sex Res., 5* (May, 1969), 126–129.

May, R. *Love and Will*. New York: W. W. Norton and Co., 1969.

McCandless, B. R. Problems of child rearing in a changing society. *Fam. Coord., 18* (July, 1969), 291–293.

McCartney, J. Overt transference. *J. Sex Res., 3* (Aug., 1966), 227–234.

McCord, W., McCord, J., and Howard, A. Familial correlates of aggression in non-delinquent male children. *J. Abnorm. Soc. Psychol., 63* (Jan., 1961), 493–503.

McCracken, R. D. *Fallacies of Women's Liberation*. Boulder, Colo.: Shields Publishing Co., 1972.

Mead, D. E. Some interaction processes in family counseling. *Fam. Perspect., 4* (Spring, 1969), 32–40.

Mead, M. Marriage in two steps. *In* Otto, H. A., ed. *The Family in Search of a Future*. New York: Appleton-Century-Crofts, 1970, 75–84.

Meltzer, B. N. Mead's social psychology. *In*

Manis, J. G., and Meltzer, B. N., eds. *Symbolic Interaction*. Boston: Allyn and Bacon, 1967, 5–24.

Middendorp, C. P., Brinkman, W., and Koomen, W. Determinants of premarital sexual permissiveness: A secondary analysis. *J. Marriage and Fam.*, 32 (Aug., 1970), 369–378.

Millett, K. *Sexual Politics*. New York: Doubleday and Co., 1970.

Millon, T. *Modern Psychopathology*. Philadelphia: W. B. Saunders Co., 1969.

Mischel, W. Chapter One in Mussen, P., ed. *Carmichael's Manual of Child Psychology*, 3rd ed. New York: John Wiley and Sons, 1970, 3–72.

Molitar, K. P. What castration does to a man. *Sexology*, 36 (Feb., 1970), 59–61.

Money, J. Variables in human eroticism. *In* Young, W., ed. *Sex and Internal Secretions*, Vol. II. Baltimore: Williams & Wilkins Co., 1961, 1383–1400.

Money, J. *Sex Research: New Developments*. New York: Holt, Rinehart and Winston, 1965.

Money, J. *Sex Errors of the Body*. Baltimore: Johns Hopkins Press, 1968.

Money, J., and Ehrhardt, A. A. Fetal hormones and the brain: Effect on sexual dimorphism of behavior. A review. *Arch. Sex. Behav.*, 3, 2 (1971), 241–262.

Money, J., Hampson, J. G., and Hampson, J. L. Hermaphrodism: Recommendations concerning assignment of sex, changes of sex and psychological management. *Bulletin of the Johns Hopkins Hospital*, 97 (1955), 284–300.

Montagu, A. *Sex, Man and Society*. New York: G. P. Putnam's Sons, 1969.

Mosher, D. L., and Greenberg, I. Females' affective responses to reading erotic literature. *J. Consult. Clin. Psychol.*, 33 (Aug., 1969), 472–477.

Mowrer, O. H., and Kluckhohn, C. A. Dynamic theory of personality. *In* Hunt, J. McV., ed. *Personality and the Behavior Disorders*. New York: Ronald Press, 1944, 69–135.

Mueller, B. J. Reconciliation or resignation: A case study. *Fam. Coord.*, 19 (Oct., 1970), 345–352.

Mulford, H. A., and Salisbury, W., II. Self-conceptions in a general population. *In* Manis, J. G., and Meltzer, B. N., eds. *Symbolic Interaction*. Boston: Allyn and Bacon, 1967, 268–278.

Murstein, B. I. Self–ideal-self discrepancy and the choice of marital partner. *J. Consult. Clin. Psychol.*, 37 (Aug., 1971), 47–52.

Murstein, B. I. Sex drive, person perception, and marital choice. *Arch. Sex. Behav.*, 3 (July, 1974), 331–347.

Nag, M. Cultural factors affecting family planning. *J. Fam. Welf.*, XIX (March, 1973), 3–7.

Narramore, C. M. *Life and Love: A Christian View of Sex*. Grand Rapids, Mich.: Zondervan Publishing House, 1956.

National Center for Health Statistics. *Age at Menopause United States 1960–1962*. Washington, D.C.: United States Department of Health, Education and Welfare, 1966.

Neubeck, G., and Schletzer, V. M. A study of extramarital relationships. *In* Neubeck, G., ed. *Extramarital Relations*. Englewood Cliffs, N.J.: Prentice-Hall, 1969, 146–152.

Neumann, F., and Steinbeck, H. Influence of the sexual hormones on the differentiation of neural centers. *Arch. Sex. Behav.*, 2, 2 (1972), 147–162.

Newton, N. Trebly sensuous women. *Psychol. Today*, 5 (July, 1971), 68–71, 98–99.

Nixon, R. E. *The Art of Growing*. New York: Random House, 1962.

Nye, F. I., Carlson, J., and Garrett, G. Family size, interaction, affect and stress. *J. Marriage and Fam.*, 32 (May, 1970), 216–226.

Oberholtzer, W. D., ed. *Is Gay Good?* Philadelphia: Westminster Press, 1971.

Offer, D. Attitudes toward sexuality in a group of 1500 middle-class teen-agers. *J. Youth and Adolesc.*, 1 (1972), 81–90.

Olim, E. G. The self-actualizing person in the fully functioning family: A humanistic approach. *Fam. Coord.*, 17 (July, 1968), 141–148.

Oman, J. B. Are you ever too old for sex? *Sexology*, XXXV (May, 1969), 698–701.

O'Neill, G. C., and O'Neill, N. Patterns in group sexual activity. *J. Sex Res.*, 6 (May, 1970), 101–112.

O'Neill, N., and O'Neill, G. C. *Open Marriage: A New Life Style for Couples*. New York: M. Evans and Co., 1972.

O'Neill, N., and O'Neill, G. C. Open marriage: Implications for human service systems. *Fam. Coord.*, 22 (Oct., 1973), 449–456.

O'Neill, W. L. *Everyone Was Brave: The Rise and Fall of Feminism in America*. Chicago: Quadrangle Books, 1969.

Osofsky, J. D., and Osofsky, H. J. The psychological reaction of patients to legalized abortion. *Am. J. Orthopsychiatry, 42* (Jan., 1972), 48–60.

Otto, H. A. *More Joy in Your Marriage.* New York: Hawthorn Books, 1969.

Otto, H. A. The new marriage: Marriage as a framework for developing personal potential. *In* Otto, H. A., ed. *The Family in Search of a Future.* New York: Appleton-Century-Crofts, 1970, 111–118.

Packard, V. *The Sexual Wilderness.* New York: David McKay, 1968.

Pavlov, I. P. *Conditioned Reflexes.* New York: Liveright, 1927.

Peterson, J. A. *Married Love in the Middle Years.* New York: Association Press, 1968.

Pfeiffer, E., and Davis, G. Determinants of sexual behavior in middle and old age. *J. Am. Geriatr. Soc., XX* (April, 1972), 151–158.

Pfeiffer, E., Verwoerdt, A., and Davis, G. Sexual behavior in middle life. *Am. J. Psychiatry, 128* (April, 1972), 1262–1267.

Pfeil, E. Role expectations when entering marriage. *J. Marriage and Fam., 30* (Feb., 1968), 161–165.

Pineo, P. C. Disenchantment in the later years of marriage. *Marriage and Fam. Living, 23* (Feb., 1961), 3–11.

Pineo, P. C. Developmental patterns in marriage. *Fam. Coord., 18* (April, 1969), 135–140.

Pinker, G. D., and Roberts, D. W. T. *A Short Textbook of Gynaecology and Obstetrics.* Philadelphia: J. B. Lippincott Co., 1967.

Plotsky, H., and Shereshefsky, P. The psychological meaning of watching the delivery. *Child Fam., 8* (Summer, 1969), 254–264.

Poe, C., and Mills, D. Interpersonal attraction, popularity, similarity of personal needs and psychological awareness. *J. Psychol., 81* (May, 1972), 139–149.

Pomeroy, W. *Boys and Sex.* New York: Delacorte Press, 1968.

Pomeroy, W. *Girls and Sex.* New York: Delacorte Press, 1969.

Popenoe, P. Premarital experience no help in sexual adjustment after marriage. *Fam. Life, 21* (Aug., 1961), 1–2.

Potts, R. L. The compulsion to expose oneself. *Sexology, 35* (Nov., 1968), 267–269.

Potts, R. L. The sex hormone all men need. *Sexology, 35* (Jan., 1969), 375–377.

Presser, H. B. The timing of the first birth, female roles and Black fertility. *Millbank Memorial Fund Quarterly, 49* (July, 1971), 329–361.

Queen, S., and Habenstein, R. *The Family in Various Cultures,* 3rd ed. Philadelphia: J. B. Lippincott Co., 1967.

Raboch, J. Penis size: An important new study. *Sexology,* (June, 1970), 16–18.

Raboch, J., and Starka, L. Reported coital activity of men and levels of plasma testosterone. *Arch. Sex. Behav., 2, 4* (1973), 309–315.

Rainwater, L. Marital sexuality in four cultures of poverty. *J. Marriage and Fam., 26* (Nov., 1964), 457–466.

Rainwater, L. Some aspects of lower class sexual behavior. *J. Soc. Issues, 22* (April, 1966), 96–108.

Rallings, E. M. Family situations of married and never-married males. *J. Marriage and Fam., 28* (Nov., 1966), 485–490.

Ramsey, G. V. The sex information of younger boys. *Am. J. Orthopsychiatry, 13* (April, 1943), 347–352.

Ramsy, J. The modern woman's guide to her own body. *Family Circle,* (July, 1973), 113–120.

Rand, L. Masculinity or femininity? Differentiating career-oriented from home-making-oriented college freshman women. *J. Counsel. Psychol., 15* (Sept., 1968), 444–450.

Rapoport, R., and Rapoport, R. N. New light on the honeymoon. *Hum. Rel., 17, 1* (1964), 33–56.

Reed, J. P., and Reed, R. S., P.R.U.D.E.S. *J. Sex Res., 8* (Aug., 1972), 237–246.

Reeve, S. Parental attitudes toward sex education in junior high school. Unpublished Master's thesis, Florida State University, 1963.

Reevy, W. R. Marital prediction scores of college women relative to behavior and attitudes. Unpublished doctoral dissertation, Pennsylvania State University, 1954.

Reevy, W. R. Child sexuality. *In* Ellis, A., and Abarbanel, A., eds. *The Encyclopedia of Sexual Behavior,* Vol. 1. New York: Hawthorn Books, 1961, 258–267.

Reevy, W. R. Petting experience and marital success: A review and statement. *J. Sex Res., 8* (Feb., 1972), 48–60.

Reinisch, J. M. Fetal hormones, the brain, and human sex differences: A heuristic, integrative review of the literature. *Arch. Sex. Behav.*, 3, 1 (1974), 51–87.

Reiss, I. L. Toward a sociology of the heterosexual love relationship. *Marriage and Fam. Living*, 22 (1960), 139–145.

Reiss, I. L. *The Social Context of Premarital Sexual Permissiveness.* New York: Holt, Rinehart and Winston, 1967.

Reiss, I. L. Response to the Heltsley and Broderick retest of Reiss's proposition one. *J. Marriage and Fam.*, 31 (Aug., 1969), 444.

Reiss, I. L. Comments on Middendorp's "The determinants of premarital sexual permissiveness." *J. Marriage and Fam.*, 32 (Aug., 1970), 379–380.

Reuter, M. W., and Biller, H. B. Perceived paternal nurturance – availability and personality adjustment among college males. *J. Consult. Clin. Psychol.*, 40 (June, 1973), 339–342.

Ridley, C. A. Exploring the impact of work satisfaction and involvement on the marital pair when both partners are employed. *J. Marriage and Fam.*, 35 (May, 1973), 229–237.

Robbins, M., and Lynn, D. The unwed fathers: Generation recidivism and attitudes about intercourse in California Youth Authority wards. *J. Sex Res.*, 9 (Nov., 1973), 334–341.

Robertiello, R. C. Encouraging the patient to live out sexual fantasies. *Psychotherapy*, 6 (Summer, 1969), 183–187.

Robertiello, R. C. Masochism and the female sexual role. *J. Sex Res.*, 6 (Feb., 1970), 56–58.

Robinson, I., and King, K. Sex attitudes and the fear of venereal disease among college students. *J. Sex Res.*, 5 (Aug., 1969), 195–198.

Robinson, I., King, K., and Balswick, J. The premarital sexual revolution among college coeds. *Fam. Coord.*, 21 (April, 1972), 189–194.

Robinson, I., King, K., Dudley, C., and Clune, F. Change in sexual behavior and attitudes of college students. *Fam. Coord.*, 17 (April, 1968), 119–123.

Rockberger, H. On the search for the orgiastic experience. *J. Sex Res.*, 5 (Feb., 1969), 57–64.

Rogers, C. R. Toward a science of the person. *In* Wann, T. W., ed. *Behaviorism and Phenomenology.* Chicago: University of Chicago Press, 1964, 109–140.

Rogers, C. R. *Carl Rogers on Encounter Groups.* New York: Harper and Row, 1970.

Rose, S. D. *Treating Children in Groups.* San Francisco: Jossey-Bass, 1973.

Rosen, L., and Turner, S. Exposure to pornography: An exploratory study. *J. Sex Res.*, 5 (Nov., 1969), 235–246.

Rosenberg, M. Which significant others? *Am. Behav. Sci.*, 16 (July–Aug., 1973), 829–860.

Rossi, A. Transition to parenthood. *J. Marriage and Fam.*, 30 (Feb., 1968), 26–39.

Rossi, P. A factor analysis of the MHP. Unpublished doctoral dissertation, Pennsylvania State University, 1955.

Rubin, I. *Sexual Life After Sixty.* New York: Basic Books, 1965.

Rubin, I., and Kirkendall, L., eds. *Sex in the Adolescent Years.* New York: Association Press, 1968.

Rubin, I., and Kirkendall, L., eds. *Sex in the Childhood Years.* New York: Association Press, 1970.

Ruderman, F. Sex differences: Biological, cultural, societal implications. *In* Epstein, C., and Goode, W., eds. *The Other Half Roads to Women's Equality.* Englewood Cliffs, N.J.: Prentice-Hall, 1971, 48–54.

Ruppel, H. J., Jr. Religiosity and premarital sexual permissiveness: A response to the Reiss-Heltsley and Broderick debate. *J. Marriage and Fam.*, 32 (Nov., 1970), 647–655.

Salmon, U. J. Rationale for androgen therapy in gynecology. *J. Clin. Endocrinol.*, 1 (1941), 162–179.

Salsberg, S. Is group marriage viable? *J. Sex Res.*, 9 (Nov., 1973), 325–333.

Sanford, N. *Self and Society.* New York: Atherton Press, 1966.

Scarvelis, S. Before sex education: A groundwork of values. *Fam. Coord.*, 17 (July, 1968), 188–190.

Schill, T., Emanuel, G., Pedersen, V., Schneider, L., and Wachowiak, D. Sexual responsivity of defensive and nondefensive sensitizers and repressors. *J. Consult. Clin. Psychol.*, 35 (Aug., 1970), 44–47.

Schmidt, G., and Sigusch, V. Changes in sexual behavior among young males and females between 1960–1970. *Arch. Sex. Behav.*, 2, 1 (1972), 27–45.

Schmidt, G., Sigusch, V., and Meyberg, U. Psychosexual stimulation in men: Emotional reactions, changes of sex behavior, and measures of conservative attitudes. *J. Sex Res.*, 5 (Aug., 1969), 199–217.

Schmidt, G., Sigusch, V., and Schafer, S. Responses to reading erotic stories: Male-female differences. *Arch. Sex. Behav.*, *3*, 2 (1973), 181–199.

Schwartz, M. S. A report on sex information knowledge of 87 lower class ninth grade boys. *Fam. Coord.*, *18* (Oct., 1969), 361–371.

Seaman, B. *Free and Female*. New York: Fawcett, 1973.

Sherfey, M. J. The evolution and nature of female sexuality in relation to psychoanalytic theory. *J. Am. Psychoanal. Assoc.*, *14* (1966), 28–128.

Shoben, E. J., Jr. Toward a concept of the normal personality. *In* Zax, M., and Strickler, G., eds. *The Study of Abnormal Behavior*. New York: The Macmillan Co., 1964, 12–21.

Shope, D. F. A comparison of virginal and non-virginal college girls. Unpublished Master's thesis, Pennsylvania State University, 1964.

Shope, D. F. The orgastic responsiveness of selected college females. *J. Sex Res.*, *4* (Aug., 1968), 206–219.

Shope, D. F. Sexual responsiveness in single girls. *In* Henslin, J., ed. *Studies in the Sociology of Sex*. New York: Appleton-Century-Crofts, 1971.

Shope, D. F., and Broderick, C. B. Level of sexual experience and predicted adjustment in marriage. *J. Marriage and Fam.*, *29* (Aug., 1967), 424–427.

Shuttleworth, F. A biosocial and developmental theory of male and female sexuality. *J. Marriage and Fam.*, *21* (May, 1959), 163–170.

SIECUS. *Concerns of Parents About Sex Education*. Study Guide No. 13. New York: SIECUS, 1971.

Siegelman, M. Adjustment of homosexual and heterosexual women. *Br. J. Psychiatry*, *120* (May, 1972a), 477–481.

Siegelman, M. Adjustment of male homosexuals and heterosexuals. *Arch. Sex. Behav.*, *2*, 1 (1972b), 9–25.

Siegelman, M. Parental background of male homosexuals and heterosexuals. *Arch. Sex. Behav.*, *3*, 1 (1974), 3–18.

Sigusch, V., and Schmidt, G. Lower-class sexuality: Some emotional and social aspects in West German males and females. *Arch. Sex. Behav.*, *1* (1971), 29–44.

Sigusch, V., Schmidt, G., Reinfeld, A., and Wiedemann-Sutor, I. Psychosexual

stimulation: Sex differences. *J. Sex Res.*, *6* (Feb., 1970), 10–24.

Simon, W., Berger, A. S., and Gagnon, J. H. Beyond anxiety and fantasy: The coital experiences of college youth. *J. Youth Adolesc.*, *1*, 3 (1972), 203–221.

Simon, W., Gagnon, J. H., and Carns, D. Sexual behavior of the college student. Paper presented at the 13th Winter meeting of the American Academy of Psychoanalysis, New Orleans, Dec., 1968.

Sporakowski, M. J. Marital preparedness, prediction and adjustment. *Fam. Coord.*, *17* (July, 1968), 155–161.

Sprey, J. On the institutionalization of sexuality. *J. Marriage and Fam.*, *31* (Aug., 1969), 432–440.

Staples, R. Sex education and public policy. *Fam. Coord.*, *21* (April, 1972), 183–188.

Staples, R. Public policy and the changing status of black families. *Fam. Coord.*, *22* (July, 1973), 345–351.

Stinnett, N., Carter, L., and Montgomery, J. Older persons' perceptions of their marriages. *J. Marriage and Fam.*, *34* (Nov., 1972), 665–670.

Stinnett, N., Collins, J., and Montgomery, J. Marital need satisfaction of older husbands and wives. *J. Marriage and Fam.*, *32* (Aug., 1970), 428–434.

Stoller, F. The intimate network of families as a new structure. *In* Otto, H. A., ed. *The Family in Search of a Future*. New York: Appleton-Century-Crofts, 1970a, 145–159.

Stoller, F. A stage for trust. *In* Burton, A., ed. *Encounter*. San Francisco: Jossey-Bass, 1970b, 81–96.

Sullivan, H. S. *Collected Works*, Vols. 1 and 2. New York: W. W. Norton and Co., 1953, 1956.

Sutker, P. B., and Kilpatrick, D. G. Personality, biographical, and racial correlates of sexual attitudes and behavior. *Proceedings of the 81st Annual Convention of the American Psychological Association*, *8* (1973), 261–262.

Symonds, C. A nude touchy-feely group. *J. Sex Res.*, *7* (May, 1971), 126–133.

Szasz, T. The product conversion—from heresy to madness. *In* McCaffrey, J., ed. *The Homosexual Dialectic*. Englewood Cliffs, N.J.: Prentice-Hall, 1972, 101–119.

Terman, L. M. *Psychological Factors in*

Marital Happiness. New York: Mc-Graw-Hill, 1938.

Terman, L. M., and Miles, C. *Sex and Personality.* New York: McGraw-Hill, 1936.

Tharp, R. G. Psychological patterning in marriage. *Psychol. Bull.,* LX (March, 1963), 97–117.

Thomes, M. M. Children without fathers. *J. Marriage and Fam., 30* (Feb., 1968), 89–96.

Thomlinson, R. Prevented births, naturalness, and Roman Catholic doctrine. *J. Sex Res., 8* (May, 1972), 73–100.

Thompson, N., Jr., McCandless, B., and Strickland, B. R. Personal adjustment of male and female homosexuals and heterosexuals. *J. Abnorm. Psychol., 78,* 2 (1971), 237–240.

Tietze, C., and Lewit, S. Interim report on the joint program for the study of abortion. *J. Sex Res., 8* (Aug., 1972), 170–188.

Tiger, L. *Men in Groups.* New York: Random House, 1969.

Tolar, A., Rice, F. J., and Lanctot, C. A. Characteristics of couples practicing the temperature-rhythm method of birth control. *Proceedings of the 81st Annual Convention of the American Psychological Association, 8* (1973), 353–354.

Twombly, G. H. Sex after radical gynecological surgery. *J. Sex Res., 4* (Nov., 1968), 275–281.

United States Bureau of the Census. Current Population Reports, Series P-25, No. 338, "Summary of Demographic Projections." Washington, D.C.: United States Government Printing Office, 1968.

United States Bureau of the Census. *Statistical Abstract of the United States: 1973,* 94th ed. Washington, D.C.: United States Government Printing Office, 1973.

United States Bureau of the Census. *USA Statistics in Brief 1973.* Washington, D.C.: United States Government Printing Office, 1973.

Vandervoort, H., and McIlvenna, T., eds. *The Yes Book of Sex: Masturbation Techniques for Women.* San Francisco: Multi Media Resource Center, 1972.

Van Vleck, D. B. *The Crucial Generation.* Charlotte, Vermont: Optimum Population, Inc., 1971.

Vincent, C. E., Haney, C. A., and Cochrane, C. M. Familial and generational patterns of illegitimacy. *J. Marriage and Fam., 31* (Nov., 1969), 659–667.

Wake, F. R. Attitudes of parents toward the premarital sex behavior of their children and themselves. *J. Sex Res., 5* (Aug., 1969), 170–177.

Wallace, D. H., and Wehmer, G. Evaluation of visual erotica by sexual liberals and conservatives. *J. Sex Res., 8* (May, 1972), 147–153.

Wallin, P. A study of orgasm as a condition of women's enjoyment of intercourse. *J. Soc. Psychol., 51* (1960), 191–198.

Wallin, P., and Clark, A. Cultural norms and husbands' and wives' reports of their marital partner's preferred frequency of coitus relative to their own. *Sociometry, 21* (Sept., 1958), 247–254.

Ward, W. D. Patterns of culturally defined sex-role preference and parental imitation. *J. Genet. Psychol., 122* (June, 1973), 337–343.

Warehime, R. G., and Foulds, M. L. Perceived locus of control and personal adjustment. *J. Consult. Clin. Psychol., 37* (Oct., 1971), 250–252.

Weikert, P. A rationale for the inclusion of masturbation as a topic in a family life and sex education program. Unpublished Master's thesis, Pennsylvania State University, 1970.

Weinberg, S. K. Incest. *In* Sagarin, E., and MacNamara, D., eds. *Problems of Sexual Behavior.* New York: T. Y. Crowell, 1968, 167–202.

White, R. W. *Lives in Progress.* New York: Holt, Rinehart and Winston, 1966.

Whitehurst, R. N. Premarital reference-group orientations and marriage adjustment. *J. Marriage and Fam., 30* (Aug., 1968), 397–401.

Whitehurst, R. N. Extramarital sex: Alienation or extension of normal behavior. *In* Neubeck, G., ed. *Extramarital Relations.* Englewood Cliffs, N.J.: Prentice-Hall, 1969, 129–145.

Wilson, C. *The Origins of the Sexual Impulse.* New York: G. P. Putnam's Sons, 1963.

Wilson, R. A. *Feminine Forever.* New York: M. Evans and Co., 1966.

Winch, R. F. *The Modern Family,* rev. ed. New York: Holt, Rinehart and Winston, 1963.

Wood, F. *Sex and the New Morality.* New York: Association Press, 1968.

Wright, M. R., and McCary, J. L. Positive effects of sex information on emotional patterns of behavior. *J. Sex Res.*, 5 (Aug., 1969), 162–169.

Wyden, P., and Wyden, B. *Growing Up Straight: What Every Thoughtful Parent Should Know About Homosexuality.* New York: Stein and Day, 1968.

Zehv, W. A new way to stimulate your sex partner. *Sexology, 36* (July, 1970a), 4–7.

Zehv, W. Sexual intercourse and illness. *Sexology, 37* (Sept., 1970b), 21–26.

Ziegler, F., and Rodgers, D. A. Vasectomy, ovulation supressors, and sexual behavior. *J. Sex Res., 4* (Aug., 1968), 169–193.

Zimmerman, C. C. *Family and Civilization.* New York: Harper and Row, 1947.

Zimmerman, C. C. The future of the family in America. *J. Marriage and Fam., 34* (May, 1972), 323–333.

NAME INDEX

SUBJECT INDEX

Numbers in italic indicate illustrations; numbers followed by a "t" indicate tabular material.